ARCHAEOLOGY, HISTORY AND CULTURE IN PALESTINE AND THE NEAR EAST

Essays in Memory of Albert E. Glock

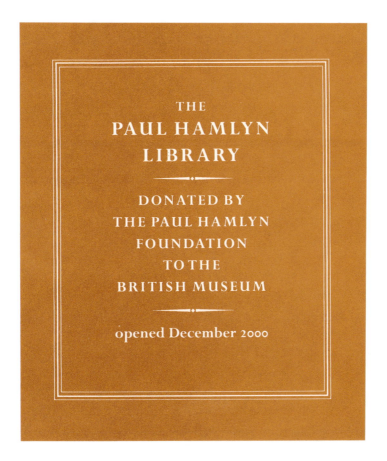

ASOR Books Volume 3

Victor Matthews, editor

ARCHAEOLOGY, HISTORY AND CULTURE IN PALESTINE AND THE NEAR EAST

ESSAYS IN MEMORY OF ALBERT E. GLOCK

edited by

Tomis Kapitan

Scholars Press • Atlanta, Georgia

ARCHAEOLOGY, HISTORY AND CULTURE
IN PALESTINE AND THE NEAR EAST
Essays in Memory of Albert E. Glock

Copyright © 1999
The American Schools of Oriental Research

Library of Congress Cataloging-in-Publication Data

Archaeology, history, and culture in Palestine and the Near East :
  essays in memory of Albert E. Glock / edited by Tomis Kapitan.
       p.   cm. — (ASOR books : v. 3)
    ISBN 0-7885-0584X (pbk. : alk. paper)
    1. Palestine—Antiquities. 2. Middle East—Antiquities. 3.
Palestine—History—To 70 A.D.—Historiography. 4. Middle
East—History—To 622—Historiography. 5. Archaeology and
history—Palestine. 6. Archaeology and history—Middle East.
7. Bronze age—Palestine—Historiography. I. Glock, Albert
E. II. Kapitan, Tomis, 1949-   . III. Series.
DS111.A75   1999
933—dc21   99–43228
                                               CIP

Printed in the United States of America
on acid-free paper. ∞

Albert E. Glock (1925–1992)

Contents

Foreword

TOMIS KAPITAN

A ny science can be subjected to social pressures that endeavor to direct research, publicize or suppress findings, and make or destroy careers. In struggles over territory, the disciplines of archaeology and history become particularly important weapons as adversaries attempt to bolster their claims to particular regions and artifacts. Appeals to prior habitation, longevity of presence, past cultural achievements, and established emotional attachment carry considerable weight in the minds of nearly everyone who considers the questions "who belongs where?" and "what belongs to whom?" Serious attempts to provide answers are inseparable from a patient examination of the historical record.

Archaeological investigation in Palestine has been especially prone to manipulation by ideological, political, and religious concerns. Initiated by Westerners interested in learning more about one of the fundamental sources of Western civilization and religion, early archaeological research in Palestine was devoted to the biblical period in its selection of sites and interpretation of data. Protestant Christians were particularly concerned to deflect criticisms of the Bible by seeking archaeological support for the historicity of biblical accounts. In the past fifty years, this focus has been paralleled by the work of Israeli archaeologists who have aimed at deepening the connection between Jews and what they regard as the ancient Jewish homeland. These efforts are understandable in their own right, but one effect of the biblical emphasis in archaeology has been to neglect the history of other peoples in Palestine, including those who populated the region during the 1600 years of Byzantine, Arab, and Turkish dominance. In particular, the history of Palestinian Arabs has rarely been the subject of archaeological investigation, and the popular Western media, while giving wide exposure to several archaeological discoveries in the Near East, has been largely silent on the Palestinians' historical presence in the land.

Yet recent years have witnessed changes in the sentiments of a significant segment of Near Eastern archaeologists as it became increasingly apparent that the historical record in Palestine is far richer and more varied than traditional biblical archaeology had portrayed it. Some have developed interests in the older communities in ancient Canaan while others have turned their attention to the historical record of more recent centuries. Neil Asher Silberman points out in the opening contribution to this volume that Albert Glock was among the first to foster this latter trend in the archaeology of the region as he embarked upon an attempt to link the contemporary Palestinian Arab community with the archaeological remains found in Palestine. Glock's fieldwork and research concerns, combined with his interests in education, led him to approach the Palestinian academic community about the importance of cataloging and preserving the cultural heritage of Palestinian Arabs. As a result, he joined the faculty at the Palestinian Birzeit University in 1976, founded the first Palestinian archaeological institute there in 1986, and instructed his students at excavations, in laboratories, and in the classroom with the aim of enhancing Palestinian credentials within the discipline of archaeology. As Silberman writes, this marked the "beginning of a grand experiment" in the archaeology of Palestine. Pursuing such an agenda under the pressures of long-term military occupation proved to be a daunting task and, at times, quite dangerous. Tragically, Glock's journey was ended by an unknown assailant on January 19, 1992, while he was still in the midst of his many projects.

This volume commemorates Albert Glock's contribution to archaeology and education in Palestine and the Near East. It includes studies by scholars who were colleagues of Glock's, knew him personally, or have been influenced and inspired by his approach. Their themes and concerns are diverse, but each discusses either the past of Palestine and its immediate neighbors, the practice of Near Eastern archaeology, or Glock's unique contribution to these areas of inquiry. Silberman's revealing memoir provides the most information about Glock's life and work, while Henry MacAdam's contribution begins with a personal account of Glock's dedication to the "cultural geography" of Palestine and its immediate neighbors. MacAdam goes on to examine early maps of Phoenicia, and devotes considerable time to discussing the similarities and dissimilarities between Strabo's and

Pliny's accounts of Phoenician geography. The essay by Thomas Ricks echoes Glock's point about the neglect of Palestinians' history throughout the period between the mid-nineteenth century and the 1970s. In describing an oral history project undertaken with faculty members and students at Birzeit University, Ricks contrasts this mode of investigation with that of archaeology, and notes that preservation of "living memories" in oral accounts is an important source for rediscovering and understanding Palestine's history.

Two of the contributors address methodological issues within archaeology. William Dever characterizes Glock's notion of *biblical* archaeology as well as *Palestinian* archaeology. He writes how his own work together with Glock's foresaw the demise of the older-style biblical archaeology, and he commends Glock's conviction that Palestinian archaeology must achieve an independent status. He advocates an interdisciplinary dialogue between biblical studies and Syro-Palestinian archaeology of the Iron Age, yet he laments the state of Syro-Palestinian archaeology in the United States. Patty Jo Watson mentions Glock's interest in ethnoarchaeology and takes up the debate about the propriety of using the methods and results of ethnoarchaeological research in archaeological interpretation. She is optimistic about the prospects for a fruitful employment of ethnographic analogy and the use of generalization within archaeology.

Two papers on pottery are especially appropriate to this volume given Glock's own concern with pottery technology as a source of information about the past. Hamed Salem gives an extensive account of contemporary pottery making techniques in different Palestinian villages. He illustrates how the procedures and materials used by potters can be a powerful tool for archaeologists in their attempts to discern trends of continuity and change since pottery production is indicative of the wider sociological, economic, and environmental factors that have shaped past and present alike. Ann Killebrew describes two main types of cooking pots from the Late Bronze II and Iron I periods that were found in four sites in Canaan. She concludes that the two types were likely to have originated from distinct communities differing considerably in their material culture.

Four of the contributions talk about some of the important findings of recent excavations in Palestine and Jordan. Nancy Lapp writes about the Early Bronze Age seals and seal impressions found in the Tell

Ta'annek excavations of the biblical site of Taanach (those that first brought Al Glock to Palestine in the early 1960s). She concludes that while the findings at Taanach fit well into the regional patterns observed in the overall Palestinian corpus, the seal-impressions are "first-time occurrences" in Palestine, and that one of the seals may have been an import from Mesopotamia. Ghada Ziadeh reports on her study of abandoned houses in the Palestinian village of Ti'innik. She conjectures that the abandonments of the village in the sixteenth century and again in the twentieth century were not sudden or unplanned, but the results of economic and political factors present in both instances. Walter Rast points out how the burial customs at a cemetery in Bad edh-Dhra' (in present day Jordan) shed light on the living society of an Early Bronze Age village that had been located at that site, indicating, for example, periodic population shifts, social hierarchies, and mechanisms of family and clan stability. Henk Franken discusses inscriptions found on wall plaster from a wall at Tell Deir 'Alla in the Jordan valley. He examines the religious background and significance of the fragmentary texts that concern a seer, Balaam, and his vision of an assembly of gods trying to prevent destruction of life on earth by a flood. Franken suggests that the structure in which these texts were found may well be the remains of an ancient sanctuary of the cult of Baal.

Two papers exemplify Glock's emphasis upon culture as a means to explaining the behaviors of past societies, discussing the importance of Near Eastern mythology in understanding cultural practices. G. R. Wright's essay concerns the Judith myth, and notes parallels between its details and those of other similar stories in the first millennium BC. There appears to have been a long established association of young women with severed heads, and Wright contends that the author of the Judith myth drew upon his knowledge of both Jewish and Greek history in composing his tale. Hugh Harcourt talks about the relevance of ancient myths in comprehending human behavior and civilized life. He is particularly interested in the Cypriot cult of Astarte, its roots in the Sumerian myths of Inanna and her Akkadian manifestation, Ishtar, who combines both love and war (hatred, destructiveness). The transformation of this goddess into the Greek Aphrodite, however, involves a conceptual shift to a figure of love and sexuality, who, unlike Athena, is not concerned with hate, violence, and warfare. Harcourt then shows how the powerful emotions of Love and Hate take on great explanatory significance in the work of Empedocles, Lucretius, and Sigmund Freud, concluding that neither of these two "immortal powers" identified by the ancient thinkers of the eastern Mediterranean can be neglected in understanding human life.

Three of Al Glock's own papers are included as appendices. The first two, previously published in truncated form, address the importance of creating a distinctively Palestinian archaeology. In them Glock summarizes the history of archaeological research in the Near East and details the manner in which the discipline has been subject to cultural biases. He proposes several steps towards creating a more balanced approach. The third essay, written during the height of the Intifada and appearing here for the first time, is a broader discussion of politics and culture in twentieth century Palestine. In a letter written in September 1991, Glock acknowledged that the essays "are already in need of repair," and that "my proposals for how to respond to the problem of the past of Palestine are subject to revision." It is helpful enough, he added, if they contribute to the discussion and "stimulate alternate proposals." A bibliography of Glock's writings reveals the scope of his intellectual concerns.

A philosopher might seem a somewhat unusual choice as editor of a volume on the archaeology, history, and culture of Palestine and the Near East. Suffice it to say that I took on the task because I came to know Al Glock quite well during the years 1981–1986 as a colleague at Birzeit University and, like many others, was impressed by his energy, insight, and commitment to both Palestinian archaeology and Palestinian education. It is these attributes, housed as they were in a remarkably unique character, that have inspired this collection.

The contributors have been admirably patient during the process of its emergence. I am indebted to Walter Rast for his review of several of the essays and suggestions for their placement, and to Victor Matthews and Billie Jean Collins of ASOR for their counsel and assistance. Most of all, I would like to express my appreciation to Lois Glock for her advice and dedication to this project, and for her enduring support of and participation in Al's bold and challenging lifework.

1   Albert E. Glock (1925–1992): A Remembrance

NEIL ASHER SILBERMAN

Al Glock was not an easy man to get to know if you were just a casual acquaintance. In his lifelong pursuit of exacting intellectual standards, he had little time or patience for those who could not share, or try to understand, his quest. Anyone who ever met him knows that he showed little interest in the social rituals, lighthearted gossip, or petty rivalries of conventional academic life. I will always remember him as tall, stern, and serious, thinking deeply before answering a question, pausing in silence to weigh all the implications before committing himself. With his thick gray hair and dark eyeglasses, he was a familiar figure in the halls of Albright Institute and in the streets of East Jerusalem—and behind the wheel of his red and white Volkswagen van, driving along the winding roads leading northward through Birzeit, Ramallah, Nablus, and Jenin, toward the village of Tiʿinnik. Yet Al Glock was by no means a public personality. Despite the devotion of family, friends, and colleagues, he seemed to prefer the role of an outsider, the role of a solitary seeker, totally committed to a life of personal exploration that ultimately proved to be far more than just an archaeological quest.

Biographical details are usually meaningful only in retrospect—when lives can be read as finished stories, as closed units of meaning, unambiguous about their ultimate direction or historical significance. And in retrospect, it is easy enough to see Al Glock's life as a classic American saga, an up-from-the-bootstraps story of a young man born in northern Idaho, trained as a Lutheran minister in the midwestern heartland, who ultimately sacrificed his life as an American expatriate teacher in the violent struggle for Palestinian nationhood. But the story as it unfolded was more nuanced in its details, less clear in its beginnings and in its end. For by the end of his career, Al Glock had ventured into the dangerous no man's land of activism that, to many, lies just beyond the boundaries of "respectable" scholarship. Consciously or unintentionally, he had entered an arena of public political struggle where historical scholarship cannot be detached from history-in-the-making. At a time when modern nations are emerging, history and archaeology almost always become the building blocks of communal identity and the moral substantiation of modern political claims. It is an area where the moral choices are hard and the stakes can be enormous, even if most academics of Al's age and background always refused (and still stubbornly refuse) to acknowledge the inevitable interconnection of scholarship with society's wider political and ideological trends. Al Glock lived a unique life because he could never be satisfied with any other. He refused to remain silent or passive in the face of social injustice, intellectual bias, or comfortable conventional wisdom. He was among the scholars who recognized that the time had come for a far reaching reexamination of the preconceptions of archaeology in both Palestine and Israel.

Family background undoubtedly influenced Al Glock's character and eventual path in life. His father Ernest, born in rural Nevada in the late nineteenth century, entered the ministry of the Lutheran Church-Missouri Synod, and in 1925 was dispatched with his wife Meta to preach the gospel in Gifford, Idaho, a small town in northern Idaho within the boundaries of the Nez Perce Reservation, where Al and his two brothers Delmar and Richard were later born. Church and ministerial responsibilities continued as the focus of the family's life even after they moved to Washburn, Illinois in 1928. Indeed, from an early age, Al seems to have inherited his father's spiritual vocation; at age 13, he was sent off to study Hebrew, Greek, and Latin at a German-style gymnasium and junior college at Concordia College in Milwaukee, one of the educational branches of the Lutheran Church-Missouri Synod. Upon graduation in 1945, he moved on to Concordia Seminary in St. Louis, where he concentrated with characteristic determination on the study of the Hebrew Bible. Yet it was there that he also began to display, according to the memories of his wife Lois whom he met there, the independence of mind that would mark him all his life. Despite his teachers' defense of the Bible's divine inspiration, Al first became fascinated with the literary-critical approach to the scriptures. In the late 1940s, he took a year abroad to visit theological centers in Europe, for some months attending classes in biblical criticism at Heidelberg University. And although he embarked on a normal pastoral career when he graduated in the spring of 1950 from Concordia Theological Seminary, there was something singular about his character that would ultimately cause him to question, and even remove himself from, the complacency of postwar American intellectual and religious life.

I do not mean to romanticize or exaggerate Al's independent spirit. For in these early years, a casual observer would have been hard pressed to distinguish him from the countless other young seminary graduates just then taking up smalltown and suburban pulpits in a nation settling into its most innocent period of postwar prosperity. Soon after he was appointed pastor of Christ Lutheran Church in Normal, Illinois (where he also served as a campus pastor for the students of Illinois State Normal College, now Illinois State University) he and Lois were married. In the years between 1952 and 1956, their four children Albert, Jeffrey, Alice, and Peter were born. Yet even with responsibilities for a congregation, student groups, and a growing family, Al never abandoned his interest in the serious study of biblical history. Lois recalls that "while doing some innovative things locally as he nurtured the young, consoled the old, fed the poor, housed some Hungarian refugees, counseled, preached short but well-researched sermons and took part in campus discussions," he also took the time and effort to drive the 120 miles up to Chicago to take additional courses in scripture and Near Eastern history and archaeology at the Lutheran Maywood Seminary.

The search for the historical and archaeological background to the scriptural text gripped him far more deeply than supervising church socials and Sunday School. Yet as a fulltime minister and part time student, he was still far from the upper echelons of American biblical and archaeological scholarship. By the late 1950s, William Foxwell Albright still stood as the benevolent father of biblical archaeology and his student G. Ernest Wright was training a generation of field archaeologists at Tell Balatah (the biblical Shechem). Wright was at the same time promoting a conservative, historically-based theological approach to the scriptures among the wider Protestant public that became known as Biblical Theology. In many circles, Protestant, Catholic, and Jewish, the hope burned brightly that the tangible discoveries of biblical archaeology might indeed revivify modern appreciation for the scriptures. And at this time, Al Glock expanded his part-time studies and became increasingly committed to joining this intellectual enterprise. In 1957, when he was offered a teaching post at Concordia Teachers College (now Concordia University) in the Chicago suburb of River Forest, he did not hesitate to accept the career shift that such a move would entail. In the next few years, as he began to devote all his time to teaching the History and Literature of the Old Testament in the light of the latest archaeological discoveries and textual insights, Al's visions widened beyond the prospect of making an occasional visit to the Holy Land, and beyond giving the same introductory undergraduate courses again and again. And by 1962, when he had received a Master of Sacred Theology Degree in Near Eastern Studies from The Lutheran School of Theology (then Maywood Seminary), he had already met with several former classmates and faculty members from Concordia Seminary, among them Carl Graesser and Delbert Hillers, and with Concordia professor A. von Rohr Sauer, to encourage the Research Committee of the Seminary to lend its official and financial support to a Lutheran archaeological project in the Holy Land.

Along with their colleague Paul Lapp (also a Concordia Seminary graduate who was completing his doctoral studies under William F. Albright and who was then serving as director of the American School in Jerusalem), they selected a promising site for excavation, Tell Taʿannek, the biblical Taanach, as the focus for a joint excavation project of the Concordia Seminary and the American Schools of Oriental Research. Their enthusiasm and the importance of this undertaking convinced the directors of a lay organization they applied to, The Aid Association for Lutherans, of Appleton, Wisconsin, to underwrite the major costs of the project at Tell Taʿannek.

A Lutheran contribution to biblical archaeology had been prominent at the dawn of the modern archaeological exploration of Palestine around the turn of the century. From 1902 to 1914, Professor Ernst Sellin, a graduate of Erlangen and professor at the University of Vienna, had embarked on a series of excavations sponsored by the

Deutsche Orientgesellschaft in an attempt to utilize archaeology to confirm the basic historical value of the Bible. No less important, he sought to undermine the radical assertions of the supporters of the Higher Criticism that the Bible was primarily a theological construct. Sellin's excavations at Shechem, Jericho, and Taanach were pioneering attempts at undertaking a conservative, German-style biblical archaeology, and although many of their specific conclusions would later be challenged, these excavations offered important evidence of the development of Canaanite and early Israelite cultures in their ancient context. Yet the outbreak of World War I and the British takeover of Palestine put an end to this initial Lutheran effort. Its close association with German universities and official societies largely disqualified it for further fieldwork under the ever-politically-sensitive British administration of Palestine during the interwar and World War II years. Now the American Lutheran Church would take a prominent role in the exploration. In the summer of 1962, Al Glock and other members of the Concordia Group joined Wright's excavation at Tell Balatah to gain field experience and prepare to mount their own excavations at Tell Taʿannek under the overall direction of Paul Lapp in the following year.

The decision to dig at Tell Taʿannek as a joint undertaking of The American Schools of Oriental Research (ASOR) and Concordia Seminary beginning in 1963 was the first step in a process that would eventually take Al Glock from a basically bibliocentric orientation into the wider worlds of anthropology and ancient Near Eastern studies. The project would also eventually transfer the geographical and cultural focus of his family's life from a stable church community in the American Midwest to the chaotic, often violent struggle between Israelis and Palestinians for self-determination and territorial sovereignty in the same small stretch of land. The site of Tel Taʿannek was situated in a sensitive border area, the minefield and barbed-wire strewn "Green Line" that separated the West Bank from pre-1967 Israel. In the course of the first season of digging, Al became thoroughly immersed in the techniques and challenges of field work, and began to see that the sequence of cultures they were uncovering belied a neat separation between "Israelite" and "Canaanite." The Hebrew Bible's seven references to the city of Taanach do not express more than a tiny facet of the city's long history, extending from the

Early Bronze Age (ca. 2700 BCE) to the rural village of Tiʿinnik that exists to the present day. In the three interrupted seasons of digging, 1963, 1966, and 1968, when modern Middle Eastern tensions and war in 1967 profoundly altered the modern circumstances of the site and its people, Al Glock completed his Ph.D. at the University of Michigan with a dissertation on "Warfare in Mari and Early Israel." During that time, he and other core staff members worked closely with dig director Paul Lapp in organizing the expedition, supervising the analysis of the finds, and trying to navigate the project through the uncertain waters of the post-1967 era. The expedition that had been conceived under the auspices of the Department of Antiquities of the Hashemite Kingdom of Jordan now found itself under the jurisdiction of the Israel Department of Antiquities.

Al Glock understood better, and expressed more clearly than any other Near Eastern archaeologist I have known, that the search for the past in this region is conducted on fairly coherent ideological lines. Although all respectable excavators attempt to be scrupulously accurate in their measurements of uncovered structures and analysis of associated finds and pottery forms, the higher levels of interpretation about political and religious history that are drawn from those tumbled stones and smashed potsherds are dependent for meaning on pre-existent logical frameworks. Those frameworks, rarely admitted or discussed, are several: Biblical, Progressivist, Nationalist, Economic Materialist. Yet each offers a neat scheme of abstract development into which a scholar can fit his or her archaeological finds. In his close contact with Palestinian colleagues and acquaintances over the years, Al grasped the fact that the archaeology of the country still maintained an antiquarian perspective, seeing the biblical periods of the country as a timeless, endlessly fascinating culture sequence with enormous significance for the western world, but with little connection to the development of the later cultures and societies of Palestine up to the present day. The trajectory of biblical archaeology rose from humble Neolithic origins to find sublime expression in the material world of the Bible ("From the Stone Age to Christianity," as W. F. Albright put it). But somehow Islam and the modern Arab inhabitants of the country were left out of the picture, ignored as orphans of history. And while the pre-1948 Jewish community of Palestine and the subsequent State of Israel celebrated their connection to the antiquities of the country, Al

Glock was among the first to devote serious thought and energy to the idea that some link between the modern Arab Palestinian community and the archaeological remains of the country could and should be found.

The tragic death of director Paul Lapp in a swimming accident off Cyprus in the spring of 1970 was a blow to the future of American biblical archaeology and it also brought about some immediate changes in the structure and plans of the ASOR-Concordia expedition to Tel Ta'annek. Where before Al had served as a senior staff member under the direction of Paul Lapp, he now assumed executive oversight of all phases of the post-excavation analysis—from initial processing of the field finds (brought directly from the site in straw baskets to the American School in Jerusalem) to the editing and publication of the final report. With greater responsibilities came longer stretches of time in Jerusalem and a more intense interest in getting the maximum data from the excavated finds. When I first met Al in 1972, he was deeply fascinated by the possibility of grouping ceramics by the composition of their material and their technique, as well as by their decorative style. I recall his laboratory in the rear of the School looking more like a machine shop than an archaeological study center, with Al wearing safety glasses and peering intently as a high speed saw whined and sheared through ancient loop handles and cooking pot rims, to reveal the pattern of grits and clay that he hoped might hold the key to understanding the secret logic and structure of the ancient potters' trade.

But Al was also deeply interested in people as well as potsherds and, in an attempt to interest Palestinian students in the technical work of the expedition, he sought out qualified draftspeople to ink the initial field plans and produce scale drawings of the excavated pottery. Shortly before his death, Paul Lapp had joined the faculty of Birzeit University with the goal of establishing a formal program for archaeological training in the leading Palestinian university and Al Glock began to teach there on a regular basis beginning in 1976. Yet by that time, the political atmosphere on the West Bank had changed beyond reckoning, as, in the wake of the 1973 War and intensifying conflict between Palestinians and Israelis, military checkpoints, burning tires, and public protests became a part of everyday life. As Al and Lois became more and more involved in the intellectual and social life of the Palestinian community of Jerusalem, Ramallah, and Birzeit, he assumed other responsibilities as the director of the Albright Institute after the departure of David Noel Freedman in 1977.   Under his editorial supervision, Walter Rast's publication of *Taanach I: Studies in Iron Age Pottery* appeared in 1978.   But more and more, Al was focused on the educational project of training a new generation of Palestinian archaeologists who might be able to craft their own meaningful vision of the link between the country's present and past.   The Institute of Archaeology at Birzeit was slowly coming together during the early 1980s, and his decision to return to Tell Taʿannek in 1985 marked the beginning of a grand experiment in rethinking the very bases of archaeology in Palestine.

Few of his colleagues could appreciate the intellectual daring of the new project he envisioned.   To most, the idea of excavating the modern Arab village of Tiʿinnek rather than the impressive biblical mound that loomed above it, seemed to be nothing less than abandoning the archaeological treasure for the archaeological dross.   Yet that distinction was part of the unspoken ideology of archaeology in the "Land of the Bible" that Al sought consciously to contest.   Who could say that a sophisticated combination of ethnoarchaeology, oral histories, and detailed studies of village structures might not provide more insight into archaeological processes and cultural transformations than some mute Iron Age monumental structure or a problematic biblical verse? Even while the already excavated Bronze and Iron Age material from Tel Taʿannek was still under intensive study, Al was determined to train his students to a meaningful link between the archaeological deposits of the country and their own reality.   Included in this volume are several of Al's papers revealing the wide range of interests he possessed. Back then, in the late 1970s and 1980s, there was probably not a single biblical archaeologist who had more than a vague inkling of what postmodernism or Critical Theory was all about; the innocent and earnest scientism of New Archaeology was all the rage then.   But Al was no ideologue, striking a fashionable intellectual pose for the attention it might garner. Al Glock was deeply dissatisfied with the unspoken biases toward certain periods and toward certain simplistic interpretations of the significance of power, nationhood, and ethnic exclusivity in the long history of the Holy Land.   And while his better known colleagues might debate issues of chronology and stratigraphy, none of them ever attained the sophistication of theoretical insight that Al Glock achieved.

Al was not a chauvinist or nationalist by inclination. He was always skeptical of the self-interested motives of people in power, and he was surely not interested in providing splendid monuments and tourist attractions for Palestinian officials to preen over. He envisioned Palestinian archaeology as something to be undertaken in the villages, where the delicate web of environment, tradition, adaptation, and rootedness provided the real fabric of Palestinian history. He did not seek to celebrate urban merchants' mansions or lavishly monumental public mosques. His interest was in starting from scratch (and this is where few, even today, understand his intentions), to work slowly and methodically backwards from the present into more remote periods, never losing touch with the modern reasons for why the search was being made. In talks, trips, and arguments about the future of archaeology in Israel, Palestine, and Jordan, Al Glock made me realize how important it is to tackle and make some sense out of the huge stretches of time and rich bodies of archaeological material that are still almost completely unknown. For all the efforts devoted to outlining the material history of the country from the Stone Age to the Crusader Period, the centuries after the fall of Acre, with their own economic ups and downs, colorful characters, and international connections, are almost completely unknown in an archaeological sense. Thanks to Al Glock and those influenced by him, that may be changing. But in the meantime, unsubstantiated, cartoon-like, orientalist images of Arab and Turkish "desolation," with all their negative political implications, continue to color the public perception of Ottoman Palestine. Arguably, they subtly undermine any prospects for respectful, peaceful coexistence in the region as well.

One day in the spring of 1987, as we were sitting in his home in Beit Hanina and discussing something or other—the Ottoman period, current Israeli-Palestinian politics, or maybe Al's latest theoretical insight—he suddenly stopped to share with me a curious item that he had recently run across in his reading: it was the sad life story of an eighteenth century Czech operatic composer named Christoph Willibald Gluck, who struggled throughout his entirely career, mostly in the shadows of the great artists of the day, to reform the conventions of opera so as to merge the drama and the music seamlessly. Al noted with an ironic smile that Gluck died in Vienna in relative obscurity and it was only in recent decades that modern musicologists had come to recognize his genius. The similarity of names and the implication of the story was telling, for Al had clearly recognized that he too would never would nor could be accepted by the mainstream in his own time.

Al Glock was well aware of his status as an outsider, and was sensitive to the delicate role he played between cultures as a tireless searcher, a digger for meaning and truth. He kept on trying, working with his students, accepting no excuses, and demanding excellence from each and every one. In his last years at Birzeit University, he struggled to navigate the stormy waters of academic politics, religious and secular radicalism, and the chaotic violence of the Intifada in order to keep his own work alive. Even as he continued to experiment with the techniques of ethnohistory, site formation processes, field technique, and historical philosophy at the village of Tiʿinnek, he could hardly avoid attracting notice for his tireless investigations and from the high level of intellectual curiosity he demanded from his students and colleagues. At the same time, he suffered the daily indignities and inconveniences of voluntarily living under military occupation and identifying himself openly and fearlessly with the cause of Palestinian nationhood. Yet even though the unfounded suspicions were many, few recognized Al Glock for the intellectual pioneer that he really was. His life and career were tragically cut short by an assassin's bullet even as he struggled to make sense of the long sequence of cultures that had so recently exploded in intolerance and violence. His archaeological quest was to explain the present and thereby shape the future. He was not interested in filling museums or digging up symbols for banknotes or postage stamps. I can only hope that there will be others to follow in the important work of reshaping the history of both Israel and Palestine. It will require political courage and a prophetic sense of urgency, lest violent, exclusivist visions of the past overwhelm all prospects for peace. "I do not know where this will lead or how it will end," Al jotted down in his notebook on May 12, 1987, in the midst of his last Tiʿinnek project, "but I do know how it began and I will show you a little of one part of the search for a meaningful picture of Palestine—that includes ALL of the story, beginning from scratch."

2 Can "Biblical Archaeology" be an Academic and Professional Discipline?

WILLIAM G. DEVER

INTRODUCTION

The late Albert E. Glock was a well-trained philologian, biblical scholar, and seminary professor who outgrew amateur-style "biblical archaeology" to become one of the first professional Palestinian archaeologists in our field in the 1970s. In addition to the two previously unpublished manuscripts presented in this volume, Glock had published two prescient but scarcely-noticed articles on Biblical and Palestinian archaeology. One appeared in *American Antiquity*, a journal that few in our field read (Glock 1985), and the other was in press from ca. 1975 on, until it finally appeared in 1986 in a rather obscure *Festschrift* (Glock 1986).[1] In this essay in memory of Albert Glock, with whom I was closely affiliated at the Albright Institute of Archaeological Research in Jerusalem, I wish to respond to the latter essay, hoping thereby to give it the wider attention it deserves.

GLOCK'S UNDERSTANDING OF "BIBLICAL ARCHAEOLOGY" AND ITS RELATION TO PALESTINIAN ARCHAEOLOGY

In his article entitled "Biblical Archaeology, an Emerging Discipline" (1986) Glock had set forth his own definition of both "biblical" and what he called simply "Palestinian" archaeology. I would paraphrase and summarize his main points as follows, first with regard to "biblical" archaeology:

(1) One must define "biblical archaeology" in such a way as to meet the "requirement" that Palestinian archaeology be a discipline independent from it.

(2) "Biblical archaeology" then becomes a related "field of study" or a "scholarly discipline."

(3) This "biblical archaeology" is a subdiscipline of biblical studies, not Palestinian archaeology, and as such has its own methods and aims apart from pure archaeology.

(4) "Biblical archaeology" can and usually should exclude fieldwork on its own, depending rather on the publications of Palestinian archaeology for its non-Biblical data.

(5) "Biblical archaeology" by nature must be interdisciplinary.

(6) "Biblical archaeology" is methodologically similar to form-criticism in Biblical studies, developing a "typology of material culture remains" rather than of texts.

(7) The ultimate aim of "biblical archaeology" is to use archaeological results in "the reconstruction of the intellectual and religious experience reflected in the biblical tradition" (1986, 100).

(8) In order to survive as an "emerging discipline," "biblical archaeology" needs to create specialized positions of its own (presumably in seminaries) alongside textual, literary, and historical criticism of the Bible.

Glock defines the other of his twin disciplines, "Palestinian" archaeology, as follows:

(1) "Palestinian" archaeology is a branch of general archaeology, whose aim is to analyze the remains of ancient ecology, settlement patterns, and technology, in "the process of reconstructing from the material evidence a deceased culture—in many places, a once-living community network" (1986, 94)

(2) "Palestinian" archaeology focuses specifically on the southern Levant; it is not simply "dirt archaeology," however, but entails analysis, research, integration, and especially publication.

(3) One of the primary functions of "Palestinian" archaeology is "to provide stable controls in dated ancient experience in the land and in the ancient Near East generally, that will permit rigorous testing of the historical authenticity of the tradition" (1986, 93).

PUTTING GLOCK'S ARCHAEOLOGY IN PERSPECTIVE

This thoughtful, articulate, and indeed prescient article was not Glock's only contribution to the "new archaeology's" impact on our disciplines in the formative years of the 1970s. He also did innovative work on ceramic technology and ethnoceramics that was well ahead of its time. In addition, he was one of the very few in the field of Palestinian archaeology to this day who has written on archaeological theory for mainstream archaeological and anthropological journals.[2]

In this essay, written more than twenty years after Glock's statement in "Emerging Discipline," I hope to put his work in broader perspective and give it a wider audience. First, one needs to appreciate where we stood in Syro-Palestinian[3] and "biblical archaeology" in the mid-1970s. The *only* critical literature at that time that addressed the challenges of the then-radical "new archaeology" were a short article of my own (1972) and a small monograph entitled *Archaeology and Biblical Studies: Retrospects and Prospects* (1974). In addition, Glock and I in 1974/75 had discussed a manuscript of mine that was soon to appear in the *Interpreters Bible Dictionary Supplementary Volume* (1976).[4] This was the extent of the discussion on "theory" in our branch of archaeology, and indeed in Near Eastern archaeology generally, when Glock wrote. That makes his contribution all the more singular.

Since Glock referred to my 1974 monograph, which we had discussed along with his manuscript, it seems appropriate to compare our early views, then update both. Glock's major stress in the 1970s was on (1) the need for "Palestinian" (my "Syro-Palestinian") archaeology to become an independent discipline, for the sake of the integrity of *both* archaeologies;[5] and (2) the possibilities for a separate "biblical archaeology," as he outlined its nature and objectives, to become an academic (if not professional) discipline.

The first of these points I had already made in 1972 and 1974; and I have insisted on this separation of our fields of inquiry in numerous treatments since the mid-1970s.[6] As the separation did begin to take place, and was in fact complete by the early 1980s, Glock did not comment further, nor did he live long enough to see the full fruition of the developments that he had advocated early on. I can only conclude that he would be gratified today—yet would not hesitate to offer critical reassessments, as I have done.[7] It is now clear that "Syro-Palestinian" archaeology's coming of age as a mature, autonomous discipline in the 1980s was inevitable, given the developing specialization and professionalism in all branches of archaeology in the 1960s onward, not least in the Middle East. It was also necessary, of course, that Syro-

Palestinian archaeology be "desacralized," as Glock also foresaw. "Biblical archaeology" of the classic style could not have survived as a respectable branch of archaeology, either in American and European academic life, or in competition with the burgeoning Israeli and Jordanian secular schools.

Even if these external challenges could have been met, along with the crisis in funding, the lack of properly archaeological aims and methods, theological biases, internal contradictions, and a largely reactionary agenda would all have conspired to hasten the death of the older style "biblical archaeology." Glock and I did not kill "biblical archaeology"; we simply foresaw its demise and wrote its obituary.

In the beginning, many amateur archaeologists and biblical scholars were threatened, or denied the reality; others passively mourned the passing of the familiar "biblical archaeology"; and a few scholars successfully made the painful transition to professional archaeological status.[8] Albert Glock was among the very few of the latter; and he must be admired for having the courage of his conviction that Palestinian archaeology *had* to achieve independent status. In this, he was right both intellectually and morally.

Elsewhere I have written regular "state-of-the-art" analyses of Syro-Palestinian archaeology's growth and development throughout the 1980s until the present.[9] It is now clear that our discipline's separation from Biblical studies—i.e. from philology and especially theology—was not only inevitable, but beneficial. Among the many lasting benefits of the "newer archaeology" are (1) broader research objectives and more explicit research designs, (2) a more interdisciplinary approach, including an ecological orientation, (3) a more sophisticated understanding not only of culture and culture change, but of approachate socio-anthropological theories, (4) the employment of more precise scientific methods in the analysis of materials, (5) a veritable explosion of new and varied field projects, meeting much higher standards of excavation, recording, and publication, (6) wider sources of funding, (7) additional and flourishing American institutes abroad, in Jerusalem, Amman, and Nicosia, (8) an upsurge in graduate enrollments in several university programs devoted specifically to Syro-Palestinian archaeology, (9) a much more professional look at annual professional meetings, including some beyond traditional Society of Biblical Literature/American Schools of Oriental Research circles, (10) the beginnings of a rapprochement with Americanist and general archaeology and, not least, (11), the production of a mass of vastly superior and more useful archaeological data that has truly revolutionized our understandings of such topics as the origins of Israel, the rise of the Israelite state, religion and cult, and the social world of the prophets.[10]

Glock did not live to see this "success story," and there are still a few who doubt it or do not grasp how far-reaching the implications of these changes are. It must be said, however, that the optimistic predictions of early architects of the "new archaeology," like Glock and myself, were predicated on one assumption: that "biblical archaeology, cut loose as it were, would not wither and die, but would develop on its own as a *complementary* field. Advocating the development of Syro-Palestinian archaeology as a separate, autonomous professional discipline did not mean, for either Glock or myself, ignoring or belittling the concerns of the "biblical archaeology" movement, as some now falsely charge.[11] On the contrary, both of us expected that the developments that we encouraged would benefit the *proper* relationship of Syro-Palestinian archaeology and biblical studies. The point of the separation of disciplines that we championed was to create a new and honest *dialogue* between two parallel, fully competent disciplines, each contributing from its own perspectives and objectives to the other. But has that happened?

Glock and I had differed in only one important particular about his second point, the future of "biblical archaeology." He characterized it, as we noted above, as not only a scholarly field of inquiry, but as an "emerging discipline." I, on the other hand, defined "biblical archaeology" over against its parent-discipline, Syro-Palestinian archaeology, as an *interdisciplinary* dialogue between biblical studies and one relatively small aspect of archaeology, i.e., the archaeology of Palestine in the Iron Age. I did not think in the 1970s that "biblical archaeology" could or should become an academic discipline, even in the rather narrow confines of theological seminaries, as Glock presumed. As a result of this conviction, I left the Directorship of the Albright Institute of Archaeological Research in Jerusalem (which Glock later directed) in 1971 to inaugurate a graduate program in Syro-Palestinian archaeology at the University of Arizona. It was my intention that this program would deliberately be affiliated with the

University's renowned Department of Anthropology and Archaeology, which had been one of the pioneers of the "new archaeology" in the 1960s and 1970s. That is where I thought the future would lie; and the anthropological thrust was part of the way I expected that the next generation of young Syro-Palestinian, archaeologists—our best hope—would be trained.

In retrospect, both Glock and I, although we stood then (and I now) on firm philosophical and pedagogical ground, were somewhat overly optimistic. Let us look first at how things have turned out for "biblical archaeology." Today it is clear to all that "biblical archaeology" has not "emerged" as a real discipline at all. On the contrary, no one any longer speaks of that possibility, or even uses the term "biblical archaeology" in scholarly discourse. If "biblical archaeology" was moribund as a discipline when Glock and I wrote in the mid-1970s, it is now dead and almost forgotten. The term itself is retained only in quotation marks, or used by some Israeli archaeologists as a sort of popular "shorthand" in English (Dever 1989).

The reasons for the failure of "biblical archaeology" to achieve Glock's goal of disciplinary status in the 1970s–1990s are numerous. Among the factors, I would note (1) the long-standing internal weaknesses noted above, (2) the failure to respond creatively to the challenges posed by both the "new archaeology" and the increasingly dominant Syro-Palestinian archaeology, (3) insufficient resolution, in facing toward the past, even to complete the publication of major previous projects (Shanks 1995), (4) the inability, with few exceptions (below), to mount, staff, and fund new field projects that would meet more recent standards, (5) inertia in the face of the challenge of the burgeoning "national schools" in the Middle East, (6) the failure to create, or even perpetuate, academic positions, especially in seminaries and (7) the fact that biblical studies meanwhile had turned away from historical studies, in favor of new "literary" approaches that had little or no use for archaeology (Haynes and McKenzie 1993).

Today "biblical archaeology" has no prospects for becoming an academic and professional discipline, unless in a very few conservative seminaries that may be willing to support it. Most American "biblical archaeologists" are seminarians or religion professors who affiliate with Israeli "joint" excavations, but receive little recognition, produce few scholarly publications, train no younger Americans for a career, and do not ever secure their own positions at home when they retire. That pattern alone, the implications of which are not sufficiently appreciated, would eliminate "biblical archaeology" as even a serious field of inquiry in North America within one generation. And Israeli and Jordanian archaeologists, who already predominate, can hardly be expected to carry on the American and European tradition. The point is simple: *their* Bible is very different; and their post-Colonial national concerns in archaeology in the Middle East will diverge increasingly from ours.

I noted above the relative success of Syro-Palestinian archaeology in achieving disciplinary status in the 1970s–1990s, compared with "biblical archaeology" and its difficulties in coming of age. Both Glock and I were confident of that success in our predictions in the early 1970s—indeed *assumed* it—in our concern for "biblical archaeology's" survival as an ancillary field. It is now evident, however, that, here too, we were overly optimistic. Syro-Palestinian archaeology *has* triumphed, in that it has become the only surviving, viable academic and professional discipline, now simply as one branch of Near Eastern (and Old World) archaeology. Specifically, Syro-Palestinian archaeology has successfully met challenges number 2, 4, 5, and 6 listed above, whereas "biblical archaeology" did not. Yet there were several *other* challenges that neither Glock nor I could have envisioned in the 1970s. The most significant turned out to be (1) the rapid and near-complete ascendancy of the "national schools," which now constitute the major threat for all the foreign schools, (2) the worsening political situation in the Middle East, (3) the retrenchment in the humanities in American academic life, which has resulted in the loss of both present and potential university positions, as well as the virtual disappearance of sources for funds for research and excavation (such as the National Endowment for the Humanities), and (4) the fact, which we must now concede, that our "courtship" of Americanist archaeology and anthropology has not really been reciprocated (Dever 1995).

The last development deserves further comment. I, in particular, had hoped finally to make "poor Palestine" a respectable and instructive case-study in the pursuit of one of Americanist archaeology's primary goals, the comparative analysis of "the rise of complex society." To enable us to contribute to this discussion, however, as we were obviously now well-equipped to do, it was necessary for Syro-

Palestinian archaeologists to be taken seriously by our would-be colleagues *as* archaeologists (one might say, as social theorists), not simply historians of antiquity, much less "Biblicists." I regret to say that by and large that ambition has not been achieved. At best, a few of our recent Ph.D.s may read an occasional paper at anthropological meetings or publish now and then in anthropological journals. Meanwhile, we have scarcely been able to place more than a handful of our recent graduates in anthropology departments—and most new Ph.D.'s we cannot place at all. Most Near Eastern Studies departments are in decline or moving to Islamic studies, and our graduates are too specialized to fit in university departments of Religion; and a fulltime Syro-Palestinian archaeologist would certainly be regarded as an esoteric luxury in all the mainstream theological seminaries I know.

Where does that situation leave *both* fledgling "disciplines"? Neither seems to have what is required for an academic discipline to thrive: (1) a place of acceptance and respect in American academic life, preferably somewhere in the humanities; (2) at least a core of secure academic and/or research positions, in whatever departments or programs; and (3) access to sufficient public and private funds to support basic research, in this case archaeological fieldwork that enables the discipline to remain competitive and to create an independent database. Syro-Palestinian archaeology has *become* a discipline, against numerous odds; but can it *survive*?

CONCLUSION

The irony, it seems to me, is that Glock, I, and others like us, having won the battle, may have lost the war. It now appears that the only major base of support for *both* "Biblical" and "Syro-Palestinian" archeology in North America is in a few enlightened conservative church circles on the one hand; and on the other hand among many educated Jewish and Christian laypeople, for whom Israel and the Bible still have irresistible appeal. This popular support is welcome, and particularly gratifying in these hard times; but clearly it is not enough to sustain *either* of the "two archaeologies" (to use Glock's term) as an academic discipline. In reflective moments, I sometimes wonder whether our campaign to "liberate" Palestinian archaeology was justified. I believe that it was, however, because all scholarly disciplines inevitably go through cycles of birth, death, rebirth, as Thomas S. Kuhn's *Structure of Scientific Revolutions* (1970) has shown.

Recently I have called for a "new style of biblical archaeology," aligned with the "post-processual, contextual, new critical-historical archaeology" now in vogue (Dever 1993). I think that Albert Glock would have spoken out with me, as courageously as he did in the mid-1970s.

NOTES

1. I am indebted to Glock for discussing this article with me in 1974/75 while the manuscript was in preparation.
2. See the reference to *American Antiquity* (Glock 1985). For Glock's other articles, see (1975; 1983).
3. For my term "Syro-Palestinian" archaeology, borrowed from Albright's original usage in the 1920s–1930s, see Dever (1972) and all subsequent publications. The essential cultural links of Palestine with Syria and "Greater Canaan" are becoming steadily clearer with continued excavations.
4. See Dever (1976). For brief histories of these two fields written after the early 1970s, especially in American scholarship, see Dever (1974; 1976; 1980; 1981; 1982; especially 1985; 1989; 1992; 1993; 1996b; and full references there).
5. The term "two archaeologies" is Glock's (1985).
6. On the need for separation of the two disciplines, so as to foster a mutual dialogue, see especially my treatments since 1974 in Dever (1976; 1980; 1982; 1985; 1992; 1993; 1996b).
7. See particularly Dever (1988; 1993; 1996b), Meyers (1984), Stager (1990).
8. In addition to Glock, other biblical scholars (all of them clergymen and/or seminary professors) who became, in my judgment, fully "professional" if not fulltime specialists, would include of course G. E. Wright himself (in his last years); many of his students, like P. W. Lapp, W. G. Dever, J. S. Holladay, J. D. Seger, L. T. Geraty, L. G. Herr, and others; and J. A. Callaway. Younger Syro-Palestinian archaeologists, entering the field in the 1980s, for instance, did not face the need for such radical shifts, since by then the field was *assumed* to be specialized, secularized, and professionalized. Israeli and Jordanian archaeologists never faced the issue of "professionalization" at all, since none had either a clerical background or any relationship with the religious establishment.

9. See the references in notes 3–7 above.
10. If "New Testament archaeology" is conspicuously absent, that is because it can scarcely be said to exist as a *discipline*. There is some excavation of Classical period sites in Israel and Jordan, but rarely related to biblical studies in any sense. For all practical purposes, "biblical" is "Old Testament" archaeology.
11. For the misunderstanding or caricature of "biblical archaeology" among "revisionist" biblical scholars who have little interest in ancient Israelite history, see for instance Lemche and Thompson (1994). For a sober view from a biblical scholar, see Drinkard (1989).

REFERENCES

Dever, W. G.
1972   Biblical Archaeology—or the Archaeology of Syria-Palestine? *Christian News from Israel* 22: 21, 22.
1974   *Archaeology and Biblical Studies: Retrospects and Prospects.* Evanston: Seabury-Western Theological Seminary.
1976   Archaeology. Pp. 44–52 in *Interpreter's Bible Dictionary—Supplementary Volume*, ed. K. Crim. Nashville: Abingdon.
1980   Archaeological Method in Israel: A Continuing Revolution. *Biblical Archaeologist* 43: 41–48.
1981a   Biblical Theology and Biblical Archaeology: An Appreciation of G. Ernest Wright. *Harvard Theological Review* 73: 1–15.
1981   The Impact of the "New Archaeology" on Syro-Palestinian Archaeology. *Bulletin of the American Schools of Oriental Research* 242: 15–29.
1982   Retrospects and Prospects in Biblical and Syro-Palestinian Archaeology. *Biblical Archaeologist* 45: 103–7.
1985   Syro-Palestinian and Biblical Archaeology. Pp. 31–74 in *The Hebrew Bible and Its Modern Interpreters*, eds. D. A. Knight and G. M. Tucker. Philadelphia: Fortress.
1988   Impact of the "New Archaeology." Pp. 337–52 in *Benchmarks in Time and Culture: Introduction to Palestinian Archaeology*, eds. J. F. Drinkard, G. L. Mattingly, and J. M. Miller. Atlanta: Scholars.
1989   Yigael Yadin: Proto-typical Biblical Archaeologist. *Eretz-Israel* 20: 44*–51*.
1992   Archaeology, Syro-Palestinian and Biblical. Pp. I: 354–67 in *Anchor Bible Dictionary*, ed. D. N. Freedman. New York: Doubleday.

1993   Biblical Archaeology—Death and Rebirth? Pp. 706–22 in *Biblical Archaeology Today, 1990. Proceedings of the Second Internatioonal Congress on Biblical Archaeology*, Jerusalem, June 1990, eds. A. Biran and J. Aviram. Jerusalem: Israel Exploration Society.

1994   Archaeology, Texts, and History-Writing: Toward an Epistemology. Pp. 105–17 in *Uncovering Ancient Stones: Essays in Memory of H. Neal Richardson,* ed. L. M. Hopf. Winona Lake, IN: Eisenbrauns.

1995   The Death of a Discipline. *Biblical Archaeology Review* 21: 51–55, 70.

1996a   Archaeology and the Current Crisis in Israelite Historiography. *Eretz-Israel* 25: 18*–27*.

1996b   Biblical Archaeology. Pp. I: 315–19 in *The Oxford Encyclopedia of Archaeology in the Near East,* ed. E. M. Meyers. New York: Oxford University.

Drinkard, J. F.
1989   The Position of Biblical Archaeology Within Biblical Studies. *Review and Expositor* 86: 603–15.

Glock, A. E.
1975   Homo Faber: The Pot and Potter at Taanach. *BASOR* 219: 9–28
1982   Ceramic Ethno-techniculture. Pp. 145–51 in *Studies in the History and Archaeology of Jordan* I, ed. A. Hadidi, Amman. Department of Antiquities.

1983   The Use of Ethnography in Archaeological Research Design. Pp.171–79 in *The Quest for the Kingdom of God: Studies in Honor of George E. Mendenhall,* eds. H. B. Hoffman, F. A. Spina, and A. R. W. Green. Winona Lake, IN: Eisenbrauns.

1985   Tradition and Change in Two Archaeologies. *American Antiquity* 50: 404–77.

1986   Biblical Archaeology, an Emerging Discipline. Pp. 85–101 in *The Archaeology of Jordan and Other Studies Presented to Siegfried Horn*, eds. L. T. Geraty and L. G. Herr. Berrien Springs, MI: Andrews University.

Haynes, S. R., and S. L.McKenzie., eds.
1993   *To Each Its Own Meaning: An Introduction to Biblical Criticisms and Their Application.* Louisville: Westminster/John Knox.

Lemche, N. P., and Thompson, T. L.
1994   Did Biran Kill King David? The Bible in the Light of Archaeology. *Journal for the Study of the Old Testament* 64: 3–22

Meyers, E. M.
  1984   The Bible and Archaeology. *Biblical Archaeologist* 47: 36–40.
Shanks, H., ed.
  1995   *Archaeology's Publication Problem.* Washington: Biblical
            Archaeology Society.
Stager, L. E.
  1990   Toward the Future: It's Just a Matter of Time. Pp. 746–55 in
            *Biblical Archaeology Today, 1990. Proceedings of the First
            International Congress on Biblical Archaeology*, Jerusalem,
            June 1987, ed. J. Amitai. Jerusalem: Israel Exploration Society.

3 Memories of Palestine: Uses of Oral History and Archaeology in Recovering the Palestinian Past

THOMAS M. RICKS

INTRODUCTION

History, some may contend, is rewritten by every generation. For historians, it is surely reexamined, rethought, and reinterpreted by every generation. Whether it be the history of early Canaanite sea peoples or the villagers of the medieval Jerusalem or the merchants of nineteenth century Jabal Nablus, researchers of history question the old and new evidence, reexamine the methodology used and seek out new perspectives from the data. Unfortunately, little of Palestine's history is being reexamined and few Palestinian historians are looking for new perspectives due in part to the social and political turbulence of occupation, the severe limitations placed on doing any field studies in Palestine, and the lack of access to archival sources or travel to archival holdings within and outside of Palestine. Indeed, much of Palestinian history is the traditional political history of great families, or leading male political and military figures. Few historians have focused on Palestine's social or economic history, or on the "everyday lives of ordinary people."[1]

The peoples whose lives are "unwritten" and whose narratives are unchronicled are generally left without a scribe or an interpreter. It is the oral historian who seeks out those unscribed and unchronicled peoples whose memories are preserved either in the oral traditions of a community or in the collective memory of the living. In interviewing

23

those with "eyewitness history" as opposed to the professional reciters of the community, the oral historian collects, transcribes and analyzes the lesser known social, economic and cultural dimensions of those with "ordinary lives."[2] In the process of "harvesting" the memories of peoples, the oral historian and the reciter pass through "layers" as it were of remembered time and place left unattended in the rush of life and its events. In part marginalized in the court chronicles by their social and economic status, and in part victimized by the men and women of power, the ordinary people of the city and countryside remain nameless and faceless in traditional Palestinian historiography. Oral history is one of several disciplines that can write their lives into the historical record as narratives of past and present generations (Swedenburg 1985/86; 1988; 1995).

Archaeologists also examine the lives of "ordinary people." Due to the nature of the discipline, archaeology is the science of everything left behind, and the recorder of small and large urban centers, homes, palaces, tools and technologies. Primarily concerned with the material cultures of a region, the archaeologist relies on a myriad of sciences and techniques to discover the bases for iron production, to understand the movement of trade, and to explain the presence of human habitation. The very contours of the land reveal many of the social, economic and cultural habits of the peoples of the region. Rather than layers of memory, the archaeologist uncovers slowly and systemically the strata of past civilizations, towns, and ordinary villages built upon by successors and unattended by the present generations. Due to the nature of field research and the archaeological data, "reading" the evidence is surely one of the more difficult tasks of archaeology.[3]

Unfortunately, Palestinian oral history and archaeology are generally little utilized as research tools in the history of Palestine and Palestinians.[4] Both disciplines require extensive field study research, systematic and careful collection of the data, and a vigorous use of corroborative evidence in order to understand their "findings" and to make any historical generalizations. Oral historians and archaeologists are both dependent on interdisciplinary and multidisciplinary approaches to their fields of study, both are open to new historical and scientific methodologies to understand more fully their evidence, and both require depositing their collected materials in repositories for other researchers to study and to utilize.

ORAL HISTORY AND ARCHAEOLOGY

Despite some similarities, oral historians and archaeologists actually conduct their research, analyze their historical evidence, and arrive at their conclusions in different ways. Unlike the archaeologist, for example, oral historians collect the "living memory" of a person or persons as the bases for their historical analyses and generalizations. In some cultures and societies, "transmitted memories" or oral traditions that are handed down from generation to generation are used as historical evidence.[5] Archaeologists, on the other hand, depend on the material culture such as pottery sherds, metal fragments, plant life or fossil deposits to begin their archaeological analyses. The tangible evidence of tool technology or metallurgical fragments left in kilns or in marketplaces serves as the bases of the generalizations.

Although apparently very distinct disciplines, both oral history and archaeology confront many of same theoretical and methodological issues. Both, for example, must begin the collection of the historical evidence in systematic and carefully defined contexts. The "uncovering" and cataloging of evidence follow rigorous procedures so as to preserve as faithfully as possible both the historical data and the conditions in which the data are uncovered . In the process of analyzing the "living memories" of eyewitnesses or the artifacts of ancient human habitation, the oral historian and archaeologist normally examine the data with an eye to internal contradictions within the evidence, and seek out external corroborative sources. Both disciplines find ways of "testing" the validity of the evidence either in the chemical laboratory or in the "remembering" of other eyewitnesses. Carbon-14 dating results, or the checking of dates, times, places or events in archival sources, are common verification practices of both fields.

Oral historians have gone beyond the random collection of "old people's nostalgia" and lost dreams. Earlier attempts to collect the memories of famous people, the Depression Years, or World War II have produced mountains of taped interviews without a proportionate amount of analysis or writing. Historians now seek out their research topics with a thesis in mind or an historical problem to solve. With the tape or video recorder in hand, following hours of preliminary research into the written and archival materials, the oral historian today sets out to accomplish the collection of oral recitations with an overarching plan in mind. Once focused on a general thesis or historical problem, the historian begins to formulate a series of interview questions, identify the appropriate age group(s) for the recitations and then identify the oral history reciters themselves. In all probability, the oral historian will be working towards the restoration of parts of a destroyed cultures, or trying to rediscover the lives of an abandoned neighborhoods, village, or town, or investigate the accomplishments of a little-known social movements. In each case, the historical narratives of the reciters usually return time and time again to a "sense of moment, object, or place" in their memories. Moreover, in the process of recording those "living memories," the historian needs to be sensitive to a range of restricting or defining factors such as the affect of ethnicity and gender in the ways the "remembering" occurs, the language in which the recitation is being given, the relationship of the historian and the oral history reciter, and the historian's place within or outside the society and culture of the oral history reciter. Ultimately, the trust that begins to occur between the historian and the reciter(s) grows as the oral history reciter unfolds the layers of memory and reveals the moments of the past. It is known that reciters reveal as much as they want the historian to know. In that regard, historical narratives are, in many cases, a *shared recitation* that resulted from the increasingly trustful, social relationship between the reciter and the historian. In that sense, all oral history is *social* history.

Some oral historians place emphasis on "collective remembering" as a way to preserve a neighborhood's memory, to rediscover individual "memory pictures," and to correct the general "community narrative."[6] Oral historians are also interested in "mapping" the memory of a place or neighborhood by asking the oral history reciters to draw a map from memory, to walk literally around and through the remembered places, and to comment on the "memory map" in juxtaposition with a professional survey map. The differences observed by the oral history reciter reveal much about the reciter's perspectives as well as adding important social and cultural dimensions to the narrative of a place and time. It is known that men remember differently than women, or Chinese-Americans from Anglo-Americans, or Native Americans from Latino-Americans because of their different needs, uses, experiences and traditions as well as class, race and gender perspectives of those places and events observed in the oral recitations.

Social historians are interested in how people used and continue to use spaces of all types in so far as the use of land is an expression of social relationships. Old markets and outdoor trading posts, homes and shops, farm lands and waterways, factories and mineral mines are essentially invested with importance *in terms of people* and their social relations with each other at a particular time and place. Thus, to remember a place in the past is to invest that place and time with a "sense of memory of place and time" and to invest in it a specific social value important and recognized not only by the individual but also by the community.

When Palestinians begin to remember their villages, their towns or the Old City of Jerusalem, their very concrete memories of places and events are immediately filled with an emotional recognition of the social relationship that Palestinians have had with other Palestinians in that place at a specific time. The idea of the village or town street or main square is invested with the specific images of *people remembered in those places*, and the reciter's own relationship with those people in those places. Palestinian students from Birzeit University who conducted oral history projects in 1983 to 1985 about their own villages found their village elders unable to complete their recitation of their memory of those places so overcome were they with their emotions and the intimate relationship that those places had with their Palestinian contemporaries, their parents and even themselves. On another occasion in 1984, during a research project with Palestinian refugees, a group of Birzeit University researchers encountered long and painful lapses when asking the refugees "what was the most precious thing that you lost?" The refugees invariably answered with "my home," "my flocks," "my children" or "my olive trees" underscoring the power of objects, places and people still very much alive in their living memories.[7] In the course of several hours of videotaping in 1995, this writer wanted to find out more about the reciter's village since the name and place of the village had not yet come up in the "remembered history" of the reciter. At the instant of mentioning the name of the old village now entirely destroyed within present-day Israel, however, the entire personality of the reciter changed to one of grief and deep sorrow though he had been joking only moments before. The taping was saved, so to speak, by a quick reference back to some incidents previously mentioned. That person's "sense of memory of a place and time" had remained so remarkably strong over the fifty years since the destruction of his village that the mere mention of its name set in motion images and fond memories that the person seemed, for a brief instant, to have been transported back in time to that very time and place.[8]

More recently, two young Palestinian researchers were carrying out an oral history project in the region of Ramallah focusing on the 1948 memories of 10 to 15 year old children now aged 56 to 61 years old who had been expelled from their homes during the 1947–1949 war. The researchers have reported that frequently reciters stopped talking entirely when asked, "what do you remember leaving behind on the day your family was evicted from your home?" Again, the strength of the images of a red coat or bicycle or favorite book caused the reciter to pause, and even to break down in many cases in the process of recalling that special object.[9] The remembered objects' assumed importance for the reciter not only in terms of the objects' relationship to the reciter and his family but also to the memory of the event and to his home now lost along with the special object. In this case, the "sense of memory of time and place" so imbued with the childhood emotions of those times and events became a "social memory of time and place." The reciters' reflections back upon a time not readily recalled became a more intense memory due to their ages at the time of the expulsion, the specialness of a particular coat or bicycle that was given to them by someone else, and the recognition of "innocence lost" at that time.

Verification of the oral historical evidence is an ongoing task for the oral historian. Archival research is usually corroborated with other written evidence, or tested by a careful examination of internal evidence, or a chemical verification of the authenticity of the manuscript. Oral historical research relies on corroborating oral recitations with other oral histories, with written primary sources, and with scientific data available for that historical period. Specifically, the oral historians search for contemporary photographs, parish records of baptism, marriage and death notices, grave stones, diaries, letters and other written primary sources. Natural phenomena and cataclysmic events verified by scientific reporting are also relied on to verify the oral recitations, such as, earthquakes, comets, solar and lunar eclipses, harsh winters and summers or plagues. The 1927 and 1936 earthquakes in Palestine were, to some Palestinians, more than a natural disturbance; given the years of the earthquakes, the subsequent 1929 "Wailing Wall Disturbances," and the 1936 all-Palestine strike, the earthquakes became harbingers of momentous political events in

Palestine. Oral reciters who remember those earthquakes speak with great authority and detail about the exact time of day of the earthquakes, where they were at the time of disasters, and their feelings about the consequences.[10] They are able to do so due to the added "memory value" of the event when upon reflection they have come to connect the natural disasters with the human struggles. Thus, with no prompting from the historian, the reciter had "pegged" the event and its details to another event enabling the reciter to be quite accurate in the "remembered history."

Archaeologists, on the other hand, begin their work with historical research and field surveys. From the outset, the "dig" is the heart of the investigative process. From the test trench to the mapping of the site, the archaeologist carefully and systematically recovers the historical evidence stratum by stratum. The painstaking recovery of unearthed artifacts, of sifting through the midden piles and pottery sherds, and in identification of each and every piece of material culture, represents one level of the archaeological discipline.

Once the materials are recovered and tagged, the researcher turns to other disciplines, techniques and specialists for assistance in verification and further identification of the findings. Field and laboratory tests, comparative analysis with similar artifacts from similar periods, and corroborative scientific data lay the bases for possible archaeological generalizations. Severe weather and climate, human tampering with the archaeological site, or previous inexperienced researchers contribute to the difficulties of recovering the archaeological past and the writing of a nearly accurate historical record. Archaeologists are further hampered by governmental interventions, changing political systems, and local or regional interference.

In the mid-nineteenth century, European scientific and military expeditions moved throughout Palestine in search of archaeological sites with biblical relevance. There was little interest in the history of Palestine or the Palestinian peoples. Indeed, the nineteenth century European archaeologists and explorers had European and Christian interests primarily on their minds; that is, the verification of Judeo-Christian roots for the recovery and preservation of their Christian, European heritage. Indirectly, such actions contributed to the increasing interest by the European nations for control of Palestine, resulting in an intensification of the religious and political struggles among the Orthodox, Protestant and Catholic churches in Palestine. The *Palestine Exploration Fund Quarterly Statement* published several articles on the need to preserve the biblical lands from the "indolent" and "ignorant" Palestinian peasantry and to place the region into the hands of the diligent and enterprising Jewish communities (Conder 1879; Finn 1879; Hauser 1900; Blyth 1917). From the 1880s onward, the rise of European (Christian and Jewish) settlements and colonies in Ottoman Palestine were justified in part by the earlier archaeological and imperial enterprises.

The archaeological surveys and digs continued through the Mandate Period under British rule into the Israeli-Jordanian-Egyptian period. It was not until the establishment of Birzeit University (1972) and the other private Palestinian universities in the 1970s that the existence of Palestinian departments of Archaeology were possible. And even then, Birzeit University's Department of Archaeology struggled for a decade before getting the appropriate national and international attention that it deserved. Dr. Albert E. Glock was the principal architect of that fledgling department and "it is in large measure due to his enthusiasm and commitment to Palestinian archaeology that a new generation of professional and locally trained archaeologists are emerging in the West Bank."[11]

BIRZEIT UNIVERSITY, ORAL HISTORY, AND ARCHAEOLOGY

I first met Al Glock in 1983 at Birzeit University's Old Campus in the village of Birzeit in the Occupied West Bank. I had just begun to teach full-time as a Visiting Professor of History in the Department of Middle Eastern Studies and had been assigned to teach the Department's seminar on historiography. In learning about Al and the Department of Archaeology, I had asked where I might find him and the Department. One of my seminar students guided me to the Department. It was not a long trip down the road from the Old Campus which was itself a set of buildings that originally belonged to the Nasir family homestead. Due to the constant growth from its establishment as a Girls' School in 1924, the University had completely outgrown its original location spilling over to buildings across one street and down another. The

Birzeit Research Center, for example, was housed at the bottom of the village ridge, and the Department of Middle Eastern Studies was housed in a new apartment building across the street and down the hill from the University's main gate. The Department of Archaeology also was "off campus," a few minutes walk towards the village center.

On entering the courtyard of a home, I then was escorted up a long flight of steps, across the open veranda into a beehive of rooms filled with earthenware, pottery sherds, boxes of material culture, research notes and classroom desks. The last room that I passed was Al Glock's and it was empty for the moment. Al was as usual showing a student assistant how to complete one form or another for a past archaeological survey when I finally met him returning to his office. I wanted him to come to my seminar and speak about archaeology and Palestinian villages. He readily accepted, we set a date for his visit and I left.

That meeting was the first of many meetings and hours of discussions about Palestine, Palestinians, and their archaeological past and present. Between 1983 and 1985, I found a number of occasions to visit Al both in his department office in Birzeit and at his home in Beit Hanina just north of Jerusalem. The seminar on "Palestinian Villages: Past and Present" continued to be popular with the students both in History and in other disciplines. Al's periodic lectures to the students on archaeological methodology and research techniques were of immense assistance in their seminar research projects on their own villages some of which were destroyed in 1948–1949, and 1967, while others were still in place. The students spent the entire semester gathering materials for their seminar presentation, collecting old Palestine passports and currency, maps and photos of the "old village," tapes of interviews with the elders about the Mandate period and the British occupation, and drawings of the old mosque and market centers. The original and copied materials, tapes, photos and maps were deposited in the Birzeit Research Center to form the basis of a largescale oral history collection, and to complement an ongoing project by Drs. Kamal Abdul Fattah and Sharif Kana'na from Birzeit's Departments of Middle Eastern Studies and Sociology respectively.[12]

In 1988, two of Birzeit University's historians, Drs. Adel Yahya and Mahmoud Ibrahim, began an oral history project on the youth, or *shibab,* who were directing and coordinating the Palestinian uprising known as the Intifada.[13] The project covered a three-year period and included over two hundred interviews of Palestinian youth in both the West Bank and Gaza Strip. The object was to let the youth who were changing the course of Palestinian history speak for themselves about the directions and accomplishments of the Intifada. Between 1989 and 1992, the oral history reciters (the youth) were interviewed in Arabic on several occasions by a team of Birzeit researchers including Drs. Yahya and Ibrahim. The interviews were then transcribed, and the tapes copied and catalogued. A collection of articles based on the oral history project of the Intifada were part of a draft manuscript published by the Tamer Institute in the Spring 1994. As part of Tamer's 1994 summer educational programs, a one-week workshop on "How to Do Oral History" was then organized and conducted at Tamer Institute in Ramallah by Drs. Mahmoud Ibrahim, Sonia Nimr, Thomas Ricks and Adel Yahya for adults and teachers of social science. The publication of *The Oral History of the Intifada* in late 1994 became the first book in Arabic to study the theories, methods and applications of oral history (Yahya, Ibrahim and Ricks 1994).

In addition to the activities of the Birzeit University historians, others have conducted oral history research projects in the West Bank and in Jordan.[14] Dr. Adnan Musallam, a professor in the Humanities Program and now Dean of Arts at Bethlehem University requires his students to conduct oral history projects as an integral part of their course work. Furthermore, a younger generation of Palestinian archaeologists, trained at Birzeit University, and in European and U.S. universities, are applying their skills and knowledge of Palestine in innovative ways including producing a television series on the ancient, medieval and modern history of Palestine based on both archaeological and oral history evidence. Others have established cultural tour agencies in Ramallah, Nablus and Beit Sahour for visits to Palestinian archaeological sites, and have begun archaeological research institutes in the West Bank and Jordan valley.[15] The Birzeit and Bethlehem initiatives in oral history and in archaeology represent long term interests in preserving and restoring the role of the Palestinian people in the historical records of the region. The recently established Palestinian Ministries of Education, of Culture and of Antiquities under the Palestinian National Authority are building on these earlier initiatives in order to create the basic national institutions for the preservation and promotion of Palestinian history and culture.

SOCIAL HISTORY AND MEMORIES OF PALESTINE

Oral history and archaeology are natural "allies" in the researching and writing of social history. Not only do both disciplines examine and seek to explain the range of social strata and institutions within a given community but also both disciplines look at the various ways a set of communities react and interact with each other over time and place. The Palestinian villages, we are told from the *sijallat* or religious court records, interacted constantly with each other as well as with the towns and market centers within a given region. They did so in terms of life rituals such as births, baptisms, and marriage, and in terms of religious and agricultural festivals in the springtime and autumn (Doumani 1995, 9–15, 54–94). The need to seek the assistance of each other in the harvesting of olives or almonds, which were labor-intensive activities, necessitated the labor of many "hands," while the occasional sheltering of families driven from their towns or villages by military forces or natural disasters literally forced the communities of the Palestinian coastal and hinterland regions into each others arms, and homes. The presence of guest rooms, granaries, and stables indicate to the archaeologists the extent of material wealth and social status of the homeowner while the remembered histories of the village or town elders clarifies the social status, the extent of social intercourse, and the role of a particular family within a larger community. Both the archaeological and oral history evidence corroborate the written records of the courts, and the literati. Indeed, the archaeological and oral history evidence raise questions and issues not found in the archival sources on Palestinian social history.

The case of the schools of Palestine is an excellent example. In the course of searching through the secondary and primary written sources on the social history of Palestinian schools over the past one hundred years, it became clear to this researcher that a contradiction existed in the historical narrative. While Palestinians both in the villages and in the towns of coastal and hinterland Palestine placed enormous emphasis on the education of both their sons and daughters, particularly from the first decades of the twentieth century, neither the villager nor the townsperson put much stock in the national schools established by Palestinian educators. Rather, Palestinians from the upper and middle classes as well as from other social sectors of the society consistently sought out the foreign missionary schools if at all possible for their children's education. It is important to remember that the same period of intense interest in mission schools coincided with the rise of local and regional nationalist activism particularly in Jaffa and Haifa on the coast, and in Jerusalem and Nablus in the Hinterland. In the process of conducting a three-year oral history project, it was found that the Palestinian oral history recitations from former students, teachers, and administrators in those twentieth century mission and national schools resolved much of the apparent "contradiction."[16]

Over the course of the eighteenth and nineteenth centuries, a number of the leading Christian Palestinian notables and urban families had sought the "protection" and assistance of the European merchants and consular officials. They had done so with greater frequency as the nineteenth century progressed and as European attempts to penetrate the hinterland region of Ottoman Palestine increased in intensity. By the beginning of the twentieth century, the urban Christian middle and upper classes were sending their sons and daughters regularly to the Christian missionary schools on the coast and in the hinterland while their Muslim counterparts attended the Ottoman schools principally in Jerusalem. The majority of Palestinians, on the other hand, had little choice but to attend the relatively few village and town schools run either by the Orthodox church or by the local Muslim leaders.

By the end of World War I, however, the social role and political fortunes of the Christian missionary schools had changed dramatically. Under the colonial umbrella of the Christian British Mandatory Government, the mission schools began to experience an enrollment boom that included both Muslim and Christian boys and girls from nearly every level of society from the urban and rural regions. The establishment of the British Department of Education contributed considerably to the increase of schools and students. Under the rubric of "government" schools, the British oversaw two types of schools in Palestine: the few elite British administered and financed schools, and all the rest administered and financed by Palestinians whose facilities and courses met the Mandate's minimum standards. Nonetheless, with an occasional Mandate subsidy for at least one government trained teacher, the "government" schools did flourish. At the same time, the mission schools nearly doubled their attendance with each decade of British colonial rule. Between 1920 and 1945, the number of girls and boys attending the missionary schools tripled while the overall numbers of Palestinian children in the elementary and secondary grades in the "government" schools had gone from a few thousand to nearly 300,000.[17]

The colonial Department of Education, staffed at the top by British personnel and administered by Palestinian Christian, Jewish and Muslim educators, set out to shape nearly every facet of Palestinian social and political life, dedicating much time to building schools, training teachers, and enforcing educational standards.[18] Part of the answer to the growth of schools and students in Mandatory Palestine is therefore the leadership of both the British Department of Education, and Palestinian educators. On the other hand, the period was one of intense political activism at the local and regional levels and accelerated emigration to the United States and to Europe. It was also a period of increasing violent confrontations between rural and urban Palestinians against the Zionist program of unlimited immigration, land purchases, settlements, and British colonial rule.

It is remarkable, therefore, that so few middle or upper class Palestinian families supported the Palestinian national schools. Rather, the trend was to attend and therefore financially support the mission and British colonial schools. Such a trend ran counter to the very visible support for other Palestinian nationalist enterprises, such as women's social organizations, political parties, certain "national" newspapers and industries.[19]

A resolution of the "historical contradiction" lies in great part in the following information, which is based on the oral history field research:

1. The clerical and administrative job opportunities in the British Mandate's civil service and law courts, and in the British Council's libraries and English-language programs, attracted the urban Palestinian families who understood that English language education insured a steady income for both Palestinian men, women, and their families, thus enhancing the familial social and economic status. The missionary and British government schools also prepared their students well for the highly-prized Palestinian matriculation certificate which essentially guaranteed a job in the British civil, military or legal services in Palestine. Thus the British and American-run schools became highly desirable for Christian and Muslim boys and girls of all ages and class background.

2. The instruction in one of the mission or government schools also meant learning subjects of importance to the European and U.S. educational and commercial institutions, thus enabling the Palestinians to enter the commercial, financial and industrial sectors of the Mandate economy. The subjects of law, accountancy, finance, marketing and banking became very popular courses in the evening professional schools in Jerusalem, Jaffa or Haifa during the 1930s and 1940s. Many such schools were conducted entirely in European languages such as the Jerusalem Evelyn Rothschild School, or the Edwin Samuel College of the Middle East located at the Jerusalem YMCA; other similar professional schools were established in Jaffa and Haifa as well.

3. In addition, the Christian and Muslim families were generally very interested in keeping their daughters in Palestine for their post-secondary schooling, for a job in the British civil, military or legal services, or, in time, for marriage to one of the marriageable Palestinian doctors, professors or lawyers returning from overseas universities.

4. Finally, the mission and British education that led to the obtaining of the Palestinian Matriculation Certificate insured a young Palestinian man or woman acceptance into the regional universities in Syria and Egypt, or, better yet, into the prestigious American University of Beirut (AUB), or universities in Europe and the United States. Palestinian men usually entered AUB directly for a four-year undergraduate education, and the women attended either the Beirut Women's College or the American Junior College before going on to AUB. While the graduates of the Egyptian and Syrian universities returned to educational and administrative jobs in Palestine, many of the AUB graduates went on to the United States for professional graduate degrees. In addition, Palestinians who did not get into regional or overseas universities frequently joined the rising emigration of Palestinian males to Europe or to the United States.[20] It was clear to Palestinians that attendance at the missionary or British government schools rather than at the national Palestinian schools ensured the kind of education that literally "got them ahead" of others. Thus, the overall prestige benefits for the Palestinian Christian or Muslim family whose son or daughter had attended one of the Christian mission or British government schools raised the social, economic and even political status of the family within the Palestinian community as a whole. The oral history recitations, therefore, of the former Palestinian students,

faculty and administrators make clear the rationale for choosing the missionary and British government schools over the Palestinian national schools.

One of the recurring themes during the oral history recitations by Palestinian women, moreover, was the range of problems such academic and career "opportunities" provided the Palestinian female. The sisters watched with dismay as their brothers were given special treatment in terms of the schools that they attended and the subjects that they studied. Even when the sisters were sent to the few prestigious women schools, such as College de St. Joseph, or the Jerusalem Girls' College or Schmidt's College for Girls, they were limited to the humanities and to "domestic" subjects appropriate for young women in a traditional society. If their interests were in areas such as science, mathematics and law, they were discouraged from thinking of pursuing those fields which were conceived as being "masculine" and more appropriate for men. The women also found fewer career paths available to them although their educational background, linguistic skills and overall matriculation scores were not infrequently higher than their brothers; the latter went off to British and U.S. colleges and universities to study science, engineering and law while their sisters stayed in Palestine or were sent to neighboring countries to study the humanities and social sciences. Two of the reciters specifically mentioned their interests in the natural sciences, which they finally pursued only after years of arguments and angry confrontations with their families. In some cases, the resentment of sisters towards their brothers and parents persist to this day.

On the other hand, nearly all the Christian missionary and British government schools had a "residency" requirement whereby the girls stayed at the school for one or two years as a "boarder" even though their families lived in the same town or were within walking distance to the school. The experience of being away from their families, their fathers and brothers, and the chance to meet girls from Christian and Muslim families from all over Palestine was truly an exhilarating and in some cases life-changing experience. Of all the impressions conveyed by the women oral history reciters, none is as strong as their love for each other, their friendships and sisterhood developed through the boarding years, and their experience of "coming of age" beyond the reach of their families and fathers. If any time was more important to the Palestinian women with diplomas from the Christian mission and government schools, it was their personal and academic maturing during those years in the foreign mission and British government schools.[21] Their disappointments and deep frustrations at having to choose subjects of less interest or attend neighboring schools of less prestige were compounded by the often early career-ending marriage arrangements that were forced upon many of them in their early twenties.

There are, of course, no written records of the Palestinian women's joys of school days or classmate bonding, nor of their frustrations or aspirations, nor the moments of academic wonderment and maturing following a lengthy research project or a flicker of intellectual awakening. Beyond the dusty pages of attendance records and curricular listings for the 1920 to 1945 Mandate period, historians can find little of interest in Palestine's educational history. The historical data that springs forth from the personal memories of the oral history reciters, however, give the historian data that is unfathomed and untapped, yet invaluable and highly useful for the social history of twentieth century Palestine. Without the oral history record, there is little that one can say about Palestinians and the Mandate-period educational boom. With the oral history narrations, however, the resilience as well as the inflexibility of Palestinian society emerges with certain clarity in the lives of the men and women who studied, graduated and married partners from their school days.

CONCLUSION

The need to begin to utilize the techniques, theoretical assumptions and research methodologies of oral historians and archaeologists in the work of recovering or "rediscovering" Palestinian history is clear. The "living memories" of the aging Palestinians pass from the historian's reach at the moment of their own passing. At the same time, potential archaeological sites are continually in danger of being molested and tampered with the passage of time. The Palestinian universities and research centers are the natural places for such training and investigations to occur, for the depositing of oral history tapes and archaeological materials, and for the holding of public seminars and conferences.

Dr. Albert E. Glock's past leadership in the archaeological field shows well what needs to be accomplished in the recovery and rediscovery process. In the introduction to *Rediscovering Palestine*, Dr. Doumani comments on the appropriateness of using of oral history in historical research:

> Finally, the reader will also note that I have occasionally made use of two other valuable but problematic local sources: published autobiographies and oral history. Both, of course, present difficulties stemming from the use of memory in the writing of history. My own skepticism about the usefulness of such sources for understanding the period under study was so ingrained that it was not until six years after I had started this project that I seriously considered probing them, and then only with narrow and carefully laid out limits. To my delight, they proved to be very useful. (Doumani 1995, 11–12)

Dr. Doumani, like the majority of Middle East and Palestinian historians, assumed the "problematic" nature of oral history to be overwhelming. Fortunately for the reader of his social history, the "experiment" into oral history was beneficial. It is hoped that others will follow his careful but resolute use of oral historiography in researching Palestine's past and present. The rewards for the oral historian, the oral history narrator and the readership are immense.

NOTES

1. See Doumani (1991; 1992; see also 1995).
2. See Burke (1993, 1) where he states, "despite a great deal of useful research on the histories of modern Middle Eastern societies, we know little of the lives of ordinary Middle Eastern men and women. Instead, we see the Middle East over the shoulders of diplomats, military officers, entrepreneurs, and bureaucrats."
3. See Glock (1987). On p. 13, he wrote, "nothing has prevented the development of archaeological theory so much as the lack of an adequate analysis of the consequences for interpretation of the fragmented and often distorted nature of archaeological evidence."
4. In the Editor's Preface to the Special Issue "Studies in Palestinian Archeology" of the *Birzeit Research Review*, No. 4 (Spring, 1987), p. 1,

Dr. Salim Tamari observed that, "one of the areas most neglected by Palestinian intellectuals working in the social sciences has been archaeology. This is an outstanding omission in view of the centrality of land and history in the motifs of current Palestinian national consciousness."

5. The bibliography on oral history is growing; see Henige (1982), Ritchie (1995), Thompson (1978), and Vansina (1985) for the basic reading on the subject.

6. Psychologists have done considerable work on the issues of "collective memory," and the cognitive processes of memory and learning; see Middleton and Edwards (1990) and Rubin (1996). Few historians, on the other hand, have investigated the issues around "remembering" and its impact on history writing; see Hobsbawm and Ranger (1983), Hutton (1993), Prins (1992), and Thompson (1994).

7. The six month field research project focused on ten refugee camps in the Occupied West Bank. The project was designed, implemented and then evaluated by a team of two faculty members and two graduate students from the Department of Middle Eastern Studies at Birzeit University (Dr. Emile Sahliyeh, Othman Sharkas, Adel Yahya and this researcher). The results were presented as a panel on Palestinian refugees at the 1985 Pugwash Conference on "Refugees: Victims or Cause of Conflict?" in Venice, Italy.

8. Oral history interview and videotape of Dr. Ihsan Abbas at his home in Amman, Jordan, September 14, 1995, by this researcher.

9. Personal communication to this writer from Rawan and Dima Damen of Ramallah, West Bank, September 1995; for a complete accounting of their project, see Damen and Damen (1997).

10. See Farwagi (1994, 25 and 29); on p. 25, he states, "on July 11, 1927 at 3:10 in the afternoon, a sudden jolt accompanied by the dull sound of the earthquake shook the building. A shelf of plates fell on our heads. We were just getting up to leave the room. Outside, the light was so intense."

11. S. Tamari, "Editor's Preface," *Birzeit Research Review* 4: 2.

12. The Birzeit Research Center is now housed in the former library building on the Old Birzeit Campus under the direction of Dr. Salah Abdul Jawad. The Center continues to research the history of destroyed and existing Palestinian villages collecting the villagers' oral history, their artifacts, photos, written accounts and land records. The massive field research, undertaken by Birzeit University's research team of Drs. Kamal Abdul Fattah, Sharif Kana'na and Albert Glock, and the Galilee Center for Social Research with Dr. Ghazi Falah, of all 418 destroyed Palestinian villages is now published in Khalidi (1992).

13. Among the many works now published on the Intifada, the following are excellent accounts of the major events in the West Bank and Gaza Strip

from 1987 to 1993: Hiltermann (1991), Lockman and Beinin (1989), and Nassar and Heacock (1990).

14. The researchers at In'ash Al-Usrah (Family Rehabilitation Society) under the leadership of Umm Khalil located in al-Bireh in the West Bank have carried out many oral history projects over the past decades on Palestinian lives, villages and neighborhoods while transcribing and preserving the tapes, and cataloguing the results. Two recent works in Arabic have appeared focusing on Palestinian children's memories and on the 1919–1947 Government Arab College of Jerusalem; that is, Daman and Daman (1997) and Al-Karmi (1995). In addition, a number of autobiographical works on contemporary Palestinian life have been published in English and French also relying in part on the use of oral history; that is Audi (1992), Chacour (1992), Farwagi (1994), Rose (1993), Sakakini (1990), and Toubbeh (1998).

15. The newly-founded Palestinian Association for Cultural Exchange (PACE) is an excellent example. Comprising Palestinian archaeologists, historians, geographers and engineers who are graduates of Birzeit, Bethlehem and Najeh universities, PACE is a non-governmental, non-profit organization whose goals are to promote awareness of Palestinian cultural heritage, to promote cultural tourism in Palestine, and to maintain relations with international organizations, institutes and universities on issues concerning the preservation and examination of Palestinian cultural treasures.

16. The project was carried out during the summers of 1993, 1994 and 1995 in the Ramallah-Jerusalem-Bethlehem area and was funded by a Senior Fulbright Research Grant from the Council for the International Educational Exchange of Scholars (CIES) based in Washington, D.C. The research included eighty Palestinian men and women between the ages of 45 and 92 who were present or former students, teachers and administrators in the fifty-two mission, national and government schools in the towns of Birzeit, Ramallah, al-Bireh, Beit Hanina, Jerusalem, Bethlehem, Beit Jala and Beit Sahour over the past seventy years (1925 to 1995).

17. The data are based on the Government of Palestine, *Annual Report on Education* published by the Government House in Jerusalem from 1919 to 1947; copies are preserved in both the London Public Record Office (PRO) at Kew Gardens, UK, and in the Israel State Archives (ISA) in Jerusalem. See Graham-Brown (1984, 14–21; 1980, 152–55).

18. See Miller (1985) which has an excellent summary of British views on rural education and social institutions such as the Boy Scout movement in Palestine. Dr. Miller notes, "the British in Palestine sought to use education for specific purposes: to maintain a stable social order and to

transmit what seemed to them universal values. They hoped thereby *to immunize the population against the nationalist emotions that seemed threatening to their concepts of order and stability*" (1985, 97; my emphasis). The same policy considerations were part of the British interest in creating a rural leadership program through the Boy Scout movement; soon, however, it was discovered that the Boy Scout troops were in fact highly politicized and involved in the Palestinian national movement (1985, 114–15).

19. See the excellent overview of women's organizations during the British Mandate in Fleischman (1995, 49).

20. Research on the emigration patterns of the Christian and Muslim Palestinian communities of Al-Bireh and Ramallah is only now beginning to connect the mission schools with the rising exodus of Palestinian males to overseas jobs and careers. Dr. Saleh Abdul Jawad, Associate Professor of History at Birzeit University, has identified the British Mandate period as the period of the "second wave" of Palestinian emigration to the United States; a period that was characterized by twice as many Christian and Muslim emigrants from Al-Bireh and Ramallah than in the previous 1890s to 1919, or "first wave" period. Dr. Abdul Jawad argues that the mission schools and their curricula were excellent preparatory training for Palestinian emigration at that time. The information is based on Abdul Jawad's unpublished paper, presented at Villanova University's Center for Arab and Islamic Studies on April 21, 1998.

21. The narratives by and about Palestinian women, their schooling and their aspirations are based on the oral history recitations by Palestinian women in Birzeit, Ramallah, Beit Hanina, Jerusalem, the Old City, Bethlehem, Beit Sahour and Beit Jala; in particular, the "remembered histories" of the following women were very important to the oral history project: Jean Zaru, Rita Giacaman, Hala and Dumiya Sakakini, May Mansur, and Aida Audeh in Ramallah and Birzeit, by Joyce Nasir and Abla Nasir in Jerusalem, and by Olge Wahbe in Beit Jala during the summers of 1993, 1994 and 1995. I am especially indebted to Dr. Ellen Fleischman of Georgetown University for her insightful comments and generous sharing of her oral history recitations that form part of her Ph.D. thesis.

REFERENCES

Abdul Jawad, S.
    1998   The Palestinian Diaspora: The Case of Al-Bireh and Ramallah
                Palestinians. Unpublished paper.

Audi, A.
1992   *From Ramallah, Palestine to Lake Wales, Florida, and In-
            between.* New York: Vantage.

Azar, G. B.
1991   *Palestine: A Photographic Journey.* Berkeley: University of
            California.

Blyth, E.
1917   The Future of Palestine. *Palestine Exploration Fund Quarterly
            Statement*: 81–91.

Burke III, E., ed.
1993   *Struggle and Survival in the Modern Middle East.* Berkeley:
            University of California.

Chacour, E.
1992   *We Belong to the Land.* New York: HarperCollins.

Conder, Lt. C. R.
1879   The Present Condition in Palestine. *Palestine Exploration Fund
            Quarterly Statement*: 6–15.

Damen, R., and Damen, D.
1994   *Atfal Filastin Ayyam Zaman: Yawmiyyat Atfal Filastin Qabl
            'Amm 1948* [The Children of Palestine Long Ago: The Daily
            Lives of Palestinian Children Before 1948]. Amman: Maktabah
            Wataniyya.
1997   *Al-Tatahjir fi Thakirat al-Tafulah* [The Expulsion in Childhood
            Memories]. Ramallah: The National Palestinian Committee for
            Education, Culture and the Sciences.

Doumani, B. B.
1991   Al-Tarikh wa I'adat al-Tarikh lil-Filastin al-'Uthmaniyya wa-l
            Intidabiyya [Historical Reconsideration of the History of
            Ottoman and Mandatory Palestine]. *Afaq al-Filistiniyya* 6:
            5–32.
1992   Rediscovering Ottoman Palestine: Writing Palestinians into
            History. *Journal of Palestine Studies* 21: 5–28.
1995   *Rediscovering Palestine: Merchants and Peasants in Jabal
            Nablus, 1700–1900.* Berkeley: University of California.

Farwagi, Z. A.
1994   *Dans et aux alentours de Jérusalem Pendant le mandat
            britannique 1922–1948.* Araya, Lebanon: Imprimerie
            Catholique.

Finn, E. A.
1879   The Fellaheen of Palestine: Notes on Their Clans, Warfare,
            Religion, and Laws. *Palestine Exploration Fund Quarterly
            Statement*: 33–48, 72–87.

Fleischman, E.
1995   *Jerusalem Women's Organizations During the British Mandate, 1920s–1930s.* Jerusalem: PASSIA Publication

Glock, A. E.
1987   Prolegomena to Archaeological Theory. *Birzeit Research Review* 4: 4–39.

Graham-Brown, S.
1984   *Education, Repression & Liberation: Palestinians.* London, UK: World University Service.
1980   *Palestinians and Their Society, 1880–1946: A Photographic Essay.* London, UK: Quartet Books.

Hauser, J. E.
1900   Notes on the History of Modern Colonisation in Palestine. *Palestine Exploration Fund Quarterly Statement*: 124–42.

Henige, D.
1982   *Oral Historiography.* London, UK: Longman Group.

Hiltermann, J. R.
1991   *Behind the Intifada: Labor and Women's Movements in the Occupied Territories.* Princeton, NJ: Princeton University.

Hobsbawm, E., and Ranger, T., eds.
1983   *The Invention of Tradition.* Cambridge, UK: Cambridge University.

Hutton, P. H.
1993   *History as an Art of Memory.* Hanover, VT: University Press of New England.

Al-Karmi, H. S.
1995   *Al-ʾIlm wa-l Taʾlim wa-l Kuliyat al-ʾArabiyya fil-Quds* [Knowledge, Education and the Arab College of Jerusalem]. Amman, Jordan.

Khalidi, W., ed.
1992   *All That Remains: The Palestinian Villages Occupied and Depopulated by Israel in 1948.* Washington, DC: Institute for Palestine Studies.

Lockman, Z., and Beinin, J., eds.
1989   *Intifada: The Palestinian Uprising Against Israeli Occupation.* Boston, MA: South End Press.

Middleton, D., and Edwards, D. eds.
1990   *Collective Remembering.* London, UK: Sage.

Miller, Y. N.
1985   *Government and Society in Rural Palestine, 1920–1948.* Austin, TX: University of Texas.

Nassar, J. R., and Heacock, R., eds.
1990   *Intifada: Palestine at the Crossroads.* New York: Birzeit University and Praeger Publishers.

Prins, G.
1992   Oral History. Pp. 114–39 in *New Perspectives on Historical Writing,* ed. P. Burke. University Park, PA: Pennsylvania State University.

Rajab, J.
1989   *Palestinian Costume.* London, UK: Kegan Paul.

Ritchie, D. A.
1995   *Doing Oral History.* New York, NY: Twayne Publishers.

Rose, J. H. M.
1993   *Armenians of Jerusalem: Memories of Life in Palestine.* London, UK: The Radcliffe Press.

Rubin, D. C., ed.
1996   *Remembering Our Past: Studies in Autobiographical Memory.* Cambridge, UK: Cambridge University.

Sakakini, H.
1990   *Jerusalem and I: A Personal Record.* Amman: Economic Press.

Shaheen, N.
1992   *A Pictorial History of Ramallah.* Beirut, Lebanon: Arab Institute for Research and Publishing.

Swedenburg, E.
1985–86   Problems in Oral History: the 1936 Revolt in Palestine. *Birzeit Research Review* 2: 30–42.
1988   The Role of the Palestinian Peasantry in the Great Revolt (1936–1939). Pp. 169–205 in *Islam, Politics and Social Movements,* ed. E. Burke III and I. Lapidus. Berkeley: University of California.
1995   *Memories of Revolt: The 1936–1939 Rebellion and the Palestinian National Past.* Minneapolis: University of Minnesota.

Thompson, E. P.
1994   *Making History: Writings on History and Culture.* New York: The New York Press.

Thompson, P.
1978   *The Voice of the Past: Oral History.* Oxford, UK: Oxford University.

Toubbeh, J. I.
1998   *Day of the Long Night: A Palestinian Refugee Remembers the Nakba.* North Carolina: McFarland.

Vansina, J.
   1985   *Oral Tradition as History.*   Revised Edition.   Madison, WI:
            University of Wisconsin.
Yahya, A.; Ibrahim, M.; and Ricks, T.
   1994   *Al-Tarikh Ash-Shafawi Lil-Intifada: Dalil Lil-Mu ʾalamin wa-l
            Bahhthin wa-l Talabah* [Oral History in the Intifada: A Guide
            for Teachers, Researchers and Students]. Ramallah, Palestine:
            Tamer Institute for Community Education.

4 Ethnographic Analogy and Ethnoarchaeology

PATTY JO WATSON

When Al Glock was building an archaeological curriculum at Birzeit University in the early 1980s, he invited me there to talk with him and his students about various theoretical and methodological concerns. I accepted the invitation, and benefitted a great deal from that opportunity and a subsequent one to meet Al, his wife Lois, and several of the Birzeit personnel including Al's students. Al's interest in my work stemmed from the fact that I have an anthropological background, thus contrasting with his own, had published on Near Eastern prehistory as well as archaeological theory, and had field experience in archaeobotanical recovery techniques as well as with ethnoarchaeology (the latter in a Near Eastern setting).

On both the study trips that he arranged for me, I stayed at the Glocks' apartment, and participated in many lively discussions with him, Lois, and the Birzeit students, ranging widely over these and related issues. Ethnoarchaeology was of particular interest to him and his students during this period, so it was often the central topic for our debates. I was strongly impressed by Al's intellect and integrity, as well by the demanding task he had taken on at Birzeit. In addition to these attributes and to his formidable scholarly characteristics, Al was a thoughtful and kindly man with a wonderful sense of humor. I cherish the memory of our brief collaboration.

INTRODUCTION

The use of ethnographic analogy was heatedly discussed in print and elsewhere during the "New Archaeology" period (ca. 1962 to 1982) in

Americanist archaeology. Al Glock, his students and I also threshed through—in some detail—the pros and cons of various views on the use of ethnographic analogy and ethnoarchaeology in archaeological interpretation. Al thought there was considerable potential in ethnoarchaeology in general, and specifically for the research he was directing at Tell Taʿannek near the West Bank town of Jenin (where one of his students later carried out an ethnoarchaeological project [Ziadeh 1984]). Because the issues surrounding ethnographic analogy and ethnoarchaeology are so central to archaeological interpretation, and because there still seems to be some serious ambivalence and confusion about the whole topic (Lamberg-Karlovsky 1989; Grayson 1993), I thought it might be useful to provide an account of the main points resulting from the most comprehensive and detailed 1970s –1980s dialogues before explicitly addressing the major sources of difficulty.

The general character of the Americanist debates and many of their highlights are delineated in Alison Wylie's substantive review, "The Reaction Against Analogy" (1985).[1] Wylie, a philosopher of science familiar with archaeological field and laboratory research, presents detailed conceptual analyses and critiques. Carol Kramer, an archaeologist who has herself carried out longterm ethnoarcheological studies in Iran and India, has provided several overviews of ethnoarchaeology in practice during the past two decades (Kramer 1979; 1982; 1994). Some twenty years ago, Donnan and Clewlow (1974), and Gould (1978) each published important edited volumes on ethnoarchaeology; Binford's 1970s ethnoarchaeological research in Alaska is well-known and highly influential (Binford 1978) as is Yellen's in Africa (1977) and Longacre's in the Philippines (1974). Together with Frank Hole, Carol Kramer and Lee Horne, I carried out ethnoarchaeology in prerevolutionary Iran (Hole 1979; Kramer 1994; Watson 1979a), and have published general commentaries on ethnoarchaeology as well (Gould and Watson 1982; Watson 1979b; 1982a; 1982b; 1993).

In what follows, I briefly summarize major agreements and disagreements among the 1970s–1980s practitioners and discussants of ethnoarchaeology before coming to some conclusions about ethnoarchaeology in the 1990s and beyond.

CENTRAL POINTS ABOUT ETHNOGRAPHIC
ANALOGY AND ETHNOARCHAEOLOGY

(1) Well over ninety-nine percent of the human past is undocumented save in the archaeological record; and that past is over. We can never experience it directly, but we can infer much about it by using physical objects and other evidence surviving from the past together with knowledge of relevant contemporary cultural and noncultural materials.

(2) "Relevant materials" are those contemporary forms, functions, and processes that seem to show significant resemblance to, i.e. are analogous to or analogs for, past forms and their hypothesized functions and processes.

(3) To interpret past cultural remains, archaeologists, explicitly or implicitly, compare their forms (including their intrasite and extrasite spatial patterning) with present ones; assesses similarities and differences between present and past forms; devise new observations on present or past materials to test hypothesized relations among the forms and functions being investigated archaeologically; and come to conclusions about past cultural functions and processes that might have produced the archaeologically observed forms.

(4) Observations on relevant present cultural materials may be obtained from published or archival ethnographic or historic accounts, or from photos, or from specially designed ethnographic and/or experimental (replicative) research. That is, the archaeologist may be able to locate relevant analogs in already available sources, or may decide to make her or his own experimental or ethnographic observations in the laboratory or in the field. The latter activity, where the archaeologist becomes an ethnographer for archaeological purposes, is now usually referred to as "ethnoarchaeology."

(5) The scope of relevant analogs sought varies greatly according to the problems or questions addressed by individual archaeologists. At one end of the continuum is matching of individual forms and functions; near the other end are attempts at deriving, via more complex inferential networks, models of prehistoric sociopolitical dynamics, or of ancient cognition.

(6) Ideally, archaeologists working with ethnographic materials and information should seek to establish what Wylie and other philosophers

of science call "relational analogies." This is done by going beyond the matching of form and function to investigation of the underlying relations structuring the ethnographically observed events and processes, and how material culture is implicated in them. That is, ethnoarchaeology is strongest when the work of its practioners is directed towards generalizing rather than particularizing goals.

(7) Archaeological interpretations are always based explicitly or implicitly on analogies with noncultural remains and processes (data drawn from the natural sciences, and from ethnography and ethnohistory) and cultural ones (data drawn from ethnographic or historic archival sources), and are always somewhat tentative; even if the interpretations check out repeatedly, they are never immune from further testing, modification, or discard.

Discussion

These seven statements summarize, somewhat abstractly, the general procedures of all archaeological interpretation, which is always based on arguments from and about analogies. Those procedures may be focused on a single artifact: for example, a two thousand year old life-size replica of a duck made very skillfully from reeds and rushes (Tuohy and Napton 1986), or oddly-shaped, badly corroded chunks of metal found in association with scattered fragments of a small ship that sank more than three thousand years ago (Bass 1967). Or they may be focused upon a more complex set of archaeological observations, such as regional changes in site sizes and populations through centuries and millennia (Sumner 1979); or upon a more extended line of inference, such as the nature and intensity of reliance on wild plants in a proto-Neolithic community (Ertuğ-Yaraş 1995).

In any case, the archaeologist goes through the same procedure of comparing cultural forms observed in the archaeological record of a now dead community or of an event long past with forms documented in a living context by ethnographers, historians, or other chroniclers. The duck effigy is constructed so that it sits upon the water and closely resembles a live duck. It was found in a place (a dry rockshelter near a marshy lake) and time (as shown by radiocarbon dating) where prehistoric people hunted ducks as indicated by paleoenvironmental, zooarchaeological, and other archaeological evidence. Ethnographic information on nineteenth and early twentieth century subsistence practices among the indigenous peoples in the same region includes descriptions of such models used as decoys. Therefore, it seems plausible to suggest that the artifact was a prehistoric decoy made by ancient hunters of wild fowl. But newly discovered archaeological and/ or ethnographic information may, at some future time, indicate that the duck effigy was much more likely to have been a cult or votive object. The original interpretation would then have to be modified accordingly.

The oddly-shaped metal objects, shown by laboratory tests to be bronze, resemble "ox-hide ingots" depicted in ancient Egyptian paintings being loaded onto boats, and mentioned in ancient texts making reference to metal-working and metal-transport. The artifacts were found together with a scattering of other material (including fragments of a wooden hull) left on the sea bottom subsequent to an ancient shipwreck, which occurred somewhat prior to 1000 BC. It seems plausible to interpret the corroded bronzes as standard ingots (raw material for the production of tools and weapons) being carried along with other cargo in the hold of an ancient ship that came to grief on the rocks of Cape Gelidonya, below which the archaeological remains were discovered, submerged 30 m below the surface of the Mediterranean.

Estimates of population size in sites or regions, and of regional changes in site and settlement patterns can seldom be more than rough approximations based on modern information, but there is a considerable literature on various means of using present data to aid in arriving at such estimates for past times and places in some world areas (Cameron and Tomka 1993; Horne 1985; Kintigh 1985; Kramer 1982; Kroll and Price 1991; Sallade 1989).

Information about gathering and use of wild plants can sometimes be obtained in contemporary communities occupying physical environments similar to those pertaining in the past. Detailed data on modern plant gathering, processing, storage, and consumption of the same species documented or inferred to have been present in ancient times can be of great help in the interpretation of past subsistence patterns, as well as of specific artifacts (e.g., sickle flints, milling stones) and architectural features (e.g., storage pits) (Ertuğ-Yaraş 1995; Wilson 1987).

This whole interpretive, analogical enterprise may sound quite straightforward, as discussed and briefly illustrated above, yet periodic protests and critiques continue to appear, inveighing against some or any use of ethnographic analogy in archaeology.[2] Because such critiques usually cover the same ground and raise the same objections, I think it worthwhile to present a summary account of those objections here.

THE TROUBLE WITH ETHNOGRAPHIC ANALOGY ACCORDING TO ITS CRITICS

Discussions concerning problematic aspects of ethnographic analogy usually reduce to two main points, one theoretical and the other methodological.

The Theoretical Objection

The theoretical objection is that observations on contemporary peoples, practices, or events cannot be legitimately applied to past situations because they are too different. The past and present are incommensurate, one cannot be translated into the other. If you try to reach the past via the present you will simply, and unavoidably, read the present into a past time and place, attributing present biases and perspectives to the past.

The most extreme statement of this view is a form of scepticism that is usually expressed somewhat like this: "No one can ever really know anything about the past, so anyone's guesses and fantasies are as legitimate as those of the archaeologist." I do not consider this radically sceptical position further here because it is uninteresting and irrelevant to practicing archaeologists. Yet at least a few commentators on archaeology have deliberately assumed such an extreme position recently (Shanks and Tilley 1987). Those with serious but less extreme worries about the difficulties in translating present observations into interpretations of the past can be addressed in the following manner.

Of course there are large and significant differences between any present community or situation and any past one. And of course there are many past societies and whole categories of societies for which we have no ethnographies or other first-hand descriptions. It does not follow, however, that we can never know anything about such past societies. If their archaeological remains are preserved, then those materials can be interpreted by reasoning systematically about contemporary observations and the ancient remains. The best way to carry out this systematic reasoning is to derive plausible interpretive hypotheses from sources (ethnographic, ethnoarchaeological, archival, experimental or replicative) corresponding as closely as possible to the case under investigation and to what is known about its physical environmental and social setting. Then these interpretative hypotheses are compared to the currently available archaeological data, to newly discovered archaeological data from the same time and place (or from closely related or otherwise relevant times and places); and to further ethnographic data as well as new ethnoarchaeologically obtained information, if any. The interpretive process, like any other kind of scholarship, is iterative and interactive between both data sources or realms of observation, the archaeological and the ethnographic. New questions arising from either or both observational realms suggest new lines of investigation, which result in more information and more questions, and so on. The scholarship in question continually involves both archaeology and ethnology, but is ultimately driven by questions about interpreting—describing and explaining—some portion of the human past. Like all scholarly work, a particular set of conclusions, no matter how carefully constructed and tested, is always liable to further checking, to modification, or to rejection by the authors or by other interested parties.

I turn now to a recent publication by a prominent scholar of West Asian and Central Asian prehistory, Carl Lamberg-Karlovsky (1989). In this paper, Lamberg-Karlovsky presents strong criticism of the sort just referred to, thus providing a concrete illustration based in Near Eastern archaeology.

Lamberg-Karlovsky begins by noting that a nineteenth century description of Tepe Yahya in Kerman Province, southeastern Iran (where he directed archaeological excavations for several seasons) contrasts significantly with the current situation there. The nineteenth century account refers to a lake, and to rice as well as wheat and barley being grown in the vicinity. There is no visible trace of the lake now, and no one remembers hearing about rice growing near Tepe Yahya a century ago, where cotton (together with wheat, barley, potatoes, and poppy seeds) was a major crop during the time Lamberg-Karlovsky's crew was working there.

Lamberg-Karlovsky also informs the reader that some of his collaborators undertook ethnoarchaeological research at a village half a kilometer south of the archaeological site during the mid-1970s, and that a survey of local flora was carried out as well.

He concludes his summary of the ethnoarchaeological and botanical observations made by his colleagues as follows:

> In the final analysis we were unable to make meaningful correlations or statements concerning the present vegetation with that recovered from our excavations. These two discrete data bases, the modern and the ancient, with significant overlaps, do not permit clearly defined statements concerning differences in climate, soil, or vegetational histories between the past and present. Similarly, when it came time to write up the report on the early periods of Tepe Yahya the ethnoarchaeological data was all but ignored (Lamberg-Karlovsky 1989, 957)

To judge from this account, Lamberg-Karlovsky expected not just significant overlap, but virtually total identity of the present community and the present vegetative patterns with those of the nineteenth century and more remote past. Because such close correspondence was not forthcoming, he rejected the modern information altogether. He has probably overstated the Yahya example for rhetorical purposes, to make his point about non-correspondence between present and past as strongly as possible. In so doing, however, he invites a rebuttal beginning with the characterization of his decision to abandon systematic actualistic studies, for the reasons given, as extremely naïve, and continuing with instructions to him about the iterative and interactive research that is always necessary in archaeological interpretation, and that always involves both present and past observations in and of themselves and in relation to each other. This is the real work of archaeological interpretation. In conclusion, such a rebuttal would surely express deep regret that the ethnoarchaeological and botanical data were never published so that other interested scholars might undertake the task abandoned by Lamberg-Karlovsky. One obvious project, for example, would have been a regional geoarchaeological study including sedimentological analyses to locate the position of the nineteenth century lake and to trace its history. Geoarchaeological research in combination with further botanical investigations in archives and herbaria would have enabled these experts to work out a developmental sequence for regional landforms and vegetation that would have provided the information Lamberg-Karlovsky wanted about the environmental setting for the various occupations at Tepe Yahya.

As to village ethnoarchaeology, Lamberg-Karlovsky elaborates his point regarding the uselessness of this kind of research (useless because present-day villages are too different from ancient ones to be relevant to archaeological problems). He reproduces a household map I published in 1979 from data previously recorded in an Iranian village where I was carrying out an ethnoarchaeological study (Watson 1979a, 127). He notes that somewhat less than fifty percent of the artifacts and features shown or listed on the map could be expected to survive archaeologically (actually, most archaeologists would probably be quite delighted with preservation that good in an open prehistoric site). He then concludes: "We are left with a five-room house, unable to determine the existence of the two stables, the location of the living room, or that the cohabitating couple had four sons and a daughter" (1989, 958).

Again, he invites rebuttal pointing out how naïve he is being to expect perfect and certain knowledge about either past or present, and how unreasonable he is to reject on that basis (i.e., that the results will not guarantee perfect knowledge) systematic study of contemporary places and situations relevant to past ones. He himself grants without question the identification of the structure as a house. Why does he not believe that archaeological data delineating relative room-sizes; the locations of hearths, storage bins, mangers, and so on (in the presence of more detailed ethnographic analogies about the expected layout and furnishings of such a village house) would not indicate possible or probable room functions that could be checked at least partially with palynological, sedimentological, and other pedological analyses, even if artifacts and artifact distributions were not especially helpful? Again, his stringent requirements for what he will accept as adequate evidence in aid of hypothetical interpretations undercuts his and other archaeologists' abilities as field workers, and as careful, intelligent interpreters of the past.

Lamberg-Karlovsky's final elaboration of his opinion that most ethnoarchaeological data are of very dubious value takes a somewhat different tack. Although his discussion (Lamberg-Karlovsky 1989, 959–61), is not very clear, he objects strongly to the study of modern and ancient Near Eastern villages within a context of specific anthropological theories about social organization and evolution. He asserts that the theories used in this way by some archaeologists are outmoded within their source areas of sociocultural anthropology. He has not, in my opinion, justified that assertion in his paper, but it is an important point that merits careful attention. His main objection, however, is that noted at the beginning of this section: because the present is very different from the past, attempts to describe the past via contemporary theoretical understandings will be so hopelessly biased and flawed as to reproduce the present in the "past" so described. Hence, again, he takes the real or potential difficulties of archaeological interpretation as a warrant for categorically rejecting explicit pursuit, not only of ethnographic analogies, but also of possibly useful present social theory.

Lamberg-Karlovsky's final point (1989, 961) seems to be that ethnoarchaeology has been promoted as a very important means to aid understanding of the past, but the results fail to measure up to these promises. Moreover, he believes that some contemporary ethno-archaeologists view their subject matter in the same deeply ethno-centric, racist way that many nineteenth century European evolu-tionists viewed "primitive" peoples: as living fossils illustrating early stages in human (European) social and cultural evolution.

This conclusion, which is not justified by Lamberg-Karlovsky's preceding, rather unclear discussion, is simply wrong, as is obvious to anyone familiar with the material he cites, or with the literature on ethnographic analogy referred to above. In that literature, this same issue is thoroughly debated; the conclusions, however, are quite different from those of Lamberg-Karlovsky (see Wylie 1985; and my seven-point summary above).

Lamberg-Karlovsky's paper is frustrating to analyze, but he does succeed in demonstrating that unclarity about the nature and practice of ethnoarchaeology as well as strong doubts about its usefulness are still present in the mind of at least one, well-known, contemporary archaeologist.

The Methodological Objection

The methodological objection is quite different from the theoretical one just discussed. It is usually phrased as a critique of the focus and scope of ethnoarchaeological research. A particular example or sometimes a whole ethnoarchaeological subcategory (e.g., investigations of contemporary hunter-gatherers, or taphonomic studies of carnivore behavior) is characterized as particularistic or even idiosyncratic, rather than aimed at defining and elucidating broad questions and theoretical issues. Binford, Grayson, Schiffer, and Tringham are among the archaeologists who have lodged these kinds of protests over the past one to two decades (Binford 1978, 359; 1980; Grayson 1993; Schiffer 1978; Tringham 1978; Yellen 1977). Binford's discussion of Yellen's ethnoarchaeological research in Africa is a good example. Binford characterizes Yellen's work among the !Kung San hunter-gatherers of the Kalahari Desert as producing low-level empirical generalizations rather than contributing to theory building at a higher, explanatory level. These generalizations or patterns are described by Yellen, Binford says, but no attempt is made to seek explanations for the specific patterns noted and described: what are the causal factors producing these patterns among the !Kung, and what is their significance for theories about human behavior in other times and places?[3]

Similarly, Grayson (1993) complains that too much ethno-archaeological work by or in the interests of zooarchaeological (faunal) interpretation consists of "cautionary tales" (e.g., documentation of the fact that modern hyenas, and hence presumably also ancient ones, can collect and damage bone in ways that may be mistakenly attributed to the work of prehistoric human hunters on the African savanna). He says that not nearly enough effort is directed at producing "general statements about the way the world works," and that too much ethnoarchaeology is inductively propelled by particularistic reactions to highly specific archaeological analyses.

I have already published a brief response to Grayson (Watson 1993), making the point that particular and general approaches are both essential and, in fact, inseparable. Ethnoarchaeologists producing cautionary tales are constructing an observational method enabling access to the subject matter of primary concern, which is that of early hominids, not ancient hyenas; and that of prehistoric human communities, not prehistoric wind, water, dog, and earthworm effects.

ETHNOARCHAEOLOGY TODAY AND TOMORROW

Although Hodder characterizes ethnoarchaeology as a transient phenomenon (1991, 108), I think it is probably going to be an integral part of archaeological practice for the foreseeable future. There are at least four reasons why this seems likely. The first is the simple observation that an archaeologist, or anyone thinking about a past situation, perceives and interprets that portion of the past, explicitly or implicitly or both, via analogy with contemporary experience.[4]

The second reason is that the kind of actualistic data archaeologists require is seldom of interest to non-archaeologists, even to those sociocultural anthropologists and ethnologists who still carry out fieldwork in relevant societies or communities.[5] Therefore, archaeologists will have to obtain their own relevant actualistic data.

The third reason is that new developments in video and in computer technology, especially mapping and computerized imagery, make ethnoarchaeology (as well as archaeology) more comprehensive and more precise. Two people with a digital laser transit can map complex terrain, architecture, features, and artifacts in a fraction of the time required with optical transits. Moreover, data can immediately be plotted at the end of each mapping episode, and are simultaneously available for computer manipulation in dozens of ways, including three-dimensional imagery (e.g., Tringham 1994). Highly sophisticated video cameras as well as automated 35 mm still cameras are now available (at prices most archaeological budgets can encompass) that are easy to use and that produce excellent visual documentation. Even very complex actualistic data relevant to a multitude of archaeological questions can be input, stored, and manipulated in laptop and desktop computers by moderately funded ethnoarchaeological projects.

The fourth reason is that so many archaeologists during the past twenty years (and continuing into the current scholarly generation) have found the results of explicitly ethnoarchaeological research to be productive and useful. In addition, several ethnoarchaeological investigations have now been followed for so many years that important information accessible only after multiple decades of study is becoming available. These include, for example, research on ceramic ethnoarchaeology begun in the 1970s in the Philippines and continuing; studies of hunter-gatherer groups in the Kalahari, begun by anthropologists and archaeologists in the 1950s–1960s and continuing, as well as investigations of various other African communities, beginning in the early 1970s and now forming an ethnoarchaeological literature of their own; as do studies of Near Eastern villages and nomads, begun in the 1960s and continuing.[6]

Another factor contributing to the vigor and bright prospects of contemporary ethnoarchaeology is the synergism noticeable here and there where ethnoarchaeologists collaborate closely with sociocultural anthropologists in addition to the usual specialists (archaeometrists, archaeobotanists and botanists, geoarchaeologists and geologists, zooarchaeologists and zoologists) involved in modern interdisciplinary archaeology.[7]

As regards the issue of particularistic vs. generalizing approaches in ethnoarchaeology, I suggest further that a particularistic focus upon traditional artifactual, architectural, and technical forms, functions, and knowledge will and should continue in all those world regions where they are still accessible. No thoughtful ethnoarchaeologist expects this information to lead directly to archaeological certainty or to serve as ready-made archaeological interpretations, but it is a precious resource in aid of archaeological inference that is rapidly diminishing and must not be ignored.

Nevertheless, should a high priority be placed upon generalizing research? Yes, because it is always better, scientifically speaking, to describe and explain groups or classes of phenomena rather than individual (particular) cases. Optimally, then, particulars would be sought and described in relation to high level questions or theories so that specific analogs would be assured of playing double roles: in localized archaeological interpretation, and also as part of theoretical constructions applicable much more broadly. In the real world of contemporary archaeology, however, complexly constrained as it is by global commercial and political configurations, a permanent state of emergency applies to detailed records of pre-industrial/pre-contemporary world system lifeways and economies. For that reason and the others just noted (see also the discussion under "The Methodological Objection" above), I continue to defend those who carefully, systematically, and particularistically document vanishing lifeways with their attendant material culture and technology, even in the absence of an explicit theoretical rationale beyond that of aiding local archaeological interpretation. Such documentation, when thoughtfully and cautiously used for either particularist or generalist purposes, is the wellspring of all present archaeological inference about the past.

ACKNOWLEDGEMENTS

I wish to thank Tomis Kapitan for inviting my contribution to this volume. Initial work on the paper was carried out at the Camargo Foundation in Cassis, France, whose Director, Michael Pretina, and Administrative Assistant, Anne-Marie Franco, were very supportive. I am also indebted to Elizabeth Monroe at Washington University for tracking down several essential references while I was working on this paper in France; and Carol Kramer kindly provided a manuscript copy of her "Ethnoarchaeology" entry for *The Encyclopedia of Cultural Anthropology*. Finally, I am deeply grateful to Jacques Chabert and Marc Keller in Paris for printing out the final-draft manuscript.

NOTES

1. See also two other papers (Wylie 1982, 1989) where Wylie specifically discusses arguments from analogy in general, and ethnographic analogy in archaeology specifically.
2. Examples from the 1950s to 1970s are discussed by Wylie (1985); see also my review of Gould's 1980 book, *Living Archaeology* (Watson 1982b); more recent examples may be found in Grayson (1993) and Lamberg-Karlovsky (1989).
3. For an extended discussion of Binford and Yellen's respective ethnoarchaeological work, see Wylie (1989, 21–22).
4. For further elaboration of this point within the archaeological literature, see Gould and Watson (1982), Watson (1982), Wylie (1989).
5. Ethnography and ethnology of the traditional sort where subsistence modes, artifacts, architecture, and, in general, relations of a culture with a specific physical environment were of concern is currently only a minority focus in angloamerican sociocultural anthropology (see Borofsky 1994). In any case, archaeologists cannot expect non-archaeological ethnographers routinely to collect highly specific and highly quantified information of the sort irrelevant to the ethnologist but essential for archaeological interpretations (e.g., spatial distributions,

dimensions, and ranges of variation for artifacts, hearths and other architectural features).

6. Longacre's Kalinga ethnoarchaeological project (Philippines) (1974, 1991; Longacre and Skibo 1994); examples of African ethnoarchaeology include David (1971), Dietler and Herbich (1993), Stone (1994), and Yellen (1977). See also the results of experimental and replicative archaeology focused upon early agriculture in the Near East in Anderson (1992).

7. Netting, G. Stone and P. Stone (1993; Netting and P. Stone are sociocultural anthropologists, G. Stone is an ethnoarchaeologist); Sahlins and Kirch (1992; Sahlins is a sociocultural anthropologist, Kirch is an archaeologist).

REFERENCES

Anderson, P., ed.
1992   *Prehistoire de l'Agriculture*. Centre de Recherche Archeologique, Monograph No. 6. Paris: Centre nationale de Recherche Scientifique.
1999   *Prehistory of Agriculture; New Experimental and Ethnographic Approaches*. Monograph 40. Los Angeles: Institute of Archaeology, UCLA.

Bass, G.
1967   *Cape Gelidoniya: A Bronze Age Shipwreck*. Transactions of the American Philosophical Society, New Series volume 57, part 8. Philadelphia: American Philosophical Society.

Binford, L. R.
1978   *Nunamiut Ethnoarchaeology*. New York: Academic.
1980   Willow Smoke and Dogs' Tails: Hunter-Gatherer Settlement Systems and Archaeological Site Formation. *American Antiquity* 45: 4–20.

Borofsky, R., ed.
1994   *Assessing Cultural Anthropology*. New York: McGraw-Hill.

Cameron, C. A., and Tomka, S. A., eds.
1993   *Abandonment of Settlements and Regions: Ethnoarchaeological and Archaeological Approaches*. Cambridge: Cambridge University.

David, N.
1971   The Fulani Compound and the Archaeologist. *World Archaeology* 3: 111–31.

Dietler, M., and Herbich, I.
1993   Living on Luo Time: Reckoning Sequence, Duration, History

and Biography in a Rural African Society. *World Archaeology* 25: 248–60.

Donnan, C., and Clewlow, C., eds.
1974   *Ethnoarchaeology.* Institute of Archaeology, Monograph 4. Los Angeles: University of California.

Ertuğ-Yaraş, F.
1997   An Ethnoarchaeological Study of Subsistence and Plant Gathering in Central Anatolia. Unpublished Ph.D. Dissertation, Department of Anthropology, Washington University, St. Louis, MO.

Gould, R. A., ed.
1978   *Explorations in Ethnoarchaeology.* Albuquerque: University of New Mexico.

Gould, R. A., and Watson, P. J.
1982   A Dialogue on the Meaning and Use of Analogy in Ethnoarchaeological Reasoning. *Journal of Anthropological Archaeology* 1: 355–81.

Grayson, D. K.
1993   Comments, in Chapter 20, "Concluding Discussion: the Role of Actualistic Studies." Pp. 349–50 in *From Bones to Behavior: Ethnoarchaeological and Experimental Contributions to the Interpretation of Faunal Remains,* ed. J. Hudson. Center for Archaeological Investigations, Occasional Paper No. 21. Carbondale, IL: Southern Illinois University.

Hodder, I.
1991   *Reading the Past.*   Second edition. Cambridge: Cambridge University.

Hole, F.
1979   Rediscovering the Past in the Present: Ethnoarchaeology in Luristan, Iran." Pp. 192–218 in   *Ethnoarchaeology: the Implications of Ethnography for Archaeology,* ed. C. Kramer. New York: Columbia University.

Horne, L.
1994   *Village Spaces: Settlement and Society in Northeastern Iran.* Washington D.C.: Smithsonian Institution.

Kintigh, K. W.
1985   *Settlement, Subsistence, and Society in Late Zuni Prehistory.* Anthropological Papers of the University of Arizona No. 44. Tucson: University of Arizona.

Kramer, C., ed.
1979   *Ethnoarchaeology: The Implications of Ethnography for Archaeology.* New York: Columbia University.

Kramer, C.
1982   *Village Ethnoarchaeology: Rural Iran in Archaeological Perspective.* New York: Academic.
1994   The Quick and the Dead: Ethnoarchaeology in and for Archaeology. Distinguished Lecture presented to the Archeology Division, American Anthropological Association, at the 93rd Annual Meeting of the AAA in Atlanta, Georgia, December 1994.

Kroll, E. M., and T. D. Price, eds.
1991   *The Interpretation of Archaeological Spatial Patterning.* New York: Plenum Press.

Lamberg-Karlovsky, C. C.
1989   Ethnoarchaeology: Legend, Observations and Critical Theory. Pp. 953–75 in *Archaeologia Iranica et Orientalis: Miscellanea in Honorem Louis Vanden Berge*, Volume II, ed. L. De Meyer and E. Haerinck. Gent: Peeters.

Longacre, W. A.
1974   Kalinga Pottery Making; the Evolution of a Research Design. Pp. 51–67 in *Frontiers in Anthropology: An Introduction to Anthropological Thinking*, ed. M. Leaf. New York: van Norstrand.

Longacre, W. A., ed.
1991   *Ceramic Ethnoarchaeology.* Tucson: University of Arizona.

Longacre, W. A., and Skibo, J., eds.
1994   *Kalinga Ethnoarchaeology: Expanding Archaeological Method and Theory.* Washington D.C.: Smithsonian Institution.

Netting, R.; Stone, G. D.; Stone, P.
1993   Agricultural Expansion, Intensification, and Market Participation among the Kofyar, Jos Plateau, Nigeria. Pp. 206–49 in B. Turner II, G. Hyden, and R. Kates, eds. *Population Growth and Agricultural Intensification in Africa*. Gainesville, FL: University of Florida.

Sahlins, M., and Kirch, P.
1992   *Anahulu: the Anthropology of History in the Kingdom of Hawaii.* Volume 1. *Historical Ethnography*, by Marshall Sahlins; Volume 2. *The Archaeology of History*, by P. Kirch. Chicago: University of Chicago.

Sallade, J.
1978   Ethnoarchaeological Investigations, 1976: Evaluating Assumptions Concerning Spatial Patterning on the Basis of Data from a Cypriote Village. Pp. 407–24 in *American Expedition to Idalion, Cyprus, 1973–1980*, ed. L. Stager and A. Walker. Chicago: The Oriental Institute of the University of Chicago.

Schiffer, M.
1978   Methodological Issues in Ethnoarchaeology. Pp. 229–47 in *Explorations in Ethnoarchaeology*, ed. R. Gould. Albuquerque, NM: University of New Mexico.

Shanks, M., and Tilley, C.
1987   *Re-Constructing Archaeology*. Cambridge: Cambridge University.

Stone, G. D.
1994   Agricultural Intensification and Perimetrics: Ethnoarchaeological Evidence from Nigeria. *Current Anthropology* 35: 317–24.

Sumner, W.
1979   Estimating Population by Analogy: An Example. Pp. 164–74 in *Ethnoarchaeology: the Implications of Ethnography for Archaeology*, ed. C. Kramer. New York: Academic.

Tringham, R.
1978   Experimentation, Ethnoarchaeology, and the Leapfrogs in Archaeological Methodology. Pp. 169–79 in *Explorations in Ethnoarchaeology*, ed. R. Gould. Albuquerque, NM: University of New Mexico.

1994   Visual Images of Archaeological Architecture. Paper presented at the 59th Annual Meetings of the Society for American Archaeology, Anaheim, California, April, 1994.

Tuohy, D. R., and Napton, L. K.
1986   Duck Decoys from Lovelock Cave, Nevada, Dated by 14C Accelerator Mass Spectrometry. *American Antiquity* 51: 813–16.

Watson, P. J.
1979a   *Archaeological Ethnography in Western Iran*. Viking Fund Publications in Anthropology No. 57. Tucson, AZ: University of Arizona.

1979b   The Idea of Ethnoarchaeology: Notes and Comments. Pp. 277–87 in *Ethnoarchaeology: Implications of Ethnography for Archaeology*, ed. C. Kramer. New York: Columbia University.

1982a   The Theory and Practice of Ethnoarchaeology with Special Reference to the Near East. *Paleorient* 6: 55–64.

1982b   Review of R. A. Gould, *Living Archaeology. American Antiquity* 47: 445–48.

1993   Comments, in Chapter 20, Concluding Discussion: the Role of Actualistic Studies. P. 350 in *From Bones to Behavior: Ethnoarchaeological and Experimental Contributions to the Interpretation of Faunal Remains*, ed. J. Hudson. Center for

Archaeological Investigations, Occasional Paper No. 21. Carbondale, IL: Southern Illinois University.

Wilson, G. L.
1987   *Agriculture of the Hidatsa Indians: An Indian Interpretation.* Minneapolis: University of Minnesota Studies in the Social Sciences, No. 9, Bulletin of the University of Minnesota (reprinted in 1987 by the Minnesota Historical Society Press, St. Paul, Minnesota as *Buffalo Bird Woman's Garden*: *Agriculture of the Hidatsa Indians*).

Wylie, A.
1982   An Analogy by Any Other Name is Just as Analogical. *Journal of Anthropological Archaeology* 1: 382–401.
1985   The Reaction Against Analogy. Pp. 63–111 in *Advances in Archaeological Method and Theory* Volume 8, ed. M. Schiffer. Orlando, FL: Academic.
1989   The Interpretive Dilemma. Pp. 18–27 in *Critical Traditions in Contemporary Archaeology*, ed. V. Pinsky and A. Wylie. Cambridge: Cambridge University.

Yellen, J.
1977   *Archaeological Approaches to the Present: Models for Reconstructing the Past.* New York: Academic.

Ziadeh, M. H.
1984   Site Formation in Context. M.A. Thesis, Department of Anthropology, Washington University, St. Louis, Missouri.

5 Implications of Cultural Tradition: The Case of Palestinian Traditional Pottery

HAMED J. SALEM

In archaeological studies of cultural tradition and change, two principles are followed. The first principle is that archaeology is a product of accurate fieldwork led by a multi-disciplinary team whose interest is collecting and analyzing data. Physics, chemistry, biology or anthropology are used in archaeological analysis. Furthermore, archaeology is not an imitation of other approaches, but an independent approach based on the development of local ideas and methods. It requires careful recording and presentation of data. The focus on environmental study and the analysis of the material culture is one method of fulfilling this strategy.

The second principle is that archaeology is not to be confused with history. They are separate fields (Glock 1983). Influenced by biblical archaeology, archaeologists in Palestine have often used historical methods to reveal the past (Trigger 1993). Archaeological records and historical documents are two different sources to explain the past. Data recovered by archaeological techniques are different from those written by historians involved in interpreting the past.

Glock's contribution to Palestinian archaeology has been to free archaeology from history and, thus, from the burden of biblical interpretations. His alternative to historical approach is a systematic anthropological study of the living traditions as a source for understanding the past. Ethnoarchaeology is an example of such research (Glock 1982). The tradition of pottery making reinforces the continuity in Palestinian archaeology. This tradition has a line going all the way back to the seventh millennium BC. The objective of this paper is to present a model of the use of an anthropological method for archaeological analysis based on the pottery traditions.

THE CONCEPT OF TRADITION

A *tradition* involves the continuous use of the same space and means of subsistence inherited from previous generations. Decades ago, Haury et al. (1955, 38) defined "tradition" as a "socially transmitted form-unit (or a series of systematically related form-units) which persists in time." Form-units can be defined as observable phenomena such as a dominant artifact type, a production technique, or an architectural element. Many traditions compose a culture. A model based on the living cultures where traditions are observed in a harmony is the best way to avoid the risk of segmenting culture and dispersing archaeological remains. The following are some examples.

The study by Magnarella (1974) in a Susurluk (Turkey) town reported on the integration of several immigrant ethnic groups as a criterion for examining cultural change. The integration of these groups into urban centers led to the formation of new towns that included specialized communities. An amalgamation of heterogeneous social traits into the town life contributed to the development and modernization of the region. Without this integration, it is difficult to understand the phenomena of urbanization.

Steward's work has influenced views about the criteria of adaptation and cultural integration. Steward (1955, 40) pointed to three aspects of cultural integration in its ecological settings:

(1) The interrelationship of productive technology and environment. The form of such technology is material culture, which varies according to technological complexity. For example, in the case of simple technology it was the natural environment the conditioned the development of material culture.

(2) The "behavior patterns involved in the exploitation of a particular area by means of a particular technology." Again the complexity of the involved technology may limit or simplify the traditional culture behavior patterns in certain areas.

(3) The effect of these behavior patterns on cultural aspects. This is more concerned with the historical domain of cultural patterns over a specific geographic spot.

In each of these aspects, there is a relation between the development of a certain technology and the environment to which it adapts.

Steward's approach influenced pottery analysis when Matson (1965) called for connecting pottery materials to the ecology. Pottery relates to technology in a specific place through clay and non-plastics. As a technological system, pottery production can be also an indicator of the social and economic system in the region.   Since then, many archaeologists have directly and indirectly translated pottery data into a specific approach to tradition and change within ethnographic research. An argument arose between those who agree that observable changes on pottery tradition mean stability and change of culture (Adams 1979; Stanislawski 1978, and Rice 1984), and those who believe that pottery traditions reflect cultural change (Longacre 1981; Peacock 1982; Annis 1985; Arnold 1985). In particular, van der Leeuw (1977) and Peacock (1982) presented a model to classify pottery systems into modes or states. Each mode of production had its own factors to endorse stability and change. For example, pottery made for the commercial market is open to change more than household production owing to the external pressure imposed on its production.

Among the most interesting surveys of continuity and innovation is that of Nicklin (1972). Based on ethnography, he listed the factors that influence pottery stability and innovation. The influence of economy, environment and the individual potter was at the core of his discussion. The work of Arnold (1985) in Guatemala is much influenced by the ecological approach. Although he was aware of the different variables that influence ceramic change, the focus of his analysis was the explanation of the mineralogy and composition of the clay fabrics. In his general conclusions, tradition and change are stimulated by the efficiency of production techniques to cope with the economic and environmental pressure as, for example, a population increase or climatic change (Arnold 1985). Rice (1984) considers the pottery-producing groups as a subsystem of a larger cultural system, and contends that through its interaction with its systemic (living) contexts we can study cultural tradition and change. Among the factors Rice listed as influencing change are the resources, manufacturing techniques, "diet" or function, social and ritual values and market demands.

Today, there is a general agreement among archaeologists regarding the causes of stability and change, thanks to ethnoarchaeological research. However, liberating tradition and change from the solely exhaustive theoretical treatment remains an enigma in the attempt to explain pottery traditions. In this sense, the tradition concept is examined first in trial and error procedures to confirm its reliability to reconstruct culture. To approach this concept, it is necessary to study continuity and change of a cultural form within appropriate time and space contexts. Pottery tradition is one form of culture that continues and changes in time. Pottery tradition and change are influenced by factors that change or stabilize other elements in material culture, and cannot be studied independently from the socioeconomic and environmental systems within which it is embedded (Peacock 1982, van der Leeuw 1984). For example, pottery is made from local clay resources accessible to the potters of that region, and knowledge of these resources is transmitted from one generation to another. Consequently, an understanding of these resources is a way of understanding culture.

AN ETHNOARCHAEOLOGICAL MODEL: LIVING PALESTINIAN POTTERY TRADITIONS

The following presentation is based on the direct observations and interviews with potters in Gaza, the town of Hebron, and the villages of el-Jib, Beit Aʿnan, Sinjil, ʿAqabet Jaber, Yʿabad, and Jabaʿ. It continues the research conducted during the mid 1970s by Glock, Rye and Landgraf (see Glock 1982; 1983; Rye 1976; 1981; Landgraf 1980). My research has been conducted irregularly since 1984. Fortunately, many potters are still alive and have good memories. They furnish useful information of the sociology, production, use and distribution of traditional pottery during the past decade.

There are two pottery traditions, the handmade tradition and the wheelmade tradition, which differ from each other in the manufacturing process. Both traditions are learned.

THE SOCIO-ECONOMY OF HANDMADE POTTERY

The dominant learning framework among Palestinian potters is family production. In the village of Yʿabad, for example, one potter learned the craft of pottery-making by watching her mother make pottery. As a ten year old, she used to sneak away from her mother to make pottery herself. While she stopped making pottery for a long time she decided to go back to it in her late thirties. Another example of is found in el-Koom village in Hebron. Haja Amnah, how in her sixties, learned to make pottery from her mother because her mother felt that the daughter would need to make her own household pottery after getting married. In these cases, pottery is produced for the potter's own household.

Another learning framework is the neighborhood network where a group of women with different skills make pottery together. Women teach each other what they learn from their ancestors. Actually, pottery is learned on the basis of neighborhood relationships, exactly as other female shared practices such as food recipes, cultivation, and oven making. Because there is no competition among the women there is no need to keep secrets from each other.

El-Jib village north of Jerusalem is a good example of this framework. It is a well-known center of making the cooking pot (*qidra*). There used to be a group of about twenty potters in the village. Today, because of aging and competition of plastic objects, only Umm Hamdan is making pottery and only on an irregular basis. (For example, Umm Abdallah died during writing this report, and I conducted the last interview with her.)

Umm Hamdan was about 65 years old, born at el-Jib. The village had more than two thousand inhabitants. She learned pottery by watching an older woman. To quote her, "whatever she does, I do the same." She also learned how to make pottery when she was helping her mother and grandmother. She continued learning from her neighbors until she mastered the craft and then started to work alone. The women are usually relatives and neighbors who are working in a network. Umm Hamdan chose pottery because she belonged to a poor family. Although she learned the craft before getting married, she mastered it after getting married to help her husband financially. She made the pottery and he took care of the marketing to nearby villages.

The el-Jib potter considers pottery-making a very difficult task. She accuses the new generations of not being hard workers and of being spoiled by modern technologies. This is one reason pottery production is not practised in the village anymore. For her, to live is to labor and so a good female is one who can produce "real" food rather than one who consumes "junk" or canned products. Today she has stopped making pottery, but continues her life as a farmer. She makes pottery on an irregular basis and only by special request. Her daily tasks are to cultivate the land, and rent olive or fig trees and market their products.

In Sinjil, pottery-making is a "network activity" which is led by a specialized potter. Haja Zu'l is in her eighties. Other women, especially those who order pottery from her, are asked to acquire the material and to crush the grog. The potter's daughter is usually the one who decorates the jars.

In Beit 'Enan, the master potter Haja Wasna is still remembered by most of the females in the village. She lived in a single room complex (4 × 4 m) with a small courtyard where she used to make pottery. No trace of the production can be found in this location found today. Umm Abdallah said she learned the craft by watching Haja Wasna and being one of her assistants. The only form she made is the storage jar (*hisha*). Her attempts to imitate small objects made on the wheel, like the water pitcher, failed, especially when making the neck. Umm Abdallah kept the same tradition, and continues to make a few jars for her own consumption and other relative woman in the village. She makes pottery in the threshing season only, when the weather helps in the firing process.

THE SOCIO-ECONOMY OF WHEELMADE POTTERY

Unlike the handmade pottery, which has more than one learning framework, wheelmade pottery is a family affair. Almost all the potters learned pottery-making from their fathers. Few of them learned the craft from a craftsman beyond the clan.

Today only a few of them are working as potters, in favor of other low paid jobs. One potter's son holds a degree in Commerce from Cairo. He prefers to work in pottery rather than being employed with a low salary. Some potters who had ceased to make pottery in the 1980s reestablished their workshop in the beginning of the 1990s because of the lack of other jobs, especially after work in Israel became difficult due to the continuous closure of the border.

In Hebron, pottery is made by a clan called "el Fakhori," whose name derives from the word Foukhar meaning pottery. There are about eleven workshops in the area south of Hebron, called el Fahs. All the workers are related. Many of them continue their fathers' traditions. The craft stayed inside the family, to avoid any competition. Both the sons and fathers are active participants in pottery making. In one workshop, the father and his three sons are working in pottery making. They claim that pottery making provides a sufficient income for all of them to survive. However, many fathers leave the choice to their sons to learn pottery making. Some actually prefer that their sons work in another craft and advise them to get a good quality education. In recent years many workshops in Hebron have produced pottery for the Israeli and European markets, especially the Netherlands). Pottery is also produced for the local market. The forms are in greatest demand are the cooking pot, the pitcher (*ʿibriq*) and the water jug (*sharba*).

Abu Ali (Salem 1986) was born in Er-Ramleh and immigrated to ʿAqabet Jaber camp in Jericho after the 1948 war. He learned pottery making from his father who, in turn, had learned it from his father. Thus, Abu Ali brought with him a pottery tradition of the coast. In ʿAqabet Jaber the potters' sons refuse to learn pottery because it is hard work and does not cover living expenses. Abu Ali is the last potter working in Palestine today who continues the Er-Ramleh tradition.

The potters of Gaza had different means of transmitting pottery traditions. Mustafa ʿAttallah had a unique learning framework. He is about 80 years old. He learned pottery making when he was a boy from another potter who is unrelated to him. His father was not a potter. In the late 1940s and early 1950s he traveled to Haifa, ʿAkka and later Lebanon. During this time, Mustafa acquired the knowledge of the white pottery or *Ibriq* tradition. When he came back to Gaza in the early 1960s, he introduced this tradition to the region. Before that the making of black pottery was the only known tradition. Mustafa learned pottery from more than one source, and taught all his sons how to make pottery. Only one of the sons is now working with him; the others have left the craft for other jobs.

In Jabaʿa, Abu Munir learned pottery from his father. He said that his grandfather had taught his father. Thirty years ago, the potter stopped making pottery. His cousin is a well-known potter of el-Jib who also learned from the fathers. The workshop continues to be run by them. Abu Munir decided to work as a painter in Israel. After the border was closed, he could no longer obtain a permit, so he decided to open a new workshop . He decided to have new forms that he created in addition to the traditional forms. He supplies to both the local market and to the Israeli market.

The point learned from the potters' sociology is the variation of the learning framework. The common learning framework is transmission via the clan. While conservatism is one way of maintaining "tradition" over time, the role of new generations is seen as "developing" the earlier style of pottery-making, as seen in the example of the Gaza potters. The change in generation may cause a change in the pottery production.

THE TECHNOLOGICAL ASPECTS:
THE POTTERY PRODUCTION CYCLE

The production cycle of Palestinian traditional pottery starts from the moment potters locate the clay sources and ends with the final forms. Five stages reflect the change and tradition of pottery-making. These are the following:

Clay Procurement and Preparation

One way of understanding the pottery tradition is to focus on the raw material used to construct a group of pots (Glock 1975). Usually, the pottery form is made from local clay known to the potters of that region. If the resources fall short, then the potter may use clay from other regions. However, the knowledge of these resources is a secret transmitted from one generation to another. Few traditional potters are willing to change the clay sources used by their fathers. The location of the source is a secret that is told only to trusted members of the family. In case of known sources like el-Jib, the source is not a secret. Often potters mix more than one clay type. In one Gaza workshop at least five clay sources are used, though at least one is local.

Three examples illustrate the form of using clay resources; namely el-Jib or Abu Ali, the Khalili and the Gaza clays. The potter of ʿAqabet Jaber uses clay from el-Jib area, which is located 50 km away. Sometimes, and particularly with large forms, he uses a mixture of local clay collected from the nearby wadi. His knowledge of both resources was transmitted to him by his father. In Hebron the potters also mix two types of clays, the local Terra Rossa and Alaleh clay. To make small souvenir forms, special clay is imported from Turkey and Holland.

Unlike the wheelmade forms, the handmade forms are produced from local clays. This is the case with the el-Jib cooking pot and Sinjil Jar. The women use the clay source from the nearby fields. A tempering agent is added to the clay. In case of el-Jib the temper comprises calcite milah which is brought from areas located about 7 km from the village. At Sinjil the temper is formed of grog, which is brought from the nearby archaeological sites

In an experiment done with five clay sources used by Palestinian potters, the Hebron clay is the best one with a shrinkage rate of 12% when fired at around 700° C, followed by el-Jib clay with a 10% shrinkage rate. The rest of the clay sources had the similar percentages: of clay fired at 650° C, the shrinkage rate of the clay from Yʿabad is 6%, Hebron-Kalaleh 11%, Hebron-Hamrah 12%, Hebron-mixed 11%, ʿAqabet Jaber 6%, Sinjil 11%, and el-Jib 10%. Potters prefer a clay with high shrinkage and usually without non-plastics.

Forming Techniques

The handmade traditions are based in the villages and carried on by women on a part time basis for both domestic use and market demands. From a technological view, the handmade pottery is classified into the traditions of making of the jar (*hesha*) and of the cooking pot (*qidra*). Both are different in the manufacturing process and the tempering agents, and a woman who can make one form does not make the other.

The el-Jib *qidra* has two horizontal handles, a holemouth plain rim, flattened base and squatted shallow carinated body. A band of incision below the rim is a typical mark of the *qidra*. The clay is fired to a yellowish red color. The *qidra* is made in the following way. The non plastics are crushed on an exposed rock in the courtyard, and then ground, usually using the same one used to grind seeds. The powder is then sieved. A paste is prepared by mixing 1.5 non-plastic piles with two clay piles (*koom*). The device used to measure the clay is called a *qobʿa* The *qidra* body is built by the coiling method. Its size is decided by the number of coils (*khabsat*). The small *qidra* needs two coils, and the larger one needs three or four coils.

Umm Hamdan mentioned three processes in building the *qidra*. The base (*kaaʿ*) is first beaten thick at a special mould (*madrab*), a process called *dareb*. Then the walls are turned by adding the coils, a process called *tedwir*. The whole vessel is cut (*tokshot*), shaved (*toksob*), smoothed (*temash*) and burnished (*temalis*) several times until it becomes thin (like the palm), by using a bamboo stick (*kasabeh*). In the last stage, the handles are added (*tethwin*). The decorations comprise only a simple incised line below the rim, which is made by a thin stick. The pots are then left to dry for two days before they are fired. The firing is done by men, usually the potter's husband or the commissioner, and the fuel used consists of a wild shrub (*natish*) collected one day before firing. The completely dried pots are carried on donkeys to the wilderness, about 2 to 4 km away. The el-Jib *qidra* is distributed in most regions of Palestine, e.g. Jaffa, Jerusalem, Ramallah and Ramleh.

The handmade storage jar, *hesha,* requires more work than the *qidra*. According to Haja Zuᶜl of Sinjil, the potmaking method is a specialized task that includes several stages and needs the labor of two or three women. She herself is specialized in building the pot hash while another does the grinding (*drees*) and another the decoration (*tazeen*).

Before building the *hesha* the clay (*teen*) and non-plastics (*shahef*) are procured from the nearby mountains. The clay is brought from the neighboring mountains when the source is exposed during digging new building foundations, while the grog is obtained from the nearby Khirab. The grog is crushed (*drees*) by the "grinding wheel" over rocks and mixed with equal quantities of clay to form the paste.

The jar is built by the coiling method (*radat*). First, a woman makes the base on a mat and leaves it to dry. She then makes another coil (*radeh*) and attaches it to the base. The size of the form is determined by the number of coils. In Beit Aᶜnan, according to Umm Abdallah, the base is made first by beating a clay ball (*hasborah*) on a wooden board, and then turned around. Three coils are added to the base, one for the body (*wasat*), the next for the neck (*raqabeh*), and the last for the rim or upper opening (*bab*). The vessel is decorated with red paint and incision by means of a chicken feather. The firing is done in the open with fuel consisting mainly of animal dung (*late ᶜe el-dwab*), but wood and cactus may also be used. The technical difference in making the two forms is that potters temper cooking pots with calcite, which absorbs heat when firing, whereas water jars are tempered with grog.

THE PRODUCTION SEQUENCE
OF THE WHEELMADE POTTERY

Palestinian potters classify pottery according to the final colors: The red tradition of Hebron, the white tradition of Haifa and the black tradition of Gaza.

The White Pottery Tradition of Haifa

The potter's workshop consists of four basic spaces, the clay preparation basins, the "wheel room", the store rooms and the kiln. Each of these has its own function. The clay is prepared by soaking it in special basins in a process called (*es-sool*). The potter uses three basins. *Joret es-Sool* (also called *fajron Gaza)* is a small deep (1 × 1 × 1 m) basin, in which the clay is soaked for one day. The second is *el-Moswall* which is a shallower and larger basin than the first, and here the clay is soaked for another day, and then moved to *el-Mansher*, the drying basin. The objective of these processes is to remove the heavy particles from the clay, and to make it well-levigated and fine enough to be used in the building stage. The clay is carried into the workshop while still moist. It is kneaded by foot and hand (*eddos or ettadwees*). The clay is cleaned from the plastic objects and from air pulps. Finally, the pot is constructed by preparing a clay hump, a process is called *ellaf.* Here another amount of sand is added to the clay.

There are three stages in building the vessel (*ettashkeel*). Turning (*ettajless*) is building and centering the base. The potter first makes the base (*ka'ab*) and then leaves the pot to dry for two hours. Throwing (*el-fateh*) is the process of opening and raising the clay body. The potter brings in the *ka'ab* after it has lost water but before it is totally dried out, and places it in a mold (*el-kaleeb*) or the mold that he has prepared for this purpose. He uses both hands, as the process involves interior and exterior pressures to raise the walls. He also uses a metal scraper with sharp edges (*el-sadef*) to move up the extra clay from the exterior. He then places the partly finished form in the sun for another two hours, while he makes the heads, neck and rim. Finally, he adds the heads and accessories (e.g. handles) to the water jar (*zeer*), pitcher (*ibriq*) and large jug (*sharbeh iraqiah*), and spouts to the *ibriq.*

The pots are left to dry for more than a week before firing. They are fired in a close updrafted kiln (*tanur* or *furon*). The kiln is loaded by placing the pot upside down. During the first stage of firing (*el-hemiah*), the potter starts the fire and preheats the kiln, and the second stage (*etadkheen)* is when the smoke start rising. The main feeding stage (*ettaghatiah*) is when the temperature reaches its maximum, after which the potter leaves the kiln to cool down. The pottery is removed the next day. The pots are decorated by bands of incision. While the roulette decoration is characteristic of the jugs, in the flower pots the rim is pinched and folded.

The Black Pottery Tradition of Gaza (et-Tatweeseh)

There are no major differences in forming and clay preparation between black pottery and the white pottery discussed above. The only difference is in firing.

There are various forms made by the potter, most of which are made in a similar way by using the wheel. The red clay (*teen ahmar*) is procured from Jabalia about 3 km away. The clay is prepared in basins similar to the way described above but in larger quantities, and stored in a basin dug into the workshop floor. Forming is done on the wheel in the *tajlees* method described above. The black pottery is a result of firing in a reduction atmosphere (*tatweeseh*), which involves the use of a special kiln with a small opening in which the pottery is smoked or carbonized (*yinakhniq*). First, the kiln is loaded with pottery and the preheating stage is the same as described above. The lower opening of the kiln is sealed with mud. The pottery should be well fired, the flame reaching to the top of the kiln. Then the potter mixes oil with leftovers of the carpenter's wood (*njara*). An opening 15 cm in diameter is left in the top door while one of 10 cm is left in the bottom. Then he mixes crude oil and *njara* (about 20–25 *tanka*), quickly feeds the mixture into the kiln, and closes the kiln openings. The black smoke gives the pottery its black or gray color. In the past they burned *qasal* (the remains of barley that are unusable as straw) and tree leaves or paper. In the preheating they used wood from lemon, orange or any other available trees. The firing continues for five to twelve hours, according to the tanur size.

The Red Pottery Tradition of Khalil

The production sequence of red pottery is similar to that of white, except in mixing the clay. The potters of el-Khalil mix the local clay (*kalaleh*) with red soil (*hamrah*) at a ratio of 1 to 2 and add local purple sand. This results is an increased proportion of iron in the clay composition. Thus, the potters are aware of the importance of the clay composition to the fired pottery. Otherwise the process is the same.

DISTRIBUTION OF THE TRADITIONS IN SPACE AND TIME

Pottery is distributed through intermediates, or by members of the potter's family. It can be exchanged for other goods or money. There have been community potters' unions in Mexico, India, Pakistan and Bengal, one task of which was to help potters to market their products.

A principle of "least movement" controls the transportation of pottery i.e. the greater the distance the pottery travels, the more likely it will be subject to breakage. Potters prefer to sell their pottery for cash to intermediates or mediators where they do not have to carry it away from the workshop. In this way they avoid the pain of selling pottery piece by piece to the local market. Pottery produced for household use is distributed within the family complex, as gifts, or produced for neighbors.

Most Palestinian traditional pottery is made for market distribution. In el-Jib, for example, female potters form a network to increase the production rate for sale in markets. Pottery was distributed by means of donkeys to Ramla and Arourah, 35 km away. With the improvement of transportation, the pottery of el-Khalil reached many cities in Palestine. Unlike the potter of ʿAqabet Jaber, who made pottery to order, the potters from el-Khalil made pottery on a regular basis. The extra pottery was stored and distributed later. Because of the distinctive ware of the painted Gaza pottery, it was found in many cities in the region. Since the Intifada, Gaza pottery is hardly found in the West Bank or in Israeli markets due to the closure of the roads and the thorough tax clearance regulations.

CONCLUSION

Pottery is a powerful tool for discerning trends of continuity and change. For a long time many Palestinian archaeologists had narrowed their scrutiny of pottery to typological and stylistic factors. But advancing technology used in pottery analysis has increased the opportunities for the archaeological use of pottery (see Franken 1969, 1971; Rice 1987). The main conclusion of this paper is that there is a need to combine technological restraints and socioeconomic and environmental considerations in order to understand continuity and change of the pottery traditions.

The distribution of Gaza pottery, for example, illustrates how this is so. For the past decade or so, the pottery of Gaza has been distributed only in the Gaza Strip, unlike in preceding decades. It can safely be assumed that Gaza pottery will be back on the market after the Israeli closure ends. Here we are dealing with a gap in a tradition: future archaeologists might mistakenly infer that the tradition of Gaza pottery had ended and was replaced by a new tradition.

On the other hand, the making of pottery by women is a good example of a tradition that ended for socioeconomic reasons. Most of the female potters stopped making pottery because pottery vessels are no longer used. Also, there is a changing role of women in Palestinian society, and many now look at a female potter as having a lower status in society. (One man said that returning to pottery making is turning us back fifty years, but one major reason is that pottery making was part of the division of labor in the society.) The basic social and economic principle is the need for household utensils so that only the items that could not be made by the females were bought from the market. But the availability and low price of household utensils has led to a gradual change in the roles and numbers of woman potters. At the same time, the harsh economical situation resulting from the Israeli closure of the Gaza and the West Bank border forced many Palestinians to look for alternatives to working in the Israeli labor market. Some potters who had previously abandoned the craft returned back to pottery production.

Other exterior factors have also influenced continuity and change of a tradition, for example how natural resources are manipulated. Almost all the Palestinian potters used not only local resources but also clay imported from neighboring regions. All are in scarce supply. While they often keep looking for the clay, none complained about the limitation of resources. When resources are exhausted in a locale, as in the case of both Gaza and Hebron potters, they have searched for alternative resources. Gaza potters mixed more than five different clays to make pottery, and by manipulating the resources in this way planted the seeds for the continuity of tradition.

Skill and knowhow are other factors. Many Palestinian male potters have mastered the stage techniques or the *tajlis* method, but some are unaware of the three stages common to Haifa and er-Ramla potters. This method is probably influenced by connection between Lebanon and Palestine. Learning about new methods also changes pottery techniques in given locales.

The study of the technology of the pottery is one method of understanding both past and present systems in Palestine. The way pottery technology is transmitted testifies to the modes of connection and continuation of cultural systems.

REFERENCES

Adams, W. Y.
  1979   On the Argument from Ceramics to History: A Challenge Based on Evidence from Medieval Nubia. *Current Anthropology* 20: 727–44.
Annis, M.
  1985   Resistance and Change: Pottery making in Sardinia. *World Archaeology* 17: 240–55.
Arnold, D.
  1985   *Ceramic Theory and Cultural Process.* Cambridge: Cambridge University.
Franken, H. J.
  1969   Excavations at Tell Deir ʿAlla. *Documenta et Monumenta Orientis Antiqui.* Leiden: Brill.
  1971   Analysis of Methods of Pot-making in Archaeology. *Harvard Theological Review* 64: 227–55.
Glock, A. E.
  1975   Homo Faber: The Pot and the Potter at Taʿanach. *BASOR* 219: 9–28.
  1982   Ceramic Ethno-Techniculture. Pp. 145–52 in *Studies in the History and Archaeology of Jordan*, ed. I. A. Hadidi. Amman: Department of Antiquities.
  1983   The Use of Ethnography in an Archaeological Research Design. Pp. 171–79 in *The Quest for the Kingdom of God: Studies in Honor of George E. Mendenhall*, eds. H. B. Huffmon, *et al.* Winona Lake, IN: Eisenbrauns.
Haury, E. W., *et al.*
  1955   An Archaeological Approach to the Study of Cultural Stability. *Seminars in Archaeology* 1955: 33–57.

Landgraf, J.
1980   Keisan's Byzantine Pottery. Pp. 51–99 in *Tell Keisan (1971–1976)*, ed. J. Briend and J. Humbert. Paris: Gabalda.

Longacre, W. A.
1981   Kalinga Pottery: An Ethnoarchaeological Study. Pp. 49–66 in *Patterns of the Past: Studies in Honor of D. Clarke*, ed. by I. Hodder, et al. Cambridge, UK: Cambridge University.

Magnarella, P.
1974   *Tradition and Change in a Turkish Town*. New York: Wiley and Sons.

Matson, F.
1965   Ceramic Ecology: An Approach to the Study of Early Cultures of the Near East. Pp. 202–17 in *Ceramics and Man*, ed. F. Matson. Viking Fund Publication in Anth. no. 41. Chicago: Aldine.

Nicklin, K.
1971   Stability and Innovation in Pottery Manufacture. *World Archaeology* 3: 13–48.

Peacock, D. P. S.
1982   *Pottery in the Roman World: An Ethnoarchaeological Approach*. London: Longman.

Rice, P.
1984   Change and Conservation in Pottery–Producing Systems. Pp. 231–93 in *The Many Dimensions of Pottery: Ceramics in Archaeology and Anthropology*, ed. S. van der Leeuw and A. Pritchard. Amsterdam: University of Amsterdam.

1987   *Pottery Analysis: A Sourcebook*. Chicago: University of Chicago.

Rye, O.
1976   Traditional Palestinian Potters. *National Geographic Society Research Reports* 1976: 769–76.

1981   *Pottery Technology: Principles and Reconstructions. Manuals in Archaeology* No. 4. Washington, D.C.: Taraxacum.

Salem, H.
1986   Pottery Ethnoarchaeology: A Case Study. Master Thesis: University of Arizona.

Stanislawski, M.
1978   Pots, Patterns and Potsherds: Ethnoarchaeology of Hopi and Hopi-Tewa Pottery Making and Settlement. *Discovery* 15: 15–25.

Steward, J.
1955   *Theory of Culture Change* 51–55; 70. Urbana: University of Illinois.

Trigger, B. G.
  1993   Early Civilizations: Ancient Egypt in Context. Cairo: American University of Cairo.

Van der Leeuw, S.
  1977   Towards a Study of the Economics of Pottery Making. *Ex Horreo* 4: 68–76.
  1984   Dust to Dust: A Transformational View of the Ceramic Cycle. Pp. 707–73 *The Many Dimensions of Pottery: Ceramics in Archaeology and Anthropology*, ed. S. van der Leeuw and A. Pritchard. Amsterdam: University of Amsterdam.

6 Late Bronze and Iron I Cooking Pots in Canaan: A Typological, Technological, and Functional Study

ANN E. KILLEBREW

C ooking pots are one of the most easily identified groups of utilitarian pots in any ceramic assemblage. They are generally descernible by the remnants of soot or signs of fire on the exterior together with a distinctive fabric or ware that is usually distinguishable from other vessels in the assemblage. During the last few decades, cooking pots have been the focus of numerous studies, either from an ethnoarchaeological perspective[1] or as a subject of examination using various characterization studies or scientific evaluations of different physical properties of this vessel—or a combination of several approaches.[2] Significant morphological variables in cooking pots are container volume, aperture diameter, flame heating factor, support factor, handle feature, and wall thickness.[3] Several other correlates of use behavior should also be considered with regard to cooking pots, including frequency and duration of heating, distance from fire, handling while hot, cooking method, and oven type. An additional aspect of the functional use of cooking pots not generally discussed in the archaeological literature is cuisine.

This paper examines the typology, technology, and function of Late Bronze II and Iron I cooking pots from four representative sites located in different regions of Canaan—Tel Miqne-Ekron,[4] Deir el-Balah,[5] Tel Beth Shean,[6] and Giloh.[7] Two main types of cooking pots appear:

Type I is a cooking bowl that has a long tradition throughout Canaan, going back to the beginning of the second millennium BC, and can be considered the "indigenous" cooking pot of the region (figs. 1, 2; Forms CA 18–20; Killebrew 1998a, 103–109). Type II is a cooking jug that appears mainly in the southern coastal plain during the Iron I period at sites such as Tel Miqne-Ekron that are associated with the Philistines (fig. 3; Killebrew 1998a, 183–84). This cooking pot differs both typologically and technologically from all known cooking pots in Canaan in the preceding Late Bronze II period.

TYPOLOGY[8]

Type I

The Late Bronze Age cooking pot from Canaan is a distinct and well-known type that evolved from the Middle Bronze Age cooking pot. Typologically, Late Bronze Age handleless cooking pots continue the general shape and everted rim profile of the Middle Bronze IIB–C restricted cooking pots, except that their vessel proportions vary and the shape becomes increasingly more carinated. During the Late Bronze II, the most common cooking pot has a folded-over everted rim with a triangular-shaped flange. These handleless cooking pots have a round base and a carinated body. The rim diameter can be both narrower or wider than the maximum body diameter at the carination. The rim is everted with a triangular shaped profile formed by folding the rim. The diameter (at its opening) averages 25 to 40 cm to approximately 15 to 20 cm in height. This cooking pot is well-known from Late Bronze Age sites in Canaan dating to the fourteenth and thirteenth centuries, and often continuing well into the twelfth century BC.

This cooking pot, designated in this paper as Form CA 18 is divided into five sub-types, a–e. It continues to develop as form CA 19 in the Iron I, retaining its folded-over rim but with a straight or slightly inverted stance and triangular profile. A variation of this cooking pot, Form CA 20, has the general body profile of the Late Bronze Age cooking pots, however the upright to inverted rim is usually thickened at the top and pinched midway down, forming a ridge at the base of the rim.

Type I, Cooking Bowl with Everted Rim

Form CA 18a (fig. 1:1–4). Cooking Bowl Form 18a is the classic Late Bronze II cooking pot with an everted rim and well-defined triangular-shaped flange. The flange can be pointed or trimmed flat, short or long, resulting in a great variety of rim profiles. The body often has a more pronounced carination and a deeper body than cooking bowl Form CA 18b. This is the most common cooking pot at Tel Miqne-Ekron (fig. 1:1, 3; Killebrew 1996, pls. 6:6–9; 8:4) and at nearby Tel Batash (e.g., Stratum VII [Kelm and Mazar 1995: fig. 4.28]). It was also popular at Deir el-Balah (fig. 1:4; T. Dothan et al. in press) and at the Iron I site of Giloh (fig. 1:2).[9] It is very rare at Tel Beth Shean Levels VII and VI (see below, Form CA 19). Numerous complete examples of Form CA 18a cooking pots are known throughout Canaan, for example, from all levels of the Late Bronze II strata at Hazor,[10] Tel Dan (Biran 1994: fig. 80:5 [Tomb 387], fig. 83:2 [Stratum VII]), and from the soundings at Khirbet Rabud (Kochavi 1974, fig. 4:6–7, 9). It appears in Fosse Temples II and III at Lachish (Tufnell et al. 1940: pl. LVIB:368, 370, 371), in thirteenth century contexts at Gezer (Dever et al. 1974, pls. 23:7, 25:5), at Ashdod (M. Dothan 1971: fig. 33:6, 7, 8 [LB II]; M. Dothan and Porath 1993: fig. 17:6 [Stratum XIIIb]), and at Tel Harasim (Givon 1992: fig. 15:1 [Stratum VI]; 1995: fig. 5:5, 6, 7 [Stratum V]). It continues to appear in Iron I contexts at sites in the Manasseh region,[11] at Shiloh (Finkelstein et al. 1993, 156 and fig. 6.47:2, 4 [Stratum V]), Tell el-Ful (Sinclair 1960, fig. 21:6), and Tell Beit Mirsim (Greenberg 1987: fig. 4:6 [Silo 15]; fig. 5:18 [Silo 14]), however the triangular flange in these cooking pots is not often as well defined as those from the Late Bronze Age levels. This cooking bowl appears during the Late Bronze II and early Iron I periods throughout Canaan.

Form CA 18b (fig. 1:5–7). This cooking pot is defined by its everted to flaring rim and much less pronounced triangular shaped flange. The folded-over rim is pressed down against the exterior body of the vessel, creating a more flattened triangular profile. The rim diameter is usually the widest part of the vessel and there is a tendency for the body to be shallower in depth than Form CA 18a. The folded-over rim can be short or long in length. Cooking bowl Form CA 18b appears at Deir el-Balah (fig. 1:5) and Tel Miqne-Ekron (fig. 1:6; Killebrew 1996, pl. 4:14, 15; 1998b: fig. 1:6), but rarely at Giloh (fig. 1:7). It is also known at Ashdod,[12] Tel Sera (Oren 1985, fig. 5:4 [Stratum IX]), Tel Harasim (Givon 1991, fig. 4:7; 1992: fig. 15:2 [Stratum V]), and Tell Beth Mirsim (Greenberg 1987, fig. 7:11, 13, 14 [Silo 6], fig. 10:2 [Silo 1],

Fig. 1. Type I Cooking Pots (Form CA 18). Scale 1:6.

No.	Form	Site	Reg. No.	Locus No.	Date	Comments
1	CA 18a	Miqne-Ekron	6.163/18	6011	LB II	Ware ME-B2
2	CA 18a	Giloh	253/1	34	Iron I	Mazar 1981: fig. 7:5
3	CA 18a	Miqne-Ekron	5.422/12	5081	LB II	Killebrew 1998b: fig. 4:4
4	CA 18a	Deir el-Balah	6211/1	138E	LB II	
5	CA 18b	Deir el-Balah	2262/1	1057	LB II	
6	CA 18b	Miqne-Ekron	6.182	6022	Iron I	Killebrew 1998b: fig. 1:6
7	CA 18b	Giloh	552/7		Iron I	Mazar 1990: fig. 6:10
8	CA 18c	Giloh	340/7	32	Iron I	Mazar 1981: fig. 7:1
9	CA 18c	Giloh	205/1	32	Iron I	Mazar 1981: fig. 7:2
10	CA 18c	Giloh	149/12	8	Iron I	Mazar 1981: fig. 7:3
11	CA 18d	Deir el-Balah	2748/2	1153	LB II	
12	CA 18d	Giloh	245/8	34	Iron I	Mazar 1981: fig. 7:6
13	CA 18e	Giloh	698/1		Iron I	Ware GI–C
14	CA 18e	Giloh			Iron I	Mazar 1990: fig. 7

Cooking Pots

Form CA 18

CA 18a

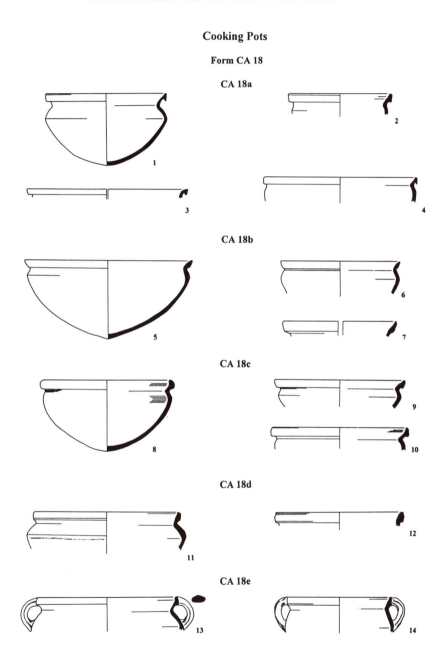

CA 18b

CA 18c

CA 18d

CA 18e

Fig. 1

Fig. 2. Type I Cooking Pots (Forms CA 19–20). Scale 1:6.

No.	Form	Site	Reg. No.	Locus No.	Date	Comments
1	CA 19a	Beth Shean	206/1	2533	Iron I	Yadin and Geva 1986: fig. 25:1
2	CA 19a	Miqne-Ekron	36.244/23	36081	Iron I	Ware ME-B2
3	CA 19a	Deir el-Balah	3585	1319	Iron I	Ware DB-B
4	CA 19a	Giloh	700/4	107	Iron I	Mazar 1990: fig. 3:7
5	CA 19a	Miqne-Ekron	4.313/27	4070A	Iron I	Ware ME-B2
6	CA 19b	Miqne-Ekron	5.100/8	5029	Iron I	Ware ME-B4
7	CA 19b	Giloh	206/2	22	Iron I	Mazar 1981: fig. 7:15
8	CA 20a	Beth Shean	184165/20	18418	LB II	Ware BS-C
9	CA 20a	Beth Shean	328/2	2533	Iron I	Yadin and Geva 1986: fig. 25:3
10	CA 20b	Beth Shean	253/2	2533	Iron I	Yadin and Geva 1986: fig. 25:2

Cooking Pots

Form CA 19

CA 19a

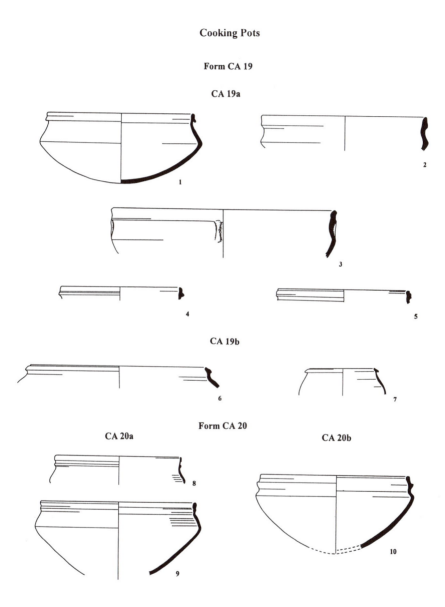

CA 19b

Form CA 20

CA 20a   **CA 20b**

Fig. 2

Fig. 3. Type II Cooking Pots (Form AS 10). Scale 1:6.

No.	Form	Site	Reg. No.	Locus No.	Date	Comments
1	AS 10	Miqne-Ekron	3.376/6	3073	Iron I	Ware ME–B3
2	AS 10	Miqne-Ekron	36.225/8	36081	Iron I	Killebrew 1998b: Fig. 10:13
3	AS 10	Miqne-Ekron	36.226/1	36081	Iron I	Killebrew 1998b: fig. 10:14
4	AS 10	Miqne-Ekron	3.439/3	3087	Iron I	Ware ME–B3

Cooking Pots

Form AS 10

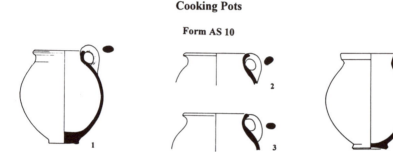

fig. 10:12 [Silo 43]). Form CA 18b cooking pots were also found at Gezer in the late thirteenth to early twelfth centuries BC (Dever 1986, pl. 33:2) and at Khirbet Rabud (Kochavi 1974, figs. 4:13, 5:6). Form CA 18b is common during the Late Bronze II and early Iron I mainly in southern Canaan.

Form CA 18c (fig. 1:8–10). Cooking Bowl Form CA 18c is typical of Form CA 18 Late Bronze Age cooking pots, but is distinguished by its concave gutter rim with either rounded or everted triangular section. This cooking pot appears in significant numbers at Giloh (fig. 1:8–10; Mazar 1981, fig. 7:1–3; 1990, fig. 6:5, 7), but is absent at the three other sites under discussion in this paper. This type seems to be confined mainly to the central hill country, at sites such as Emek Reph'aim (Jerusalem),[13] Tell el-Ful (Sinclair 1960, pl. 21:16, 18), and Mount Ebal (Zertal 1986/87, fig. 14:6). These cooking pots date to the Iron I period and are found in the central hill country in Canaan.

Form CA 18d (fig. 1:11–12). Cooking bowl Form CA 18d is defined by its slightly everted, nearly upright rim stance. The rim is still folded over and retains a slightly triangular profile. The rim diameter is more restricted than Forms CA 18a–c, and in the Deir el-Balah examples (fig. 1:11) the carination of the body is more pronounced. A few similar cooking pots are also known from Giloh (fig. 1:12; Mazar 1981, fig. 7:6). Cooking bowl Form CA 18d appears at Ashdod (M. Dothan 1971, fig. 81:9 [Stratum XIV]; M. Dothan and Porath 1993, fig. 9:11), in Stratum III at Tel Sippor (Biran and Negbi 1966, fig. 7:7), in Fosse Temples II and III at Lachish (Tufnell et al. 1940, 369), at Tel Harasim (Givon 1991, fig. 4:8 [stratum V]), and Tell Beit Mirsim (Greenberg 1987, fig. 8:21 [Silo 6]). It appears mainly in southern Canaan during the Late Bronze II and early Iron I periods.

Form CA 18e (fig. 1:13–14). This form is distinguished by two fragmentary cooking pots from Giloh, which are unusual because of the addition of two vertical handles from the rim to the shoulder. Though A. Mazar (1990, 89) classifies them as belonging to his Type B, owing to their everted triangular rim profile, I have combined them into one version of the Form CA 18 cooking pot.

Summary. The majority of the Late Bronze II cooking bowls belong to Forms CA 18a and 18b. Form CA 18a is the dominant cooking pot at most Late Bronze II sites. Though there have been several scholars who have attempted to trace a chronological development of cooking pot rim profiles during the fourteenth to thirteenth centuries BC (see, e.g., Amiran 1969, 135–40; Wood 1985, 388–96) there is no clear stratigraphic evidence in published excavation reports for a well-defined development of Late Bronze II cooking pots. Statistical analysis of Late Bronze II cooking pots at Tel Miqne-Ekron has not indicated any discernible evolution of this form until the Iron I period. At Deir el-Balah, cooking pot Forms CA 18a and 18b appear together with a large variety of rim profiles. I suggest here that we are dealing with typological variations created by individual potters or in different workshops. Form CA 18d is closely related to later Iron I cooking pots and may foreshadow the appearance of the classic Iron I cooking pot, here represented by our Form CA 19.

Type I, Cooking Bowl with Vertical to Inverted Rim

Form CA 19a (fig. 2:1–5). Cooking bowl Form CA 19a is characterized by a great diversity in the vertical rim stance and triangular profile. Often the bottom of the folded-over lip is upturned, forming a low ridge on the outer part of the rim. The rim can also be slightly inverted with a short triangular section. This cooking pot is found in several Iron I loci at Deir el-Balah (fig. 2:3; T. Dothan et al. in press), Level VI at Tel Beth Shean (fig. 2:1), Strata VII and VI at Tel Miqne-Ekron (fig. 2:2, 5), and in significant numbers at Giloh (fig. 2:4; Mazar 1981, fig. 7:9, 12, 16, 17; 1990, fig. 3:7). The cooking pots found at Giloh often have a "short" triangular-shaped rim and constitute part of A. Mazar's (1981, 23) cooking pot Type B. Nearly identical cooking pots appear in large numbers at Tell el-Ful (e.g. Sinclair 1960, pl. 21:7–10), Tell Qasile,[14] and Tel Batash (see, e.g., Kelm and Mazar 1995, fig. 5:12). These shorter, triangular-shaped rim profiles seem to be a regional variation of cooking bowl Form CA 19a.

The shape and rim profile are typical of Iron I cooking pots in the Manasseh region,[15] at Gezer (see, e.g., Dever 1986, pl. 39:7 [Stratum XI]), Deir ʿAlla (Franken and Kalsbeek 1969, 120, Iron Age cooking pot Type 1), Megiddo (Loud 1948, pl. 85:16, Cooking Bowl 21 [Stratum VI]), and Dan (Biran 1994, fig. 98:7 [Stratum V], fig. 103:3, 4 [Pit 3127]). Cooking bowl Form CA 19 appears in significant quantities at Tell Qasile,[16] Izbet Sartah (Finkelstein 1986, fig. 6:12 [Type 12:65]), and at other Iron I sites throughout Canaan.[17]

Form CA 19b (fig. 2:6–7). This cooking pot is similar to Form CA 19a, except for its inverted rim. The few examples from Giloh and Tel Miqne-Ekron belong to the short triangular-rimmed type, however the longer, inverted, triangular flange is a very popular shape in Canaan during the Iron I, perhaps continuing into the Iron II period.[18] Similar cooking pots are known from Tell el-Ful (Sinclair 1960, pl. 21:1, 3) and those with a slightly longer flange at Mount Ebal (Zertal 1986/87, fig. 17:6).

Type I , Cooking Bowl with Infolded Rim

Form CA 20a (fig. 2:8–9). The body profile of cooking bowl Form CA 20a is very similar to that of Form CA 18, however the vertical rim, with its distinctive ridged profile and thickened top, is characteristic of a group of cooking pots prevalent in Levels VII and VI at Tel Beth Shean. It appears at other sites in the Jordan Valley, such as Deir ʿAlla, where it appears at the end of the Late Bronze II period in Phase E (see e.g. Franken 1992, fig. 5–9:6, 10), continuing into the Iron I levels (Franken and Kalsbeek 1969, 119, fig. 26), where it is classified as Late Bronze cooking pot Type 2. This cooking pot is possibly known from Megiddo, Stratum VII.[19] The distribution of cooking bowl CA 20a is concentrated mainly in the Jordan Valley and is perhaps also found in the Jezreel Valley.

Form CA 20b (fig. 2:10). This cooking pot belongs to the same typological and technological family as CA 20a. Its distinguishing feature is its inverted, ridged rim. It first appears at Tel Beth Shean Level VI (fig. 2:10) and is also a well-known form in Iron I levels at Deir ʿAlla, where it is defined as Iron Age cooking pot Type 2 (Franken and Kalsbeek 1969, 124: fig. 28).

Type II, Globular Cooking Jug

A second type of cooking pot was found in twelfth century BC levels at Tel Miqne-Ekron, located in the southern coastal plain of Philistia. Cooking Jug Form AS 10 is a closed cooking pot and has the shape of a globular jug with one or two handles from the rim to the shoulder, and a flat base (fig. 3; Killebrew 1998a, 183–84). It usually has a simple or slightly thickened everted rim. At Tel Miqne-Ekron, this cooking jug reaches a maximum height of ca. 20 cm, with a maximum diameter of ca. 18 cm, and is generally fairly uniform in size. The aperture ranges from 9 to 12 cm in diameter. Dark black soot is found on the exterior surface of these cooking jugs, clearly confirming their use as cooking vessels. These twelfth century cooking pots from Tel Miqne-Ekron (Killebrew 1998b, 397) first appear in Stratum VII alongside Mycenaean IIIC:1b and related wares. It is the most popular cooking shape in the early Iron I levels at this site almost replacing the traditional indigenous cooking pot of the Late Bronze and Iron I periods. Fragmentary examples of this cooking jug appear in the Iron I pits at Deir el-Balah.

Cooking Jug Form AS 10 is also well-known from Ashdod, where they appear in Strata XIIIb (M. Dothan and Porath 1993, fig. 17:4, 5) and XII (M. Dothan and Porath 1993, fig. 34:2, 7) and date to the Iron I Philistine levels. They also make a debut at Tell ʿAitun[20] and possibly at Beth Shemesh (Grant and Wright 1938, pl. LXI: 27–31) and Tell Qasile (Mazar 1985, fig. 41:1 [type CP 3: 53]). This cooking jug bears no resemblance typologically to the typical indigenous cooking pots of the Late Bronze and Iron I periods. However, similar single- and double-handled cooking jugs are a form well-known in Cyprus in the Late Cypriot IIC and IIIA periods. The single-handled cooking jug, sometimes with a round base, appears at Hala Sultan Tekke (Öbrink 1979, 23, fig. 111 [F 6171]; Åström et al. 1983, figs. 318, 49), Pyla-Kokkinokremos (Karageorghis and Demas 1984, pls. XX:102; XXXVI:102; XX:104; XXXVI:104, classified as Coarse Handmade Ware), Maa-Palaeokastro,[21] Athienou (T. Dothan and Ben-Tor 1983, fig. 50:7–8), Enkomi (Dikaios 1969, pl. 106:3), Kourion (Daniel 1937, pls. II–III, V), and along the southern coast of Anatolia (e.g. Tarsus, see Goldman 1956, pl. 324: 1220–21).

Similar cooking jugs are also found, although in smaller quantities, in the Aegean.[22] However, the typical Late Helladic cooking pot is usually placed on a tripod and classified by Furumark (1941, 640) as Form 95, FS 320, the tripod cauldron (see also Mountjoy 1985, fig. 5.22:376, 377 from Phylakopi). The long history of this cooking pot type on a tripod has been traced on Crete.[23] Though its body is similar in shape to our Form AS 10 cooking jug, its placement on three legs clearly distinguishes it from the Tel Miqne-Ekron examples. Thus, typologically, the closest and most numerous parallels come from Cyprus and Tarsus.

These cooking jugs are found on the southern coast of Canaan during the Iron I period, slightly earlier on Cyprus during the Late Cypriot IIC and IIIA, at Tarsus on the southern coast of Anatolia, and in the Aegean during the Late Helladic IIIC period.

Summary

The two main types of cooking pots, Types I and II, appearing in Canaan during the Late Bronze II and Iron I, typologically derive from two very different potting traditions. The Type I cooking bowl has a long and well-known indigenous development, beginning at the dawn of the second millennium and continuing well into the end of the Iron Age. The Type II cooking jug which has no local antecedents prior to its sudden appearance at several Iron I sites in the southern coastal plain associated with the Philistines. It is an Aegean-inspired form, known from the west, especially on Cyprus and at Tarsus on the southern coast of Anatolia. Typologically, these two cooking pots types can be identified with two very different groups of potters and consumers— Type I with the indigenous population of Canaan, and Type II with a new population group whose origins lie to the west and is identified with the biblical Philistines.

TECHNOLOGY[24]

An examination of the technology used to produced cooking pots of the Late Bronze II and Iron I periods is based on the petrographic thin section analysis of forty cooking pots from Tel Miqne-Ekron, Deir el-Balah, Beth Shean, and Giloh. This technique was selected owing to the diverse types of information that can be obtained, including the choice and provenience of raw materials, the mixing of clays and tempers, as well as formation techniques and the firing temperature.[25] One of the main applications of petrographic examination and the identification of minerals is the determination of the raw material source; this most effective when minerals of a limited geological distribution are identified within the clay body. In these instances, it is a relatively easy task to pinpoint an area (or areas) from which a particular vessel is most likely to have originated.[26] The examination of thin sections of ceramics can also aid in the study of ancient technology regarding methods used in fabric preparation (clay "recipe"), shaping of the clay vessel, and firing conditions.[27]

Thin sections are formed by affixing a small fragment of pottery to a glass microscope slide, which is then ground with a diamond lap or abrasive powder until it is ca. 0.03 mm thick. Most of the minerals in the pottery are transparent at this stage and can be studied and identified under the petrographic (i.e., polarizing) microscope. Clay-sized minerals are too fine-grained to enable identification under the microscope, so analysis of minerals is limited to coarser inclusions, either naturally occurring in the clay or added by the potter as temper (Hodges 1965, 198; Peacock 1970, 379; Tite 1972, 25).

In order to describe and discuss the thin sections so that they would be relevant to archaeological questions regarding these ceramic assemblages, and in order to facilitate handling the large number of samples, the samples were divided into main groups having similar petrographic features (= ware or fabric). A "petrographic group" includes vessels that share petrographic affinities in both clay type (matrix) and temper, and therefore may serve as an independent technical criterion for the classification and interpretation of ceramic assemblages.[28]

The starting point for any petrographic analysis is a general knowledge of the exposed geological formations and raw materials availabe in the region of the site.[29] Ideally, locating sources of raw materials is essential in any attempt to distinguish between local and imported pottery and enables the testing of hypotheses relating to the sources of clays used for the pottery production.[30] To achieve this goal, the geology of the four sites discussed here is briefly described as a first step in our petrographic analysis.

TEL MIQNE-EKRON

Geology

Tel Miqne-Ekron is located at the eastern end of the coastal plain, near the western flanks of the Shephelah, along the southern bank of Nahal Timna, a tributary of the Nahal Soreq wadi system. The area of the eastern coastal plain includes outcrops of the Pleset Formation,[31] which overlies the Zor'a Formation (Maresha Member).[32] To the east, in the Shepehlah, a rather homogeneous picture is evident with the Zor'a Formation ('Adulam Member)[33] overlying the Taqiye Formation.[34] Local bedrock visible on the surface today includes Eocene chalk and chalky marl on the outcrops of low hills several hundred meters east of the tell, as well as a few outcrops of Neogene beachrock (A. M. Rosen unpublished). Present-day soils are remnants of Mediterranean brown forest soils, water-logged vertisoils near the wadi, and alluvial soils in the valley surrounding the site (Rosen n.d.; Ravikovitch 1970).

Ancient Clay Sources

Approximately 2 km west of Tel Miqne-Ekron, a modern quarry cutting through approximately 20 m of sediment accumulation reveals three different sediments: a red hamra; a greyish-beige grumusol, and the sediments from an ancient wadi system that penetrated the two other sediment layers.[35] The clay in this region can be characterized in general as smectite-rich.[36]

The lowest level visible in the modern section is a quartz-rich hamra clay. A grumusol clay sits on top of the hamra, and recently a prehistoric site, probably Acheulean in date (Marder et al. in press) was found at the base of the grumusol soil, where it comes into contact with the hamra. This provides an approximate date for the beginning formation of the grumusol unit. Also visible in this quarry section is an ancient wadi system which cuts through the grumusol clay. This calcareous clay has moderate quantities of sand-sized quartz and a larger quantity of silt-sized quartz. The ancient wadi clay is similar to the grumusol clay when examined under the petrographic microscope (fig. 4 top).

Tel Miqne-Ekron Ware Groups

In a comprehensive study of the Late Bronze II and Iron I pottery assemblage from Tel Miqne-Ekron, five main ware groups were distinguished. All the Type I cooking pots from Tel Miqne-Ekron belong to Ware Groups B2, B4, and C. One non-locally produced Iron I cooking pot has been classified as Ware Group D. Most of the Type II cooking jugs belong to Ware Group B3.

Type I Cooking Bowls

ME-B2 (fig. 4 middle). The majority of the Tel Miqne-Ekron cooking pots were produced out of ware ME-B2. Ware Group ME-B is a silty calcareous clay matrix containing some fine and sandy quartz (4–10%) with different types of temper. The clay has an eolian source (loess) and a fluvial source similar to the wadi clay sampled in the vicinity of Tel Miqne-Ekron. However, moderate to large quantities of limestone and shell temper (generally › 10%) were added to the matrix of sub-type ME-B2, distinguishing it from the other sub-types of Ware ME-B. Pieces of *kurkar* also appear occasionally. This group consists of Late Bronze II and Iron I cooking pots in the local Canaanite tradition, with a composition similar to cooking pot ware from Deir el-Balah (see below, Ware DB-A2) and from the Lachish potters' workshop (Magrill and Middleton 1997, 69).

ME-B4. Only one sample, an Iron I cooking pot, belongs to this sub-group of Ware Group ME-B. The calcareous matrix, typical of ME-B wares, is distinguished by the appearance of crushed calcite temper (4–10%), which is extremely rare in this assemblage.

ME-C (fig. 4 bottom). These vessels have been grouped together because of their temper, which is characterized by a relatively large amount of sand-sized quartz (20–30%). Two cooking pots have a calcareous matrix with clearly visible foraminifera. Two other cooking pots have a non-calcareous matrix, similar to the *hamra* clay sediment near to the tell. A few shells are also present in the ware of these two vessels. Limestone and kurkar occasionally appear as temper in the matrix. This group is made up of Iron I cooking pots in the Canaanite tradition.

ME-D. The Late Bronze-style cooking pot of ME-D, with its non-calcareous clay, is not locally produced. The temper includes large quantities of sandy quartz (> 10%) and large rounded pieces of limestone.

Type II Cooking Jugs

ME-B3 (fig. 5 top). The calcareous matrix of this group is can be defined as almost a pure loess matrix, with sandy quartz and straw occasionally added to it. Only Aegean-style Iron I cooking jugs appear in this group and differ from the Type I cooking bowls owing to the lack of shell temper added to its matrix.

DEIR EL-BALAH

Geology

The site of Deir el-Balah, located 1.7 km east of the Mediterranean shoreline, belongs to the coastal plain extending from Khan Yunis to Caesarea. This geographical region includes the coastal cliff, as well as a series of longitudinal ridges and *marzevot*, or trough features. Two ridges, the first 2 km east of the coast and the second 2 km further east, consist of friable calcareous sandstone (*kurkar*). The trough between the two ridges contains a stiff brown silty, clayey sand sediment.[37] The sediments upon which the site was constructed were deposited during the Holocene period, between 5,500 to 3,000 years BP. This date is based on the C-14 dating of land snails and the discovery of an Early

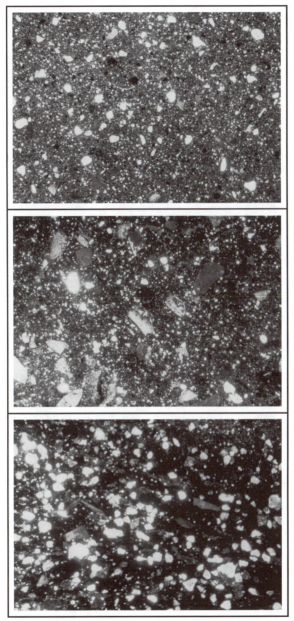

Fig. 4. Petrographic Ware Groups, Tel Miqne-Ekron. Top) Wadi Clay Sample (width: 3.5 mm); middle) Ware Group ME-B2 (width: 3.5 mm); bottom) Ware Group ME-C (width: 1.75 mm).

Bronze site within the layer. This stable sand evolved into a soil upon which the site is located; is the sediment presently used for agricultural activities in the Gaza Strip (Bakler in press).

Ancient Clay Sources

Two sediment layers were revealed while excavating a large square pit measuring ca. 20×20 m, which had been dug during the initial phase of settlement at the site. It is suggested that this pit originally served as a clay quarry, as it consisted of sandy silts and silts resembling residual and cummulic dark brown soils and residual quartzic-psammic arid brown soils.[38] The upper yellow sediment included quartz sand and silt in a calcareous silty matrix belonging to a loess clay and classified here as Ware DB-A. Feldspar, hornblende, epidote, and pyroxene occur in small amounts (Goldberg et al. 1986, fig. 32:7). The lower, brown sediment is similar but somewhat coarser than the yellow sediment, with a larger percentage of sand-sized quartz and smaller quantities of silt-sized quartz. Land snails in the brown sediment indicate a fluvial origin for this loess clay (Goldberg et al. 1986, fig. 32:8; Goldberg and Rosen in press).

Deir el-Balah Ware Groups

The Deir el-Balah Late Bronze II–Iron I assemblage is divided into three main ware groups. Most of the cooking pots belong to Ware Group A, subtype A2, and cooking pots produced out of a non-local clay is defined as Ware Group B.

DB-A: This ware is by far the most common group at the site and includes most of the locally-made pottery. It is characterized by a silty calcareous matrix and belongs to a loess clay. It is distinguished by traces of feldspar, chert, and mica, and by the heavy minerals pyroxene, epidote, and hornblende. This is the typical matrix of the local sediments found at the site in the quarry of Deir el-Balah.

Type I Cooking Bowls

DB-A2 (fig. 5 middle). The matrix of this ware is defined by the moderate amounts of shell temper (4–10%) added to the matrix. Small

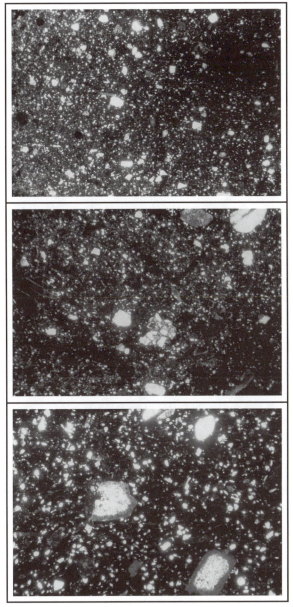

Fig. 5. Petrographic Ware Groups, Tel Miqne-Ekron and Deir el-Balah (cross-polarized light). Top) Ware Group ME-B3 (width: 3.5 mm); middle) Ware Group DB-A2 (width: 3.5 mm); bottom) Ware Group DB-B (width: 1.75 mm).

amounts of *kurkar* occasionally appear in the ware. All of the vessels of this ware are Late Bronze cooking pots with a variety of rim profiles. The rounded shell temper is similar to the temper added to Canaanite-style cooking pots at Tel Miqne-Ekron (Ware ME-B2) and seems to be the same clay recipe used to produce typologically identical cooking pots from the Lachish potters' workshop (Magrill and Middleton 1997, 69–70).

DB-B (fig. 5 bottom). This ware group is characterized by its non-calcareous clay. It includes small quantities (1–3%) of mudballs, *kurkar*, chalk, and a moderate amount of shell (4–10%). Only one vessel, an Iron I cooking pot, is assigned to this group.

Type II Cooking Jugs

DB-A1. This is the most common version of Ware DB-A, which is characterized by moderate to high quantities of silty quartz (10–30%). The amount of sand-sized quartz temper varies, and occasionally *kurkar* fragments also appear. The ware is almost identical to the loess clay sediments (both the lower brown and upper yellow layers) at the site and very little additional preparation was invested in the clay before it was used in the production of vessels. Occasionally signs of straw temper are evident in the matrix. One Iron I cooking jug (Form AS 10) was produced using this paste.

TEL BETH SHEAN

Geology

Geologically, Tel Beth Shean is located in a very diverse region. Igneous basalt outcrops appear in the eastern hills of the Lower Galilee to the north, and sedimentary limestone and chalk deposits belonging to the Eocene period form the Mt. Gilboa range to the south. In the Beth Shean and Jordan Valleys, calcite-rich alluvial sediments rest on Upper Pleistocene travertine and Lisan deposits. Most of these sediments are exposed within a 1 km perimeter of the tell. This rich variety of raw materials is reflected in the ceramics petrographically examined here.[39]

Tel Beth Shean Ware Groups

Three main locally produced ware groups have been defined in the Level VII ceramic assemblage sampled.[40] Ware BS-C, exclusively used in the production of cooking pots, is a calcareous clay with large amounts of limestone and calcite temper added to the matrix.

Type I Cooking Bowls

BS-C (fig. 6 top). Ware BS-C is characterized by a very calcareous clay matrix with a small number of foraminifera. The temper includes large quantities of crushed calcite and limestone minerals (› 10%) with small amounts of silty and sandy quartz (1–3%). Occasional basalt grains appear in the matrix. Cooking pots comprise Ware BS-C.

GILOH

Geology

Giloh is located to the south of Jerusalem, on a hill opposite and north of Beit Safafa. The greater Jerusalem area is situated in the Judean and Samarian hills (or central hill-country), which comprise a series of hills forming a chain extending from north to south through the center of Israel. The Jerusalem area sits on bedrock of limestone, dolomite, and chalk layers dating to the Late Cretaceous period. Two main groups are visible, the earlier Judea Group and the later Mt. Scopus Group (Gill 1996). The hill where Giloh is situated consists of the Weradim Formation, overlying the exposed Kefar Shaul Formation. These rest on the Aminadav Formation; all are part of the Judea Group.[41] These formations consist of dolomite (Weradim and Aminadav Formations), limestone (Weradim, Kefar Shaul, and Aminadav Formations), and chalk (Kefar Shaul Formation). In the nearby Nahal Refaim, outcrops of the Moza Formation are exposed (Arkin et al. 1976).

Clay Types

Three main local clay types were used in the production of the entire Giloh assemblage. All cooking pots were produced out of one ware, defined as Ware Group C.

Type I Cooking Bowls

GI-C. Ware GI-C is a non-calcareous, silty *terra rossa* clay. Terra rossa is a soil type that is widely available in the central hill-country and in many other regions of Israel (Glass et al. 1993, 277). Thus, the exact source of these vessels cannot be determined solely on the ware, however this clay is available in the Giloh area. I have divided the cooking pot ware into two sub-groups based on the temper appearing in it.

GI-C1 (fig. 6 bottom). This group contains only cooking pots. It is defined by the moderate to large quantities of crushed calcite added as a temper to the matrix (5–15%). Sandy quartz also appears in significant amounts (4–10%). This well-known ware is referred to as the "Terra-Rossa + Calcite" group in Iron I vessels analyzed from Shiloh (Glass et al. 1993, 277). The group is easily definable by the naked eye because of the large amounts of angular calcite crystals that form the main tempering component. The angular edges of the calcite indicate that the potter crushed it intentionally before using it as temper.[42]

GI-C2. Only one example, a cooking pot, has been assigned to this group. The matrix of GI-C2 is a non-calcareous clay similar to Ware GI-C1. A coarse sandy quartz (10–15%) and limestone (1–3%) temper is the main component. No crushed calcite appears in the matrix.

Summary

At Late Bronze II levels at Deir el-Balah, Tel Miqne-Ekron, and Tel Beth Shean, potters used the same clay to produce cooking pots that were used to create other locally produced vessels (Wares DB-A, ME-B, and BS-C [similar to BS-B]), respectively). The defining factor was the type of temper intentionally added to the paste by the potter. In Canaanite-style cooking pots from Deir el-Balah and Tel Miqne-Ekron, the vast majority of the cooking pots were formed out of a paste containing relatively large amounts of shell and smaller amounts of limestone that were intentionally added to the local clay (Wares DB-A2 and ME-B2, respectively). This well-known temper was added to cooking pot wares to strengthen them and to reduce the damage due to thermal shock.[43]

The Late Bronze II and early Iron I cooking pot wares from Tel Beth Shean and Giloh are also distinctive from other vessel types (Wares BS-C and GI-C, respectively). Though the clay matrix of cooking pots at Beth Shean is calcareous and the matrix of the Giloh vessels is non-

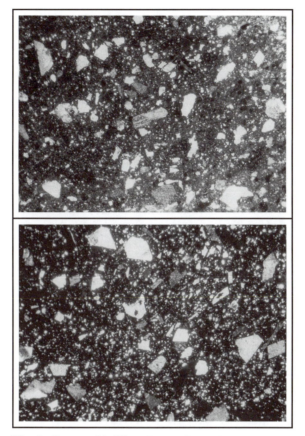

Fig. 6. Petrographic Ware Groups, Beth Shean and Giloh (cross-polarized light). Top) Beth Shean: Ware Group BS-C (width: 3.5 mm); bottom) Ware Group GI-C1 (width: 3.5 mm).

calcareous, both wares are defined by their relatively large quantities of crushed calcite temper, which is well-known already in the Chalcolithic and Early Bronze Ages (Goren 1987; Porat 1989, 45–47). This type of temper in Iron Age cooking vessels is well-known also at Tell es-Saʿidiyeh[44] and at other Iron Age sites such as Hazor (Shenhav 1964), Tel Dan (Slatkine 1974), and Tel Hadar (Shoval et al. 1989). Shoval et al. (1992) observe that crushed monocrystalline calcite tempers are very common in Iron Age cooking pots, where they assisted in preventing defects in vessels due to thermal shock caused by rapid heating or cooling. He notes that crystalline calcite is a superior tempering material over other types of calcite, such as limestone, since the former decarbonized at a higher temperature than the latter.

The only cooking vessel that did not use a calcite temper such as crushed calcite or shell is the Iron I Aegean-style cooking jug (Wares ME-B3 and DB-A3). The main temper in this loess clay is small quantities of sand-sized quartz and an even smaller amount of limestone. Once again, this represents a complete break with local cooking pot manufacturing traditions of the Late Bronze Age at Tel Miqne-Ekron and the surrounding regions.

The type of ware utilized in the production of cooking pots is also a reflection of the formation techniques. Nearly all of the Type I cooking bowls used a heavily tempered ware, either fairly large pieces of shell or crushed calcite. This coarse ware would have been most suitable for handmade vessels, using either a coil or mold and coil technique, as has been reconstructed by H. J. Franken and J. Kalsbeek in their replication study of the Late Bronze II and Iron I pottery at Deir ʿAlla (Franken and Kalsbeek 1969, esp. 73–100). In contrast, the Type II cooking jug used a clay with moderate amounts of silty and sandy quartz, but lacking the coarse temper used in the clays of the Type I cooking bowls. Visual examination of this vessel type from Tel Miqne-Ekron and of published examples from the Aegean indicates that this cooking jug was produced on a fast wheel, which was the technique used to produce most of the Tel Miqne-Ekron Iron I Aegean-style vessels.

FUNCTION

The morphology and technology of a ceramic vessel often reflects the functional uses of the pot. The divergent shapes and technology used to produce Type I and II cooking vessels indicate that these cooking vessels served very different purposes. The relatively wide aperture, an "open" though slightly restricted shape, would enable several different cooking methods, including steaming, frying, simmering, and boiling. The round base is not suitable for placement on a flat surface while cooking; it was probably "suspended" above the heated fuel, perhaps resting on the small opening of domed ovens. The narrow opening of the Type II (Form AS 10) cooking jug hints at the method by which the contents were cooked. In his study on cooking technologies in the prehistoric American southeast, K. E. Sassaman (1995, 226) has noted that quartz temper, the temper of choice for the Type II cooking jug potters, was ideal when a cooking vessel was heated directly, while other types of temper were better suited for indirect heating. Also the shape of cooking pots reflects functional use. In the above-mentioned study by Sassaman (1995, 226, and Table 18.1), he notes that restricted vessels were more suited for direct heating. I suggest here that the contents inside these cooking pots were boiled. The walls of the Type II cooking jug are thin, which is especially useful in boiling. The flat base would have allowed the cooking pot to rest directly on the heated surface and the handle would have permitted easy removal. The relatively uniform size and small volume of this cooking pot, in comparison with the Late Bronze Age cooking pot, may indicate that smaller portions were being prepared in this pot; it may also reflect the number of people that participated in any given meal. The paucity of larger cooking bowls (Type I) in the early Iron I Philistine levels at Tel Miqne-Ekron may suggest that much of the food was cooked directly over an open fire or hearth.

Aspects of functional use are also reflected in the types of ovens used during the Late Bronze II and Iron I periods. Ovens often indicate how the contents of cooking pots were heated, an area of research seldomly investigated. Cooking ovens are frequently uncovered during the course of excavation, but little thought has been given to how the ovens were used. Two types of ovens were generally excavated at sites in Canaan: a partially subterranean, circular oven with straight sides and open at the top, or a circular, domed oven with a small aperture at the top. The former oven was probably used for baking bread while the latter was most likely used for cooking. The cooking pot could have been placed on top of the domed oven, over the coals below. At Tel Miqne-Ekron, open hearths have been uncovered in the courtyards of several structures dating to the twelfth century BC. Similar hearths are known from the Aegean world and may have been used for heating, roasting, or other methods of cooking (Karageorghis 1998; Karageorghis and Demas 1988, 60–61).

As described above, different cooking pot forms and types of cooking installations most likely reflect diverse traditions of cuisine.[45] This should be examined also in light of other aspects of material culture, such as faunal and floral remains or eco-artifacts. These studies of diet, environment, and animal management provide invaluable information on foodways, an especially resilient and conservative element in human cultures. Diet, as any other element of material remains, can be as distinctive a marker of cultural identity. Ethnographic studies have shown that people tend to resist change in their ways of preparing and consuming foods (Hesse 1986, 17). An important aspect of foodways is cuisine;[46] it is suggested here that cuisine is reflected by the containers that cooked the food.

Coinciding with the sudden change in cooking vessels at Tel Miqne-Ekron and Ashdod at the beginning of the twelfth century, a shift occurred in the animal production systems that supported Tel Miqne-Ekron. Based on Hesse's examination of faunal remains in the Field INE sondage there, he concluded that during the twelfth century BC, pigs and cattle became more important in the economy at the expense of sheep and, particularly, goats.[47] In several studies, pig raising has been linked with newcomers to a region. Though pig husbandry at Tel Miqne-Ekron and Ashkelon was short-lived (perhaps only a century in length), it does mark a change in diet and would also indicate a different cuisine for the twelfth century BC recent inhabitants at Tel Miqne-Ekron (Hesse and Wapnish 1997, 248, 263).

CONCLUSIONS

This investigation of Late Bronze II and Iron I Age cooking pots illustrates the unique properties of this type of utilitarian vessel. Typologically, both cooking pot types are shaped to serve a specific function. Types I and II cooking pots reflect two distinctly different cultural traditions and most likely indicate different functional aspects of their use. Technologically, these cooking vessels are distinguished from other contemporary vessels by their distinctive tempers, which in most cases were added to local clays. These special tempers, usually a form of calcite in Type I cooking pots, were added in order to reduce the effects of thermal stress on the cooking pot as a result of repeated heating and cooling. Probably owing to these considerations and as evidenced by this study of Late Bronze II and Iron I cooking pots, these wares as a group demonstrate greater conformity than those of other vessel types, seldom deviating from the standard clay recipe used by a specific potter or workshop.

In addition to the two distinctive typological traditions of Types I and II, two very different technological traditions are clearly evident. Potters of Type I cooking pots added significant amounts of calcite (either shell or crushed calcite) to the local clays, while the potters of Type II cooking jugs did not include calcite in their pastes and the wares of their cooking vessels were characterized by silty and sandy quartz.

These two cooking pot types, with very different typological and technological traditions, are not only a chronological indicator, but most likely reflect two very diverse groups of people with very different foodways. Cuisine, a variable seldomly considered in archaeological interpretation, undoubtedly played a very important role in the morphological development of cooking pots and tablewares. The archaeological and historical evidence at Tel Miqne-Ekron reveals a rather sudden change in material culture associated with the appearance of a new dominant cultural group, referred to as the Philistines in biblical sources. This change is evident not only in the "luxury" tablewares, but also in more utilitarian vessels such as the cooking pot. I propose that the Type II cooking jug should be interpreted as an imported cultural and technological tradition with a different functional use than indigenous Type I cooking bowl, reflecting a different cuisine. This cooking jug is just one of many elements of Philistine material culture that demonstrates a western, Aegean-inspired source, whose immediate origins point to Cyprus.

NOTES

This study is dedicated to Albert Glock, whose research on ancient and traditional pottery and potters was especially influential on my investigation of Late Bronze and Iron Age pottery in Canaan.

1. See e.g. DeBoer and Lathrap (1979, 116–17), Henrickson and McDonald (1983, 631), Annis and Geertman (1987), Schiffer (1990).
2. See e.g. Linton (1944), Plog (1980, 85–87), Smith (1988 and references there), Annis and Jacobs (1989/90), Bronitsky and Hamer (1986), Rice (1987, 207–43).
3. See Smith (1988) for a summary of these morphological variables.
4. The excavations at Tel Miqne-Ekron were directed by Professors Trude Dothan of the Hebrew University of Jerusalem and Sy Gitin of the Albright Institute of Archaeological Research. I would like to thank Professors Dothan and Gitin for their permission and support to use the

results of the excavations in Field INE, which was under my supervision from 1984–1988 and 1994. For a general overview of the excavation results, see Gitin and Dothan (1987), Dothan and Gitin (1993, 1051–52). Regarding the excavations in Field INE, see Killebrew (1986; 1996), T. Dothan (1989; 1992; 1995; 1997; 1998a).

5. The excavations at Deir el-Balah were directed by Professor Trude Dothan. I would like to thank Professor Dothan for her permission to publish and use this material for my dissertation. For a summary of the excavations at the settlement and cemetery, see T. Dothan (1972; 1973; 1979; 1981; 1982; 1985a, b; 1987; 1993; 1998b), and T. Dothan et al. (in press).

6. The cooking pots described in this paper originate from Levels VII and VI at Tel Beth Shean and have been excavated by A. Rowe (1925–1928) and G. M. FitzGerald (1930, 1933), Y. Yadin (1983), and A. Mazar (1989–1996). See Mazar (1993a, b; 1994a; 1997a, b, c) for a summary of the excavations on the tell. I would like to thank Professor Amihai Mazar for allowing me to use the material from Area NA in this study and in my dissertation.

7. The site was first discovered during surveys in the region conducted by M. Kochavi in 1968. Salvage excavations were directed by A. Mazar between 1978 and 1982 (see Mazar 1981; 1990; 1993c; 1994b for reports on these excavations).

8. The "Form Numbers" (CA 18–20; AS 10) of cooking pots used in this paper are part of a comprehensive typology of Late Bronze and Iron I pottery, which appears in my dissertation (1998a). CA refers to pottery that belongs to the indigenous "Canaanite" style pottery in Canaan during the second millennium BC. AS indicates pottery locally produced in Canaan, but demonstrating a strong Aegean-style influence.

9. It is one of the types designated by Mazar (1981, 20–23) as cooking pot Type A (1981, fig. 7:5, 11, 14, 16; 1990, figs. 3:3; 6:11).

10. See, e.g., Yadin *et al.* (1958, 120, Pls. LXXXV:23, CVII:1-7, CXXVII:1-9, CXLV:6-9; 1960, Pl. CXXX:5, 6).

11. Zertal (1991:39) defines this type as cooking pot Type A.

12. A complete example, similar to fig. 1:6, appears in Stratum XIV (late thirteenth century BCE) of Area G at Ashdod (M. Dothan and Porath 1993, fig. 12:10; see also fig. 9:15 [Stratum XVI]).

13. Edelstein and Milevski (1994, fig. 12:1–2, 6), where they are found with a Nineteenth Dynasty scarab.

14. Mazar (1985, 52). Mazar's Type 1a; and see footnotes 70–72 for detailed comparative material.

15. Zertal (1991), cooking pot Type B: 39. Our Forms CA 19a and 19b are included in Zertal's Type B.

16. Mazar (1981), cooking pot Type 1a: 52. Mazar notes that this type is most common in the Iron I period.
17. For a detailed discussion of the comparative material, see Mazar (1981, 52), Finkelstein (1986, 65).
18. See Zertal's cooking pot Type C (1991, 39). This is equivalent to Mazar's Type 1b at Tell Qasile (1985, 52–53); and for detailed comparative material, see Mazar (1985, nn. 73–77). See also, e.g., Gezer (Dever 1986, Stratum XI: pl. 39:6), Tel Dan (Biran 1994: Stratum VI: fig. 93:5; Stratum IV: fig. 104:9–12).
19. This cooking pot may possibly appear on the Stratum VII ceramic typology chart published by Shipton (1939, Stratum VII chart - no. 59).
20. Edelstein and Aurant 1992, figs. 2 (jug on left) and 10:9, where they are classified as "jugs."
21. Single- and double-handled cooking pots; see e.g. Karageorghis and Demas (1988, pls. LX:692; CLXXXIII:692; LX:578; CLXXXIII:578; CIX:387; CCXI:387).
22. See, e.g., Lefkandi (Popham and Milburn 1971, fig. 2:5), and Perati (Iakovidis 1969, pl. 62:720); double-handled cooking pots are known from Phylakopi (see Mountjoy 1985, 196, fig. 5:22:379; 207 fig. 5:29:543).
23. On Crete, this cooking pot resting on a tripod has been discussed by Martlew (1988) and Haggis and Mook (1993).
24. This section is part of a comprehensive study of the technology of Late Bronze II and Iron I pottery assemblages from Tel Miqne-Ekron, Deir el-Balah, Tel Beth Shean, and Giloh appearing in my unpublished dissertation (see Killebrew 1998a, Chapter IV). The ware groups which appear in this section are based on a study of all the major ceramic typology groups found at these sites.
25. Following the application of advanced chemical analyses, such as Neutron Activation Analysis and others, to ceramic studies, petrographic thin section analysis experienced a decline in popularity. Recently, however, petrography has undergone a revival due to the limitations of several of these chemical analyses that have become evident with time (see e.g. Lemoine *et al.* 1982). The relatively inexpensive cost and quick results of petrography have enhanced the attractiveness of this method. Ideally, for best results, one should combine thin section analysis with a chemical analysis (Lazzarin et al., 1980; Maggetti and Galetti 1980; Hughes *et al.* 1982; Maggetti and Schwab 1982; Maggetti et al. 1984; Maniatis et al. 1984; Goldberg et al. 1986; Schubert 1986; Hamroush 1992). See Porat (1989, 13–14) and Vaughan (1995) for a summary of the advantages and disadvantages of petrographic analysis.
26. The first study to establish the importance of this technique in

archaeology was A. Shepard's work (1942) on the Rio Grande Glaze-Painted pottery from New Mexico. Due to the varied geology of the region, it was possible to distinguish between the products of different areas based on the various mineral tempers. Shepard was able to relate the ceramic sequence to cultural innovations at particular locales and to changes in trade patterns. This technique has been used in countless ceramic studies in order to assist in establishing the provenience of ancient pottery.

27. See Vaughan (1995) for a summary of the advantages and disadvantages of petrographic analyses.

28. See Porat (1989, 25) and Glass *et al.* (1993, 272) for a discussion of the criteria useful in defining fabric groups which are a result of both human and natural factors. See Whitbread 1989 who also stresses the importance of studying the clay matrix of pottery.

29. See, e.g., Masucci and Macfarlane (1997) for a recent study that successfully employs a regional geological survey with a provenance study of ceramics from Ecuador.

30. Porat (1989, 16–19) and bibliography noted there; for a similar approach, see Day (1989).

31. The Pleset Formation is a calcareous pebbly sandstone. It is exposed in the Lower Shephelah and coastal plain in the Kefar Menahem–Tel Zafit area. It is Pliocene–Lower Plesitocene in date (Buchbinder 1969, 9).

32. The Zor'a Formation (Maresha Member) is a white globigerinal chalk covered by a thick nari crust. It is found mainly in the regions of Lachish, Beth Guvrin, and Tel Maresha (Buchbinder 1969, 9).

33. Exposed at many spots in the Shephelah, the Zor'a Formation (Adulam Member) consists of white and silicified chalks with alternations of flint beds and nodules. It overlies the Taqiye Formation and is dated to the Lower to Middle Eocene period (Buchbinder 1969, 5).

34. The Taqiye Formation is a marl consisting of a lower member of chalky shales and an upper member of hard silicified chalk and chalky shales. The latter is exposed in Nahal Soreq along the slopes of the Zor'a Hills and along the southern slopes of Ha'ela Valley. It is Paleocene in date (Buchbinder 1969, 5).

35. Sediments were identified by Dr. Paul Goldberg during a visit to the quarry site.

36. Regarding the importance of locating ancient clay sources and quarries, see Buko (1995).

37. P. Goldberg's brown "nazaz" or residual sandy grumusol.

38. See Goldberg et al. (1986) for a detailed description and petrographic illustrations of the natural clay sediment; see also Dan *et al.* (1976).

39. For a detailed description of the geology of the Beth Shean region see

Shaliv *et al.* (1991). Due to budgeting constraints, it was impossible to conduct clay sampling and a geological survey of the area. Unfortunately, no recent detailed geological map of the Beth Shean Valley has been published.

40. McGovern *et al.* (1993) petrographically sampled forty-three ceramic objects presumed to be locally produced. However, the mineralogical description of the samples lack a general profile of the ware and a division of the specimens into main groups. Moreover, no photographs were published of the petrographic thin sections. It is thus very difficult to correlate their descriptions with the ware groups I discerned. More recently, A. Cohen-Weinberger (1998) has published a short article describing several petrographic wares typical of selected Egyptian pottery shapes from Level VI at Tel Beth Shean.

41. The Judea Group, which forms the Judean hills, comprises mostly hard limestones and dolomites. To the west, the Judea Group forms the synclinorium of the Shephelah region upon which formations of the Mt. Scopus/HaShephela Group were laid (Buchbinder 1969, 3). See also Gill (1996) for further details regarding the geology of the Jerusalem area.

42. The potter was required to mine calcite from naturally-occurring veins in limestones and then crush it before adding it as temper (see e.g. Glass 1978). This labor-intensive activity was probably dictated by market demand. See Glass *et al.* (1993, 277) for a detailed discussion of this ware and its appearance in the pottery from Shiloh.

43. For a description of the effects of heating and cooling on ceramic cooking pots, see Amberg and Hartsook (1946), Kingery (1955), Bronitsky and Hamer (1986; regarding a commentary on this article, see Feathers 1989), and Rice (1987, 367–68) for a discussion of thermal properties of clay; see Woods (1986) for an alternative view regarding thermal stress. See also Braun (1983) for a discussion of the physcial properties of cooking pots. See Feathers (1989) and Matson (1989) for a detailed discussion of the use of shell as temper in clays and the effects this temper has on different aspects of pottery manufacture.

44. See Vilders (1993; 1996). She also notes that organic temper was added to the cooking pot paste; for the effects of organic material as temper in pottery, see Skibo et al. (1989).

45. See also Killebrew (1992) and Yasur-Landau (1992). Regarding its significance as an ethnic indicator, see Bunimovitz and Yasur-Landau (1996, 92–93).

46. Cuisine has been defined by J. Goody (1982, vii) as (1) the products of the kitchen; (2) foods that are associated with a particular culture; and (3) highly elaborated forms of cooking (see Grantham 1992, 9–15 for a summary of the social ramifications of cuisine).

47. The shift placed a greater emphasis on intensively herded stock in contrast to the earlier, more extensive forms of herd management during the Late Bronze Age. The evidence suggests that pigs and cattle reflect less contact or interaction with hill country pastoral production that, based on the faunal evidence, characterized the Late Bronze Age society (Hesse 1986).

REFERENCES

Amberg, C. R., and Hartsook, J.
  1946   Effect of Design Factors on Thermal-Shock Resistence of Cooking Ware. *American Ceramic Society* 25: 448–52.
Amiran, R.
  1969   *Ancient Pottery of the Holy Land.* Jerusalem: Massada Press.
Annis, M. B., and Geertman, H.
  1987   Production and Distribution of Cooking Ware in Sardinia. *Newsletter Department of Pottery Technology (A Knapsack Full of Pottery Archaeological Miscellenea Dedicated to H. J. Franken)* 5: 154–201.
Annis, M. B., and Jacobs, L.
  1989/90 Cooking Ware from Pabillonis (Sardinia): Relationships Between Raw Materials, Manufacturing Techniques and the Function of the Vessels. *Newsletter Department of Pottery Technology* 7/8: 75–131.
Arkin, Y.; Braun, M.; Buchbinder, B.; Diamant, E.; Itzhaki, Y.; Lasman, N.; Rot, I.; and Shachnai, E.
  1976   *Jerusalem and Vicinity, Geological Map 1:50,000.* Jerusalem: Geological Survey of Israel.
Åström, P.; Åström, E.; Hatziantoniou, A.; Niklasson, K.; and Öbrink, U.
  1983   *Hala Sultan Tekke 8 Excavations 1971–79.* SIMA Vol. XLV: 8. Göteborg: Åström.
Bakler, N.
  in press Geological Background of the Deir el-Balah Archaeological Site, Gaza Strip. In *Excavations in the Cemetery and Settlement at Deir el-Balah*, eds. T. Dothan *et al.* Qedem. Jerusalem: The Hebrew University of Jerusalem.
Biran, A.
  1994   *Biblical Dan.* Jerusalem: Israel Exploration Society.
Biran, A., and Negbi, O.
  1966   The Stratigraphical Sequence at Tel Sippor. *Israel Exploration Journal* 16: 160–73.

Braun, D. P.
1983   Pots as Tools. Pp. 107–34 in *Archaeological Hammers and Theories*, eds. J. A. Moore and A. S. Keene. New York: Academic.

Bronitsky, G., and Hamer, R.
1986   Experiments in Ceramic Technology: The Effects of Various Tempering Materials on Impact and Thermal-Shock Resistance. *American Antiquity* 51: 89–101.

Buchbinder, B.
1969   *Geological Map of HaShephela*. Jerusalem: The Geological Survey of Israel.

Buko, A.
1995   Clays for Ancient Pottery Production: Some Current Problems of Analysis. Pp. 29–36 in *The Aim of Laboratory Analyses of Ceramics in Archaeology April 7–9 1995 in Lund, Sweden In Honour of Birgitta Huth*, eds. A. Lindahl and O. Stilborg. Kung. Vitterhets: Historie Och Antikvitets Akademien.

Bunimovitz, S., and Yasur-Landau, A.
1996   Philistine and Israelite Pottery: A Comparative Approach to the Question of Pots and People. *Tel-Aviv* 23: 88–101.

Cohen-Weinberger, A.
1998   Petrographic Analysis of the Egyptian Forms from Stratum VI at Tel Beth-Shean. Pp. 406–12 in *Mediterranean Peoples in Transition Thirteenth to Early Tenth Centuries BCE*, eds. S. Gitin, A. Mazar and E. Stern. Jerusalem: Israel Exploration Society.

Dan, J.; Yaalon, D. H.; Koyumdjisky, H.; and Raz, Z.
1976   *The Soils of Israel* (Pamphlet NO. 159). Bet Dagani: The Volcanic Center.

Daniel, J. F.
1937   Two Late Cypriote III Tombs from Kourion. *American Journal of Archaeology* 41: 56–85.

Day, P. M.
1989   Technology and Ethnography in Petrographic Studies of Ceramics. Pp. 139–47 in *Archaeometry Proceedings of the 25th International Symposium*. Amsterdam: Elsevier.

DeBoer, W. R., and Lathrap, D. W.
1979   The Making and Breaking of Shipibo-Conibo Ceramics. Pp. 102–38 in *Ethnoarchaeology: Implications of Ethnography for Archaeology*, ed. C. Kramer. New York: Columbia University.

Dever, W. G.
1986   *Gezer IV: The 1969–71 Seasons in Field VI, The "Acropolis."*

Jerusalem: Annual of the Nelson Glueck School of Biblical Archaeology.

Dever, W. G.; Darrel Lance, H.; Bullard, R. G.; Cole, D. P.; and Seger, J. D.
1974   *Gezer II: Report of the 1967–70 Seasons in Fields I and II*, ed. W. G. Dever. Jerusalem: Hebrew Union College.

Dikaios, P.
1969–71 *Enkomi Excavations 1948–1958*. Mainz: von Zabern.

Dothan, M.
1971   *Ashdod II–III The Second and Third Seasons of Excavations 1963, 1965, Soundings in 1967*. ʿAtiqot 9–10. Jerusalem: Israel Department of Antiquities and Museums.

Dothan, M., and Porath, Y.
1993   *Ashdod V Excavations of Area G, The Fourth–Sixth Seasons of Excavations 1968–1970*. ʿAtiqot 23. Jerusalem: Israel Antiquities Authority.

Dothan, T.
1972   Anthropoid Clay Coffins from a Late Bronze Age Cemetery near Deir el-Balah (Preliminary Report). *Israel Exploration Journal* 22: 65–72.

1973   Anthropoid Clay Coffins from a Late Bronze Age Cemetery near Deir el-Balah (Preliminary Report II). *Israel Exploration Journal* 23: 129–46.

1979   *Excavations at the Cemetery of Deir el-Balah*. Qedem 10. Jerusalem: The Hebrew University of Jerusalem.

1981   Deir el-Balah 1979, 1980 (Notes and News). *Israel Exploration Journal* 31: 126–31.

1982   Gaza Sands Yield Lost Outpost of the Egyptian Empire. *National Geographic* 162: 738–69.

1985a   Aspects of Egyptian and Philistine Presence in Canaan during the Late Bronze–Early Iron Ages. Pp. 55–75 in *The Land of Israel: Cross-Roads of Civilizations*, ed. E. Lipinski. Orientalia Lovaniensia Analecta 19. Leuven: Peeters.

1985b   Deir el-Balah: The Final Campaign. *National Geographic Research* 1, no. 1: 32–43.

1987   The Impact of Egypt on Canaan during the 18th and 19th Dynasties in the Light of Excavations at Deir el-Balah. Pp. 121–35 in *Egypt, Israel, Sinai: Archaeological and Historical Relationships in the Biblical Period*, ed. A.F. Rainey. Tel Aviv: Tel Aviv University.

1989   The Arrival of the Sea Peoples: Cultural Diversity in Early Iron Age Canaan. Pp. 1–14 in *Recent Excavations in Israel: Studies in Iron Age Archaeology*, eds. S. Gitin and W. G. Dever. Annual of the American Schools of Oriental Research 49. Winona Lake, In.: Eisenbrauns.

1992   Social Dislocation and Cultural Change in the 12th Century B.C.E. Pp. 93–98 in *The Crisis Years The 12th Century B.C.: From Beyond the Danube to the Tigris*, eds. W. A. Ward and M. Joukowsky. Dubuque, IA: Kendall/Hunt.

1993   Deir el-Balah. Pp. 343–47 in *The New Encyclopedia of Archaeological Excavations in the Holy Land,* Vol. 1. Jerusalem: Israel Exploration Society.

1995   Tel Miqne-Ekron: The Aegean Affinities of the Sea Peoples' (Philistines') Settlement in Canaan in Iron Age I. Pp. 41–59 in *Recent Excavations in Israel: A View to the West*, ed. S. Gitin. Dubuque, IA: Kendall/Hunt.

1997   Tel Miqne-Ekron: An Iron Age I Philistine Settlement in Canaan. Pp. 96–106 in *The Archaeology of Israel Constructing the Past, Interpreting the Present*, eds. N. A. Silberman and D. Small. JSOT Supplement Series 237. Sheffield: Sheffield Academic.

1998a   Initial Philistine Settlement: From Migration to Coexistence. Pp. 148–61 in *Mediterranean Peoples in Transition Thirteenth to Early Tenth Centuries BCE*, eds. S. Gitin, A. Mazar and E. Stern. Jerusalem: Israel Exploration Society.

1998b   Cultural Crossroads: Deir el-Balah and the Cosmopolitan Culture of the Late Bronze Age. *Biblical Archaeology Review* 24: 24–37, 70, 72.

Dothan, T., and Ben-Tor, A.
1983   *Excavations at Athienou, Cyprus 1971–1972.* Qedem 16. Jerusalem: Institute of Archaeology, Hebrew University of Jerusalem.

Dothan, T.; Brandl, B.; Gould, B.; Killebrew, A. E.; and Lipton, G.
in press   *Excavations in the Cemetery and Settlement of Deir el-Balah.* Jerusalem: The Hebrew University of Jerusalem.

Dothan, T., and Gitin, S.
1993   Miqne, Tel (Ekron). Pp. 1051–59 in *The New Encyclopedia of Archaeological Excavations in the Holy Land*, Vol. 3, ed. E. Stern. Jerusalem: Israel Exploration Society.

Edelstein, G., and Aurant, S.
1992   The "Philistine" Tomb at Tell ʿEitun. *ʿAtiqot* XXI: 23–41.

Edelstein, G., and Milevski, I.
1994   The Rural Settlement of Jerusalem Re-evaluated: Surveys and Excavations in the Raphʾaim Valley and Mevassert Yerushalayim, *Palestine Exploration Quarterly* 126: 2–23.

Feathers, J. K.
   1989   Effects of Temper on Strength of Ceramics: Response to Bronitsky and Hamer. *American Antiquity* 54: 579–88.

Finkelstein, I.
   1986   ʿIzbet Sartah An Early Iron Age Site Near Rosh Haʿayin, Israel. Oxford: British Archaeological Reports.

Finkelstein, I.; Bunimovitz, S.; and Z. Lederman
   1993   *Shiloh: The Archaeology of a Biblical Site*, ed. I. Finkelstein. Monograph Series of the Institute of Archaeology, Tel Aviv University. Tel Aviv: Tel Aviv University.

Franken, H. J.
   1992   *Excavations at Tell Deir ʿAlla. The Late Bronze Age Sanctuary.* Louvain: Peeters.

Franken, H. J., and Kalsbeek, J.
   1969   *Excavations at Tell Deir ʿAlla.* Vol. I. Leiden: Brill.

Furumark, A.
   1941   *The Mycenaean Pottery Analysis and Classification.* Stockholm: Victor Pettersons.

Gill, D.
   1996   The Geology of the City of David and its Ancient Subterranean Waterworks. Pp. 1–28 in *Excavations at the City of David 1978–1985 Directed by Yigal Shiloh Vol. IV Various Reports*, eds. D. T. Ariel and A. De Groot. Qedem 35. Jerusalem: The Hebrew University of Jerusalem.

Gitin, S., and Dothan, T.
   1987   The Rise and Fall of Ekron of the Philistines: Recent Excavations at an Urban Border Site. *Biblical Archaeologist* 50: 197–222.

Givon, S., ed.
   1991   *The First Season of Excavation at "Tel Harasim" 1990 Preliminary Report 1.* Tel Aviv (in Hebrew).
   1992   *The Second Season of Excavation at "Tel Harasim" 1991 Preliminary Report 2.* Tel Aviv (in Hebrew).
   1995   *The Fifth Season of Excavation at Tel Harassim (Nahal Barkai) 1994 Preliminary Report 5.* Tel Aviv (in Hebrew).

Glass, J.
   1978   Petrographic and Technological Analyses. Pp. 8–9; 43–44; 50; 117 in R. Amiran, *Early Arad: The Chalcolithic Settlement and Early Bronze City I.* Jerusalem: Israel Exploration Society.

Glass, J.; Goren, Y.; Bunimovitz, S.; and Finkelstein, I.
   1993   Petrographic Analyses of Middle Bronze Age III, Late Bronze Age and Iron Age I Pottery Assemblages. Pp. 271–86 in *Shiloh:*

The Archaeology of a Biblical Site, eds. I. Finkelstein, S. Bunimovitz and Z. Lederman. Tel Aviv: Institute of Archaeology, Tel Aviv University.

Goldberg, P.; Gould, B.; Killebrew, A.; and Yellin, J.
  1986   Comparison of Neutron Activation and Thin-Section Analyses on Late Bronze Age Ceramics from Deir el-Balah. Pp. 341–51 in *Proceedings of the 24th International Archaeometry Symposium*, eds. J. Olin and J. Blackman. Washington D.C.: Smithsonian Institute.

Goldberg, P., and Rosen A. M.
  in press Geological Observations at Deir el-Balah. In *Excavations in the Cemetery and Settlement of Deir el-Balah*, eds. T. Dothan *et al.* Jerusalem: The Hebrew University of Jerusalem.

Goldman, H.
  1956   *Excavations at Gözlü Kule, Tarsus Volume II: From the Neolithic through the Bronze Age.* Princeton: Princeton University.

Goody, J.
  1982   *Cooking, Cuisine and Class: A Study in Comparative Sociology.* New York: Cambridge University.

Goren, Y.
  1987   *The Petrography of Pottery Assemblages of the Chalcolithic Period from Southern Israel.* Unpublished M.A. thesis, Hebrew University of Jerusalem (in Hebrew).

Grant, E., and Wright, G. E.
  1938   *Ain Shems Excavations (Palestine) Part IV (Pottery).* Haverford, PA: Haverford College.

Grantham, B. J.
  1992   *Modern Buqata and Ancient Qasrin: The Ethnoarchaeology of Cuisine in the Golan Heights.* Unpublished MA Thesis, University of Alabama.

Greenberg, R.
  1987   New Light on the Early Iron Age at Tell Beit Mirsim, *Bulletin of the American Schools of Oriental Research* 265: 55–80.

Haggis, D. C., and Mook, M. S.
  1993   The Kavousi Coarse Wares: A Bronze Age Chronology for Survey in the Mirabello Area, East Crete. *American Journal of Archaeology* 97: 265–93.

Hamroush, H. A.
  1992   Pottery Analysis and Problems in the Identification of Geological Origins of Ancient Ceramics. *Cahiers de la Céramique Ägyptienne* 3: 39–51.

Henrickson, E. F., and McDonald, M. M. A.
  1983   Ceramic Form and Function: An Ethnographic Search and an Archaeological Application. *American Anthropologist* 85: 630–43.

Hesse, B.
  1986   Animal Use at Tel Miqne-Ekron in the Bronze Age and Iron Age. *Bulletin of the American Schools of Oriental Research* 264: 17–28.

Hesse, B., and Wapnish, P.
  1997   Can Pig Remains be Used for Ethnic Diagnosis in the Ancient Near East? Pp. 238–70 in *The Archaeology of Israel Constructing the Past, Interpreting the Present*, eds. N. A. Silberman and D. Small. JSOT Supplement Series 237. Sheffield: Sheffield Academic.

Hodges, H.
  1965   *Artifacts An Introduction to Early Materials and Technology.* London: Royal Opera Arcade.

Hughes, M. J.; Cherry, J.; Freestone, I. C.; and Lease, M.
  1982   Neutron Activation Analysis and Petrology of Medieval English Decorated Floor Tiles from the Midlands. Pp. 113–22 in *Current Research in Ceramics: Thin-Section Studies*, eds. I. Freestone, C. Johns and T. Potter. British Museum Occasional Paper No. 32. London: British Museum.

Iakovidis, S.
  1969/70 *Perati: To Nekrotafian.* Athens: Archiologike etairia en Athenais.

Karageorghis, V.
  1998   Hearths and Bathtubs in Cyprus: A "Sea Peoples'" Innovation? Pp. 276–82 in *Mediterranean Peoples in Transition: Thirteenth to Early Tenth Centuries BCE*, eds. S. Gitin, A. Mazar and E. Stern. Jerusalem: Israel Exploration Society.

Karageorghis, V., and Demas, M.
  1984   *Pyla-Kokkinokremos: A Late 13th Century BC Fortified Settlement in Cyprus.* Nicosia: Department of Antiquities, Cyprus.
  1988   *Excavations at Maa-Palaeokastro 1979–1986.* Nicosia: Department of Antiquities, Cyprus.

Kelm, G. L., and Mazar, A.
  1995   *Timnah A Biblical City in the Sorek Valley.* Winona Lake, IN: Eisenbrauns.

Killebrew, A. E.
  1986   *Tel Miqne-Ekron Report of the 1984 Excavations Field INE/SE,*

ed. S. Gitin. Jerusalem: Albright Institute of Archaeological Research.

1992 Functional Analysis of Thirteenth and Twelfth Century BCE Cooking Pots. Paper presented at the annual meeting of the American Schools of Oriental Research, San Francisco.

1996 *Tel Miqne-Ekron Report of the 1985–1988 Excavations in Field INE: Areas INE.5, INE.6 and INE.7 The Bronze and Iron Ages. Text and Data Base (Plates, Sections, Plans)*, ed. S. Gitin. Jerusalem: Albright Institute of Archaeological Research.

1998a Ceramic Craft and Technology During the Late Bronze and Early Iron Ages: The Relationship Between Pottery Technology, Style, and Cultural Diversity. Unpublished Ph.D. Dissertation. Jerusalem: Hebrew University of Jerusalem.

1998b Ceramic Typology and Technology of Late Bronze II and Iron I Assemblages from Tel Miqne-Ekron: The Transition from Canaanite to Philistine Culture. Pp. 279–304 in *Mediterranean Peoples in Transition: Thirteenth to Early Tenth Centuries BCE*, eds. S. Gitin, A. Mazar and E. Stern. Jerusalem: Israel Exploration Society.

Kingery, W. D.
1955 Factors Affecting Thermal Stress Resistance of Ceramic Materials. *Journal of the American Ceramic Society* 38: 3–15.

Kochavi, M.
1974 Khirbet Rabud = Debir. *Tel-Aviv* 1: 2–33.

Lazzarin, L.; Calogero, S.; Burriesci, N.; and Petrera, M.
1980 Chemical, Mineralogical and Moessbauer Studies of Venetian and Paduan Renaissance Sgraffito Ceramics. *Archaeometry* 22: 57–68.

Lemoine, C.; Walker, S.; and Picon, M.
1982 Archaeological, Geochemical, and Statistical Methods in Ceramic Provenance Studies. Pp. 57–64 in *Archaeological Ceramics*, eds. J.S. Olin and A.D. Franklin. Washington DC: Smithsonian Institution.

Linton, R.
1944 North American Cooking Pots. *American Antiquity* 9: 369–80.

Loud, G.
1948 *Megiddo II: Seasons of 1935–39*. Chicago: University of Chicago.

Maggetti, M.; and Galetti, G.
1980 Composition of Iron Age Fine Ceramics from Chatillon-s-Glane and Heineburg. *Journal of Archaeological Science* 7: 87–91.

Maggetti, M.; and Schwab, H.
  1982   Iron Age Fine Pottery from Chatillon-s-Glane and Heineburg.
            Archaeometry 24: 21–36.
Maggetti, M.; Westley, H.; and Olin, J. O.
  1984   Provenance and Technical Studies of Mexican Majolica Using
            Elemental and Phase Analysis. Pp. 151–91 in *Archaeological
            Chemistry III*. Advances in Chemistry Series 205. Washington:
            American Chemical Society.
Magrill, P., and Middleton, A.
  1997   A Canaanite Potter's Workshop at Lachish, Israel. Pp. 68–74 in
            Pottery in the Making World Ceramic Traditions, eds.
            I. Freestone and D. Gaimster. London: British Museum.
Maniatis, Y.; Jones, R. E.; Whitbread, I. K.; Kostikas, A.; Simopoulos, A.; C.
Karakalos, H.; and Williams, C. K.
  1984   Punice Amphoras Found at Corinth, Greece: An Investigation of
            their Origin and Technology. *Journal of Field Archaeology* 11:
            205–22.
Marder, O.; Kalaily, H.; Rabinovich, R.; Gvirtzman, G.; Wieder, M.; Porat, N.;
Ron, H.; Bankirer, R.; and Saragusti, I.
  in press The Lower Paleolithic Site of Revadim Quarry, Preliminary
            Results. *Journal of the Israel Prehistoric Society.*
Martlew, H.
  1988   Domestic Coarse Pottery in Bronze Age Crete. Pp. 421–14 in
            *Problems in Greek Prehistory: Papers Presented at the
            Centenary Conference of the British School of Archaeology at
            Athens Manchester April 1986,* eds. E. B. French and K. A.
            Wardle. Bristol: Bristol Classical.
Masucci, M., and Macfarlane, A.
  1997   An Application of Geological Survey and Ceramic Petrology to
            Provenance Studies of Guangala Phase Ceramics of Ancient
            Ecuador. *Geoarchaeology* 12: 765–93.
Matson, F. R.
  1989   Shell-Tempered Pottery and the Fort Ancient Potter. Pp. 15–31
            in *Pottery Technology Ideas and Approaches,* ed. G. Bronitsky.
            London: Westview.
Mazar, A.
  1981   Giloh: An Early Israelite Settlement Site near Jerusalem. *Israel
            Exploration Journal* 31: 1–36.
  1985   *Excavations at Tell Qasile Part Two The Philistine Sanctuary:
            Various Finds, the Pottery, Conclusions, Appendixes.* Qedem
            20. Jerusalem: The Hebrew University of Jerusalem.
  1990   Iron Age I and II Tower at Giloh and the Israelite Settlement.
            Israel Exploration Journal 40: 77–101.

1993a   Beth-Shean Tel Beth-Shean and the Northern Cemetery. Pp.
         214–23 in *The New Encyclopedia of Archaeological
         Excavations in the Holy Land* Vol. 1, ed. E. Stern. Jerusalem:
         The Israel Exploration Society.

1993b   Beth Shean in the Iron Age: Preliminary Report and Conclusions
         of the 1990–1991 Excavations. *Israel Exploration Journal* 43:
         201–29.

1993c   Giloh. Pp. 519–20 in *The New Encyclopedia of Archaeological
         Excavations in the Holy Land* Vol. 2, ed. E. Stern. Jerusalem:
         The Israel Exploration Society.

1994a   Four Thousand Years of History at Tel Beth-Shean, *Qadmoniot*
         27 (107–108): 67–83 (in Hebrew).

1994b   Jerusalem and Its Vinicity in Iron Age I. Pp. 70–91 in *From
         Nomadism to Monarchy Archaeological and Historical Aspects
         of Early Israel*, eds. I. Finkelstein and N. Naᶜaman. Jerusalem:
         Israel Exploration Society.

1997a   Four Thousand Years of History at Tel Beth Shean: An Account
         of the Renewed Excavations, *Biblical Archaeologist* 60: 62–76.

1997b   Iron Age Chronology: A Reply to I. Finkelstein, *Levant* XXIX:
         157–67.

1997c   The Excavations at Tel Beth Shean during the Years 1989–94.
         Pp. 144–64 in *The Archaeology of Israel Constructing the Past,
         Interpreting the Present*, eds. N. A. Silberman and D. Small.
         JSOT Supplement Series 237. Sheffield: Sheffield Academic.

McGovern, P. E.; Harbottle, G.; Huntoon, J.; and Wnuk, C.
1993   Ware Composition, Pyrotechnology and Surface Treatment. Pp.
         80–94 in *The Late Bronze Egyptian Garrison at Beth Shean:
         Study of Levels VII and VIII*, eds. F. James and P. McGovern.
         Philadelphia: The University Museum, University of Pennsyl-
         vania.

Mountjoy, P.
1985   The Pottery. Pp. 151–208 in *The Archaeology of Cult The
         Sanctuary at Phylakopi,* ed. C. Renfrew. London: The British
         School of Archaeology at Athens.

Öbrink, U.
1979   *Hala Sultan Tekke 6 A Sherd Deposit in Area 22.* SIMA Vol.
         XLV:6. Göteborg: Åström.

Oren, E. D.
1985   Architecture of Egyptian "Governors' Residencies" in Late
         Bronze Age Palestine, *EI* (Nahman Avigad Volume) 18:
         183–99 (in Hebrew).

Peacock, D. P. S.
  1970   The Scientific Analysis of Ancient Ceramics: A Review. *World Archaeology* 1: 375–89.
Plog, S.
  1980   *Stylistic Variation in Prehistoric Ceramics Design Analysis in the American Southwest.* Cambridge: Cambridge University.
Popham, M., and Milburn, E.
  1971   The Late Helladic IIIC Pottery of Xeropolis (Lefkandi): A Summary. *BSA* 66: 333–67.
Porat, N.
  1989   Composition of Pottery—Application to the Study of the Interrrelations Between Canaan and Egypt During the 3rd Millennium B.C. Unpublished Ph.D. Dissertation, Jerusalem: Hebrew University.
Ravikovitch, S.
  1970   Soil Map. *Atlas of Israel.* Section II/3. Tel Aviv: Survey of Israel.
Rice, P. M.
  1987   *Pottery Analysis.* Chicago: University of Chicago.
Rosen, A. M.
  n.d.   *Miqne-Ekron Geoarchaeological Report on the 1984, '85 and '86 Seasons.* Unpublished report.
Sassaman, K. E.
  1995   The Social Contradictions of Traditional and Innovative Cooking Technologies in the Prehistoric American Southeast. Pp. 223–40 in *The Emergence of Pottery Technology and Innovation in Ancient Societies,* eds. W. K. Barnett and J. W. Hoopes. Washington, D.C.: Smithsonian Institution.
Schiffer, M. B.
  1990   The Influence of Surface Treatment on Heating Effectiveness of Ceramic Vessels. *Journal of Archaeological Science* 17: 373–81.
Schubert, P.
  1986   Petrographic Modal Analysis—A Necessary Complement to Chemical Analysis of Ceramic Coarse Ware. *Archaeometry* 28: 163–78.
Shaliv, G.; Mimran, Y.; and Hatzor, Y.
  1991   The Sedimentary and Structural History of the Bet She'an Area and its Regional Implications. *Israel Journal of Earth Sciences* 40: 161–79.
Shenhav, H.
  1964   *Petrographic Analyses of Pottery from Hazor Excavations.*

Unpublished M.Sc. Thesis, Geology Department, Hebrew University of Jerusalem (in Hebrew).

Shepard, A. O.
1942   *Rio Grande Paint Ware: A Study Illustrating the Place of Ceramic Technological Analysis in Archaeological Research.* Washington: Carnegie Institute.

Shipton, G. M.
1939   *Notes on the Megiddo Pottery of Strata VI–XX.* Chicago: University of Chicago.

Shoval, S.; Erez, Z.; Kirsh, Y.; Deutsch, Y.; Knafo, R.; Kochavi, M.; and Yadin, E.
1989   Mineralogy and Petrography of Groups of Pottery from Tel Hadar (abstract). *Geological Society of Israel Annual Meeting, Ramot, April 1989*: 151.

Shoval, S.; Gaft, M.; Beck, P.; Kirsh, Y.; and Yadin, E.
1992   The Preference of Monocrystalline Calcite Temper Upon Limstone Ones in Preparation of Iron Age Cooking Pots. P. 137 in *Israel Geological Society Annual Meeting, 1992 Ashqelon 30 March – 1 April*, ed. B. Polishook.

Sinclair, L. A.
1960   *An Archaeological Study of Gibeah (Tell el-Ful).* Annual of the American Schools of Oriental Research 34–35. New Haven: ASOR.

Skibo, J. H.; Schiffer, M. B.; and Reid, K. C.
1989   Organic-tempered Pottery: An Experimental Study. *American Antiquity* 54: 124–46.

Slatkine, A.
1974   Comparative Petrographic Study of Ancient Pottery Sherds from Israel. *Museum Haaretz Yearbook* 15–16: 101–14.

Smith, M. F., Jr.
1988   Function from Whole Vessel Shape: A Method and an Application to Anasari Black Mesa, Arizona. *American Anthropologist* 9: 912–22.

Tite, M. S.
1972   *Methods of Physical Examination in Archaeology.* London: Seminar.

Tufnell, O.; Inge, C. H.; and Harding, L.
1940   *Lachish II: The Fosse Temple.* London: Oxford University.

Vaughan, S. J.
1995   Ceramic Petrology and Petrography in the Aegean. In: Science and Archaeology: A Review, ed. P. E. McGovern. *American Journal of Archaeology* 99: 115–17.

Vilders, M.
  1993   Some Remarks on the Production of Cooking Pots in the Jordan
            Valley. *Palestine Exploration Quarterly* 125: 149–56.
  1996   Some Technological Features of Tall as-Saʿidiyya Cooking
            Pots. Pp. 597–601 in *Studies in the History and Archaeology of
            Jordan V*. Amman: The Hashemite Kingdom of Jordan.
Whitbread, I. K.
  1989   A Proposal for the Systematic Description of Thin Sections
            Towards the Study of Ancient Ceramic Technology. Pp. 127–38
            in *Archaeometry Proceedings of the 25th International
            Symposium*. Amsterdam: Elsevier.
Williams, D. F.
  1979   Ceramic Petrology and the Archaeologist. Pp. 73–76 in *Pottery
            and the Archaeologist*, ed. M. Millett. Occasional Publication
            No. 4. London: Institute of Archaeology.
Wood, B.G.
  1985   Palestinian Pottery of the Late Bronze Age: An Investigation of
            the Terminal LBIIB Phase. Unpublished Ph.D. Dissertation,
            University of Toronto.
Woods, A.J.
  1986   Observation on the Cooking Pot in Antiquity. Pp. 157–72 in:
            Ceramics and Civilization Vol. II: Technology and Style, ed.
            W. D. Kingery. Columbus, OH: The American Ceramic
            Society.
Yadin, Y.; Aharoni, Y.; Amiran, R.; Dothan, T.; Dunayevsky, I.; and Perrot, J.
  1958   *Hazor I: An Account of the First Season of Excavations 1955*.
            Jerusalem: Magnes.
  1960   *Hazor II: An Account of the Second Season of Excavations 1956*.
            Jerusalem: Magnes.
Yadin, Y.; and Geva, S.
  1986   *Investigations at Beth Shean the Early Iron Age Strata*. Qedem
            23. Jerusalem: The Hebrew University of Jerusalem.
Yasur-Landau, A.
  1992   The Philistine Kitchen—Foodways as Ethnic Demarcators.
            Eighteenth Archaeological Conference in Israel, Abstracts, 10.
            Tel Aviv.
Zertal, A.
  1986/87   An Early Iron Age Cultic Site on Mount Ebal: Excavation
            Seasons 1982–1987: Preliminary Report. *Tel-Aviv* 13–14:
            105–65.
  1991   Following the Pottery Trail Israel Enters Canaan. *Biblical
            Archaeology Review* 17: 30–49, 75.

7 Abandonment and Site Formation Processes: An Ethnographic and Archaeological Study

GHADA ZIADEH-SEELY

The focus of this paper is the abandonment of the village of Ti'innik in both the sixteenth and twentieth centuries. The data presented here are based on an ethnographic study of site formation processes, conducted between 1982 and 1983 (Ziadeh 1984), as well as the archaeological evidence from the 1985–1987 excavation of that Ottoman village. The excavation at Ti'innik was divided into the early Ottoman site (sixteenth–eighteenth centuries) and the late Ottoman site (nineteenth century to the present). The latter included the excavation of one house that was studied ethnographically.

During the past thirty-five years, archaeologists interested in understanding the dynamics of archaeological formation have recognized that abandonment and refuse are primary factors in shaping the archaeological record. Abandonment is particularly important because it fossilizes the last human action before it becomes part of the archaeological record. The abandonment process is what determines the types, frequencies and distribution of artifacts in a specific locus. This subject had been discussed at length by Ascher (1968), Schiffer (1972; 1975; 1976; 1983), Stevenson (1982), Eidt (1984) and most recently by Joyce and Johannesen (1993) and Rothschild *et al.* (1993).

The Ti'innik case is particularly significant because it analyzes abandonment within the context of a still inhabited and growing settlement. In contrast to many studies that take place following the total abandonment of a settlement, this study provides us with a chance to observe firsthand the more complex dynamics of abandonment not as the final phase in the settlement's life but as an essential and integral stage in the living cycle of a settlement (Ascher 1968). Because the settlement is still inhabited, the abandoned buildings usually pass through a phase of reuse before they completely collapse becoming part of the archaeological record. Due to the reuse phase the classification of material deposits into clear categories of primary, secondary, abandonment and *de facto* refuse is not applicable (Reid 1985, 22).

Although total abandonment of settlements is frequently encountered in the archaeological record, gradual intra-site abandonment is not only far more frequent, it is an integral part of the archaeological record. Therefore, ethnographic observations connecting human behavior to abandoned buildings are critical in explaining the presence of certain materials in specific contexts. This type of a study should help in making the distinction between materials related to the original phase of occupation and those accumulating subsequent to abandonment. Such distinction is crucial in making inferences regarding the function of an excavated structure. In this study a structure is considered to be "abandoned" when it no longer retains its original function.

Ti'innik is a small Palestinian village located on the northern border of the West Bank just five miles southeast of Megiddo. The present village, established around the middle of the nineteenth century, is situated on the eastern slops of Tell Ta'annek, a site that had been occupied intermittently since 2700 BC. The village population of 539 people (in 1983) belongs to fifteen different extended families. Until the 1967 Arab-Israeli War, agriculture was the main source of income. Following the war, unskilled wage labor began to supplement the income of most households. Extended families in Ti'innik used to live in *ahwash* (the singular is *hawsh*). A *hawsh* consists of several single room houses enclosing a common courtyard. The houses were built with dirt and undressed soft limestones. The flat roofs were constructed with twigs and branches with a layer of dirt on top were supported by on eor two arches. Inside the house the floor was divided into two levels, 50 cm apart. The lower part, normally the part close to the entrance, was used for domestic activities as well as sheltering animals at night or during the rainy season. The upper part of the floor was where people slept, ate and socialized. Since the 1960s, concrete has begun to replace the traditional building material thus dramatically changing the layout and the appearance of the village. The new houses, which consist of several rooms, are no longer clustered around open courtyards (fig. 1).

ABANDONMENT AT TIʿINNIK

With the help of the village plan and three aerial photographs dating to 1917, 1944 and 1968, thirty-one cases of abandonment were identified over the last sixty-five years. Three of the abandoned structures had been dismantled completely without leaving a trace. Although it is difficult to date precisely the abandonment of each structure, the earliest abandonment of an existing structure dates back to the 1920s. Abandonment at Tiʿinnik is a slow continuous process that can be witnessed today. With a few exceptions, most of the abandoned buildings are old single room houses located at the core of the village. For the most part, the former inhabitants of these buildings still live in the village. More than one factor contributed to the abandonment of the old houses, among which is the population growth, the relative economic prosperity, and the replacement of the traditional building material. Lower infant mortality and longer life expectancy during this century increased the population. Old single room houses, used for centuries, could no longer accommodate three generations of the same family. The younger generation often moved into new a house, leaving the old generation behind. Population growth coincided with two other important factors, reinforcing the abandonment of the old houses. On the one hand, the availability of concrete as a substitute to the traditional building material made the new houses much more durable with minimal maintenance. On the other hand, availability of cash resulting from wage labor made the purchase of new building materials possible. In addition to the practical aspects the attraction of the new concrete houses lay in their becoming a symbol of status and wealth. Thus, we find some of the old abandoned houses in relatively good condition.

At the time of the study there were twenty-eight old abandoned structures in Tiʿinnik. With the exception of five structures, the rest were being reused in one form or another. The fate of an abandoned house depends on many factors, such as the condition of the building at the time of abandonment, whether or not the former residents left the

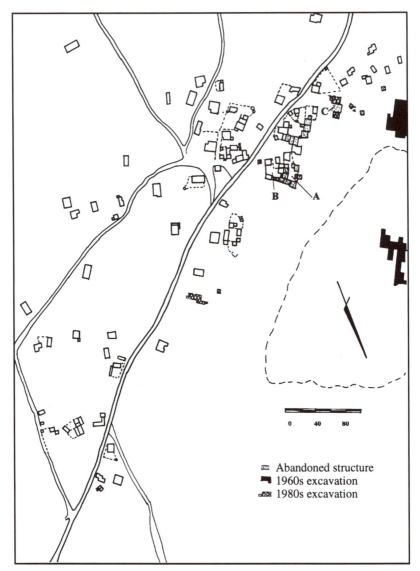

Fig. 1. Village plan showing the location of abandoned structures.

village permanently, and the interest and need of the former inhabitants. In the few cases where the former residents left the village permanently, the buildings collapsed shortly afterwards due to the lack of annual maintenance. With permanent abandonment, old houses fall prey to natural forces such as rain, wind and sun speeding its decay. With the decay came the scavenging of building materials. The wooden beams used to support the dirt roof were often pulled down and reused as fire wood. Also, the few well-dressed stones used in constructing entrances and arches were reused in building other structures such as baking ovens (*tabûn*) and chicken coops, often built inside the walls of a collapsing building. Less promising structures turned into dump areas for the neighboring households.

If the owners of an abandoned building or their descendants remained in the village however, the old house was either used for a secondary function such as a storage space or an animal shelter or was simply locked up and left to decay. The most recently abandoned buildings were likely to be turned into a storage space. The storage phase usually began with abandonment itself where few items, thought to be of little value in the new house, were left behind. Over time other objects, such as agricultural implements, animal fodder and fuel began to accumulate in the abandoned house. All the factors determining the secondary function of an abandoned building are interdependent. For example, the proximity of the original inhabitants to the abandoned structure affects the frequency of its maintenance, which in turn determines the way in which the building is reused. The interest of those people who reuse the building for a specific function also determines the level of care it receives.

Table 1 shows that the most common reuse of abandoned buildings, 13 out of 28 structures, is for sheltering animals, storage or both. The second most common reuse is a dump area; 6 out of 28 structures. It is worth noting that all of the abandoned structures that are used as dump areas belong to people who abandoned the village permanently. Another five of the abandoned structures no longer serve any function. Despite the fact that 60% of the unused building are in an advanced stage of decay, the presence of the original owners of these buildings in the village protects the buildings from turning into a dump area.

When abandoned buildings are used for sheltering animals, the level of decay determines the type of sheltered animals. If a building is in an advanced state of decay only chickens or rabbits are sheltered within its walls. By contrast, valuable animals, such as cows, goats and horses, are sheltered in abandoned buildings that are structurally sound, and definitely have a strong roof.

Table 1. Percentage of Destroyed Buildings in Each of
Eight Categories Characterized by Reuse Function

Category	Frequency	Destruction Rate
1. Not used	5	60%
2. Baking facility, *Tabûn*	3	100%
3. Baking facility & chicken coop	1	100%
4. Animal shelter	4	25%
5. Storage & animal shelter	5	0%
6. Storage	4	0%
7. Dump & chicken coop	2	100%
8. Dump area	4	100%

ABANDONMENT AND DESTRUCTION

Destruction caused by natural forces affects both inhabited and abandoned buildings. However, the impact of the weather depends on factors such as the age of the building, the quality of the structure, and the interest of the owners in maintaining the structure. Naturally abandoned houses are affected far more than inhabited ones mainly because of the lack of annual maintenance necessary to the longevity of a mud and stone structure. From an archaeological perspective, the impact of weather on abandoned buildings is critical because it accelerates the process of archaeological formation. When inhabited structures are damaged by weather, repair is often speedy. If similar damage occurred to an abandoned building its repair depends on the vitality of its secondary use to the owner. During the winter of 1982/83, I was able to record seven incidents of destruction caused by heavy winter rains. Some of the structures were still in use at the time of collapse, whereas others had been abandoned long before. I attempted to keep a record of the period of time it took to repair each of the damaged structures as an indicator of the need and importanceof the structure to the people who use it.

The first structure to be repaired immediately was a baking oven (*tabûn*) on which the owners depended to provide them with bread. In another case where a cave entrance leading to a *tabûn* collapsed, it took two months before any repair was done. The repair was delayed until the weather improved because the family was allowed to share the use of another baking facility belonging to relatives. During the same winter, two features collapsed in a single complex. These were an old stone and dirt room used as a kitchen and the courtyard wall. Surprisingly, priority was given to the courtyard wall which was reconstructed within ten days. At Ti'innik, courtyard walls are built to a height of two meters in order to shield the women, who carry on most of their domestic tasks in the courtyard, from the eyes of men in the village. The kitchen room, which was old and beyond repair, was left as is. In the long run, the young family living in these rooms, one man with his two wives and one child, will clear away the rubble and build a new concrete room in its place. The other three features that were damaged during that winter, a cave used occasionally as an animal shelter, an abandoned building used as a dump area, and a chicken coop, were not repaired by the following summer. Structures that stand a very little chance of being repaired are either abandoned structures or structures whose repair is not cost effective, such as the old kitchen room and the chicken coop.

ABANDONMENT AND REFUSE

Archaeologists studying abandonment pay special attention to the distribution and density of the remaining artifacts. Such evidence is used to determine the nature of abandonment, i.e. whether planned or unplanned and, if planned, did the people intend to return? If a site had been abandoned abruptly, the artifact frequency is expected to be much higher than if the abandonment was planned. In cases of planned abandonment one expects to find two types of byproducts; materials left behind because they were considered of little value and refuse that accumulated as people, knowing that they were leaving, would relax there cleaning habits. Hording, or storing away objects that are of value, is a strong indicator of people's intention to return to the site (Stevenson 1982).

At Ti'innik most of the abandoned houses contained two types of artifacts. The first comprises items considered to have little value, such as old ceramic vessels, threshing boards, and tin cans. The second type depends on the secondary function a house performs. The temporary retention of potentially recyclable artifacts and the economy of effort are major factors behind artifact accumulation in abandoned buildings (Joyce and Johannesen 1993, 139). The inventory also depends on whether the owners remain in the village, which functions as a deterrent against scavenging and discarding by other people in the village. Unless the abandoned building is used as a dump, most of the accumulated materials are inorganic, long-lasting objects that have a reasonable chance of becoming part of the archaeological record. A detailed study of artifact repertoire and distribution has been carried out in three complexes (*ahwash*) representing different stages of abandonment. One was totally abandoned, the second was almost completely abandoned with the exception of one room while the third was only half abandoned. These *ahwash* comprised seventeen rooms and three enclosed courtyards.

The first of the three complexes consists of eight single room houses, (*beût*, sing. *beit*) and a courtyard (complex A, see fig. 2). Only one of the rooms, room 8, was still occupied by an elderly widow. This room, constructed with cement, is a recent replacement of an older stone and dirt room. It is very likely that with the death of the old widow the complex will become totally abandoned. One of the rooms in the complex is no longer usable. The rest were being used for storage and animal sheltering. The complex initially housed four brothers and their families. Each of the families occupied two adjacent rooms. The courtyard, where many domestic activities took place, was shared by all four.

The abandonment of this complex was gradual. It began during the 1950s with the abandonment of rooms 5 and 6. The last two rooms to be abandoned in 1978 were room 11 and 12. The extended family that owns the complex continues to live in the village at the present. At the time of the study, two of the abandoned houses, rooms 5 and 6, had lost their original roofs. Whatever artifacts were left in room 5 remain buried under the collapsed roof. The debris of the fallen roof in Room 6 was cleared and a new tin-sheet roof was added, making the room usable for the occasional sheltering of animals. The inventory of artifacts in room 6 includes an old ceramic vessel, four (20 liter) tins, a plastic bucket, a handful of nails, an ash tray and a cover for a metal barrel. The 20 liter tins are commonly used to store, sell and transfer olive oil and kerosene. Aside from the ceramic vessel, probably left behind with the abandonment, the rest of the artifacts are post

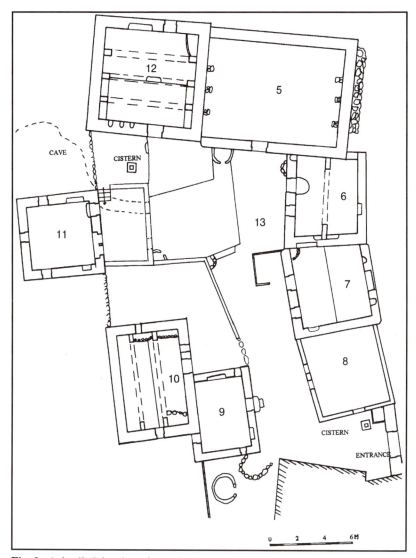

Fig. 2. A detailed drawing of complex A.

abandonment. Post abandonment objects are kept in the room because they have little use at the moment. However, people will not discard them just in case one day they can be recycled.

Room 7 are used both as a storage and an animal shelter. The old wooden roof was replaced with a new concrete one. The room has abuilt-in trough on the lower floor, part of the original construction.

Two metal sheet storage bins used for storing grain are a recent replacement for the clay bins found in these houses. The repertoire of artifacts includes three ceramic storage jars, two (20 liter) tins, one large plastic barrel, a large copper cooking pot, a pile of straw and one unfired clay *tabûn*, a kerosene heater and a copper coffee grinder. The artifacts in this room could be divided into two categories. Dead storage includes items that are not useful, such as the ceramic jars, the broken coffee grinder and the nonfunctioning heater. Live storage refers to items such as the stack of straw fed to the animals during the winter months, the unfired clay *tabûn*, waiting to replace the current one, as well as the large cooking pot used on special occasions and feasts.

Rooms 9 and 10 belong to the third family. These rooms were abandoned in the early 1960s. Room 9 used to function as a guest house thus it lacks the basic features found in a single room house. Room 10 contains the usual features of a single room house, split floor level, troughs on the lower floor and clay storage bins on the upper floor. The two rooms are in relatively good condition except that Room 9 is currently without a door and thus cannot be used for storage. While room 9 is used for sheltering animals, room 10 is used primarily for storage. The contents of room 9 are what I consider to be dead storage, including four (20 liter) tins, two plastic buckets and the cover of a metal barrel. By contrast, the inventory of room 10 includes two large copper and two small aluminum cooking pots, three ceramic storage jars and one basin, one plastic and one metal barrels, a metal oven, a plastic bucket, a shovel, a ladder, a tea pot, a glass bottle and five tin cans. For the most part the artifacts that accumulated after abandonment are either for seasonal use or are of no use at all.

Rooms 11 and 12, which belong to the fourth family, were abandoned in 1978. The old wood and dirt roofs in both buildings were replaced with concrete ones. The architectural features in each of the rooms suggest that Room 11 was used as a guest room, whereas Room 12 was used for daily living. Following the abandonment, both rooms were turned into storage spaces. Room 11 contains the following items: a pile of straw, several brooms, a straw basket, two aluminum cooking pots and five (20 liter) tins. Most of these objects belong to the live storage category. Room 12 contains the only functioning example of a clay storage bin (*khabieh*), as well as a more recent version of a storage bin made of metal sheet. A pile of charcoal, used for heating, and a pile of straw (animal fodder), are indicators of live storage. Six glass bottles, six (20 liter) tins, one jerry can, a copper lid, a straw basket, a serving tray, a grinding stone, a wooden box, a manual sewing machine, five ceramic vessels, two clay beehives, a sledge plate and a drainage pipe are objects that were either left behind or stored there. Knowing the original and secondary function of both rooms leads to the conclusion that most of the artifacts in room 11 resulted from secondary use while the artifacts in room 12 are a mixture of objects that were left behind with the abandonment and objects that were stored after the abandonment.

Finally, the courtyard (fig. 2.13) shows clear evidence of abandonment with the construction of a *tabûn* and two chicken coops. Traditionally, such installations are located outside the complex for sanitary reasons. A wide range of objects such as old shoes, plastic buckets, tins and bottles are scattered all over the courtyard floor. These objects are further indicators that the courtyard was turning into a discard area following abandonment.

The second complex (complex B, fig. 3), adjacent to the first one, consists of six rooms and a large courtyard. While three of the rooms were still occupied by an elderly widow and her daughter, the other three rooms were abandoned and in an advanced state of decay. In the past, the complex housed the families of two brothers, one of whom left the village in the early 1960s. The three functioning rooms have been converted into specialized areas. Room 14, the oldest room in the complex that carries the features of a single room house, was used as a kitchen. It contained one clay and two metal sheet storage bins, a stove, a cupboard, a ceramic jar and several pots, pans, china dishes and glasses. Room 16 was used mainly for storing mattresses. It contains several mattresses and one large mirror. Room 15 functioned as a guest room, with six armchairs, a TV set, a table, two cupboards and a bed. Despite the apparent specialization, the kitchen continued to be used for living and sleeping, especially during winter.

Two of the three abandoned rooms (17 and 19) no longer have roofs. Room 17, which is smaller than average, had the remains of a raised platform, suggesting it might have been used as a kitchen. A can, a broken bottle, and a metal cover of a barrel were scattered on the floor in no particular order. The room was basically not used except for the

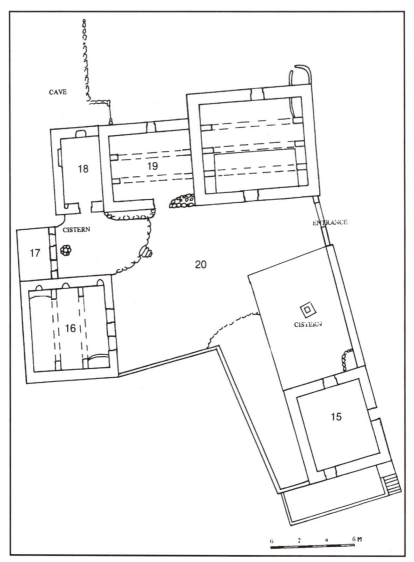

Fig. 3. A detailed drawing of complex B.

occasional discard of an odd object. Room 18 had one clay storage bin and a small ceramic vessel, remnants of the original occupation. A metal stake planted in the dirt floor, used for tying animals, was the only evidence for the secondary function of the room. Room 19, which is the closest to the functioning section of the complex, contained the largest collection of objects. The collection included a stack of branches used to start a fire, two metal troughs, a wooden crib, a shoe, a hoe, a ploughing blade, three tins, three cooking pots and a straw basket. None of the artifacts reflect the original function of the room. These objects had accumulated as a result of the secondary use of the room as a storage/ dump area, which is often the case when the occupants of the house leave the village permanently. The courtyard (fig. 3.20) is divided into two sections. The part that links the functioning rooms are kept clean and tidy with flower pots, plants and a hearth while the abandoned section is used to store away/dump unused items such as a sledge plate, a wooden door, two barrels, two cooking pots and a plastic jug. This complex is useful in differentiating living spaces from abandoned ones. While artifacts in abandoned rooms are scattered haphazardly, objects in a living space are stored along the walls thus leaving the center space clean and empty.

The third complex (complex C, fig. 4) consists of three adjacent rooms built in a straight line with a courtyard in front. All three rooms were missing a roof and the front wall. The collapse debris was 1.5 m high in some places. Only a small portion of the courtyard wall remains standing to the south while the rest, including the front gate, having disappeared. This *hawsh* was built some time during the last part of the nineteenth century as a farm house for an Ottoman appointed tax collector. Following the first world war, the family lost its influence. Thus the house fell into abandonment during the 1920s. A careful analysis of the aerial photograph dating to 1944 shows that the original roofs of all three rooms had fallen by that time. According to oral information, the house was reoccupied after 1948 by two Palestinian refugee families from the Haifa area. This second phase of occupation lasted until the early 1960s.

In 1982 the decaying complex was used for a variety of activities by neighboring families. In Room 1 (see fig. 4), which still contains piles of collapse deposits, a chicken coop was built in the corner over the rubble. A half cut jerry can was used to provide the chickens with water. Room 3 has only one chicken coop built over the high deposits of collapse debris. Room 2 was extensively occupied with one *tabûn* structure, four chicken coops and a stone lined area used for drying animal dung. Dry animal dung is used as fuel for the *tabûn*. A few artifacts were scattered on the ground. These include a mortar, a jerry

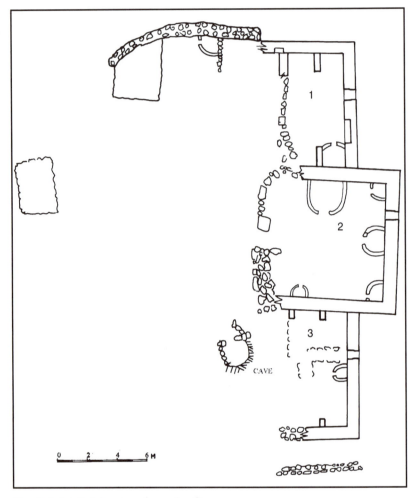

Fig. 4. A detailed drawing of complex C.

can, a cooking pot and four different size tins. Most of these objects
were reused for feeding and watering the chickens. The courtyard had
several built-in features including an entrance to a cave where a *tabûn*
was installed, one chicken coop, and two stone lined areas for drying
animal dung. The courtyard contained few scattered artifacts, six
shoes, four cans, two plastic buckets, one (20 liter) tin, a wooden door
and a metal barrel. All artifacts have very little value and were simply
discarded.

The detailed study of artifact distribution in abandoned buildings involved seventeen rooms and three courtyards totaling an area of 1542 m². The total artifact count in this area was 177 objects of varying sizes and values. The average distribution of objects per square meter is 1.1 objects for every ten square meters. There is a strong correlation between the secondary use of an abandoned structure and the frequency of the artifacts, as shown in Table 2. It seems that the highest frequency of artifacts, 0.354 per square meter, is found in abandoned buildings used for storage and animal shelter. The second highest frequency of artifacts, 0.245 items per square meter, is found in abandoned buildings used as discard areas. There is a fine line between items found in a storage space and discard area. Most often the items found in a storage/ discard area are unusable items that are cast aside in the hope that the object might be reused some time in the future. Areas that combine the functions of discard and domestic activity show the lowest frequency of artifacts (0.05) mainly because the domestic activity areas require a large space, such as courtyards thus reducing the concentration of artifacts. Inhabited rooms rank third in artifact density per square meter. Another distinction is the location of artifacts in inhabited areas, found usually along the walls. In contrast, artifacts found in dump and storage areas are scattered all over the floor.

ARCHAEOLOGICAL EVIDENCE
(LATE OTTOMAN PERIOD)

Two years following the ethnographic study, complex A was excavated. The excavation was limited to rooms 1 and 3 mainly because most of the debris in room 2 had been cleared out by the current users. Archaeological evidence suggested that the building witnessed not two but three phases of occupation. When old neighbors were asked again about the history of the building they informed us that the building was also occupied during the 1930s by a family of shepherds from a nearby village.

The excavation shows that each of the rooms had two front walls. The later wall was inset 1 m from the original one. Two layers of clean clayish debris found over the floors in each of the rooms were attributed to the collapse of the roof. The roof of the first room collapsed after the second phase of occupation (ca. 1935–1944). The second room's roof

Table 2. Frequency of artifacts in abandoned buildings.

function	area/m^2	artifacts	installations	artifacts/m^2
closed	80	0	0	0
dump	98	24	7	0.245
domestic use/dump	78	40	20	0.053
storage/animal shelter	207	70	5	0.338
inhabited	409	43	2	0.105
total	1542	177	34	0.114

collapsed following the last abandonment, just before 1967. The original floors in both rooms were divided into two levels similar to other single room houses in the village dating to the same period. During the second phase, both floors were adjusted by raising the lower floor to the level of the upper floor, leaving a small depression near the entrance. In both rooms a thick deposit of collapsed roof and walls were found between the floors of the second and third occupational phase. This layer was caused by an extended period of abandonment between the late 1930s and late 1940s. The third floor in both rooms were redivided into lower and upper floors. With this phase, the front, eastern wall in both rooms was rebuilt using the same stones of the original walls except the foundation. This last phase was followed by the abandonment and collapse of the roofs and the walls. The last phase in the history of the complex was the secondary use phase, which was recorded ethnographically.

Because each abandonment of this complex was planned and took place in the context of a thriving settlement, we did not expect to find many artifacts. The artifacts found in the fill between the first and the second floors in room 3 were the metal components of a saddle, a stirrup and buckles, and two spoons. Similar items were found in Room 1: a horseshoe, a small metal bell and a bronze bullet shell. The major findings in the fills above the second floor in room 3 were two aluminum plates, an iron lock, a metal fragment and a bottle fragment. The objects found over the third floor in room 1 were an aluminum bowl, an aluminum plate, a padlock and a chain, several fragments of cloth and plastic, two shoes and a glass bottle. The artifacts on the third floor in room 3 included an iron spatula, an earring, a buckle, a key and a fragment of a bone comb. None of these artifacts are different from those found in abandoned houses in the village today. The absence of large numbers of artifacts in the abandonment deposits tends to support the oral information regarding the abandonment of the complex. Knowing that the abandonment of this house was planned with no intention of returning, I believe that only objects of little value or hard to carry were left by the original inhabitants. The rest of the objects were discarded by the neighboring families.

ABANDONMENT DURING THE
EARLY OTTOMAN PERIOD

In 1985 we began our search for the early Ottoman village of Ti'innik. Our knowledge of the Ottoman village came from two sixteenth century tax records dating to 1538 (Bakhit and el Hmud 1989a) and 1596 (Bakhit and el Hmud 1989b). The location of that village was unknown to us at the time. To complicate matters further, and due the absence of well-stratified sites in Palestine dating to the Ottoman period, we did not know what to look for. Following a surface survey of the eastern slopes of the tell, we were able to identify one area that produced ceramics that did not match the ceramics of any known period. These ceramics were handmade with coarse clay tempered with straw and crushed stones. The surface was often slipped and/or burnished, and then covered with geometrical designs painted in white, red and brown. This type of ceramic was similar to those found in ethnographic collections.

The 1985–87 excavation proved to be very profitable. Within ten centimeters of the surface we began to encounter the remains of several buildings. Out of ten strata the sixth to the ninth were assigned to the Early Ottoman period. The artifacts in these layers were dominated by the handmade, geometrically painted ceramics. Dating these strata depended on two types of evidence. First, the presence of light gray, tobacco pipes in stratum 7 and red tobacco pipes in stratum 9. Archaeologist believe that the light gray pipes first appeared in the Ottoman Empire some time during the early part of the seventeenth century while the red pipes are dated to the end of the seventeenth century (Simpson 1990; Robinson 1985). Therefore, Strata 7, 8 and 9 must be given a seventeenth century post quem date. The presence of white-slipped green glazed ceramics in stratum 5 dates to the fourteenth century (Pringle 1986, 147). Thus we were able to date stratum 6, the first stratum with hand made ceramic to the sixteenth centuries.

Stratum 6 (fig. 5) included the remains of three of rooms constructed in a similar fashion to the present *ahwash* of the village. Further similarities were evident in the architectural details inside each room. As in the case of the late Ottoman single room houses, the floors in all three rooms were divided into two levels. The presence of troughs on the lower floors suggested that these rooms actually housed livestock as well as humans. Stratum 6 ended with the gradual abandonment of all three houses, at the same time archaeological evidence seems to indicate that the settlement was not entirely abandoned. Evidence supporting this claim came from the contents of the layers above the floor inside the rooms. The floors of the three rooms were cleared of almost all artifacts associated with the living phase. The only objects we found were a handmade jar found on the lower floor of the eastern room and an incomplete green glazed bowl found on the upper floor of the western room. The absence of artifacts on the living floors is an indicator of planned abandonment, scavenging, or both.

The rooms became dumping areas for the neighboring sixteenth century residents of Ti'innik. This conclusion was reached by the presence of heavy deposits of broken ceramics above the collapse debris in all three rooms. Attempts to mend these pots proved that none of the vessels were intact when they were deposited. Furthermore, several pieces of the same vessels were found in adjacent rooms. The above evidence leads to the following conclusions. First, these deposits are likely to be discard layers. Using abandoned rooms as secondary refuse disposal is common ethnographically as well as in the archaeological record (Montgomery 1993, 158). Second, the discard must have been produced by people who live in the vicinity of the abandoned rooms, which means that the settlement was still inhabited at the time the rooms in stratum 6 were abandoned.

Stratum 7 produced the remains of another single room house with a split floor plan, in addition to a part of a courtyard. The lower floor in the house had troughs, indicating that the house used to shelter animals as well as humans. As in the case of stratum 6, the floor of the house and the courtyard in stratum 7 were almost empty except for a single wheel-thrown large jar found on the lower floor of the room. Post abandonment layers in this stratum were shallow in comparison to those in stratum 6. Much of the evidence was probably cleared away with the construction of stratum 8. Stratum 8 was badly eroded due to

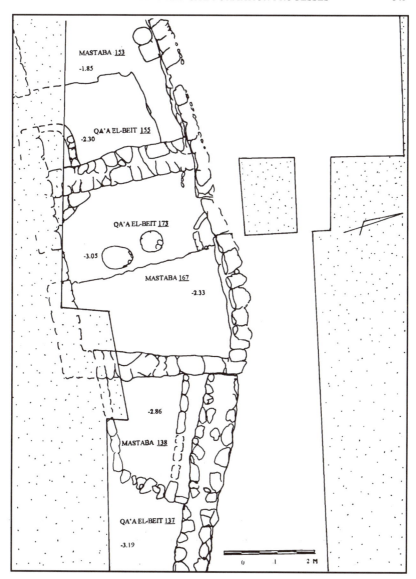

Fig. 5. Early Ottoman houses in stratum 6.

its closeness to the surface. The fragmentary evidence in this stratum included the corner of a building, and a dirt surface with patches of packed small stones. Stratum 9 has no architectural remains. It consisted mainly of thirteen pits of various sizes and shapes. Although these pits were originally intended to function as grain silos (Sandys, 1673), at the time of excavation these pit were packed with ash and ceramic fragments. The existence of these silos in that location meant that the settlement has shifted, turning the old location into threshing floors and grain silos. Judging by the intensity of the ceramic contents in these pits, it was evident that the early Ottoman village was still occupied by the end of this stratum. The appearance of red tobacco pipes in this stratum tends to suggest the end of the seventeenth or the beginning of the eighteenth century as the date for the last stratum. The abandonment of the early Ottoman village must have followed that date. The site remained abandoned until the middle of the nineteenth century when it was resettled by the ancestors of the present population.

Stratum 6 is the only stratum that can be dated to the sixteenth century, the date of the two tax registers. According to those registers, the population of Ti'innik grew from nine *khâna* in 1538 to thirteen *khâna* by 1596. A *khâna* is thought to refer to a taxable married adult male. The population of the sixteenth century is estimated by multiplying the number of *khâna* by a factor of six or seven (McCarthy 1987) and adding to the result the number of unmarried adult males referred to as *mujarrad*. The population figures for Ti'innik show a 40% increase between 1538 and 1596. The population growth meant that the abandonment of the three excavated houses could not be attributed to a general decline of the village. This situation is analogous to the present village were we find abandoned houses despite the fact that the population is growing. This leaves us with two potential explanations for the abandonment in stratum 6. It could be that the excavated houses were abandoned because they became old houses and could not accommodate the population growth, as in the case of the current village. The other possibility, which is more plausible, is that abandonment was caused by a general population mobility in the region due to economic hardship and political instability.

Evidence for such mobility can be detected from the growth and decline patterns of settlements in the Marj Ibn 'Amir area during the sixteenth century. Table 3 is a comparative list of *khâna* in forty-one villages in the Marj Ibn 'Amir area.

A comparison of the *khâna* figures in 1538 and 1596 shows that eight villages became totally abandoned. Another fourteen villages witnessed partial abandonment due to the decline in population. Although eleven villages, including Ti'innik, witnessed a normal population growth rate, another eight villages show a population influx that exceeds the average population growth rate for the district. In light of the total abandonment of some villages, migration from one village to another is a likely explanation of the unusual increase in the population of these eight villages. It is also worth noting that three new villages were settled during the same period. Total and partial abandonment of 50% of the villages and the large population growth in 20% of the villages reflects a great deal of mobility in the Marj Ibn ʿAmir area during the sixteenth century. Such mobility could be attributed to the political instability and economic depression following the Ottoman invasion of the Levant. The general economic deterioration is best-illustrated by the radical change in the ceramic tradition. The dominant ceramic type in the pre-Ottoman period was the wheelthrown, elaborate, glazed type. The glazed wheelthrown ceramic, which required a specialized line of production, was suddenly substituted with a crude, handmade type. The handmade ceramics were likely to be produced by individual households for personal use (Ziadeh 1995).

CONCLUSION

Gradual intrasite abandonment is not limited to the modern village. Archaeological evidence from the early Ottoman village shows that such process dominated the life cycle of the settlement for two hundred years before the village was abandoned permanently. Extrapolating from the ethnographic evidence, it seems that none of the abandonment phases of the early Ottoman village were sudden or unplanned. If this were the case one would expect to find larger quantities of artifacts on the living floors. Although it is difficult to make definite statements regarding the cause for the abandonment of the early Ottoman village, some of the present causes for abandonment might be applicable to the past. However, the historic particularities of the twentieth century make this ethnographic case unique. A case in point is the introduction of new building material, which encouraged the abandonment of functioning buildings. The availability of cash and waged labor is another factor particular to the twentieth century that promoted the construction of new buildings at the expense of repairing older ones. Economic hardship and political and social instability are probably

Table 3. Demographic Change in Sixteenth Century
Villages of the Marj Ibn ʿAmir Area.

Village	Population in 1538	Population in 1596	Growth Rate
Rummanah	16	12	partial abandonment
Tiʿinnik	9	13	normal growth
Solam	18	26	normal growth
Naʿura	14	3	partial abandonment
ʿAindor	9	4	partial abandonment
Zirʿin	9	4	partial abandonment
Nuras	15	16	moderate growth
ʿArrana	15	17	moderate growth
Jalama	19	16	partial abandonment
Kharruba	4	3	partial abandonment
Kufr Dan	18	9	partial abandonment
Beit Qad	7	20	above normal growth
Jalbun	12	0	total abandonment
Sandalah	5	8	normal growth
Akamda	12	0	total abandonment
ʿArbuna	5	14	above normal growth
Jenin	12	8	partial abandonment
el-Muhaffar	6	0	total abandonment
Heiruz	6	0	total abandonment
Deir Ghazala	9	5	partial abadonment
ʿArʿara	8	8	no change
ʿAnin	7	8	moderate growth
ʿAba	14	14	no change
Umm el-Fahim	6	24	above normal growth
el-Yamun	37	28	partial abandonment
Sirin	34	45	normal growth
Sibghin	8	6	partial abandonment
Umm et-Tut	4	0	total abandonment
el-Bireh	37	54	normal growth
Jadd	7	5	partial abandonment
Danna	10	5	partial abandonment
Tira Qiblieh	5	0	total abandonment
Tira Shamalieh	3	0	total abandonment
Qiffin	14	27	above normal growth
el-Lajjun	23	41	above normal growth
Zabda	7	26	above normal growth
Deir Marwan	8	0	total abandonment
Sheik Bureik	23	22	partial abandonment
Salem	6	9	normal growth
Rihana	11	20	above normal growth
Jba Siwar	3	12	above normal growth

some of the most consistent factors behind abandonment both past and present. Finally the aging of buildings should be considered as a constant factor for abandonment, although the duration of the building depends on the cultural, economic and environmental background.

The artifact distribution and frequency in recent abandoned buildings seems to have parallels in the archaeological record. The objects associated with the living phase, for example, are minimal both past and present. As in the case of the present village, where the majority of the people who abandoned the buildings remain in the village itself, the storage dump secondary use of abandoned places is dominant. The turning of the sixteenth century houses into dump areas suggests that the former occupants had left the village permanently.

REFERENCES

Ascher, R.
    1968   Time's Arrow and the Archaeology of a Contemporary
            Community. Pp. 43–52 in *Settlement Archaeology*, ed. C.
            Chang. Palo Alto: National Press Books.
Bakhit, M., and el-Hmud
    1989a   *Dafter Muffassal, Nahiat Marj Bani ʾAmir wa Twabiʾha wa
            Lwahiqha Allati Kanat fi Tasarruf al-Amir Turabay Sanat 945
            A.H./1538 A.D.* Amman: Jordan University.
    1989b   *The Detailed Dafter of al-Lajjun, Tapu Dafteri No. 181, 1005
            A.H./1596 A.D.* Amman: Jordan University.
Eidt, R. C.
    1984   *Advances in Abandoned Settlement Analysis: Application to
            Prehistoric Anthrosoles in Columbia, South America.* Milwau-
            kee: University of Wisconsin.
Joyce, A., and Johannesen, S.
    1993   Abandonment and the Production of Archaeological Variability
            at Domestic Sites. Pp. 138–53 in *Abandonment of Settlements
            and Regions, Ethnoarchaeological and Archaeological Ap-
            proaches*, eds. C. Cameron and S. Tomka. Cambridge:
            Cambridge University.
McCarthy, J.
    1987   Factors in the Analysis of the Population of Anatolia,
            1800–1878. *Asian and African Studies* 21: 33–63.
Montgomery, B.
    1993   Ceramic Analysis as a tool for discarding processes of Pueblo
            abandonment. Pp. 157–64 in *Abandonment of Settlements and*

Regions, Ethnoarcheological and Archaeological Approaches, eds. C. Cameron and S. Tomka. Cambridge: Cambridge University.

Pringle, D.
1986   *The Red Tower*. London: British School of Archaeology in Jerusalem Monograph Series No. 1.

Reid, J. J.
1985   Formation Processes for the Practical Prehistorian: An Example from the Southeast. Pp. 11–33 in *Structure and Process in the Southeastern Archaeology*, eds. R. Dickens and H. Ward. Birmingham, Alabama: University of Alabama.

Robinson, R.
1985   Tobacco Pipes of Corinth and of the Athenian Agora. *Hesperia* 54: 149–201.

Rothschild, N. *et al.*
1993   Abandonment at Zuni Farming villages. Pp. 123–37 in *Abandonment of Settlements and Regions, Ethnoarcheological and Archaeological Approaches*, eds. C. Cameron and S. Tomka. Cambridge: Cambridge University.

Sandys, G.
1673   *Travels, Containing an History of the Original and Present State of the Turkish Empire*. 7th edition. London: John Williams, Jr.

Schiffer, M.
1972   Archaeological Context and Systemic Context. *American Antiquity* 37: 156–65.
1975   Archaeology as Behavioral Science. *American Anthropologist* 77: 836–48.
1976   *Behavioral Archaeology*. New York: Academic.
1983   Toward the Identification of Formation Processes. *American Antiquity* 48: 675–705.

Simpson, S. J.
1990   Ottoman Clay Pipes From Jerusalem and the Levant: A Critical Review of the Published Evidence. *Society for Clay Pipes Research, Newsletter* 28: 7–16

Stevenson, M. G.
1982   Toward an Understanding of Site Abandonment Behavior: Evidence From Historic Mining Camps in the Southwest Yukon. *Journal of Anthropological Archaeology* 1: 237–65.

Ziadeh, M. G.
1984   *Site Formation in Context*. Unpublished M.A. Thesis, St. Louis: Washington University.
1985   Ottoman Ceramics from Ti'innik. *Levant* 27: 209–45.

8 Early Bronze Age Seals and Seal Impressions from Taanach

NANCY LAPP

The excavation at Tanaach in 1963, 1966, and 1968 was the project that first brought Albert Glock to Palestine. When Paul Lapp, the Director of the excavations, was accidentally drowned in 1970, the Taanach materials became Al's responsibility. Many of his years in Palestine and at Birzeit University were dedicated to the study and publication of this data. After Al Glock's death, a Publication Committee and numerous other contributors, and now the Institute of Archaeology at Birzeit University, have been concerned with the final publication of these materials.

In the spring of 1995, I spent several weeks at the Institute studying these extraordinary finds. When examining the excavation materials, I found several Early Bronze Age seals and seal impressions that previously had not been recognized as being from that era. This is undoubtedly because they were found in later contexts, thus unfortunately not stratified. However, their typology and motifs are characteristic of this period and add to the growing corpus of known seals and impressions from this time. It is appropriate that these be published in a volume dedicated to Albert Glock.[1]

Among the artifacts are two probable Early Bronze seals, and two hitherto unrecognized Early Bronze seal impressions. The two seal impressions that were previously published are also presented, with updated information.

CONTEXT

All the seals and impressions were found in contexts that included later material as well as diagnostic sherds of the Early Bronze Age.

This is undoubtedly why they have not been dated to the Early Bronze Age until recently, as the Palestinian seals and impressions of this period become better known. When the final stratification of the Early Bronze Age at Taanach has been studied and published, it may well be ascertained that some of these specimens, particularly Seal Impression No. 1555, are from clear Early Bronze Age contexts.

As to their place within the Early Bronze Age, one must consider the period of Early Bronze occupation at Taanach. All preliminary studies indicate Early Bronze occupation only during the latter part of EB II to before the end of EB III, approximately 2850 BC–2500 BC (P. Lapp 1967, 7; 1969, 4). It can therefore be concluded that the Taanach seals and impressions belong to this time.

THE CYLINDER SEALS

No. 662 (fig. 1)
  Findspot: SW 5–2 locus 107, basket 210
  Context date: MB–LB (pottery field reading)
  Material: limestone[2]
  Seal size: 24 mm high, 12 mm diameter
  Motif: cross hatching on one side, irregular vertical and
                          diagonal lines on the remainder; border grooves

This is a rather primitively carved cylinder seal. On one side is a small section of the net motif; in another area there are diagonal lines that probably were meant to be developed into the net motif, but vertical lines indicate other trial endeavors, and even a drill hole may indicate an effort to undertake a more difficult composition.

Crude attempts are found on seals from Jericho and Gezer (Kenyon 1960, fig. 27:4; Kenyon and Holland 1983, fig. 368:3; Macalister 1912, pl. 28:21), and on an unfinished seal from Khirbet ez-Zeraqon (HZ 88-413). A poorly carved net pattern from Zeraqon (HZ 87-269)[3] contrasts with the intricately cut bone seal with the net motif from Lahav (Seger *et al.* 1990, 5, fig. 6b). The net design is rather common as a Palestinian seal impression alone or in combination with other geometric motifs.[4]

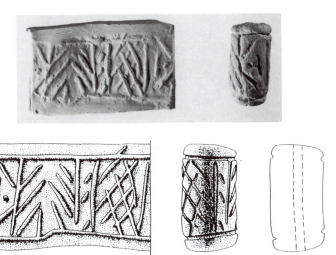

Fig. 1. Cylinder Seal No. 662.

No. 736 (fig. 2)[5]

Findspot:	SW 5–2 locus 118, basket 232
Context Date:	LB (pottery field reading)
Material:	blue stone
Seal size:	17 mm high, 8 mm diameter
Motif:	2 horned animals (antelopes?); running border grooves

The seal is well-carved, with the bodies of the animals rounded and deep. There are no parallels to this style of the "animal file" in the Palestinian seal and seal impression corpus. But the animal file is a common theme on Mesopotamian and Syrian seals, and although an exact parallel cannot be found, several features of the Taanach motif are commonly found on Near Eastern seals.

Most of the Mesopotamian parallels are dated to the Jamdat Nasr period, or classified in the Jamdat Nasr style, i.e. Early Bronze I in Palestine. They are usually identified as goats or antelopes. Striking characteristics in the Taanach seal are the long horns and legs represented by tent-shaped lines. These characteristics are found in seals published from the Diyala (Frankfort 1955, nos. 378, 379, 493, 526; Buchanan 1966, nos. 32, 110 [British Museum collection]).

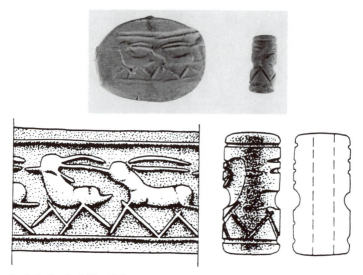

Fig. 2. Cylinder Seal No. 736.

Sometimes the bodies are deeper and more rounded, but often slenderer than the Taanach specimen, and the deep and wide necks continuing to the heads are not found (cf. Collon 1987, no. 21; Buchanan 1966, no. 29; 1981, no. 178; Teissier 1984, nos. 11, 12). Many have fillers above or around the animals.[6] The Taanach seal has no fillers, but the horns and legs are lengthened to fill all the space.

When Ben-Tor published his first corpus of Palestinian seals and impressions of the Early Bronze Age no seal imported from Mesopotamia had been found in Palestine (Ben-Tor 1978, 9), and as far as can be determined, none has as yet been published. The Taanach seal, No.736, could well be the first Mesopotamian imported seal into Palestine during the Early Bronze Age to become known. The motif is a common one in Mesopotamian seals, and the stone is probably imported. It also is better engraved than many of the local seals. It could have been produced in Syria, but it is not particularly a Syrian style. The seal was perhaps carved in Mesopotamia during the Jamdat Nasr period or under Jamdat Nasr influence, but it did not become a part of the Taanach repertoire until Taanach's occupation about 2850–2500 BC.[7]

SEAL IMPRESSIONS

No. 1897 (fig. 3)

Findspot:	SW 2–25 locus 160, basket 431$_5$
Context Date:	MB IIC–tenth c. (pottery field reading)
Fragment size:	35 × 30 mm
Impression on:	probably impressed near widest part of a closed vessel
Vessel ware:	handmade; 5Y 6/2 pinkish gray with wide 5/1 gray core; no slip, burnish, or wash
Motif:	geometric; fragmentary; horizontal lines in rhomboids and triangles, fragment of spiral or circle motif; no dimensions possible

The motif is incomplete, but there is enough to indicate that it is typical of the geometric patterns common among the plentiful impressions now known from northern Palestine and Transjordan. The motif includes the rhomboids, triangles, and concentric circles (or spirals) of Ben-Tor's class I-D (Ben-Tor 1978, 5–6). All these impressions are from the north (the Galilee, Golan Heights, or northern Transjordan), along with more now published from Beth-Yerah (Esse 1990), a large corpus from Zeraqon,[8] and some from Ebla in Syria (Mazzoni 1993, figs. 9–10, A47 and pl. 73). The previously published impressions from Taanach, Nos. 1844 and 1845, presented again below, are related types. It should be noted, however, that the spiral and circle, sometimes with other geometric motifs, are now known from the Dead Sea Plain sites of Bab edh-Dhra᾿ and Numeira,[9] on a sherd from

Fig. 3. Seal Impression No. 1897.

Umeiri (N. Lapp 1991, 242–43), and on sherds from Tell es-Sukhne North (Chesson *et al.* 1995, 119 nos. 17 [SN93-1], 18 [SN93-2], 120 [all sherds probably part of same vessel]). Thus, there are at least regional varieties outside of northern Palestine and Transjordan.[10]

No. 1844[11] (fig. 4)

Findspot:	NW 8-1 locus 9, basket 12
Context date:	EB III (pottery field reading)
Fragment size:	75 × 75 mm
Impression on:	shoulder of closed vessel with metallic ware, vertical combing
Motif:	angular spirals with concentric rhomboids between them; fragmentary; no lower border groove present size: 29+ mm high
Published:	Ben-Tor, *Cylinder Seals of the Third Millennium B.C.*, fig. 3:16, pl. 3:16

No. 1845   (fig. 5)

Findspot:	SW 4-7 locus 201, basket 304$_3$
Context date:	EB III–MB IIA (pottery field reading)
Fragment size:	60 × 70 mm
Impression on:	shoulder of closed vessel with metallic ware, diagonal combing
Motif:	spirals with herring bone design between them fragmentary: top border groove present size: 55 mm length (?)
Published:	Ben-Tor, *Cylinder Seals of the Third-Millennium B.C.*, fig. 4:8, pl. 4:8

The above two impressions were published and discussed by Ben-Tor in his corpus of Palestinian seals and impressions. The motif has been furthered discussed (N. Lapp 1989, 3–5; Esse 1990, 30*–33*), and only the new evidence cited above, that this class of motif has also been found in central and southern Transjordan, needs to be mentioned. The corrected dates for these two impressions should be noted. Since they were found with the Early Bronze material directly below the succeeding Middle Bronze material, Ben-Tor concluded that they came from the end of Early Bronze, thus EB IV (see N. Lapp 1989, n. 6; Ben-

Fig. 4. Seal Impression No. 1844.

Fig. 5. Seal Impression No. 1845.

Tor 1978, 43, 89). Since the end of Taanach Early Bronze was earlier, these sherds cannot be placed in EB IV, but probably during the EB II–III occupation, approximately 2850–2500 BC.

No. 1555 (fig. 6)

Findspot:	SW 6–6 locus 186, basket 338
Context date:	EB III, MB IIC (pottery field reading)
Fragment size:	43 × 35 mm
Impression on:	Probably a clay stopper
	5 mm hole upper side of one edge; opposite side is broken, revealing hole, which probably goes through; handmade, blackened all visible surfaces, perhaps by local fire rather than intentional firing; no slip, burnish, or wash
Motif:	two animals, tête-bêche, one horned (gazelle or antelope?), the other with large head (lion), with

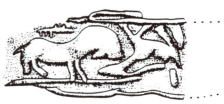

Fig. 6. Seal Impression No. 155.

> unidentified fillers above animals; irregular border
> grooves; impressed lengthwise and continued over
> edge; size: 12 × 32 mm; motif repeated

One of the original and primary uses of seal impressions was to ensure the security of goods and documents. Small and valuable objects were packed in jars, baskets, or mats, and a piece of cloth or skin was stretched over or around the vessel and tied with a string. Then a lump of clay was laid over the wrapping and a cylinder seal was rolled on it in such a way that it would be necessary to break the seal to reach the contents (Frankfort 1939, 9, and fig. 1). A cylinder seal was used rather than a stamp seal because it could be rolled to cover extended surfaces. Sometimes the shape of the clay is that of the neck of a jar, or examination of the underside of the pieces of clay on which the seals were rolled show patterns of baskets, the grain of wood, or the imprint of cloth or string.[12] One of the first uses was to secure clay balls containing tokens relating to economic transactions; later they were rolled across tablets bearing numerical signs, and still later, writing (Collon 1987, 113, figs. 491–495). From the end of the third millennium, authentic documents, thus tablets and their envelopes, were one of the largest groups of clay objects using seal impressions (Teissier 1984, xxii).

Tanaach No. 1555 shows the impression of a cylinder seal on a lump of clay, thoroughly blackened and broken at one end (the left in the photograph). A hole appears near the edge (top in the photograph) in the unbroken end and near the same edge where the object is broken. On the opposite side (bottom middle) the edge is slightly broken and also shows a small hole (cf. Buchanan 1981, no. 429, where the string hole on the lower edge is also broken). The object is probably a lump of clay applied over and around string to secure something. It was impressed by a rolled seal on the smooth or front side, continuing to the broken end and around the unbroken end. The break to get at the contents may have occurred in antiquity, but at some time the stopper was burned, and all that has been recovered is the hard baked blackened object with the seal impression. There is no obvious impression of fabric on the reverse side, but it is rough and unfinished. This is the first cylinder seal impression to be found on such an object in the Palestinian corpus.

The motif, a horned animal and a lion in the tête-bêche arrangement, with maximal filling of the space, is similar to others known from northern Palestine and especially Byblos in coastal Syria (cf. esp. Dunand 1937, pl. 133:3232; Saghieh 1983, pl. 33:12613, 11298, 11572). The space fillers cannot be defined, though possibly a fish is meant to be depicted above the lion. There may be an object, possibly a bush, behind the horned animal, but on the edge of the object the motif is hard to distinguish. There may have been a poor attempt to roll the seal again above the motif.

The similar impressions from Byblos date to the first urban settlement at Byblos, EB II in Palestine. The Taanach motif, belonging to Ben-Tor's Class II-B, "Animals in tête-bêche Arrangement" (Ben-Tor 1978, 9, 55), fits well Ben-Tor's conclusions concerning Class II, "Animal motifs." He concludes that "the center and perhaps also the origin of this type lies in Byblos ... it appears plausible that, although the vessels were produced at [Palestinian sites], they were impressed there by seals which were imported from Byblos. Another possibility is that the vessels from these [two] sites are originally from Byblos, where they were also impressed" (1978, 104). Ben-Tor includes in this statement all of his Class II, but with the recovery of several animal motifs in the excavations at Bab edh-Dhra᾽ and Numeira on the southern Dead Sea Plain it is known that the use of animals on seals was much more widespread.[13] However, the tête-bêche arrangement did not appear at the Dead Sea Plain sites and the Taanach find still limits this attribute to northern Palestine and Transjordan.

TAANACH SEALS AND IMPRESSIONS
AS PART OF THE PALESTINIAN CORPUS

Taanach fits well into the regional patterns that have been recognized in the Palestinian corpus. Geometric impressions with triangles, rhomboids, and circles, and the tête-bêche animal arrangements have long been recognized as northern Palestinian motifs. In addition, however, the presence of a seal impression on a clay sealing (probably a stopper), and perhaps an imported Mesopotamian Early Bronze seal, are first-time occurrences in Palestine. Perhaps even more important, Taanach shows that the study of older excavated material may turn up hitherto unknown contributions to the Palestinian corpus.

NOTES

1.   The writer owes a special debt of appreciation to Al Glock's wife, Lois. She not only helped make accessible the materials while I was on the West Bank, but she has continued to assist me in obtaining photographs and drawings. Lois has done an admirable job of organizing and making available the Taanach materials for their final publication, and most specifically, assured the continuation of Al's work through the Institute of Archaeology at Birzeit University. I would also like to extend thanks and credit to Bishara Zogbi and Robert Laos who helped with the drawings, to Dereich Photography for some of the photographs, and to Gary A. Cooke of Solutions International, Inc. who analyzed the limestone cylinder seal.

2.   Gary A. Cooke of Solutions International, Inc. analyzed the cylinder's material by means of X-ray Diffraction. He reports: The "surface was examined using copper radiation on a Philips XRG-3100 unity equipped with a graphite monochrometer and a theta compensation slit. The sample was scanned from 4 to 64°20 using normal run parameters. Peak positions and intensities from this run were tabulated and used to identify the phases present. The dominant phases that were identified include calcite, quartz and a clay mineral (probably kaolinite). This is consistent with the cylinder being composed of fine-grain limestone or marl."

3.   The Zeraqon information is possible through the courtesy of S. Mittmann and personal communication with M. Flender.

4.   Ben-Tor (1978), Class I–B and others in combination; also to be noted are several yet unpublished from Zeraqon.

5.   Unfortunately Seal no. 736 was unavailable to the writer to examine first-hand and the following discussion is based on the drawings, photographs,

and Object Registration Book description. Thus, the "blue stone" as described in the Object Registration Book could not be analyzed further, and certain determination that the seal was an import cannot be made.

6. For example, Teissier (1984, nos. 9–12). Collon thinks the ladder above the animal file may represent enclosures (Collon 1987, no. 21).

7. If the seal could be examined first hand, analysis might throw further light on its origin.

8. Ibrahim and Mittmann (1994), and personal communication with M. Flender. To be noted particularly, among others, are HZ88-352/370, HZ88-398, HZ88-100, and HZ87-121.

9. N. Lapp (1989, 3–5) and others to be published in the final publications of the Dead Sea Plain excavations.

10. The evidence at present seems to indicate that the Dead Sea Plain sites developed their own regional style, influenced by those of other regions. The different motifs found on the seals and impressions from the Dead Sea sites are varied, often related but not identical to those of other parts of Palestine and the ancient Near East.

11. The present location of this sherd and the next, nos. 1844 and 1845, is unknown, and they were not available for study. Information and the discussion here is drawn from their previous publication, drawings, photographs, and Taanach field reports.

12. Cf. Buchanan (1981, nos. 425, 427), with basket marks or flat base; cf. also the EB III "plugs" from Tarsus (Goldman 1956, fig. 398:1–8).

13. Note that at least one impression from Numeira is definitely within the "Byblos tradition" (N. Lapp 1989, 7–9).

REFERENCES

Ben-Tor, A.
   1978   *Cylinder Seals of Third-Millennium Palestine.* Cambridge, MA: American School of Oriental Research.

Buchanan, B.
   1966   *Catalogue of Ancient Near Eastern Seals in the Ashmolean Museum I: Cylinder Seals.* Oxford: Oxford University.
   1981   *Early Near Eastern Seals in the Yale Babylonian Collection.* New Haven and London: Yale University.

Chesson, M. *et al.*
   1995   Tell es-Sukne North: An Early Bronze Age II Site in Jordan. *Paleorient* 21/1: 113–23.

Collon, D.
   1987   *First Impressions: Cylinder Seals in the Ancient Near East.* Chicago: University of Chicago.

Dunand, M.
1937　　　*Fouilles de Byblos I, 1926–1932.* Paris: Guenther.

Esse, D.
1990　　　Early Bronze Age Cylinder Seal Impressions from Beth Yerah. In *Eretz-Israel* 21, Jerusalem: Israel Exploration Society: 27*–34*.

Frankfort, H.
1939　　　*Cylinder Seals: A Documentary Essay on the Art and Religion of the Ancient Near East.* London: Macmillan.

1955　　　*Stratified Seals of the Diyala Region.* Chicago: University of Chicago.

Goldman, H.
1956　　　*Excavations at Gözlü Kule, Tarus II.* Princeton: Princeton University.

Ibrahim, M., and Mittmann, S.
1994　　　Excavations at Khirbet ez-Zeraqon, 1993. *Newsletter of the Institute of Archaeology and Anthropology, Yarmouk University* 16: 11–15.

Kenyon, K. M.
1960　　　*Excavations at Jericho I.* London: British School of Archaeology in Jerusalem.

Kenyon, K. M., and Holland, T.
1983　　　*Excavations at Jericho V.* London: British School of Archaeology.

Lapp, N.
1989　　　Cylinder Seals and Impressions of the Third Millennium B.C. from the Dead Sea Plain. *Bulletin of the American Schools of Oriental Research* 273: 1–15.

1991　　　EB III Seal Impression. Pp. 242–43 in *Madaba Plains Project: The 1987 Season at Tell el-ʿUmeiri and Vicinity and Subsequent Studies*, ed. L. G. Herr *et al.* Berrien Springs, MI: Andrews University.

Lapp, P. W.
1969　　　The 1968 Excavations at Tell Taʿannek. *Bulletin of the American Schools of Oriental Research* 195: 2–49.

1967　　　Taanach by the Waters of Megiddo. *Biblical Archaeolgist* 30: 2–27.

Macalister, R. A. S.
1912　　　*Gezer III.* London: John Murray.

Mazzoni, S.
1993　　　Cylinder Seal Impressions on Jars at Ebla: New Evidence. Pp.

399–412 in *Aspects of Art and Iconography: Anatolia and its Neighbors*, eds. M. Mellink, E. Porada, T. Özgüç. Ankara: Türk Tahih Kurumu.

Saghieh, M.
1983   *Byblos in the Third Millennium B.C.* Wilts, England: Aris & Phillips.

Seger, J. *et al.*
1990   The Bronze Age Settlements at Tell Halif, Phase II Excavations, 1983–1987. Pp. 1–32 in *Preliminary Reports of ASOR-Sponsored Excavations 1983–1987*, ed. W. Rast. Baltimore: Johns Hopkins University.

Teissier, B.
1984   *Ancient Near Eastern Cylinder Seals from the Marcopoli Collection.* Berkeley: University of California.

9 Society and Mortuary Customs at Bab edh-Dhra'

WALTER RAST

Those who have visited the Early Bronze Age site of Bab edh-Dhra' in Jordan are acquainted with the way the paved road from Kerak to the Dead Sea bisects the site. The road passes between the settlement and the cemetery, effectively separating these two components, the town to the north, the cemetery to the south (see the map in Schaub and Rast 1989, 23, fig. 2). Ironically, the modern road highlights an important problem for the interpretation of Bab edh-Dhra'. How are these two parts of the site related to each other? What can the two sets of data tell us about the way people lived during the third millennium BC, and how can these data, taken together, throw light on social aspects of the Early Bronze population? With its rich and well-preserved evidence from both areas, Bab edh-Dhra' offers the chance to venture explanations that may apply not only to this site but also to conditions at other sites of the third millennium BC. At the very least, the circumstances at Bab edh-Dhra' are feasible ones for testing questions of the meaning of mortuary data for problems of social organization.[1]

Although the late Paul Lapp's three seasons of work at Bab edh-Dhra' from 1965 to 1967 dealt mainly with the cemetery and its tombs, the limited excavations he conducted at the town site during the second season of 1965 already suggested the problem of exploring relations between the cemetery and town. We shall return below to the way his excavations first opened up the problem of relating the cemetery and town evidence. Before doing so, we must review how the focus on the cemetery at the time led to Lapp's unique conclusions about periodic shifts in the population at Bab edh-Dhra'. During the first season of excavations in 1965 it became evident that the earliest burials were shaft tombs hewn into Lisan marl of the site. These tombs were dated by Lapp to EB IA. Stratigraphically later than the shaft tombs was a circular brick structure dating to EB IB, the main type of tomb during this phase, while shaft tomb interment also continued into EB IB. Again, above the EB IB tombs were rectangular structures, also of mudbrick, dating to EB II–III.[2] On the basis of the great mass of human skeletal material found in the EB IB and EB II–III buildings, Lapp called these structures "charnel houses," although the term should not suggest that human remains were originally placed into the tombs as disarticulated burials, since from EB IB onward the common practice in these buildings was primary burial, with subsequent movement of decomposed remains against the back and side walls of the structures. Thus the burial customs of EB IB and EB II–III were different from the secondary burials in the EB IA shaft tombs. Finally, during EB IV the occupants again practiced a form of shaft tomb burial, while at the same time retaining the custom of primary interment followed by later removal of earlier skeletal remains against the bases of the tomb walls. Thus the EB IV phase suggested a mixed pattern in comparison with what had preceded.

One of Lapp's achievements, therefore, was to have determined the stratigraphic history of the cemetery, both with respect to the different types of tombs in relation to each other and in specifying more precisely the artifactual record at the site. He observed changes in burial disposition, recording in detail the placement of the human remains in the tombs. The excavations in the cemetery also brought to light a great quantity of Early Bronze Age pottery, providing rich material to compare with other sites, especially the Jericho tombs.

This earliest work in the cemetery showed a development in which each phase of the Early Bronze Age could be seen to be followed by the next. This perspective received further clarification during the second season of excavations in 1965, when the first attempts were made to explore the walled remains about 500 m northeast of the cemetery. Here the surprises that met the excavators were considerable, especially since it had become commonplace following the 1924 survey by Albright, to view the Bab edh-Dhra' "enclosure" as a ritual rather than an urban settlement. The 1965 excavations brought an entirely new understanding, by showing that these ruins were indeed those of an Early Bronze Age town, with a succession of phases dating to that period. At the same time, it was evident that the data in the town area correlated closely with the artifactual evidence from the cemetery.[3]

The town site excavations were thus the point at which Lapp dealt with the implications of the reinforcing evidence from the two areas of the site (P. Lapp 1966c, 10–12). For the earliest phase of EB IA the lack of evidence for settlement at and around the town site confirmed Lapp's initial intuition that the shaft tomb burials were the work of nomadic pastoralists who transported the disarticulated skeletal remains of their deceased members for reburial in the shaft tombs. The succeeding phase of EB IB, characterized by its line-group painted pottery, represented a shift of some sort, although Lapp's evidence at the town site was too meager to lead him to conclude that it was precisely during EB IB that occupation began on a village level. What became especially clear during Lapp's only work at the town site was the correlation between the EB II and EB III town evidence and that from the "charnel houses" in the cemetery. Preliminary examination showed correspondences in the pottery and other artifacts at both areas.[4] As for the latest phase, for which Lapp preferred the term EB IV, only meager evidence for this phase appeared in the excavations at the town site, and indeed the relation between the town and the cemetery in this final phase remained unclear for Lapp (P. Lapp 1975, 110).

Thus it became evident already in the second season of Lapp's excavations that the great cemetery that had become so well-known through its numerous tombs, could also be related to an equally long-lived settlement spanning the length of the Early Bronze Age. Although this discovery was a breakthrough, the restrictions put upon his work at the time did not allow Lapp to integrate fully the implications of what he had uncovered. In a programmatic article published in 1968, Lapp still preferred to see the cemetery as a burial ground for occupants of the "cities of the plain," located elsewhere toward the southern end of the Dead Sea basin. And thus he bypassed the possibility that the cemetery might contain information for interpreting the living community at the town site itself (P. Lapp 1966c, 25). The view of Bab edh-Dhra' as a regional cemetery was as far as Lapp was able to take the problem before his untimely death.

At the same time, on the basis of the evidence he had, Lapp wrestled with the the problem of explaining the shifts in occupation occurring between EB IA and EB IB, again in EB II and III, and finally the transition from EB III to EB IV. Lapp proposed the theory that during EB II and III an external group under Egyptian support dominated the native EB I population, and that this imposition from the outside was a factor in the emergence of urbanism in the southeast Dead Sea plain (P. Lapp 1970, 112–14). The situation was reversed when in EB IV the native population reasserted itself, precipitating the collapse of urban life. Although his theory has not received broad support, Lapp's attempts in this direction were a step toward dealing with the social and political dimensions of his results.

The subsequent work at Bab edh-Dhra' carried on by the Expedition to the Dead Sea Plain brought additional support to Lapp's stratigraphic conclusions.[5] The new excavations confirmed that the earliest use of Bab edh-Dhra' occurred during EB IA. At this time the cemetery was used predominantly for clan or family interments, the vast majority of them consisting of secondary burials. During the following EB IB phase, a major shift to sedentary village life occurred, following which in turn a fluorescence of urban development took place during EB II and EB III. Finally, in the aftermath of the disastrous events that terminated the EB III town at Bab edh-Dhra', a new or returning group of occupants took charge of the site during the final phase of the Early Bronze Age. Both the earlier and later excavations and surveys have shown, therefore, that the Bab edh-Dhra' cemetery is related to the settlement and that the lifeways of the Early Bronze Age occupants of the southeast Dead Sea plain can best be examined through a study of both sets of information. This returns us to the point posed: How are the burial data to be understood in relation to the living occupants at Bab edh-Dhra'?

The problem may seem simple, given the fact that a good number of Early Bronze Age sites in Jordan and Israel have produced data from settlements and cemeteries. For example, Jericho yielded material from the tombs and settlement that compare in quantity and richness to that from Bab edh-Dhra'. Despite such a wealth of material from sites like Jericho, however, what has not attracted much discussion is the problem of interpreting the data from the living community and the tombs in relation to each other.

Two factors retarded efforts to deal with this issue at Bab edh-Dhraʾ. One was the way the site and the surrounding region came to be discovered and eventually explored. During the nineteenth and early twentieth centuries, the southeastern Dead Sea plain attracted explorers lured by this largely unknown region. The fact that the area was a *terra incognita* contributed to its mysterious nature, while those who carried on their explorations returned with tales of the exotic environment of the southeastern Dead Sea plain.[6] The 1924 survey added a further element to this perspective by proposing that Bab edh-Dhraʾ had been a center of ceremonial activity for a populace living elsewhere in the southeastern Dead Sea region, including perhaps the people of ancient Sodom (Albright 1924, 7). Such interpretations, fascinating though they were, put constraints on the way the material remains were studied. In this context the success of Lapp's 1965 excavations at the town site represented an entirely new understanding of Bab edh-Dhraʾ, and eventually would open up new perspectives on the region as a whole.

A second factor that would naturally have some effect on the interpretation of the evidence at Bab edh-Dhraʾ was the absence in Palestinian archaeology generally of developed thinking regarding methods for integrating burial evidence in relation to settlement systems. A perusal of the bibliography of the 1960s shows that at the time Lapp was working at Bab edh-Dhraʾ, the issue of how to explore mortuary remains for their social significance was not an issue of discussion by Palestinian archaeologists. Callaway's article on Early Bronze Age burials came the closest, but his contribution to the subject was brief and barely touched on broader matters of relationships and interpretation (Callaway 1963, 74–91). Even the first two volumes of the Jericho publications, valuable as a depository of information on the tombs and their contents, contained no substantive discussion of the relation of the tombs to the Early Bronze Age settlement (Kenyon 1960b; 1965). Bloch-Smith's recent work on burial practices in ancient Judah, and thus restricted to the Iron Age, may be cited as the first effort to broaden the discussion to include a concern for what burial evidence may contribute to a larger understanding of a society. At the same time, while Bloch-Smith makes occasional reference to the social implications of burial, her main interest is to provide "a new categorization of Iron Age tomb types and burial remains," and thus her study pays relatively brief attention to theoretical problems (Bloch-Smith 1992, 17–18).[7]

Several contributions by scholars working in areas other than the Middle East are of aid in dealing with the methodological issues of relating mortuary remains to social organization. The well-known study of Binford in 1971 argued that the "mortuary practices of any society are conditioned by the form and complexity of the organizational characteristics of the society itself" (Binford 1972, 235). Binford critiqued the views of a variety of theoreticians to test his thesis. Above all, he took issue with Kroeber who viewed burial customs as so "affect-laden" and driven by emotion as to not be usable for evaluating the normal patterns of the living society. For Kroeber the behavior exhibited in mortuary evidence was "unstable," and varied independently of behavior relating to "biological or primary social necessities."[8]

In refuting Kroeber's and others' rejection of an integration of mortuary and cultural data, Binford reassessed the published results of forty sample societies (see his list in 1972, 228–29). His study led him to reason that, whether dealing with an agriculturalist society, or that of hunters and gatherers, a correlation could be established between the treatment of the dead and the social pattern of the society. Thus in a society of agriculturalists, where role and status differentiation would be more likely to occur, the treatment of the deceased in regard to body preparation, grave location, and tomb and burial layout would correspond to the social persona of the deceased person. On the other hand,"hunters and gatherers should exhibit more egalitarian systems of status grading," in contrast to settled agriculturalists (Binford 1972, 230).

Binford's proposals have come up against criticism, and some have rejected his correlation of mortuary data and social organization. Hodder discussed Binford's proposals on burial customs in the framework of a broader critique of the new archaeology's stress on process, systems, and adaptation. For Hodder, archaeology must take into greater account the "individual" as a culture-maker, since all material objects are reflections of the decisions, actions, and behavior of individuals, and consequently a more abstract concentration on processes will obscure specific results, one of the promises of archaeology. Between a burial practice and a living society there must be assumed an acting individual, or a group of acting individuals, but also individuals who held attitudes and ideas about death, all of which have left an imprint on the archaeological data relating to mortuary practices.[9]

Hodder cited as support for his critique of Binford a study by Parker Pearson of recent burial practices in Cambridge, England, which showed that "even a highly differentiated society of the type found in Cambridge today might choose to bury its dead in an 'egalitarian' fashion" (Hodder 1991, 2). The conclusion to be drawn is that an adequate explanation of burial practices is not to be found in generalizations, but in the "ideas, beliefs and meanings which interpose themselves between people and things. How burial reflects society clearly depends on attitudes to death" (Hodder 1991, 3). This latter viewpoint returns the discussion to a more idealist interpretation, precisely the point that Binford rejected.

It will be useful, then, to turn to specific data from Bab edh-Dhra', and to make several proposals about what this information may tell us when the cemetery and settlement data are taken in correspondence. We begin with the earliest cultural horizon, that of the EB IA shaft tomb people, whose settlement pattern at Bab edh-Dhra' was most likely seasonal and non-sedentary. The excavations into the lowest levels of the town site in Fields I, II, IV, XI, XII, XIII, and XIV, as well as below the EB II and III town wall in Fields II and XIII, showed that the first permanent settlement in all these areas occurred during EB IB. Evidence for EB IA settlement of any kind was absent in all the fields, just as Lapp had also discovered. The extensive surveying activity around the town site, as well as throughout the cemetery area, also turned up a hiatus as far as structures dating to EB IA were concerned. A number of stumps of stone and brick walls in Areas H2 and H4 had no associated pottery, and could not be dated securely to EB IA. Only in Area J2, some 200 m southwest of the town site, was there some suggestion that a first attempt at settling down on the long term may have been made during EB IA, but even this evidence is tenuous since the main settlement in Area J2 dated to EB IB (Schaub and Rast 1984, 36–39).

It is consequently justifiable to speak of the EB IA society at Bab edh-Dhra' as having been non-sedentary, at least on the basis of the evidence thus far obtained. An object like the wooden staff in Tomb 114N must have belonged to a person who had made his livelihood by tending sheep and goats, and it thus seems to be an indicator of pastoralism (Froehlich and Ortner 1982, 263–64, fig. 74). If we can presuppose such a nomadic pastoralist interpretation in general for the EB IA shaft tomb population, the question that would follow would be how the mortuary data of EB IA throw light upon the social organization of the people of this phase. Do the burials and tombs of EB IA evidence a relation to the social structure of the EB IA group, after Binford's view, or do they relate to a different sphere from that of the living society, as others would argue?

What is striking about the many EB IA tombs excavated by Lapp and the more recent expedition is the formality in the practice of burial. The customs are followed universally by all members of the community, and can be grouped as follows:

Minimal Variability
- Tomb construction—little variation in cutting shaft tombs and their features
- Matting—evidence found in many tombs for the bed of matting on which burials were placed; evidence disappeared in some tombs
- Number of individuals—usually around four or five, but no more than ten
- Sex and age—no separation, all represented

No Variability
- Bone stacks in center of chamber
- Crania in line to left of bone stack
- Pottery clustered around chamber walls

Variability
- Maceheads
- Basalt bowls
- Beads
- Figurines
- Other personal objects

Those features listed under minimal or no variability are community-related, while those categorized under variability are person or gender-related. The great number of shared community-related items suggest that the EB IA society was a cohesive organization. Some burials had a greater quantity of pottery vessels than others, indicating moderate differentiation in ranking of families or clan groups in particular tombs. Special objects also served to distinguish individuals and family groups. But none of these are sufficient to suggest that the EB IA society was nonegalitarian. Even the related but clearly differentiated tombs in Cemetery C shared the basic formality of the tombs of Cemetery A (Schaub and Rast 1989, 185).[10] Thus the EB IA tombs provide a window into the social organization of this nonsedentary people.

At the same time, the formal elements have to be viewed as the group's way of coping with separation from the deceased. The conventional dispositions of burials in the shaft tombs, along with the close grouping of tombs to one another, were not simply nonreflective elements of tradition, but served to integrate the deceased members into a community apart from the living society, while assuring that they were still related to the latter. These practices would thus have the effect of stabilizing the family and clan in the face of loss of their members. Thus there are dimensions in the evidence that are not explainable simply in terms of social processes alone. Viewed from the perspective of the discussions about burial and social organization, the EB IA tombs would suggest that interments such as these are complex enough not to be placed in an either/or classification regarding their relevance for social organization or for a completely separate sphere related to the experience of death.

With the EB IB phase, a new pattern of mortuary treatment was introduced, one that continued through EB II and III. This was the practice of constructing buildings in which the dead could be placed. During EB IB these houses were of round shape, carrying over a mental template from the shaft tombs to these brick structures built partly below surface. Thus the EB IB phase evidenced its transitional character following EB IA to the town life of EB II and III. That is, during this transition the pervasive pastoralism of EB IA was replaced by settled village life with its subsistence base in agricultural production. In the two examples of circular EB IB mortuary structures excavated (Tombs 53, G1), only nonvariable features were identified. That is, in all cases the same elements were found.[11]

- Round house construction of plano-convex bricks, stone-slab framed doorway

- Primary burials deposited
- Remains of earlier inhumations repositioned within the tomb following decomposition; clusters of human bone and crania from a single person were placed against the walls of the chambers
- Pottery and other objects were also spotted near the skeletalized clusters

The two EB IB charnel houses from Bab edh-Dhra' point, first of all, in the direction of their relevance for social organization during this phase. The fact that articulated burial was first broadly practiced during EB IB at Bab edh-Dhra', in contrast to the predominant tradition of secondary burials of EB IA, correlates exactly with the stratification at the town site mentioned above, where the first evidence for permanent settlement at the site appeared in the basal levels. Somewhat deviant, however, is the circular form of these tombs. Thus far no circular buildings dating to EB IB have been found among EB IB domestic structures at the village site, where all the buildings thus far uncovered have been rectilinear. Thus there is a disjunction in architecture between the dwellings of the EB IB occupants and their burial structures.

At the same time, EB IB tomb construction was conventional, with the two examples thus far excavated conforming in every way. The burials and goods deposited in them also followed the same pattern. In contrast to the preceding EB IA shaft tombs, however, EB IB charnel houses contained a larger number of burials, suggesting that the familial relation of those interred was broadened to include a wider number who could be buried in a tomb. Perhaps now a clan or tribe claimed ownership of a particular tomb, but in any case these features in the EB IB tombs correspond to the developments of a settled community. As far as symbols of status in the burials in EB IB tombs are concerned, excavation results have highlighted no clear patterns, and it appears rather that the EB IB society was still essentially egalitarian. Such data would conflict with Binford's principle noted above, that the burials of agriculturalists should denote some form of status differentiation.

In the case of the EB IB burials, therefore, the social dimension of the tombs may be paramount. It is difficult to identify features belonging to a sphere outside of the practical needs following death, but no doubt such dynamics were present, and probably lie concealed in the data.

The creation of common repositories in which to place the deceased members signals collective participation in burial rites. The fact that the brick structures were house-like buildings, although in rounded form, implies the idea of the community persisting beyond death, but now in "quarters" shared by a broader spectrum of the society's members. Thus the ideological side of burial also manifests itself here.

Perhaps the most difficult phase to assess in relation to the questions of how burials reflect the living society, is that of the so-called urban period of EB II and III. During these two phases, the charnel houses, now in rectangular form, were greatly expanded in size, no doubt in response to the need for larger facilities caused by an increase in population. Quite in contrast to the small numbers of burials in the EB IA and IB tombs, the EB II and III charnel houses contained anywhere from forty to more than two hundred individuals. These figures are estimates since it is impossible to quantify in a final way the EB II and III charnel house populations until the skeletal material has been fully reconstructed (currently being finalized by Michael Finnegan). Clearly the larger numbers of burials in the EB II and III charnel houses indicates at the very least that the deceased were not always from the same immediate family, and thus a shift in conception of social organization was taking place during the urban phase at Bab edh-Dhra'. Correspondingly, the charnel house burials may be designated communal interments, since the familial line was not as dominant in the decision about who would qualify for placement in a tomb.

The phenomenon of communal interment during EB II and III, therefore, may be considered in relation to the emergence of early state formation in the southeast Dead Sea valley during this period, of which Bab edh-Dhra' is the prime example among the Dead Sea sites (Rast, in press). The dynamics of state formation brought change not only to the social make-up of the population at Bab edh-Dhra', but their effect was substantial on units like the family or the clan. The needs of the emerging state in regard to construction, such as the erection of town walls or public buildings, called forth a labor force that included specialized skill and activity. Other major undertakings like water management in regard to the agricultural needs of the southeast Dead Sea valley similarly placed individuals of varying backgrounds together. In the process, laborers of unrelated family backgrounds participated in mutual activity, with the result that new forms of interpersonal relationship coalesced. As a consequence of the emergent economy of EB II and III and its technological innovations, therefore, major revisions of the social structure took place.

The questions about the EB II and III charnel houses arise in this context, To what degree do the charnel house burials reflect these changes? Can a direct link be made between the evidence at the settlement and the practices in the charnel houses, or do the latter belong to a domain discontinuous with the social realia of the settlement? Callaway's conclusions about EB II and III burial practices led him to a very negative judgment, based on the presupposition that the condition of the remains as they were found reflects directly on the behavior of the living society:

> The careless treatment of skeletal remains [during EB II and III] shows some departure from the more careful preservation of skulls in the earlier period. This may represent a deterioration in traditions due to the influx of new people, or it may be an influence of increased prosperity in an urban environment. Both possibilities may have contributed to the general picture of decay reflected in late burial customs (Callaway 1963, 87).

The EB II and III charnel houses evidence many similarites among one another, together with a greater amount of variability in some practices:

Minimal or No Variability
* Construction features: rectangular buildings made of rectangular, form-made mudbricks; doorways flanked by stone slab door jambs, stone slab lintels, and slab blocking stone; small forecourt behind doorway; buildings cut partly into natural slopes; floors within building cobbled
* Primary burial practiced; as new, articulated burials were deposited, skeletal remains and crania were transferred as clusters toward the walls of the building
* Pottery associated with burial clusters

Variability
* Difference in size of buildings between all examples excavated

- Difference in numbers of people buried
- Objects deposited: daggers, crescentic axe-heads with some burials, jewelry with others, in one charnel house jewelry of gold
- Burning in some houses, not in others
- Some variability of pottery quality between some buildings

The first thing that becomes apparent in the excavation of the charnel houses at Bab edh-Dhra᾿ is the extreme amount of displacement of burials in the houses. This same condition was observed in the large Early Bronze Age cave tombs at Jericho, where Kenyon concluded that "complete bodies were originally placed in the tomb, but that subsequently the remains were ruthlessly disturbed to make place for later burials"[12] This judgment, similar to that of Callaway, cannot be accepted, since varying explanations are possible for the scattered human remains in the tombs of this period—including erosion or later pillaging of the tombs. What is important for the question of the social meaning of EB II and III tombs, however, is the practice of burial in large, collectively shared buildings. In contrast to the charnel houses of EB IB, the structures of these later phases were able to handle greater numbers of interments. That this evidence correlates with the emergence of a primitive state society at Bab edh-Dhra᾿ also suggests that the mortuary evidence for these phases is reflective of the social shifts occurring.

At the same time, the burial practices of EB II and III intimate hidden ideological incentives. That burials in the charnel houses were organized by functionaries associated with what have been proposed as sanctuaries at Bab edh-Dhra᾿, throws a different light on the evidence.[13] When a townsman/woman at Bab edh-Dhra᾿ died, it was not necessary as in earlier times for the family to construct a tomb. The charnel house as a "corporate facility" in Binford's terms (1972, 234) stood ready to receive the deceased, and had indeed been built by town laborers assigned this task. What remained was the rite of burial, carried out under the auspices of the sanctuary personnel, with the participation of larger numbers of occupants of the town. That such sanctuaries and their personnel existed in Palestine during EB II and III has become an increasing possibility through the study among other things of the seal impressions at various sites containing what is arguably a scene of cultic celebration at temples or sanctuaries of this period.[14] The placement of the skeletalized earlier burials against the walls of the charnel houses, then, would be best explained not as an act of careless disregard of the dead, but rather as being in accord with the public rites, which included preparing a place within the communal mortuary structure for later burials.

It is, of course, the aspects of the rite of burial for which we have so little evidence. Yet such a conditioning factor must be assumed. Thus, in the case of EB II and III burial in the charnel houses, a one-sided choice between social process or ideological explanation appears inadequate, at least from the perspective of the evidence at Bab edh-Dhra'. The answer must lie somewhere between the two, or in a combination of both perspectives.

For the EB IV phase at Bab edh-Dhra' the evidence is limited, since only a handful of tombs and settlement data has been excavated. This phase is still far from being adequately studied at Bab edh-Dhra', despite the fact that Schaub very early published one of the tombs of this phase (Schaub 1973, 2–19). The evidence has now to be examined together with the data from Khanazir, near the southernmost extremity of the southern Ghor. This latter site, called Abu Irshareibeh, was discovered by the MacDonald survey, and was subsequently excavated by the Expedition to the Dead Sea Plain, Jordan in the winter of 1989–1990. The site consists of tombs made of two main components: a rectangular enclosure wall of crude, natural stones within which was usually a single shaft tomb, with both the shaft and chamber usually being stone-lined (MacDonald 1992, 69, fig. 13 and photo 8).

Judging from the tomb and settlement evidence, therefore, a major shift occurred in the occupation of the southern Ghor following the demise of the EB III towns of Bab edh-Dhra' and Numeira. That the region reverted entirely to pastoralism is unlikely, since Bab edh-Dhra' has evidence of clusters of mudbrick dwellings dating to EB IV. At the same time, the evidence from Khanazir has brought forth no indications of sedentization, and thus a good part of the southern Ghor was occupied by nomadic pastoralist groups during this phase.

The burials of EB IV correlate once again with the social shift occurring, since they were no longer enclosed structures in the charnel house style, but shaft tombs, reminiscent of the earlier ones from EB IA. At the same time, multiple, successive burials continued to occur, suggesting that whether pastoralist or not, the population did not wander far from the region. The much smaller number of burials in the EB IV tombs, in comparison to the preceding charnel houses, also shows a reversion to family- or clan-oriented interments. It is impossible, without further evidence, however, to assess anything with regard to the possible ideological motives implied in these burials, but it is clear that they do present important data for the changes occurring in the society of this phase.

In conclusion, it may seem too easy to argue that in studying burial practices at Bab edh-Dhra᾿ one should take into account both the social processes and the ideologies that influenced the nature of the data. Nonetheless, this study would maintain that evidence for both influences is abundantly present, and that to choose the one over the other is to obliterate important aspects of this rich material, widely recognized as some of the most important third millennium BC mortuary evidence we possess from the ancient Near East.

NOTES

1. It is an honor to participate in this memorial volume for Albert E. Glock. Al was a stimulating scholar in a variety of projects we shared through the years—including writing biblical commentaries, participating in professional undertakings, and working together on the expedition to Tell Ta᾿annek. Al's contributions to the theory and methods of modern archaeology, including social archaeology, were an ongoing stimulus to many of us who were privileged to work with him. He was the right person at the right time to direct the new Institute of Archaeology at Birzeit University, laying a solid foundation based on current theory and practice. Fortunately, he was able to achieve many of his goals for the institute before his life was sadly cut short. For Glock's ideas on such subjects as social archaeology see Glock (1985). The notion of social archaeology has for several decades profited from the works of Colin Renfrew. Renfrew's development of this theme first took form in a short essay entitled at *Social Archaeology: An Inaugural Lecture at the University, 20th March 1973* (Renfrew 1973), followed later by the basic volume *Approaches to Social Archaeology* (Renfrew 1984).

2. One EB IB round charnel house was excavated under Lapp's direction in 1967, and a second by the Expedition to the Dead Sea plain in 1977. See n. 25. For reports on Lapp's work, see the preliminary communication on the cemetery at Bab edh-Dhra᾿ in Lapp, P. (1968a). Lapp's interpretations of Bab edh-Dhra᾿ are found in his three programmatic studies,

1968b, 1968c, and 1970. Lapp's controversial theories about the identity of the peoples of the Early Bronze Age are discussed in his 1966a.

3. A discussion of the various publications presenting the interpretation of Bab edh-Dhra ᵓ by Albright and other members of the 1924 survey can be found in Schaub and Rast (1989, 16–18). For Lapp's initial communication on the discovery of the Early Bronze town at Bab edh-Dhra ᵓ see Lapp, (1966b).

4. The forthcoming publication of the Bab edh-Dhra ᵓ town site, presently being completed by Schaub and Rast with other members of the Expedition to the Dead Sea Plain, will include a full correlation of the town site and cemetery pottery, including the groups excavated at the town site by Lapp. This will offer a major contribution of new material, along with some new approaches, to Early Bronze Age ceramic studies.

5. The newer work directed by R. T. Schaub and W. E. Rast is known as the Expedition to the Dead Sea Plain. Between 1975 to 1983 the expedition conducted seasons in the Bab edh-Dhra ᵓ cemetery and town, and at the nearby EB III town of Numeira, south of Bab edh-Dhra ᵓ . In late 1989 and early 1990 the expedition uncovered EB I tombs and Neolithic occupation at Feifa, south of Ghor es-Safi, while excavating a number of previously unknown EB IV tomb types near Khanazir at the south extremity of the southern Ghor. An Iron II walled settlement at Feifa was also exposed in a small section on the southeast side. The Expedition to the Dead Sea Plain is a regional, interdisciplinary study of the population and settlement of the southeastern Dead Sea valley during the height of its occupation in antiquity, namely the Early Bronze Age (3300–2000). Lapp's work has been incorporated into the publication plans of the expedition, and the first volume of the expedition was devoted to his results in the cemetery between 1965 and 1967 (see note 3). The second volume, devoted to the town site of Bab edh-Dhra ᵓ , is currently being finished and will appear in the near future. A third volume dealing with the EB III town at Numeira is also underway, while a fourth volume focusing on the skeletal biology from the Bab edh-Dhra ᵓ cemetery is under preparation.

6. See the discussion of earlier explorations in Schaub and Rast (1989, 15–16).

7. Bloch-Smith's remark in n. 1 on p. 18 that "burials are most commonly presented from the social perspective" certainly does not apply to Palestine. In fact, not one of the studies to which she refers after making this statement is by a Palestinian archaeologist.

8. Binford (1972, 215–16) cites Kroeber's view in great detail. The original article is found in Kroeber (1927).

9. See Hodder (1991, 1–18, esp. 2) for a criticism of Binford's views on

mortuary practices. Cf. similar remarks made earlier by Adams to the effect that "processual understanding of changing patterns of social organization will never be obtained from the mortuary cult alone." (Adams 1966, 21).

10. Schaub has suggested to me that the predominance of Fine Wares in some EB IA tombs might indicate social status. See his remarks on these wares in Schaub and Rast (1989, 274).

11. Tomb A 53 was published in Schaub and Rast (1989, 209–32); a preliminary report of Tomb G 1 is found in Rast and Schaub (1981, 62–65, figs. 23–24).

12. Kenyon (1960b, 53); also Kenyon (1960a, 123), where she writes, "it would seem that even before the flesh had completely decayed it was no longer felt necessary to treat the body with any reverence. The skull alone remained worthy of care, and it alone was left with any consistency in the tomb."

13. For the EB II and III structures designated "sanctuaries" at Bab edh-Dhra', see Rast and Schaub (1981, 27–31), and Schaub and Rast (1984, 50–51).

14. The relevant class in Ben-Tor's discussion is Class III, one sub-class of which represents most likely a scene of communal prayer or cultic dancing. (Ben-Tor 1978, 58–61). A sherd with seal impression representing a cultic dancing scene was found in such a context, in the sanctuary courtyard at Bab edh-Dhra'. See N. Lapp (1989, 5–7).

REFERENCES

Adams, R.
1966   *The Evolution of Urban Society.* Chicago: Aldine.
Albright, W.
1924   The Archaeological Results of an Expedition to Moab and the Dead Sea. *Bulletin of the American Schools of Oriental Research* 14: 1–12.
Ben-Tor, A.
1978   *Cylinder Seals of Third-Millennium Palestine.* Bulletin of the American Schools of Oriental Research Supplement No. 22. Cambridge, MA: American Schools of Oriental Research.
Binford, L.
1972   Mortuary Practices: Their Study and Their Potential. Pp. 208–43 in *An Archaeological Perspective.* New York: Seminar.
Bloch-Smith, E.
1992   *Judahite Burial Practices and Beliefs about the Dead.* JSOT/ASOR Monograph Series 7. Sheffield: JSOT.

Callaway, J.
1963   Burials in Ancient Palestine: From the Stone Age to Abraham. *Biblical Archaeologist* 26: 74–91.
Froehlich, B., and Ortner, D.
1982   Excavations of the Early Bronze Age Cemetery at Bab edh-Dhraʾ, Jordan, 1981: A Preliminary Report. *Annual of the Department of Antiquities of Jordan* 26: 249–67.
Glock, A.
1985   Tradition and Change in Two Archaeologies. *American Antiquity* 50: 464–77.
Hodder, I.
1991   *Reading the Past: Current Approaches to Interpretation in Archaeology.* 2nd ed. Cambridge: Cambridge University.
Kenyon, K.
1960a   *Archaeology in the Holy Land.* New York: Frederick A. Praeger.

1960b   *Excavations at Jericho, Volume One: The Tombs Excavated in 1952–54.* London: British School of Archaeology in Jerusalem.
1965   *Excavations at Jericho Volume Two: The Tombs Excavated in 1955–58.* London: British School of Archaeology in Jerusalem.
Kroeber, A.
1927   Disposal of the Dead. *American Anthropologist* 29: 308–15.
Lapp, N.
1989   Cylinder Seals and Impressions of the Third Millennium B.C. from the Dead Sea Plain. *Bulletin of the American Schools of Oriental Research* 273: 1–15.
Lapp, P.
1966a   *The Dhahr Mirzbaneh Tombs: Three Intermediate Bronze Age Cemeteries in Jordan.* American Schools of Oriental Research Publications of the Jerusalem School, Archaeology: Volume 4. New Haven: American Schools of Oriental Research.
1966b   Bab edh-Dhraʾ. *Revue Biblique* 73: 566–61.
1968a   Bab edh-Dhraʾ. *Revue Biblique* 85: 86–93.
1968b   Bab edh-Dhraʾ Tomb A 76 and Early Bronze I in Palestine. *Bulletin of the American Schools of Oriental Research* 189: 12–41.
1968c   Bab edh-Dhraʾ, Perizzites and Emim Pp. 1–25 in *Jerusalem Through the Ages: The Twenty-Fifth Archaeological Convention.* Jerusalem: Israel Exploration Society.
1970   Palestine in the Early Bronze Age. Pp. 101–31 in *Near Eastern Archaeology in the Twentieth Century: Essays in Honor of Nelson Glueck,* ed. James A. Sanders. Garden City, NY: Doubleday.

1975   The Cemetery at Bab edh-Dhraʾ. P. 110 in *The Tale of the Tell: Archaeological Studies by Paul W. Lapp*, ed. Nancy Lapp. Pittsburgh Theological Monograph Series Number 5. Pittsburgh: The Pickwick Press.

MacDonald, B.
1992   *The Southern Ghors and Northeast 'Arabah Archaeological Survey.* Sheffield Archaeological Monographs 5. Sheffield: University of Sheffield.

Rast, W.
in press   Early Bronze Age State Formation in the Southeast Dead Sea Plain, Jordan. *Studies in the Archaeology of Israel and Neighboring Lands in Memory of Douglas L. Esse*, ed. Samuel R. Wolff. Chicago/Atlanta: The Oriental Institute of the University of Chicago/The American Schools of Oriental Research.

Rast, W., and Schaub, R. T, eds.
1981   *The Southeastern Dead Sea Plain Expedition: An Interim Report of the 1977 Season.* Annual of the American Schools of Oriental Research, Volume 46. Cambridge, MA: American Schools of Oriental Research.

Renfrew, C.
1973   *Social Archaeology: An Inaugural Lecture at the University, 20th March, 1973.* Southampton: University of Southampton.
1984   *Approaches to Social Archaeology.* Cambridge, MA: Harvard University.

Schaub, R. T.
1973   An Early Bronze IV Tomb from Bab edh-Dhraʾ. *Bulletin of the American Schools of Oriental Research* 210: 2–19.

Schaub, R. T., and Rast, W.
1984   Preliminary Report of the 1981 Expedition to the Dead Sea Plain, Jordan. *Bulletin of the American Schools of Oriental Research* 254: 35–60.
1989   *Bab edh-Dhraʾ : Excavations in the Cemetery Directed by Paul W. Lapp (1965–67).* Reports of the Expedition to the Dead Sea Plain, Jordan Volume 1. Winona Lake, IN: Eisenbrauns.

10 Balaam at Deir ʿAlla and the Cult of Baal

HENK FRANKEN

During the excavations in 1967 at Tell Deir ʿAlla in the Jordan Valley, numerous pieces of plaster fallen from a mudbrick wall bearing inscriptions were discovered. This very fragmentary text was originally written by an expert scribe on a vertical wall. The language appears to be an early form of Aramaic, and dates from about the first half of the eigth century BC. The fragments have been published (Hoftijzer and van der Kooij 1976) and have generated many studies concerning its language and the interpretation. In 1989 a symposium was held in Leiden on the results of ten years of study of the text (Hoftijzer and van der Kooij 1991). It appeared that little had been written about the archaeology of the text (van der Kooij 1989), and still less about its religious background. The following approach to the archaeological and religious setting of the Balaam text starts with a general characterization of ancient Semitic sanctuaries and speculates on the *dramatis personae* and possible interpretations of some of the archaeological finds, and suggests an interpretation of the building.

The text, as reconstructed, relates the visions of a seer Balaam Bar Beor, whose name occurs several times. This Balaam is known as the famous seer who was summoned by the king of Moab, Balak, to curse the Israelites asking free passage through his land on their way to Palestine (Numbers 22–24).

In these Deir ʿAlla plaster fragments, Balaam is introduced as a seer who had a vision in the night of an assembly of gods, comprising both *elohim*, and *shadday* gods who apparently try to prevent a goddess *šmš*(?) from destroying life on earth by a flood. The texts are fragmentary and the translation is, in many instances, uncertain. El seems to occur in the texts but the name of the god Baal is not found in

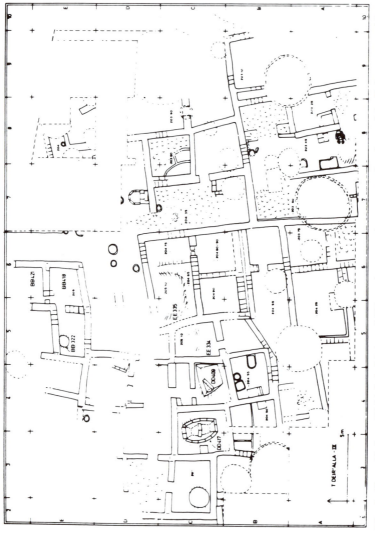

Fig. 1. Plan of "phase IX," labeled "phase M" in early excavation reports, the phase of the Balaam texts. After Hoftijzer and van der Kooij (1991, 19).

the preserved fragments. The room on whose walls the text was once written forms part of a larger complex.

To identify the complex as a sanctuary, archaeologists would like to have architectural parallels. The only broad parallel in Palestine and Jordan would be the Late Bronze Age sanctuary from the same site, where a cella and adjacent buildings were in existence until the twelfth century BC (Franken 1992). There is clearly a central unit there that can be interpreted as a cella. Such a cella has not yet been found in the eighth century complex. From the plan alone (fig. 1), one would not immediately interpret the complex as a sanctuary and, had a religious text not been found, it would be difficult to say what its function was. How could this building function as a sanctuary without a cella, the place where the god manifests itself, and without other elements one normally expects to find associated with sanctuaries? What made a site or a building in the ancient Near East a holy site or a sanctuary? The archaeological approach is not the only way to answer this question.

To solve the problem whether the "Balaam building" was a sanctuary, it is best to start from a general interpretation of the meaning of sanctuaries in the Levant and beyond. For this approach to the question one finds guidance in the work of G. R. H. Wright. On several occasions he published architectural analyses of temples in Palestine (Wright 1985). But his definition of what is a sanctuary or temple is largely dependent on definitions derived from religious literature. This is clear from much of his work, and I refer to his study of Cypriot rural sanctuaries (1992), which combines analysis of architecture with evidence about ancient religions. Wright compares the situation on Cyprus with two neighboring cultural regions. One of these is the Syro-Palestine, where, he writes, "the archaeological record is negligible but there is very interesting information available from literary reference, meaning here, significantly the Bible." This reference is to the biblical information about the Baal cult in Palestine.

In this and several other studies, notably about Shechem as a religious center of the country, Wright demonstrates that the sanctuary is seen in antiquity as the divine center of the world, with as the main symbols the *omphalos*, the tree, the rock, and the primeval waters. These elements of religious perception are primary elements in Near Eastern religions, and he refers to them as "religious constants" (Wright 1987).

How constant are these elements and how widely were the ideas accepted? For this I refer to the work of Palache (1920). His study was based entirely on Semitic texts that were then available. Using Hebrew, Arabic and other sources dating from the earliest to Medieval Jewish and Arabic literature, Palache showed that very ancient concepts persistently recur in later and very much later religious thinking. The characteristic symbolic elements are tree, water, and stone (connected with mountains or high places); these together form a central holy place. Such was still the case in the Christian and Islamic periods, and the Church Fathers as well as Rabbinic and Islamic writers mention these elements.

Palache sketched the problems that arise when open air sanctuaries are replaced by temples (1920, 35). However these four elements (the *omphalos*, the tree, the rock and the primeval waters) are still associated with temple buildings (1920, 59). Thus there is no real difference in the concept between an open air sanctuary or "height" and sanctuaries as buildings, since both comprehend the water source or pond and the stone (as according to tradition there was one in the temple of Jerusalem), which are understood to be at the center of the land. The idea of the pre-existence of these elements is also developed in ancient literature: the holy place existed before the creation of the world.

Fundamental to these concepts is that God chooses the place of the sanctuary, which is the natural point of departure of cosmologies found, with variations, among all Semites. Palache distinguished between ancient popular or traditional beliefs (1920, 127) and the development of theological or philosophical systems constructed to explain the meaning of such religious institutions like myth and cult in a quasi-scientific fashion. This tendency is already manifest in the writings of Josephus. In his treatment of the religious meaning of ancient "symbolism," Palache showed the influence of nineteenth century liberal thinking.

Whereas Palache has clearly worked out the ancient concepts relating to the sanctuary, one finds the truly religious meaning of these images studied and described in the works of Brede Kristensen. The title of his main work, *Life Out of Death*, is an appropriate expression of his reconstruction of Egyptian, Greek and Semitic religions. The central theme is the mystery of life. This mystery is expressed abundantly in the religions of the ancient world, each in its own fashion, but as a concept common to all of them. Life originates in death, rises out of death, and religion is concerned with the relationship between the world of the gods and nature. The relationship is realized or materializes through the daily activities in the ritual, not only in sanctuaries but in most critical moments in daily life, agriculture, and everything related with death and the grave, and is found to be connected with the holiness of water, tree, mountain or rock.

The great merit of his numerous studies in ancient religions is his focus on truly religious elements, rather than on a desanctified "structural" analysis. As an example, I mention his interpretation of the labyrinth because the Deir ʿAlla building is somewhat labyrinthic in its layout and size. For the area, it was unusually large and complicated.

The mythical building with intricate passages from which nobody can find the way back is generally considered to be a symbol of the underworld. Whether this image was connected with the palace at Knossos is unimportant in this connection. The Labyrinth represented, at any rate, the innermost recesses of the earth, or the night sky, the two interchangeable locations of the Kingdom of Death. Greek writers describe the Labyrinth as an obscure grotto or a dark cave, or a prison from which nobody escapes. In early Christian art and symbolism the Minotaur is equated with Satan, while Theseus is Christ, who descended into the underworld (hell) to defeat the arch enemy and the power of death for his own salvation and for that of all mankind. This Christian interpretation of the myth shows that its meaning was understood correctly (Kristensen 1992, 190). The Labyrinth had a long afterlife and the idea spread in western Europe (Doob 1992).

These symbols and the religious interpretations of the sacred place or sanctuary as a cosmos in itself, representing the divine world, would as much seem to constitute the general guide to the understanding of sanctuaries in Egypt, the Near East and the Greek world as the specific layout of a building.

In a recent work, Lundquist has connected these symbols, which he calls "the heavenly landscape," with other similar elements, but his efforts are directed toward state temples, which the Balaam sanctuary is unlikely to have been (Lundquist 1987).

Turning now to the more local religious or mythological scenery, there are several aspects to be considered in relation with features that may have been or were connected with the Deir ʿAlla sanctuary.

Balaam's presence is manifested in the sanctuary as a "Sepher," or book of Balaam, was the basis (*Vorlage*) for the writing on the wall. Gressmann (1913) has already pointed out that the texts of the biblical Balaam are to be dated to the time of the Israelite prophets. In those days the Balaam cult became a threat for the people and the religion of Israel. Balaam may have been a seer in Transjordan, whose deeds and words were authoritative for local religious practices. However, his pagan, but nevertheless critical, prophecies as preserved on wall plaster make him contemporary with, and nearly put him in accordance with, critical prophets like Jeremiah.

Hoftijzer compares many of Balaam's sayings with Jeremiah. In the translation by Weippert (in Hoftijzer and van der Kooij 1991, 157) *am* is the leading goddess and the *elohim* or *shadday* ask her to punish the world:

> Thou mayest break the bolts of heavens
> in the clouds let there be gloominess and no brilliance
> darkness and not thy radiance
> thou mayest cause terror by the gloomy clouds
> but do not be angry forever
> for the swift is reproaching the eagle
> and the vultures brood over the ostrich.

This is a tentative translation and the next lines of the text are corrupt. However, it seems clear that the meaning of the lines that follow is the same as the sayings about the swift dominating the eagle and the vulture serving the ostrich. The stork is superior to the hawk and the owl to the heron, which is an unnatural situation. The world seems to be in complete disorder (Hoftijzer and van der Kooij 1991, 174). As far as I can determine, the meaning is that the augur (who derives his signs from birds) can no longer do his vital work: the signs can no longer be trusted or understood. In this way one can no longer be sure about the agricultural calendar or of the right time for rituals in the public and private sphere.

There are other motifs not mentioned in the text that derive from ancient Near Eastern mythology. We may infer that the patriarch Jacob was remembered in the area. According to the stories preserved in Genesis, Jacob returned from exile as a rich man (Genesis 32). On entering the land where he came from, he meets with troubles. The first is his crossing of the river Jabbok, identified with the Zerqa. He waits until his caravan has reached the other side of the river. Then he meets the demon of the stream. The ensuing fight lasts until dawn, when the demon has to go. But in agreement with a far more general myth, Jacob has extracted a secret from the demon about the future (Frazer 1918, 410). His name is changed to Israel and he will be the father of a great nation. At the same time he is mutilated; his hipbone is dislodged and he becomes lame. This is given as the reason why the Israelites do not eat the flesh and muscle of the hip of sacrifical animals (Gen 32:32). This not eating those parts was common practice in the ancient Near East. Again the feature of the lame hero is a rather well-known element in the legends of king–heroes, whose handicap is also their means of survival (Graves 1961, 324 and 1957, 92.2; Ogden 1997).

After this Jacob has to face a dreaded meeting with his twin brother Esau, and again one is reminded of a not uncommon element of the saga. Jacob held on to Esau's leg when the latter was about to be born (Genesis 25, 26; cf. Stricker 1975, 265). Hosea reproaches his people for this treacherous fact (Hosea 12:4). Then Jacob moves towards Succoth (which in popular biblical atlasses is identified with Tell Deir ʿAlla, cf. Franken 1992, 166–71), where he builds "booths" (= *succoth*) for his flocks. This is certainly an euphemism or a substitute for an earlier tradition, which may have related that Jacob built a sanctuary for the local gods or numina: a "Beth Jacob," if not "Beth Israel." Jacob may have been known locally as the founder of the sanctuary. On a pottery stand dating from the beginning of the Iron Age at Deir ʿAlla, of which unfortunately only one half has been preserved, two large figures with raised arm and hand are depicted, separated from each other by a "net" or trellis pattern. This scene may have been inspired by the nightly engagement of Jacob with the angel (Franken and Kalsbeek 1969, 200, no. 51).

The question of the function of the writing on the wall takes us back to Balaam. At the symposium on the Deir ʿAlla text the question was raised as to why the Balaam text was written on the wall. The text is called *Sepher Balaam*, the "book" of Balaam, and attempts were made to answer the question on the basis of its literary genre (Dijkstra, in Hoftijzer and van der Kooij 1991, 216). If, as Weippert thinks, (Hoftijzer and van der Kooij 1991, 164), this is a narrative told to introduce the sayings of some important person, a god or a seer, and to hand them down to posterity, one could see a function for the writing on the wall. The Balaam of the text on the plastered wall is already a hero of a relatively remote past. In this fashion it was supposed at the symposium that the room with the texts was a little chapel belonging to a village, or at least standing between ordinary dwellings to which there was an easy access. But this is not the case. The area that was excavated under my supervision in 1967 revealed one large complex of about twenty rooms all belonging to one structure, including the collapsed wall of the text. The excavated area was not large enough to expose the entire building. Moreover, the room of the text was not an ordinary little "chapel," because it could not be entered on floor level, as is shown below.

I would suggest that the function of writing in such a semi-permanent fashion is a primary function. It is not educational but magical in the sense that it describes and represents a situation existing through the creative power of the divine word, and written down to make the word visible, if not for the general public then for the "initiated." It is a compelling statement like the word of Amos addressed to Amaziah. The latter tells Amos (Amos 7:12–17), to go away from Bethel and back to Judah where he came from, but Amos' answer puts Amaziah in a hopeless position and reveals his future fate that his wife will be taken by the enemy to become a woman of the streets, his children will be killed and he himself will be burried in unclean soil. The force of these words lies not with the mortal person who utters them but in the fact that they are divine words put in the mouth of a prophet. The case is similar to that of Numbers 20–22. The king of Moab cannot influence Balaam because the God of Israel has put the words in his mouth (Lods 1949, 244). While seemingly hidden in a dark corner, Balaam's prophecies are no less real than when first spoken. They haunt the people even more than when spoken in the street, because, having been fixed in writing, they certainly will create the disaster, if people do not heed these words (Pedersen 1940, 117; cf. Kristensen 1992, 35). Amos' words were remembered as being spoken two years before an earthquake occurred, maybe the same earthquake that destroyed the buildings at Tell Deir ʿAlla. But people did not experience an earthquake as a natural phenomenon as it is conceived in a secular world. Nature was divine and the earthquake a terrible realization of God's will (Ps 104:32; cf. Judg 5:4; Ps 68:8; Hab 3:6; Nah 1:5).

From the Old Testament, and certainly from the New Testament, one gets the impression that Balaam was a foreigner who was not accepted in Israel. However, there must have been other traditions about this seer. Balaam blesses the people in a manner comparable to the blessing of Abraham by Melchizedek (Gen 14:18–20). Moreover at a time when some early Christians thought of Balaam as Satan (Rev 2:13–14), Josephus expresses a different view, (quoted in *TWNT* I 522). Also, in early Christianity Balaam was known as the prophet of the "star of Israel" and one finds him depicted in the catacomb of Priscilla in Rome (first half of the third century AD) pointing to the star for Mary and her child (Num 24:17). According to the text on the wall, Balaam's fate was that of the Israelite prophets. There is a text fragment that describes the purely negative reaction of his audience to his words, exactly as with the receptions of Amos and Jeremiah.

Balaam's words on a wall in Deir 'Alla in the eighth century BC were a symbol of cosmic destiny under which human destiny is subsumed. They were put there to keep the life of the people in order.

We have no evidence of Balaam coming to Deir 'Alla or when this took place. If the seer Balaam was originally at home in Midian or Edom, his fame may have already travelled with the caravans (Franken 1992, 175) at an early date. Since the eastern half of the tell contains substantial buildings dating back to the twelfth century onward it is to be expected that there was a continuous tradition of sanctuaries through the Late Bronze and early Iron Age, and Balaam or traditions about his prophecies may have come to the site at any time during those periods. These prophecies may have been rephrased or adapted if not invented by the priestly scribe and his fellow priests who were the guardians of the Balaam traditions.

Not much can be said about Baal: the name is not mentioned in the text, and the narrative is not a mythological story like the ones found in Ugarit. Nor is the height an open air sanctuary. There is, however, mention in the text of the mythological meeting of the *elohim* (such as is also referred to in the Old Testament), including a goddess who has the power over the heavenly water sluices, and of *El*, all of which is reminiscent of Ugarit, but it is clear that such images were also current in Israel in the eighth century BC, stemming from a common Canaanite substratum. Current views on the Baal cult in Palestine are descibed by Wenning and Zenger (1986), and the relation between Baal and

Yahweh by Pedersen (1940, 503–509). Jer 23:18 and 22 relates that the true prophet must have attended the council (*basod*) of Yahweh, a concept known in Israel as well as in surrounding countries. The Bible associates Balaam with the Baal heights in the land of Moab. Balak the king takes him to the Baal's height where he sacrifices, and it is there that God put His words in the mouth of Balaam (Numbers 22:41, 23:5; Pedersen 1940, 118).

We do not know of there having been a third movement in religious matters in the area. There was a genuine Yahwistic movement in Israel and there were the Baal cults. If the choice is between the two for the Deir ʿAlla region, then the cult was that of Baal or a local Baal. However, if one tries to look at the Baal cult—not through the eyes of the Hebrew prophets—but as manifestation of a religious and mental attitude towards the mysteries of life, one finds that there must have been far more to "Baal" than the pleasures of enjoying heavenly blessings in the shadow of green trees on top of hills accompanied by sexual aberrations. I refer again to Kristensen who insists that such religious imagery concerns the mystery of "raising up life out of death." For instance the green tree was the manifestation of life rising out of death and not only in priestly thinking but generally in the common peoples' perception of nature. Even today in many villages around the Mediterranean the tree is the giver of life and health. Possibly one of the best-known at present may be the holy tree of modern Paphos on Cyprus with all the votive rags hanging from its branches, and which grows from an underground chapel.

There probably was a sacred tree on the hill of Deir ʿAlla. During the first years of the excavation we found a "cistern," 8 m in diameter, which was tentatively attributed to the same level where later the texts were found, some 30 m west of the text room (Franken and Kalsbeek 1969, 62). The base of this pit was never reached in later seasons but it goes down into levels of the tenth century BC or earlier. While excavating the pit, it became clear that it could never have held water, there were no traces of plaster. When found, the east wall was heavily damaged. Naturally one thinks of a pit although we could not find a purpose for it. If one supposes that a tree was planted at an early stage of the sanctuary in the Iron Age that was meant to be a holy tree, then while the debris from destruction and erosion accumulated around the tree during the following ages, (the tell grew 9 m in height between the twelfth and the eighth century BC) the area had to be kept free while both tree and tell grew higher and so a hole from which the tree emerged was kept open. We know that trees did grow in the last centuries on the tell, because we found holes left by the roots in the upper layers.

It is rather difficult nowadays for us to understand that our materialistic or purely commercial or romantic attitude towards nature was not the attitude in ancient times. The earth was the seat of wisdom in that it possessed the secret of life, and true wisdom was to understand that the mystery of life was manifest in the primeval rock or *bama* height and in the tree growing on it. Would ordinary village people have been aware of this? I think that they were. Reverence towards rock or tree or spring and the celestial bodies combined with awe and fear from an emotion of deep respect are the normal attitude in pre-modern societies because there is no clear mental distinction between nature and the divine world (cf. Kristensen 1960, 32–36 on the concept of nature in antiquity, and Pedersen 1940, 508). Failure nowadays to see this is caused by the fact that for us the symbol is dead. A symbol is in our days merely a reminder, a sign, not a reality. But in "primitive" religion, or indeed in popular awareness, the symbol is the reality, the incarnation so to speak, of what is symbolized; or to put it differently: the actual presence of the magical value or power it symbolizes.

We think of Baal in Palestine as associated with "heights." Boyd Barrick remarks that "we have no guarantee that any example of the *bâmâh* phenomenon has yet been discovered ..." (Boyd Barrick 1975, 594), and the question as to whether the inhabitants of the Deir ʿAlla region in the Iron Age considered the tell on which the Balaam sanctuary stood to be a *bâmâh* cannot be answered. The association of the Bâmoth-Baal and Balaam in Num 22:41 may only indicate a customary association of pagan rites and sorcerers with high places by the biblical writer, but the association did exist in the mythology from Ugarit (cf. the throne of Baal on mount Saphon). The Balaam inscription was written on a plastered wall of one room that was part of a large building that stood on a fairly high artificial hill, high enough to allow people on a clear day, standing on the Mount of Olives to see the whitewashed walls of this building. The combination of the artificial hill (tell) with the building on top, the Balaam text and a number of associated objects justify the present attempt to interpret the ruins as the remains of a Baal height. And it seems that the overall characteristics and symbols of ancient Near Eastern religion also support this interpretation.

Let us now examine the building complex containing Balaam's words. Figure 1 shows a plan of the excavation of "phase 9." Starting with the north–south wall between sqares A-E 6 and A-E 7, we find on the east side paved courtyards and what seem to be ordinary houses with domestic installations, which may have been the living quarters of the priests. The latter have been described by van der Kooij (1989, 82). Among the finds in these houses were several antlers of fallow deer, known to have been used in apotropaic rites (cf. Pauly-Wissowa, II, 1182). There was even a terra-cotta figurine of a stag (van der Kooij 1989, 105).

West of this area is the north–south wall, continuing to the south in the unexcavated parts of the tell. Then right in the center of the plan, in squares B-C/5-6, built against this wall on the west side, is a small rectangular complex of three rooms. The northwest corner was destroyed almost down to ground level by an earthquake. The text was written on the east face of this west wall and it was found lying in debris covering the next room to the west. These three rooms could not be entered through a door. Somehow a visitor had to go down into the complex from above, probably through the southeast room. This is not the only room without a door; on the plan one finds at least one other room without a normal door and walls still standing one meter high. This is not as unexpected as it may sound. For Palestine one may point to stands for incense burners with windows with snakes or doves emerging from them, but no doors. Models of one room sanctuaries on Cyprus may have no door or a locked door but access through the roof (Tatton-Brown 1979). This suggests that a cave is represented. The sanctity of the cave is the same as that of the underworld, conceived as the realm of death (Kristensen 1960, 361). That is why the grotto is a place of mystery, and where the mysteries of the gods of the underworld are revealed. Thus it is the seat of the oracle. Van der Kooij writes, "the evidence from the room of the plaster text does not indicate a cultic center of the settlement but allows for the reconstruction of another kind of religious center, not yet archaeologically known" (1991, 23). This is correct to a certain degree since the room can only be interpreted as a cella when compared with certain shrines found in Palestine. Van der Kooij wishes to isolate the room from the rest of the building, but this is not warranted archaeologically. The room with two adjacent rooms on the south is an integrated part of one large complex as indicated above and cannot be said to parallel the houses to the east of it. The room with the writing on the wall, however, occupied a special place in the entire complex. It was the place of revelation where the seer "saw" the meeting of the gods. Such places were found in the Near East and around the Mediterranean in classical times and they are always interpreted as grottos or subterranean places where contact between the living and the divine world or the netherworld was established. There the seer conjures up the dead person whose advice is sought (Pedersen 1940, 482) and "sees" the meeting of the gods. Such a place existed outside the walls of Jerusalem (Franken and Steiner 1990, 125). Many such places are known from Greece under the general name of *megara* (Rhode 1898, 117), and are always a grotto or imitation of it.

The seer gave oracles, had dreams, interpreted dreams and was a healer. But the place of the oracle was indicated and fixed by divine revelation (Gen 28:16–17). Where the oracle is, is the sanctuary, and when the sanctuary has such inaccessible rooms as is the case here, they share in the holiness of the place and the building takes the nature of a maze or labyrinth (Kristensen 1992, 190). Only the savior Theseus (Balaam) can deliver its victims from perdition.

On the northwest side the traces of the sanctuary have eroded away, but to the west and the south the building continues in the unexcavated parts of the tell. All rooms west of the line indicated above belong to that one building. There may have been open spaces and some rooms seem to have had reed matting as a cover, but that they form one complex is virtually without doubt. The three rooms of the text were not an isolated little "chapel" in the midst of ordinary dwellings. In the light of what was said above about the meaning of the Semitic sanctuary and its symbolism and in the light of the meaning of the plaster texts, no matter what variant readings and interpretations are given, the archaeological evidence suggests a large religious building with many rooms.

This is indeed a slight turn away from the popular view that there was nothing more to the Baal cult than fertility rites in which sacred men and women played a dominant role. Natural fertility is something quite different from the concept that life has to be created anew every day through the cult and that the ultimate answer to the mystery of life

Fig. 2. The inscribed flint stone, register number DA 2000. Height 14 cm. After Hoftijzer and van der Kooij (1976, pl. 19.b).

Fig. 3. a) inscribed jar (reg. no. DA 2846); b) libation goblet (reg. no. DA 1990); c) "symbolic" loom weight (reg. no. DA 2006). After Hoftijzer and van der Kooij (1976, pl. 16.b).

comes out of the realm of death. As far as any connection can be postulated between Balaam, his sanctuary, and Baal, we are dealing with a Near Eastern Iron Age religion with all the characteristic general features of a religion concerned with the mystery that life comes out of death. At this time there is not yet a mystery religion like the Hellenistic ones but the notion of mystery existed (Kristensen 1992, 102). What the mystery cult involved has always been a carefully kept secret. Thus the "Homeric hymn" to Demeter (Dimier, n.d.) contains a warning. One may not reveal or even try to pry into the cultic performances and initiations, because awe for the gods ties one's lips together. "Blessed is the person who is initiated in these mysteries" (*Hist.* I: 479–480): Herodotus writes in the same vein about the nightly mysteries of Osiris near Sais in Egypt (*Hist.* II: 170). But the idea is much older and widely spread (Widengren 1969, 556; Dibelius 1956, 42).

In the north of the complex, four rooms used for weaving were found. In each one many loom weights were found, and in one corner four objects lying close together: an inscribed flint (fig. 2), a libation goblet and an oversized loom weight (fig. 3b, c), and somewhat further off an inscribed jar (fig. 3a).

These objects should not be treated as isolated finds. It seems that persons who came to weave in these rooms poured libations and kissed the "stone of *shar 'a*" (the flint), while the oversized loom weight symbolized their status as weavers.

I will now comment on two objects of special importance from the excavations. The first is the flint. This sacred stone (fig. 2), is of interest since it has a sheen from regular handling or kissing and an inscription *eben shar 'a*. Some like to see this as an ordinary weight, but there is also the associated jar with the inscription "for *Shar 'a*." In the archaeological context it rather seems that *Shar 'a* is a local numen or deity. No contemporary texts are known in which the name occurs but in Arabic as spoken by the Beduin *shar 'a* is the drinking place and *Shar 'a el kebir* refers to the river Jordan. Since in the Iron Age there was still a living stream immediately on the north side of the tell one may surmise that Shar'a was a local river numen and the inscribed stone the seat and source of fertility. As the *betil* or stone is one of the most important and in fact most holy objects in Semitic religions, this stone is in my opinion a rather important and fairly unique archaeological object, deserving more consideration than to be called an ordinary weight (van der Kooij 1989, 101).

The second object is a terra-cotta figurine found in an intrusive context. This terra-cotta figurine (fig. 4) is a fetish. In the archaeological literature of Palestine no distinction is made between image and fetish. According to Kristensen, the image is a deliberate repetition that can occur again and again, ever anew. This continual repetition presupposes the continuing reality of that which is repeated. This refers to the cult image. In the Old Testament the cult image of a god is a *statue* made of wood and covered with precious metal (Galling 1977, 99). I think that the popular terra-cottas of so called nude goddesses clasping their breasts are a modern archaeological myth (Franken 1995, 233–36). The ones found in great numbers in Jerusalem were not goddesses, not naked and mostly do not clasp their breasts but the hands rest on the belly. In Cave I at Jerusalem (Franken and Steiner 1990, 125), hundreds of complete and undamaged pots were found, but these terra-cottas were all smashed. When in use they were covered with whitewash and painted in red colors, suggesting robes, and most of them still retain traces of this. They were fetishes, only possessing spiritual powers when a "charmer," so to speak, has loaded them with magical power for one specific purpose and moment. Such a moment may be a ceremony on the occasion of illness or childbirth. Then, when the ceremony is over, the fetish has to be destroyed and the spell broken.

A clear example of this from the Near East is the Ugaritic legend of king Krt. The god Latpan (=El) appeals to the gods to expel the demon who took possession of king Krt, but none answers. Latpan decides to act himself. A figurine is made from clay and dung, (used as a temper in the clay). This is "loaded" with a magic formula directed against the demon Tannin and the effect is that the demon leaves the body of the king, taking the illness with it. The intermediary in this act is a woman whose name is "she who removes." Even today the ceremony is a normal procedure in cultures where people still believe that demons cause illnesses.

Our figurine is of such a nature. She has a tambourine indicating her involvement in some festival and she has a drop of menstruation blood. She represented probably a "vestal virgin," permanently or temporarily dedicated to a goddess as priestess. Menstruation must have been of vital importance for her in her position. There was a need for this blood in rituals, of which there are clear examples in antiquity. Menstruation

Fig. 4. The fetish of a "vestal virgin" (reg. no. DA 56). Height 10 cm. After *VT* 10 (1960), pl. 13.a.

blood was used in a ritual in the Jordan Valley according to Josephus and Pliny the Elder (*Natural History*, VII: 66). The Dead Sea was considered the vulva of the earth goddess and the bitumen that came to the surface of the sea and was used for many purposes was her menstruation blood. When this tar was collected in some kind of barges it could only be unloaded at the shore in a magical act using menstruation blood and urine. This is just one example of the use of menstruation blood in cult or ritual (Graves 1961, 166 and Josephus 1980, 262). Superstition about menstruation blood was still common in western Europe after the first World War (Lévy-Bruhl 1931, 388 and *passim*). Like the inscribed stone, this fetish seems to be a unique archeological object.[1] Also complete terra-cotta votive models of legs were found on occasion indicating that the sanctuary had a healing function.

I have sketched the way people would have looked at a Baal's height. It is a place of constant renewal of life, a holy place, where the netherworld manifests itself, and a place of revelation of the will of the gods. On the Deir ʿAlla "height" the magic word of the prophet was found, written on the wall of a dark room to be entered through a hole, like a grotto. It was the place where a seer entered into the assembly of the gods. There were also the rooms reserved for weaving like those found in the temple in Jerusalem (2 Kgs 23:7). A stone with a divine name, a libation vessel and a "symbolic" loom weight were found grouped together in a corner of one of these rooms. There were the legends of the ancient local heros and demigods—Balaam the seer and Jacob the Lame—and the fetish of a "vestal virgin." Whereas in Palestine possible remains of structures on the ancient Baal heights seem to have disappeared through human destruction and erosion, Deir ʿAlla may have preserved an architecturally developed version of a *bama* or Baal's height such as existed in the days of the great Israelite prophets.

NOTES

1. Outside the definition given above, this fetish performed another "magical act" when excavated. It was found in a medieval grave that was dug into the ruins of the sanctuary, and thus originally it comes from that level. But it came to light at the very moment when some local visitors started a fierce argument with our workmen accusing them of digging up Muslim graves. Our foreman took the figurine and asked the visitors, since when did Muslims bury their dead with such shameful images? This cut the argument short.

REFERENCES

Boyd Barrick, W.
   1975   The Funerary Character of "High-Places." *Vetus Testamentum* 25: 565.
Dibelius, M.
   1956   *Botschaft und Geschichte*. Tübingen: Fortress.
Dimier, L.
   n.d.   *Les Hymnes Homériques*. Paris: Garnier.
Doob, P. R.
   1992   *The Idea of the Labyrinth from Classical Antiquity Through the Middle Ages.* Ithaca: Cornell University.
Franken, H. J.
   1992   *Excavations at Tell Deir ʿAlla, The Late Bronze Age Sanctuary.* Leuven: Peeters.

1995   Cave I at Jerusalem: An interpretation. Pp. 233–40 in *Trade, Contact, and the Movement of Peoples in the Eastern Mediterranean*, eds. Stephen Bourke and Jean-Paul Descoeudres. Mediterranean Archaeology Supplement 3. Sydney: Meditarch.

Franken, H. J., and Kalsbeek, J.
1969   *Excavations at Tell Deir 'Alla*, Vol. I. Leiden: Brill.

Franken, H. J., and Steiner, M. L.
1990   *Excavations at Jerusalem 1961–1967*, Vol II. London: Oxford University.

Frazer, J. G.
1918   *Folk-Lore in the Old Testament*, Vol. II. London: Macmillan.

Galling, K.
1977   *Biblisches Reallexikon*. Tübingen: Mohr.

Graves, R.
1957   *The Greek Myths*. London: Penguin.
1961   *The White Goddess*. London: Farrar, Straus, Giroux.

Gressmann, H.
1913   *Mose und seine Zeit*. Göttingen: Vanderhoeck and Ruprecht.

Hoftijzer, J., and van der Kooij, G.
1976   *Aramaic Texts from Deir 'Alla*. Leiden: Brill.

Hoftijzer, J., and van der Kooij, G., eds.
1989–91   *The Balaam text from Deir 'Alla Re-evaluated*. Proceedings of the International symposium held at Leiden, 21–24 August 1989. Leiden: Brill.

Josephus
1980   *The Jewish War*. Translated by G. A. Williamson. London: Penguin.

Kooij, G. van der
1989   *Picking Up the Threads*. Leiden: State Museum of Antiquities.

Kristensen, W. B.
1954   *Symbool en werkelijkheid*. Arnhem: Van Lochum Slaterus.
1960   *The Meaning of Religion*. The Hague.
1992   *Life Out of Death*. Leuven: Peeters.

Lévy Bruhl, L.
1931   *Le Surnaturel et la Nature dans la Mentalité Primitive*. Paris: F. Alcan.

Lods, A.
1949   *Israël des Origines au Milieu du VIII' Siècle*. Paris: Albin Michel.

Lundquist, J. M.
1983   Studies in the Temple in the Ancient Near East. Ph.D. Dissertation, Lund University.

Ogden, D.
1997   *The Crooked Kings of Ancient Greece*. London: Duckworth.
Palache, J. L.
1920   *Het Heiligdom in de Voorstelling der semitische Volken*. Leiden: Brill.
Pedersen, J.
1940   *Israel, its Life and Culture*. London: Humphrey Milford.
Rhode, E.
1898   *Psyche*. Freiburg: Mohr.
Stricker, B. H.
1975   *De Geboorte van Horus*, Vol. III. Leiden: Ex Oriente Lux.
Tatton-Brown, V.
1979   *Cyprus B.C., 7000 Years of History*. British Museum Publications 188. London: British Museum.
Wenning, R., and Zenger, E.
1986   Ein bäuerliches Baal-Heiligtum im Samarischen Gebirge aus der Zeit der Anfänge Israels. *Zeitschrift der deutschen Palästina-Vereins* B.102: 75–86.
Widengren, G.
1969   *Religionsphänomenologie*. Berlin: de Gruyter.
Wright, G. R. H.
1985   *Ancient Building in South Syria and Palestine*. Leiden: Brill.
1987   *As on the First Day: Essays in Religious Constants*. Leiden: Brill.
1992   The Cypriot Rural Sanctuary, an Illuminating Document in Comparative Religion. Pp. 269–83 in *Studies in Honour of Vassos Karageorgis*, ed. G. C. Ionides. Nicosia.

11 The Head Huntress of the Highlands

G. R. H. WRIGHT

A t "Bethouliah" in the hill country of Samaria, a lurid tale has been portrayed. Although the tale overtly falls in the category of Hellenistic "sex and violence" romance, it incorporates other basic motifs and on this account warrants attention of a different nature than has been accorded in the commentaries.

The "history" of Judith and Holofernes[1] has never been accepted as canonical by Christian consensus, nor has it been received by Judaism.[2] Yet of all the apocrypha it probably remains the most widely known to the laity—indeed it has constituted a prolific source of inspiration in all forms of art (painting, sculpture, music) exceeding by far most themes drawn from the canonical scriptures.[3]

The substance of the story is as follows: The King of Assyria was challenged in his supremacy by the Median king and, accordingly, sought to marshall all his subject nations in battle against the insurgent. However, the peoples of the West, from Cilicia to Egypt, disregarded his call, considering that the Great King stood alone and was doomed. Yet five years later the King of Assyria conclusively defeated his Median rival and decided to punish severely the Western nations who had disobeyed his summons. Accordingly he dispatched an immense army under Holofernes, his commander-in-chief, to subjugate those regions, ordering Holofernes to hold those who submitted to attend spoliation and deportation at the hands of the king while extirpating absolutely all those who made any opposition. In pursuance of this commission, Holofernes first dealt with the northerly regions (Cilicia etc.) and then turned south towards Arabia. Next he attacked the coastal regions of Phoenicia, which forthwith made their submission. However the people of Israel decided to defend their upland territory and took all necessary measures to this end—laying in stocks of provisions, fortifying the frontier towns and occupying the passes that led up into the highlands.

At this point the explanatory background is concluded and the action of the story begins. Holofernes and his army are in possession of the Plain of Esdraelon and threatening the hill country by advancing beyond Dothan and concentrating their forces against the town of Bethouliah, thus making it the Israelite outpost. At a council of war Holofernes accepts the advice of his subject allies (Moabites and Ammonites) not to force the mountain pass but to seize the water supply of Bethouliah (a spring below the city) and reduce the town by starvation and thirst.

At the extremity of their endurance, when the townspeople had virtually prevailed upon the elders to submit, a beautiful and wealthy young woman (recently widowed) named Judith takes it on herself to save the situation. She called the elders to her house, rebuking them for their readiness to submit and commanded them to leave matters in her hands. She then adorned herself in seductive finery and taking a bag of delicacies she went out of the City Gate attended by her maid-servant and walked across to the Assyrian outposts by the spring. There she stated that she wished to submit to Holofernes and inform him of a secret route by which he could subjugate the whole hill country without loss.

All were struck with her incredible beauty, most of all Holofernes. Furthermore she gained credence for wisdom and devotion by a fabricated story about the imminent sinning of the Israelites against their own religious laws, entailing abandonment by their all-powerful God. In pursuance of this plan, Judith and her maid were able to come and go about the camp and out to the front lines, where she prayed regularly and awaited God's sign of the Israelites' impending sin. Eventually on the fourth night, Holofernes arranged a private banquet at the conclusion of which (after much wine had flowed) he expected to enjoy the favors of the beautiful Israelite woman. However in the upshot when all have been dismissed from the tent except Judith, Holofernes had made himself dead drunk and Judith beheaded him with his own sword. She put the severed head in the provision bag that her maid had always carried in their comings and goings through the camp. Then together mistress and maid with their trophy made their way as usual to the spring where she was accustomed to bathe and pray.

However on this occasion she continued on up to the gates of Bethouliah. At her summons she was let in and displayed to the townsfolk the severed head of the Assyrian commander-in-chief as token of God's mercy on their plight.

Judith then gave wise council of war, how to transfer the situation into the utter and final route of the enormous Assyrian army after it has been thrown into irreversible panic by the discovery of the headless body of the commander-in-chief. All these things transpire according to plan. Intelligence is sent to the rest of the country and all Israel join in the pursuit and spoliation of the fleeing enemy host. When this is concluded, a triumphal procession to Jerusalem is made and led by Judith, and a triumphal psalm is sung. Then the major spoils are dedicated in the temple of the one true God. Thereafter Judith lived to a great age (105), and during this time no one dared to threaten the Jews. Thus Jerusalem and all the land was saved by the prowess of a woman beautiful and brave, wise and devout whose name means "Jewess."

Expressed as above in summary form it is possible to regard the account as historical or pseudo-historical in intent. However as soon as any detail of time or place is considered, then it is clear that there was never any intention to present the story as factual, indeed it was specifically taken out of any factual context (cf. Buttrick 1962, 1025). Its geography is that of the Argonautica or of the Odyssey. That is to say, within a recognizable overall framework (of north to south), unknown or legendary place names are introduced for which there is no map reference.[4] As for the historical details, these are an inspired essay in anachronism. All this is now recognized, and in fact the various commentaries on the book present virtually the same picture.

The book clearly falls into two parts: the rather labored account of the circumstances leading up to the drama (chapters 1–7), then follows (chapters 8 to 16) a first-rate piece of storytelling.[5] It has an urgent, dream like (surrealist) quality, with no trace whatever of the fabulous or supernatural. Only the compelling essentials of the narrative are introduced and these marshalled in perfect order. Indeed the control exercised by the author over his narrative is such as to suggest a lurking irony of expression.[6]

Regarding the composition of the book, nothing is known other than what can be deduced from internal evidence. The book has been

206 ARCHAEOLOGY, HISTORY AND CULTURE IN PALESTINE

transmitted in Greek with the nomenclature drawn from the Septuagint, although linguistic evidence suggests that it was translated from a Hebrew original.[7] As to the date of composition, both by express statement and by implication, this is lowered many intervals from the ostensible "historical" setting. On the face of it the action is dated ca. 620 BC by the reference to the all powerful King of Assyria as protagonist, but this comes down to ca. 587 BC since this king is named Nebuchadnezzar. Further, reference to the capture of Ecbatana brings the date down again to ca. 550 BC, while the juncture of Jewish History is stated to be soon after the return from captivity entailing a date a few decades later. Finally the names of the army commander Holofernes and his chamberlain Bagoas are Persian and historical, being those of commanders in a punitive campaign directed by Artaxerxes III against Egypt, ca. 335 BC.

Thus the very explicit anachronisms provided by the author give a time range of exactly three centuries for the historical setting of the action and invoke a melange of Assyrian, Neo-Babylonian and Persian ascriptions in one event. However all the internal evidence suggests that the period depicted is Maccabean (note the anti-religious attitude of the invader). Thus it should be a Seleucid Greek who is the tyrannous potentate (i.e. Antiochos IV or Nikanor) bringing the date down to the middle of the second century BC (Moore 1984, 46). Yet a concluding item makes the date of composition still later. The action takes place in Samaritan territory, which is represented as under the dominion of Jerusalem. This can only be after the campaigns of John Hyrkanus at Shechem and Samaria later in the second century BC (Buttrick 1962, 1025). Thus the date of composition of Judith is probably as late as the first century BC.

The upshot of these deductions would seem to be that the Book of Judith was written not earlier than the first century BC by a knowledgeable, intelligent Jew with a distinct literary talent.[8] Since he is at pains to mention the town Dothan for no very good reason, then it has been conjectured that this was his home town (Torrey 1945, 91). Its propogandistic tone suggests that the composition of the book was a *piece d'occasion*. In such an event, two sets of circumstances can be adduced. Either the book was an exhortation to the Jews to behave bravely in the face of a threat to their religion and independence, or it was a call to resistance against (newly imposed) foreign subjection.[9] In either set of circumstances the obvious historical juncture would seem to be the Roman annexation by Pompey in 63 BC.[10]

Various explanations have been suggested for harmonizing the melange of earlier detail with the later date of composition. Firstly there is the obvious suggestion that the present form of the story represents an accretion of earlier stories or versions so that the anachronistic details are fossils so to speak (Moore 1984, 52). More to the point is the supposition that the ill assorted names of the foreign sovereign and his commanders are code names for contemporary figures whom it would be dangerous to mention by name, e.g. Antiochos IV, Nikanor, Pompey, Hadrian or whomever.[11] In general something of this sort can be assumed to obtain, while the sustained anachronisms are most likely an advertisement of the fact that the tale is intended to speak to the present and is not to be thought of in any way as history (Buttrick 1962, 1025; Hastings 1982 II, 283).

Whatever the precise shade of argument used to account for Nebuchadnezzar, King of Assyria, and his general, Holofernes, different considerations apply to the principal figure Judith. Since her name means simply Jewess, there can be no doubt that she is intended to stand for the Jewish people, courageous, daring, wise and most devout.[12] However it has been thought that she is not simply an *ad hoc* invention but that the figure has a definite forerunner with a local habitation and a name. This proposition immediately advances the question of identifying the scene of the action. It is possible to reconstruct several Hebrew originals for the Greek Bethoulia/ Baitoulia, e.g. House (= Temple) of God, House (= Temple) of the Ascent/Rise. No such names can be found on a map of any period, but House of the Ascent suggests Shechem (Moore 1984, 150–51). Shechem is clearly the only major site that fits the topographical details incorporated in the story. Accordingly Torrey's identification of Bethoulia with Shechem proposed a century ago (Torrey 1899, 164) is as cogent as ever and would require specific disproof to be abandoned (Torrey 1945, 91; cf. Buttrick 1962, 1025; Moore 1984, 159). In this fashion Judith has been seen as a renewed version of a famous "woman of Shechem," a popular heroine whose daring acts belonged to the time of Artaxerxes III and his army commander Holofernes (ca. 335 BC).[13] It may very well be that a saga of a manslaying woman was current at Shechem at that time, but to maintain, as do the commentators, that it took its origin from the deeds of an historical Shechemite woman is another matter (*DB Suppl.* 4, col. 1320). Here evidence of a different order must be considered.

In the first place, of course, some history is involved in the question, but this is best regarded as "historical background." If at a juncture not far removed from the composition of the Book of Judith a leader of note lost his head in dramatic circumstances at Shechem, then it would be nothing exceptional. Heads roll in history, and a number of notable heads were cut off and carried about in the region during the Judith period. Some of them are worth mentioning.[14]

The fifteen years or so at the middle of the second century BC were a turbulent period in the affairs of Syria and Palestine encompassing internecine struggle within the house of Seleucus, Ptolemaic ingression, and the standing problem of the special status of the Jews.[15] On two occasions, one in 161 BC (1 Macc 7), and the other in 147 BC (1 Macc 10–11), military defeat led to the decapitation of the vanquished leader. Nikanor, a high ranking officer of state during the reign of Antiochos IV and his successor Demetrios I, was given command of several campaigns against the Jews. In 161 BC he was defeated by Judas Maccabeus at Kfar Salama near Beth Horon, being mortally wounded in the battle. His head was cut off by order of Judas and taken to Jerusalem for exhibition. The day of victory was made a public festival called Nikanor's Day (1 Macc 7:47).[16] Then fifteen years later in 146 BC something similar befell the pretender Alexander Balas who claimed to be a natural son of Antiochos IV and had thus ousted Demetrios I. He was constantly supported by the Jews but after owing his fortune to Ptolemy VI Philometer he incurred the latter's enmity.[17] Eventually Balas was defeated by Philometer's invading Egyptian army in a battle near Antioch and fled to seek the protection of an Arab sheik. However the latter betrayed him and cut off his head and sent it to Philometer (1 Macc II, 16–17).

This was not the end of such doings. There was a recrudescence a century later when Rome had supplanted the Seleucids as the imperial power in the region.[18] It was ushered in by one of the most sensational events of ancient history—the defeat and death of Crassus near Harran in 53 BC at the hands of the Parthian army. His head was cut off to be presented to the Parthian king at a banquet (Colledge 1986, 37–42; Perowne 1956, 40). Following this, the Parthians were active in

Palestine and interfered in the struggle between Herod and the Hasmoneans. During the course of this struggle, Herod's brother Joseph was defeated and beheaded by the Hasmonean general Pappos in 39 BC. However two years later, in 37 BC, Herod avenged his brother. He slew Pappos and cut off his head and sent it off as an occasion for family rejoicing (Perowne 1956, 60).

Thus, at the two most likely historical settings of the Judith story, half a dozen celebrated heads were put on show. These instances certainly made the theme of the decapitation of a military commander a topical one, but no one of them can be reckoned the historical *Vorlage* of the Judith story. The essence of this story is the dramatic appearance of a woman bringing a severed head: it is therefore difficult to assert that the story of Judith was founded on recent historical events since none of those cited involve a woman. Indeed, the history of any age contains little record of such circumstances. Nonetheless they are not a novelty. They constitute a familiar tableau that may be called "The Invention of the Head," and the most telling way of continuing the argument may be to present an overview of the Judith story in relation to this known ichnographic device.

This matter is introduced conveniently via the fate that befell Crassus.[19] The story is well-known. After the harrowing defeat of the legions (where Crassus bore himself with distinction) his head was severed (Plutarch XXXI) and carried off for the delectation of the Parthian king (Plutarch XXXII). It followed the king to Armenia where a banquet was being celebrated with appropriate entertainment on the occasion of a dynastic marriage alliance. The entertainment included a performance of Greek tragedy (*The Bacchae*) and when the head was brought in, the protagonist, the celebrated Jason of Tralles, was inspired to seize it and break into Agave's famous lines: φέρορεν ἐξ ὄρεος / ἕλικα νεότερον ἐπι μελαθρα / ακαρίαν θηραν (Plutarch XXXII; Plutarch misquotes the first line, cf. *Bacchae* 1170). If that was his association we can only follow him.

Agave, in her infatuation, is tragically made to rehearse the tableau that is the present concern. In the denouement of the play she appears bearing the severed head of her son. She thus presents a horrible travesty of the motif that everyone knew: The Invention of the Head by a (nubile) woman (here parodied by a demented mother unwittingly displaying the head of the son she has murdered; see *Bacchae*).

Perhaps the archetypal Greek instance of the motif is in the Orpheus legend where the Thracian women, wild with rage and jealousy, bore off the severed head and cast it into the river.

> When by the rout that made the hideous roar
> His gory visage down the stream was sent
> Down the swift Hebrus to the Lesbian shore ...

It has been remarked that the Judith story has been one of the most prolific of graphic representation in the Bible[20]—including a number of celebrated Renaissance masterpieces (Moore 1984, ills. 4–9). The latter depict various episodes of the story, e.g. the actual beheading (Donatello). However all representations include the head and the favored device is the Invention of the Head—Judith with the severed head (Michelangelo). And now a striking fact must be mentioned: at roughly the same time as this tableau of Judith and her head was devised, an exact doublet of it was taking form in the region, that is, Salome with the head of John the Baptist.[21] Finally, as a curtain to this specimen exhibition, the same scene is encountered a thousand years later in perhaps the most striking contribution of western European Christianity to religious imagery: the Grail legend.[22] The central point of the ritual described in this is the sacramental presentation of the Grail by the Grail Maiden(s). Whatever esoteric symbolism the Grail may be invested with, in some versions of the legend the receptacle contained a severed head when it was sacramentally presented.[23] This once again manifests the compulsion to assign the severed head to the keeping of a (young) woman.

The upshot of this brief survey is straightforward enough. The Judith story in its culminating expression reproduces a figure (the woman bringing in the severed head) that is standard in a variety of legends from different regions and ages, but that is virtually unparalleled in history. Thus commonsense deduction suggests that the Judith author found the basic model for this story in legend not in recent historical events (as is commonly asserted). The Book of Judith is a saga—it is the story of a mighty hero; or what in a later context would be the story of a national saint. In it operates the familiar succession of *Les saints successeurs des dieux (paiens)*, i.e. the Hebrew saint Judith (the Jewess) embodies a pre-Israelite legend of a sometime God. Is it possible to recognize this legend from which the author derived his idea for a story of a superhuman woman set in and about Shechem at the end of the pre-Christian era—i.e. at a time when that ancient religious center of Israel had finally ceased to exist as a town?

Perhaps the most direct way to construe Bethouliah/Baitoulia etc. (the name given to the scene of the action) is simply (of) the Virgin (*Hbr Betulah*), i.e. the place (of the Temple of) the Virgin.[24] If there is any substance in this, then there is not far to seek for the mythical fore-runner of Judith—it is the goddess Anat, one of the best established goddesses known to the Western Semites.[25] She figures prominently in the Ugaritic legends where her divine epithet is regularly "the virgin" (*btlt*).[26] This epithet however does not refer to her corporeal status, it relates to her will. She is no one's creature but her own. She does or works her own will. This is so by definition since she is above all a warrior goddess, and as the poet correctly perceived, the happy warrior must possess this quality:

> So keep I fair through faith and prayer
> A virgin heart in work and will.

(I.e. she must not be conditioned by shackling personal relationships.)

Anat appears as a "companion" to Baal, her brother (possibly her step brother)/husband, notably in the Baal–Mot cycle[27] and in the legend of Aqhat.[28] Since, as everyone has realized, these two compositions work over the same theme,[29] they may be taken together so that the lacunae are reduced somewhat. First of all, in no particular context, a picture is painted of Anat's character. She is shown engaged in insensate slaughter of men—piling up severed heads (and hands) about her person as trophies (Caquot et al. 1974, 157–61; Gordon 1949, 17–18). Thus is established her violent murderous nature by way of the motif of the maiden with the severed head. Next, in an endeavor to redeem Baal from the bonds of death, Anat is shown in armed conflict with Mot (Death) whom she utterly annihilates, cutting him up into small pieces which she roasts and grinds (Caquot et al. 1974, 260; Gordon 1949, 45). In none of this, however, appears any reference to female guile and deception.

On the other hand, when we come to the Aqhat legend, details bring us appreciably closer to the Judith story. The myth of Baal's death and his eventual return to life aided by his sister's onslaught on Death is brought down to earth and set among princely heroes (i.e. it is transformed into legend or saga). Here Danel, the just king, plays the part of El; Aqhat (his son) of Baal; and Pgt (Aghat's sister "the maiden") of Anat. However since the deroulement of the action includes interludes in heaven, the divinities mentioned appear twice over—once in person and once in simulacrum. In the case of Anat, her role as a goddess is a very negative one and her role as a princess is the positive one.[30]

The essentials of the action are as follows. After prolonged mourning for Aqhat, during which all nature shares in the affliction (Caquot et al. 1974, 441–49; Gordon 1949, 94), Pgt (usually vocalized Pughat, Paghat) seeks out his slayer so as to avenge him (and secure his return to life) (Caquot et al. 1974, 455–56; Gordon 1949, 100). Unfortunately the achievement of her mission is not extant. However the preparations for it are very revealing. Pgt resolves on a combination of violence and trickery. She arms herself well with sword and dagger but conceals this beneath woman's clothes (Caquot et al. 1974, 456–57; Gordon 1949, 101). She then goes to find the "villain." He is a soldier by calling (Caquot et al. 1974, 437 [*m h r* = soldier, gallant], cf. 159; Gordon 1949, 92), specifically characterized as a "drinker" (Caquot et al. 1974, 437 [*s t* (+ Hbr *soteh*) = drinker], cf. 457) and his actions show him to be honorable and decently behaved. He demurred at the assassination he was called on to perform at superior behest (Caquot et al. 1974, 438–39; Gordon 1949, 92) and he receives Pgt in straightforward friendly fashion inviting her to drink with him (Caquot et al. 1974, 457; Gordon 1949, 100). And that is where the tablet breaks off, leaving Pgt with breast "like a snake" ready to deceive her host (Caquot et al. 1974, 458; Gordon 1949, 101).

Surely the combination of these two Ugaritic compositions provides sufficient evidence to assert the mythical/legendary background to the story of Judith. It comported the slaying of the death demon/enemy officer at a drinking party in the pavillion among tents by a murderous and deceitful goddess/young woman who carries off heads. All this action is manifestly set against a background of seasonal or cyclical affliction (drought and death) and its relief. The Aqhat legend from Ugarit is one version of this motif; the Judith author used as his source another similar version, a Canaanite one, the substance of which eventually went back to a basic myth possibly as domiciled in the old Canaanite religious centre of Shechem.[31]

If the preceding inquiry has correctly adduced the basic source for the Judith story, it now remains to hazard some explanation for the widespread prevalence of this motif (mythogem) of a young woman who has dealings with death in token of which she carries a severed head and to indicate how the Judith author found to hand a universal theme very appropriate to his purpose.

To begin in our own times: Jud 13:13, 18–20, depicts a sensational spectacle (tumultuous, joyful reception at the entrance to the city for a warrior returning with a severed head). This spectacle is not unique nor even is it highly unusual, for in certain parts of the world such a scene was a regular occurrence more or less into the present century. On his return, the successful head hunter in the Malay archipelago (e.g. in Borneo) was always greeted in this fashion, as the bearer of blessings upon the community (cf. Furness 1977, 65; Roth 1968, 167).

Head hunting was perhaps the feature of life in that region that most caught the attention of the outside world and numbers of people made close records of it from firsthand observation.[32] In the light of this there is no doubt that head hunting was not a random, incidental activity but was a highly regulated activity, in fact, a rite. Like many other customs, its ultimate significance or rationale was by no means always clear to its practitioners, and sometimes they gave confused and insignificant explanations of it. However the basic purport as evidenced in practice was generally understood. The significance of severing heads and their retention in and about the dwellings of the head hunters was a rite designed to release beneficent forces that would secure the blessings of the earth (material and spiritual) for the possessors of the head.[33] This is made clear by the occasions for taking and displaying heads, for example, seasonal agricultural ones, new enterprises in the way of plantations, and marriages: i.e., occasions where fortune could bring wealth, destruction or death.

In this connection, an aetiological legend from Borneo, which has been noticed several times, is rather graphic and worth quoting in substance (Furness 1977, 60).[34] A Dayak chieftain in Sarawak, ca. 1900, said to his interlocutor, "No Tuan, No, The custom (of head hunting) is not horrible. It is an ancient custom ... it brings us blessings, plentiful harvests and keeps off sickness and pain." Its traditional origin he then gave as follows. The great chief Tokong while bivouacing on a down-stream war expedition was spoken to by Kop (the frog). Kop told him that the chief and his people erred in taking only the hair of slain enemies and should take the whole head in a manner which Kop then demonstrated. Although repelled by this advice, the party eventually decided "to give it a try." And after successfully taking heads they found their return magically facilitated. The current was reversed, and like a flash, their boat was carried upstream and they reached home in no time at all. There they found that during the fifteen days they had been absent their newly planted rice crop had ripened for harvest. People who had been sick at their departure were now well, the lame could walk and the blind could see. Henceforward, not unnaturally, they decided to adhere to Kop's custom. All this clearly means to say that the Dayaks of Borneo adopted this custom from some "uncivilized" aboriginal people and found it beneficial, without ever understanding (the mystery) of its rationale.

The chief's story also points to the long anteriority of the custom in history. Ritual head hunting was prominent in several historical cultures and there is no difficulty in taking the tradition back to the period of the Judith story and its congeners.[35] Classical authors were most struck by its incidence among the Skyths (see Herodotus *Hist.* 4.6.4) and the Celts (see Diodoros V.29.4–5; Strabo IV 4–5). Particularly among the latter a wealth of information exists (both literary and archeological), extending from Medieval times to antiquity.[36] Fortunately, medieval Celtic romance encapsulated the custom in a manner that makes explicit its functional significance. The second branch of the Mainogion (a Welsh cycle of ca. the eleventh century AD) recounts the legend of Bran the Blessed, a Welsh king who warred (tragically) in Ireland and who possessed a magic cauldron, a vessel of regeneration, healing and plenty. At length dolorously wounded Bran instructed his companions to behead him and retain the severed head among them as a talisman (it is called the "noble head"). In the upshot the head was miraculously preserved without decay and kept Bran's followers together with good counsel in a paradisal state of plenty for eighty-seven years, after which it was buried in London to conserve the inviolability and prosperity of the realm (Ford 1977, 70).

In short, human sacrifice and division of human remains as typified in beheading is shown to be always in the interest of promoting salvation, deliverance from evil or "increase of life" (cosmic, social, individual). This is true among modern head hunters, as among pre-christian Celts and the Ugaritic representatives of ancient Near Eastern figures of myth and ritual, Anat, Baal and Mot.

All the foregoing well and truly accounts for the appropriateness of one half of the essential *personae* of the Judith story, the head (of Holofernes). However it affords little explanation for the other figure, the beautiful, young woman (Judith, the Maiden, Virgin Anat). Head hunting, as stated, is attested in many ages and places, yet never have the historical protagonists been women. On the other hand, myth and legend and romance concur in associating a young woman with the severed head. Why?

First of all the apparent gap can be narrowed. If in practice women do not obtain severed heads, they retain them. Generally speaking the heads kept in their houses by modern head hunters were treated with great respect. As befitted possessors of "mana," they were not to be handled lightly, but when it was necessary to carry them about on ceremonial occasions, this was done by women (Furness 1977, 65). Perhaps the most notable ceremonial occasions in which the heads took part were agricultural festivals (e.g. harvest festivals). Here, in the course of lavish feasting, the best of fare was offered to the heads by women and indeed rice was forced between their lips (Roth 1968, 173).

A similar picture is presented in modern times from a quite different tradition, that of the survival of a skull cult in the regional catholicism of Middle America.[37] In Guatemala a small community of Mayan stock kept three skulls on a side altar in the church and on the occasion of certain agricultural festivals one skull (in turn) is taken on procession through the village. Those households who have need of its blessings invite it to a ceremonial feast where it is received by the nubile woman of the household, given a place of honor, and offered the best food (Reina 1962, 27–35).

Clearly both the above customs are basically fertility and abundance rites based on the *date dabitur* principle linking (young) women and skulls. Literary reflection of such rites can be seen in the Welsh version of the Grail legend where the Grail maidens bear in a grail containing a severed head (Loomis 1930, 39–62; Weston 1923, 273–78; Goetinck 1975). Another such association is in the legend of John the Baptist, where the head is given into the keeping of the perverted maiden

Salome (Harrison 1916, 216–19; Wright 1988a, 415–25) (to dance with, according to general understanding, as did the womenfolk of the head hunters in Borneo at the "Feast of the Head").

These varied instances of women associated with the severed head demonstrate that a basic image is involved and further explanation probably belongs to the psychological plane[38] which is out of place here. However it may be possible to continue with the matter historically. If so, this would indeed arrive at the historical origin of a renowned symbol, "Death and the Maiden."

During the preceding generation a surprising body of evidence has been revealed of a very ancient skull cult or cult of the severed head (often fashioned into realistic effigy by delicate plaster modeling). These heads, which were apparently obtained in connection with the custom of secondary burial, were retained in the houses of pre-pottery Neolithic times (eighth to seventh millennia BC) and apparently indicated a cult of ancestor veneration.[39] In the nature of things, direct material evidence of their association with living women cannot be looked for, though some circumstantial evidence may be suggested of this association.

Such skulls have been found near the central hearths and also contained within wall benches—which were probably sleeping places (as indeed was the vicinity of the hearth) (Mellaart 1975, 96, 101–102, fig. 47; 1965, 82). One of the most striking discoveries made by modern anthropologists during the nineteenth century was that very primitive people did not generally subscribe to the physiological understanding of human reproduction. On the contrary, they asserted that this was affected by congress between young women and some manifestation of a defunct ancestor, so that all life took its origin literally as "life out of death."[40] One token of this understanding survives in the widespread custom of paponymy (see Hartland 1894, 220–23; Frazer 1909 III, 298).

In these circumstances it is possible to envisage that the skulls of the Neolithic skull cult served as vectors in the process of human fertility,[41] a process that might be considered a cult for which the earliest houses served as temples (cf. Raglan 1964).

Perhaps an attenuated survival of this understanding can be seen in certain beliefs associated with modern head hunting. Most observers have remarked on the fact that women often seem to be the instigators of the practice (Roth 1968, 181). For example, in Borneo, women would not marry a suitor unless he could offer a head as a marriage gift (i.e. unless he had "touched meat" as they phrased it); and an aetiological legend referred this custom back to a demand by the daughter of the great ancestor now living on the evening star (Roth 1968, 163). The obvious rationale is that without a head there was no guarantee for the man's potency, hearkening back to an original belief that it was the head itself that was the progenitor.

Should there be any substance in these speculations they would constitute an historical origin for the later image of the woman and the severed head—i.e. Death and the Maiden. However it must be noted that this congery does not *per se* account for the "head huntress" figure of myth and legend, e.g. Anat and Judith. Nothing is evident concerning who "took" these heads in Neolithic times and certainly there is no direct evidence to suggest this was done by (young) women.[42] Nevertheless conjectures have been made in this connection on the basis of very early wall paintings.

Principally at issue here is the famous Neolithic site of Çatal Hüyük in southern Turkey (seventh to sixth millennia BC) (Mellaart 1967). At this site there was ample direct evidence of a skull cult maintained in connection with funerary practices. Detached skulls were found set about the floors of rooms (Mellaart 1967, figs. 14, 15) or given separate burial, while disposal of the dead was by way of secondary burial following an excarnation in some way or another (Mellaart 1975, 101; 1965, 86). These practices are common in the Neolithic sites of the Near East.[43] However at Çatal Hüyük, exceptionally, considerable mural decoration was preserved, including motifs that were unmistakably of funerary significance (Mellaart 1967, 98). Among these were scenes where minatory birds of prey appear together with headless bodies to indicate that the heads had been ravaged off by the predators (Mellaart 1967, figs. 46, 47; 1965, fig. 62). This manifestly refers to exposure of the dead to predatory birds after the manner still kept up by modern Parsees, yet some versions of the birds of prey depict them with recognizably human legs (Mellaart 1965, fig. 66), and it has been deduced that "vulture priestesses" effected or presided over this work (Mellaart 1965 fig. 86), in which case these figures would stand behind the traditional vulture headdress of the mother goddess in token of her destructive role as "terrible mother."[44] This would also explain the concerns that the mother goddess is invested with in the Pyramid Texts for the severed head of the deceased Pharaoh.[45] Equally, this neolithic mortuary priestess could also be the ultimate reality that stands behind the persistent configuration in later myth, legend and romance of the "head huntress," a woman shown taking, holding or handling a severed head.

The above considerations have led the inquiry far distant from the Judith narrative. On all counts it is fitting to conclude by returning to the story.

The overall consonances that the model of the Judith story was a myth of slaying of the demon of dearth and death[46] to ensure the salvation/survival of communal life.[47] The essential demonstration is always in the detail, and in the Judith story there are two strange details that have no bearing upon the plot and whose significance is unexplained by anything within the story. It can only be concluded that their presence is to be explained by something outside the story. In other words, they appear in the story as fossils from an earlier age, and the author was compelled to include them because he found where they were functionally significant within his model. These two "meaningless" details in the Judith story are (1) the net (draped about Holofernes' divan) and (2) the fire (lit by the inhabitants of Bethouliah when Judith brings in the head).

The net. This is mentioned emphatically and insistently (Jud 13:9, 13:13, 16:19). After the slaying, Judith notices it and takes it, apparently as a trophy (13:9). All the commentators are puzzled about the action and give various trivial explanations.[48] Furthermore, when the spoils of war are dedicated in Jerusalem, again the net is singled out for attention (16:19). Yet this net plays no functional part in the story. The action would have transpired in exactly the same way without any mention of it. But, it may be interjected, the net could have been made functional. Judith could well have entangled the drunken Holofernes in this net so as to deprive him of the possibility of warding off her strokes. A prototype for this immediately comes to mind in the similar circumstances at the climax of the Agamemnon where Clytemnestra entangles Agamemnon in a net-like robe so he can be the more conveniently dispatched by the sword.[49] In fact we are here dealing with manifestations of a basic symbol that occurs in many mythologies.[50] It signifies the network from which there is no escape, in which we are all trapped—the web of fate, universal order;[51] and it is often the attribute of the Goddess who is reckoned a weaver (of destiny), e.g. Greek Athena and Egyptian Neath, the two deities who are most identified with Anat.[52] This net is often present in the myths of the slaying of the adversary, the monster who prevents the world.[53] Marduk has the net when he tackles Tiamat[54] and more immediately to hand, Asherat instructs Kothar to use the net as a fisherman when he is to overcome Yam.[55] There can be no doubt that the mythical figure who stood behind Holofernes was netted before, at, or after being despatched by the sword. Chaos was subdued to the bonds of cosmic order, and that is why the Judith author conspicuously retained it in his story.

The fire. When Judith walks back to the Gate of Bethouliah carrying Holofernes' severed head, it is still night, or at least it is not yet day. She announces herself and is let in and when she tells her story and exhibits the head, all those on the scene immediately light a great fire so that they can see the head (Jud 13:13). The lighting of a fire is instinctively felt to be a suitable reaction, but hardly so that those present can see the head. All they have to do is to bring lamps or torches or go to where these are found. Yet we recognize that the lighting of a bonfire is a suitable mark of recognition of Judith's victorious deed, for here again is a basic symbol that is immediately relevant to the myth behind the Judith story. With the slaying of the demon who has threatened the community with death, a new life is inaugurated, and lighting a great fire is exactly the symbol for this.[56] It is the new fire for old that indicates the return of new life and salvation—and nature's model for this is the return of the sun. Such fire rites (festivals, ceremonies) are always enacted at a time consonant with this return of the sun, seasonal as diurnal (of our Christmas Yule fires).[57]

It is also possible that another salient property appearing in the story can be subject to mythological analysis, even though it plays a highly functional role in the action and is not obviously a fossil from a mythological past. The property concerned is the bag that Judith's maid carries about everywhere and that enables the murderess to carry off the head unobserved.[58] This bag contains choice food offerings, the rich sustenance of the earth. Like many other bags or baskets, it should originally have symbolized the earth, i.e. the source of all riches.[59] Placing the severed head in the bag was probably a ritual act designed to restore or ensure the earth's yield of blessings in the face of dearth.[60] The aspect of the severed head as a good provider is attested in a number of legends, the most obvious case being the famous story of Bran in the Mabinogion (Ford 1977).

The conclusion to the foregoing remarks is that the Judith author took a basic image of cosmic effect that survived in local legends and applied it in political analogy as a work of fiction intended as a national morale booster. He did this as a very competent man of letters, possessed of talent and wide scholarship in both languages current in his milieu, Greco-Roman Palestine. Whether or not his work served its political purpose, it was certainly very readable with nothing ridiculous or primitive about it. Today it would sell well or be adapted for radio.

NOTES

1. For standard introductions and commentaries see Metzger (1961, 43), Torrey (1945, 88), Buttrick (1962, 1023), Hastings (1928 III, 822–24), Moore (1984), Enselin (1972).
2. The Book of Judith appeared in the Septuagint and on this account is regarded a canonical by the Roman Catholic and Greek Orthodox Churches but is not recognized by other (e.g. protestant) Churches. It never gained a place in the Palestinian canon of the Jewish scriptures.
3. Compare Mozart's very dramatic oratorio Bethulia Liberata and the well known masterpieces of Renaissance Art by Donatello, Michelangelo, Mantegna and Botticelli (cf. for convenience, Moore 1984, ills. 4–9). A complete fine arts biography of Judith is to be found in Montly (1978, 37–42).
4. Holofernes' obvious plan of campaign is to march westward across the Gezira to Cilicia (and further into southern Anatolia), then south from Aleppo to Damascus and beyond into Ammonite and Moabite territory, next to cross the Jordan at Beth Shan or the like and march westward to the Phoenecian coast via the Plain of Esdraelon. However every effort is made to confuse and obscure this natural itinerary—for example, Put and Lud could signify Anatolian regions but they could also refer to Africa. For a detailed study see Stummer (1947).
5. The bipartite structure is unmistakable with noticeable difference in literary quality between the two parts; the first part long drawn out, the second part very moving (Buttrick 1962, 1023).
6. This quality of (literary) irony has been made much of by Moore (1984, 78–85): "the storyteller had a mind and a perspective which are best described as essentially and profoundly ironic."

7. For a brief account of the texts and versions (Greek, Hebrew and Latin) see Hastings (1928 II, 822–23).

8. The literary quality of Judith has always evoked praise. It has been called, for example, "a masterpiece of ancient ... narrative art .... The book displays a high degree of excellence in story telling" (Hastings 1928 II, 824). As to the author's knowledgeability, Judith certainly evidences his close familiarity with the bible, echoing e.g. Genesis (34); Judges (4:4–42 and 15:2–31); also Esther and Daniel. Additionally it is possible to read into Judith some acquaintance with Greek literature. The close parallel has been noted between the preliminary scene to the invasion of Jewish territory by Holofernes and that to the invasion of Greece by Xerxes (as given in Herodotus VII). N.B. the defence of the narrow pass, the conversation of the potentate with the local defector and the advice of the latter (Momigliano 1982, 227–28).

9. I.e., it was resistance literature (Moore 1984, 46).

10. If, as it seems, Judith was written after the successful campaigns of John Hyracanus against Shechem and Samaria and probably in the first century BC, there seems little point in disguising references to Antiochos IV and his campaigns—except in the sense that these events were so recent as to make an extravaganza somewhat ridiculous.

11. Hastings (1928 II, 823): "present or recent history disguised under significant names." Cf. Moore (1984, 46).

12. This allegory was forcibly expressed by Luther in the preface to Judith in his translation of the Bible. "Judith in the Jewish people represented as a chaste and holy widow." Luther goes on to complete the allegory by representing Holofernes as the heathen and explaining Bethouliah as derived from the Hebrew for virgin (thus indicating the purity of the land of Israel) (Metzger 1961, 43).

13. It is clear that the only coherent historical references relate to this period. Holofernes and Bagoas are attested as commanders of the punitive expedition dispatched by Artaxerxes III against Phoenecia and Egypt. Towards the end of the reign of Artaxerxes II (ca. 300 BC) Egypt interfered in the Syro-Palestinian coast land leading to a Phoenecian revolt. The Jews became involved in the unrest. When Persia restored order, measures were taken against the Jews—Jericho was destroyed and many people were carried off into captivity in Babylonia and Hyrcania see Oesterly (1932, 139–41).

14. An immediate account of these events is contained in the first Book of Maccabees, although this cannot be regarded in any way as objective history. However all the events are also recorded by several Greek historians.

15. A convenient general background to this period can be found in the classic works of Bevan (1927).

16. For Nicanor see Hastings (1928 III, s.v.).
17. For Alexander Balas see Bevan (1927, 303–305).
18. A brief account of the dramatic struggle between Rome and Parthia as it affected Syria can be found in College (1967), and also Perowne (1956).
19. The standard source is Plutarch, *Crassus* XXIII.
20. A convenient survey appears in Montly (1978, 37–42).
21. According to Josephus, writing a generation or so after the events, Herod had John executed ca. 30 AD (*Antiquities of the Jews* XVIII.V). The legend involving the perverse eroticism and evil machinations of the womenfolk appears in all the gospels, its principal statement being Mark 6:17. For some outline of its subsequent development see Wright (1988a, 417–25; 1992, 22–36).
22. The critical literature on the Grail is endless. A convenient *mise-en point* with indications of origins is Loomis (1963).
23. E.g., in the Peredur version, see Goetinck (1975), and cf. Loomis (1930, 39–62) and Weston (1923, 273).
24. This construction has not been much favored by the commentators.
25. The literature on Anat is now very extensive. For recent monographs see Kapelrud (1969) and Cassut (1971). A convenient summary account is given in Caquot et al. (1974, 85–92). A good analysis appears in Edzard (1965, 235–41).
26. Cf. Caquot et al. (1974, 89). The invariable formula is simply (The) Virgin Anat or The Maid Anat (does, says thus and thus).
27. The association was emphasized by Gordon (1943). A convenient source with succinct commentary is Caquot et al. (1974, 144). A similar but earlier work is Gordon (1949, 3).
28. See Caquot et al. (1974, 401–80), Gordon (1949, 84–103). Now see also the encyclopedic monograph, Margalit (1989).
29. See Caquot et al. (1974, 409–10), citing views of Aisleitner, Eissfeldt, Dussaud, Stocks, Kopelrud.
30. For a good commentary see Caquot et al. (1974, 402–15). *Pgt* as a common noun = young girl, daughter; i.e. as a name it is exactly equivalent to the Greek *kore*. However in this text the close association of *Pgt* with water sources suggests the sense of springs possibly parallel to Anat; cf. the Greek *pege*; note also the famous springs near Damascus, Ain Figi.
31. To avoid overloading the discussion with side issues, the relationship between Palestinian and Ugaritic versions of the myth has been stated in the broadest evolutionary fashion. However it is quite possible to adduce very definite argument for the diffusion of such a myth to Palestine (and to Ugarit!). The relevance of Ugaritic texts to Israelite tradition—or rather, how to explain the manifest parallels that are apparent—has been

a much discussed subject. However the motif referred to here, as exemplified specifically in the Aqhat legend, constitutes a very special issue. It cannot be overlooked that of all the Ugaritic texts this legend displays the greatest affinities with the Old Testament. Daniel (Aqhat's father) is cited by Ezekiel (1:14, 20) as a by-word for rectitude. And this special position seems hardly accidental since intrinsic evidence in the text appears to localize the setting of the story in Galilee about the shores of Lake Genessereth, and thus much nearer at hand to Shechem than to Ugarit (see Margalith 1981, reaffirming the earlier perceptions of Barton and de Vaux). It has been maintained that the legend was carried to Ugarit by a dynasty deriving from the Rephaim tribes of the region, Danel's home being Bashan (Margalith 1981, 151–58). The goddess Anat was certainly known to the Canaanites (cf. the Beth Shan stele [ca. 1200 BC], which shows an Egyptianised Anat who is invoked as "Antit, Lady of Heaven and Mistress of all the Gods,") (Gray 1965, 229 fig. 23). For evidence from Biblical onomastics and its concentration in Northern Israel see Kapelrud (1969, 10–12), and Edzard (1965, 236–37). On the other hand, Gordon (1967) appears to take the simple position that "the Ugarit Epic of Anat was (*itself*) known to the Hebrews."

32. An encyclopedic account of the subject is given in Roth (1968, 140–83).

33. Cf. Roth (1968, 143): "to make their rice grow well, to cause the forest to abound with wild animals, to enable their dogs and snares to be successful in securing game, to have the streams swarm with fish, to give health and activity to the people themselves and to ensure fertility to their women."

34. It is also given in more summary form in Furness (1899, 14–15); and it is quoted, e.g. in Hastings (1928, 239).

35. For a brief outline, see Meslin (1987, 222–23). Cf. also *Encyclopedia Britannica* (1971 17, 201–203).

36. For summary information see MacCana in Eli 6, 2256) with good bibliography (note Lambrechts [1954], and Sterck [1981]).

37. For the background in classical Middle America see Moser (1973).

38. E.g. in the ghastly Tibetan Chod (= severing) exercise, the emanation that decapitates the practitioner is visualized as a woman with a sword.

39. For example, at Jericho, Mureybit, Tell Abu Hureyra, and Ain Ghazal (see Mellaart 1975, 47, 50, 54, 59, 60–62, 78, 96, 103, 119). An effective survey of the custom is H.-D. Biernert (1991, 9–23).

40. It was the researches of Spencer and Gillen (1969) on the aborigines of northern and central Australia that originally defined the question. The very extensive ambit involved in this subject was covered by two encyclopedia anthropologists, Frazer (1909) and Hartland (1894; 1909; 1921). A good animation of the understanding is given by Malinowski (1954, 215, 271).

41. It seems obvious that the disposition of mortal remains near the hearth fire (cf. the classical Lares) and sleeping places associates the dead ancestors with the creation of life. Equally it has been taken for granted that the retention among the living of the severed head is a cult practice to link the dead and the living as closely as possible; see Wright (1995). For the potency of the head, see Wright (1988b, 51–56).

42. This is precisely the milieu that exemplifies the limitations of archaeological evidence.

43. See note 39.

44. Best-known as the headdress of Isis.

45. E.g., "Mut will give you back your head" in *Pyramid Texts I*: 110 (available in Faulkner 1969).

46. Parallel with the terrible, destructive might of Holofernes (the mythical monster) there is implicit another negative side to this figure. If caricatured as in folktale, the character of Holofernes falls into the category of the foolish, gullible giant. His over credulous (and over indulgent) nature invites deception and destruction by shrewd mortals. There are two hundred variants of the type in Stith Thompson's Standard Index (I nos. 1000–1199).

47. Anat comes out strongly in the Ugaritic texts as the deity who "kills and makes alive again," i.e. brings life out of death (cf. Gray 1965).

48. This matter is summarized in Moore (1984, 227) where the author gives a list of previous explanations advanced for Judith's taking the net and so introducing it into the narrative (e.g. "to substantiate her story," a woman's attraction to finery etc). He then goes beyond these "explanations" by saying "more pleasure is provided the reader by leaving some details out than by explaining them in full."

49. Cf. Agamemnon 115: Cassandra "Is it a net of death"; 1381: Clytemnestra "Round him as though to catch a haul of fish I cast an impassable net ... so that he should neither escape nor ward off doom"; Cheophoros 989; Orestes: "it is a net, a hunting net you might call it."

50. Cf. generally Webs and Nets in Eliade (1987 15, 367–68). The cosmic sense of the imagery is clearly indicated in China "The Net of heaven is wide meshed but lets nothing through" (cf. Wilhelm 1925). For the significance of the net as the net of fate and world order in Egypt see Kristensen (1949, 67–76). For the biblical application see Lurker (1973, 102–103; note also Eisler 1921). In the East this net assumes a sinister, negative aspect; it is the attribute of "Crooked" Varuna in India.

51. As evoked by the poet: "The branches close above our eyes, the skies are in a net. And what is it beneath the skies, that we would most forget?"

52. For Neath see Edzard (1965, 379–80), Bonnet (1971, 516–17), and Kristensen (1992, 155, 158), for Neath and Athena as weavers (of

destiny). The most striking and interesting evidence for the identification of Anat with Athena occurs in Cyprus. A bilingual rock cut inscription near Lapethos (*Larnaka tés Lapethou*) makes the identification directly (CIS I 95). While at Idalion there are separate inscriptions in Greek and in Phoenecian referring to the sanctuary on the western Acropolis indicating that the Goddess was known both as Anat and Athena (RES 453, 1209, 1210). See Caquot et al. (1974, 88), and Ohnefalsch-Richter (1893, 16, 223, 299). The Lapethos bilingual is extremely interesting in the present context. As Anat, the Goddess is characterized as "force/strength of life," which is exactly the idea of the Indian Shaki, and that of the anima in modern psychology. While Athena is characterized by the epithets *Soteira Nike*, surely the exact epitome of the Judith figure, who was indeed Anat the victorious savior.

53. For cosmogonies by way of combat with the monster see Eliade (1987 4, 95, 432) and Wakeman (1973).

54. Marduk has the net when he tackles Tiamat. See *Enuma Elish*, trans. Speiser in Pritchard (*ANET* 66–67): "He then made a net to enfold Tiamat .... Close to his side he held the net, the gift of his father Anu." After he had slain Tiamat, Marduk turned against her followers "thrown into the net, they found themselves ensnared." In one version Marduk nets the monster before cutting off her head, the exact model for the logical reconstruction of Judith's murder.

55. "Take a net in your hand ... a large net raise up against Yam." This matter is commented on by Gaster in his translation of Baal and Yam (1961, 177–78).

56. For fire as a life symbol, see Wright (1987, 156–57); cf. Gaster (1961, 293–94) for comparative background. It is, of course, also possible to refer the compulsive introduction of the fire at this juncture to another (utilitarian) connection. It is very general practice that heads taken in head hunting are "cured" for keeping. Thus virtually the first thing done with the head on safe return is to hang it up over an open fire so that it can be desiccated and smoked. In this way vestigial traces of primitive ritual may obtain here.

57. See Gaster (1961, 270–75) for comparative background. The immediate connection is the Yuzgat Tablet, which Gaster characterizes as a Hittite Yuletide Myth.

58. It is interesting to note that this boy also turns up as a property in the Aghat Legend. Here essentially the same slaying scenario is run through twice, once with a divine protagonist (Anat) and once with his princess surrogate *Pgt*. In the former killing Anat equips herself with a bag in which she conceals her bravo (both disguised as vultures?) and thus makes an air strike on her victim (for a good commentary, see Gaster 1961, 354–55).

59. Note especially the basket called the "mystery chest" which contained the sacred objects of the Eleusinian mysteries. In spite of the secrecy it is known that these comprised pastries, and sweetmeats among other things—symbols of the produce of the earth. Equally the chest of the Dionysos cult which contained similar images of renewal and mystery is, of course, life out of Death. There are also exact parallels in Egypt connected with the Osiris cult. For general consideration see Kristensen (1949, 221–26, fig 65).

60. Cf. the *epopteia* and the initiates logion at Eleusis: "Having done the act I put again into the basket" (Clement of Alexandria, *Protepticus*, II, 21). Needless to say the significance of these phrases has been very variously interpreted (see Eliade 1958, 110–11).

REFERENCES

Bevan, E.
  1927   The House of Seleucus. *A History of Egypt under the Ptolemaic Dynasty*. New York: Methuen.
Biernert, H.-D.
  1991   Skull Cults in the Prehistoric Near East. *Journal of Prehistoric Religion* 5: 9–23.
Bonnet, H.
  1971   *Reallexikon der Agyptishen Relgionsgeschichte*. Berlin: de Gruyter.
Buttrick, G. A. *et al*.
  1962   *The Interpreter's Dictionary of the Bible*. New York: Abingdon.
Caquot, A.; Sznycer, M.; and Herdner, A.
  1974   *Textes Ougaritiques I. Mythes et Legendes*. Paris: Éditions du Cerf.
Cassut, U.
  1971   *The Goddess Anath*. Jerusalem: Magnes.
Colledge, M.
  1967   *The Parthian Period*. Leiden: Brill.
Eisler, R.
  1921   *Orpheus the Fisher*. London: Kessinger.
Eliade, M., ed.
  1958   *Rites and Symbols of Initiation*. New York: Spring Publications.
  1987   *The Encyclopedia of Religion*. New York: Macmillan.
Enselin, M. S.
  1972   The Book of Judith. *Jewish Apocryphal Literature* VII. Leiden: Brill.

Edzard, D. O. *et al.*
1965   *Götter und Mythen im Vorderen Orient: Wörterbuch der Mythologie.* Stuttgart: E. Klett.

Faulkner, R. D.
1969   *Ancient Pyramid Texts.* Oxford: Aris & Phillips.

Ford, P. K.
1977   *The Mabinogion.* London: University of California.

Frazer, Sir J.
1909   *Totemism and Exogamy* I–IV. London: Macmillan.

Furness, W. H.
1977   *The Home-life of Borneo Head Hunters. Its Festivals and Folk Lore.* Reprint of the 1902 edition. London: AMS

Gaster, T.
1961   *Thespis: Ritual, Myth, and Drama in the Ancient Near East.* New York: Norton.

Gordon, C. H.
1943   *The Loves and Wars of Ba'al and Anat.* Princeton: Princeton University.
1949   *Ugaritic Literature.* Rome: Pontificium Institutum Biblicum.
1967   *Ugarit and Minoan Crete.* New York: Norton.

Goetinck, C.
1975   *Peredur: A Study of Welsh Tradition in the Grail Legend.* Cardiff: University of Wales.

Gray, J.
1965   *The Legacy of Canaan.* Leiden: Brill.

Harrison, J.
1916   The Head of John the Baptist. *Classical Review* 30: 216–19.

Hartland, E. S.
1894   *The Legacy of Perseus.* London: Gordon.
1909   *Primitive Paternity.* London: D. Nutt.
1921   *Primitive Society.* London: D. Nutt.

Hastings, J.
1928   *Dictionary of the Bible.* New York: Scribner's.

Kapelrud, A. S.
1969   *The Violent Goddess. Anat in the Ras Shamra Texts.* Oslo: Universitets Forlaget.

Kirstensen, W. B.
1949   *Het Leven uit de dood* Haarlem: Ervin F. Bohn.
1992   *Life Out of Death.* Louvain: Peeters.

Lambrechts, P.
1954   *L'exaltation de la tete dans le pensée et dans l'art des Celtes.* Brugge: De Tempel.

Loomis, R. S.
1963   *The Grail Peredur.* Princeton: Princeton University.
1930   The Head in the Grail. *Revue Celtique* 47: 39–62.
Lurker, M.
1973   *Wörterbuch biblischer Bilder und Symbole.* Munich: Otto
          Wilhelm Barth.
MacCana, P.
1987   The Celtic Head Cult. Pp. 225–26 in *Encyclopedia of Religion* 6,
          ed. M. Eliade. New York: Macmillan
Malinowski, B.
1954   *Magic, Science and Religion and Other Essays.* New York:
          Doubleday Anchor.
Margalit, B.
1981   The Geographic Setting of the Aqhat Story. In *Ugarit in
          Retrospect,* ed. G.D. Young. Winona Lake, IN: Eisenbrauns.
1989   *The Ugaritic Poem of Aght.* Berlin: de Gruyter.
Mellart, J.
1965   *Earliest Civilizations of the Near East.* London: New York:
          McGraw-Hill.
1967   *Çatal Hüyük: A Neolithic Town in Anatolia.* New York:
          McGraw Hill.
1975   *The Neolithic of the Near East.* London: Thames and Hudson.
Meslin, M.
1987   Head. Pp. 221–25 in *The Encyclopedia of Religion* 6, ed. M.
          Eliade. New York: Macmillan.
Metzger, B. M.
1961   *An Introduction to the Apocrypha.* Oxford: Oxford University.
Momigliano, A.
1982   Biblical Studies and Classical Studies: Simple Reflections about
          Historical Method. *Biblical Archaeologist* 45: 224–28.
Montly, P.
1978   Judith as Androgyne. *Anima* 4: 37–42.
Moore, C. A.
1984   *Judith.* Anchor Bible. New York: Doubleday Anchor.
Moser, C. L.
1973   Human Decapitation in Ancient Meso-America. *Dumbarton
          Studies in Precolumbian Art and Archaeology No. 11.*
          Washington, D.C.: Trustees for Harvard University.
Ohnefalsch-Richter, M.
1893   *Kypros, the Bible and Homer: Oriental Civilization, Art, and
          Religion in Ancient Times.* London: Asher.

Osterly, W.
1932   *A History of Israel*. Oxford: Oxford University.
Perowne, S.
1956   *The Life and Times of Herod the Great*. New York: Abingdon.
Raglan, Lord F. R. S.
1964   *The Temple and the House*. New York: Norton.
Reina, R. E.
1962   The Ritual of the Skull in Guatemala. *Expedition* 4.4: 27–35.
Roth, H. L.
1968   *The Natives of Sarawak and British North Borneo*. reprint of 1896 edition. Kuala Lumpur: University of Malay.
Rowe, A.
1931   *The Topography and History of Beth Shan*. Philadelphia: Publications of the Palestine Section of the Museum of the University of Pennsylvania.
Spencer, B., and Gillen, F. J.
1969   *The Native Tribes of Central Australia*. Reprint of 1899 edition. New York: Dover.
Sterck, C.
1981   *La Mutilation Rituelle*. Saarbrucken.
Stummer, F.
1947   *Geographie des Buches Judith*. Stuttgart: Kath.
Torrey, C. C.
1899   The Site of Bethulia. *Journal of the American Oriental Society* 20: 160–72.
1945   *The Apocryphal Literature*. New Haven: Yale University.
Wakeman, M. K.
1973   *God's Battle with the Monster*. Leiden: Brill.
Weston, J.
1923   Notes on the Grail Romances. *Romania* 49: 273–78.
Wilhelm, R.
1925   *Lao Tse und der Taoismus*. Stuttgart: F. Frommann.
Wright, G. R. H.
1987   *As On the First Day*. Leiden: Brill.
1988a   The Noble Head in Transjordan. *Damaszener Mittenlungen* 3: 417–25.
1988b   The Severed Head in Earliest Neolithic Times. *Journal of Prehistoric Religion* 2: 51–56.
1992   *Obiter Dicta*. London.
1995   The Houses of the Dead and of Birth. Pp. 15–26 in *Studies in Honour of J. Basil Hennessy*. Mediterranean Archaeology Supplement 3. Sydney.

APPENDIX I

During the preceding discussion, on numerous occasions references have been made to the account in Genesis 34 of the discomfiture by Simeon and Levi of the gentile Shechemites. This was considered significant by the Judith author who mentioned it at various junctures and overtly regarded it as in some measure a parallel that could be used to justify and magnify the deeds of Judith. Although on the face of it, it is apparent that the two episodes have a basically similar cast of features, it is perhaps not obvious how narrowly they can be brought into relationship when their component elements are isolated out. These comprise in both instances four items: foreign incursion, rape, deceit, and slaughter.

Consider the following table:

Simeon and Levi	Judith
Foreign Invaders (Hebrews at Shechem).	Foreign Invaders (Gentile "Assyrians" at Shechem).
"Rape" (of Hebrew girl, Dinah, by gentile notable, Shechem son of Hamor the Hivite).	"Rape" (*in mentem* of Hebrew woman, Judith, by gentile commander, Holofernes).
Deceit (by Hebrews, Simeon and Levi, of gentile Shechemites and their leaders).	Deceit (by Hebrew woman, Judith, of gentiles and their commander, Holofernes).
Slaughter by Hebrews, Simeon and Levi, of gentile Shechemite leader and other citizens	Slaughter by Hebrew woman, Judith, of gentile commander Holofernes, and later of bulk of his army.

As an instance of closer affinity, that in each case the "rape" must be put in quotation marks, since it is doubtful whether any court would so assess it today. In fact the delectus exists solely in the Hebrew religious code regarding association of Hebrew women with gentiles. In both instances the gentile is shown to have behaved most considerately.

The likeness in structure between the two Shechem episodes is a fact. What if anything is to be inferred from it is best left to individual understanding since this may be based on very disputed theory. There is, of course, a (polar) difference in the upshot. The actions of Simeon and Levi evoke shame with recrimination; those of Judith salvation with rejoicing.

APPENDIX II

Some commentators have observed that the Judith author had a knowledge of Greek literature. Momigliano has drawn attention to the extended parallel between the tactical situation at the opening of Holofernes' campaign against Israel and that of Xerxes against Greece in 480 BC as recounted in Herodotos VII; in both cases there is an unexpected defence of a narrow pass in the face of vastly superior forces prompting the invader to question a "renegade" in his service (Momigliano 1982, 227–28). While by no means the end of the matter, this is a telling observation, and there is other material of similar interest. Indeed it is possible to see well-known episodes in Greek history as providing models for various tactical details of the action in Judith.

In the first place it is surprising how similar in spirit is the interlocution between the grandee and the renegade, with the emphasis of the renegade on his absolute truth and sincerity, and the evocation of consequent ridicule. The Spartan Demeratos says to Xerxes (*Hist.* VII.209), "you heard from my mouth at a former time when we were setting forth to go to Hellas, the things concerning these men; and having heard them you made me an object of laughter (laughing stock) because I told you of these things which I perceived would come to pass; for to me the greatest of all ends is to speak the truth continually before you, O King" while Achior (the leader of the Ammonite levies) says to Holofernes (Jud 5:5): "My Lord if you will allow your servant to speak, I will tell you the truth about this nation that lives in the hill country near here; and no lie shall pass my lips," and further (Jud 5:21): "But if these people have committed no wickedness leave them alone my Lord for fear the God they serve should protect them and we become the laughing stock of the world."

Equally, or even more to the point, is the following circumstance: Staring out of Judith's plan of campaign at the "Assyrian Camp" is the image of another famous battle in Greek history, a battle that marked the end of the century ushered in by Thermopolae, as it marked the end of Athenian glory. Judith's plan rests on her ability to escape from the "Assyrian Camp" since hers is not a suicide mission; indeed it would not work the deliverance of the Jewish people if it were. Moreover, it is immediately apparent to the reader that the "escape route" evidences a notable cleverness.

There is nothing very remarkable in a physically attractive woman finding an opportunity to assassinate in private an eminent man (as Charlotte Corday [and Tosca] demonstrate). But afterwards to return unscathed out of the gates of hell "that is the task, that is the labor" (*hoc opus, hic labor est*). And it is precisely "the intelligence disposed here which stamps Judith's deeds as rather wonderful. For she made nice use of a device highly esteemed in the art of war, that of misleading the enemy. But did the author invent *ad hoc* Judith's clever tactics?

He represents Judith as establishing a routine in the Assyrian Camp whereby she regularly goes out of the camp to the spring, which is actually in no man's land between the camp and the beleaguered city. She and her maid do this on the pretence of making their necessary ritual ablutions and praying to the national God of her people (only effective in home territory). All this constitutes reasonable grounds for her otherwise very suspicious movements. Having effectively lulled suspicions, she is able to make her escape in the most direct way and mislead the enemy.

It is doubtful that Judith's scheme is an obvious device likely to occur of itself to any writer of romance. On the other hand it is exactly paralleled in the historical circumstances of the Athenian defeat at Aegaspotami in 405 BC by the Spartans under Lysander. The events are reported by Xenophon in *Hellenika* II.7.20–28 (and they are also recapitulated twice by Plutarch, once in his life of Alcibiades, and once in his life of Lysander). It is worthwhile giving abstracts of the two ruses. First Judith's stratagem (Jud 12:5):

> Shortly before the morning watch she got up and sent this message to Holofernes: "My Lord, will you give orders for me to be allowed to go out and pray." Holofernes ordered his bodyguard to let her pass. She remained in the camp for three days, going out each night into the valley of Bethoulia and bathing at the spring. When she came up from the spring she prayed the Lord the God of Israel to prosper her undertaking to restore her people. Then she returned to the camp purified. On the following day Holofernes gave a banquet for his personal servants only (as an occasion for seducing Judith, but instead she beheads him). Then the two of them (she and her maid) went out together as they had usually done for prayer. Through the camp they went, and round that valley and up to the hill to Bethoulia till they reached the Gate.

Now let us examine Lysander's stratagem. The Athenian fleet has followed the Spartans to the Chersonese where Lysander has taken the town of Lampsacus on the Asiatic shore and stationed his fleet there. The Athenians take their station at Aegospotami opposite on the European shore less than two miles away:

> When early dawn came Lysander gave the signal for his men to take breakfast and embark upon their ships and after making everything ready for battle … he gave orders that no one should stir from his position or put out. At sunrise the Athenians (sailed over from Aegospotami and) formed their ships in line for battle at the mouth of the harbour. Since however Lysander did not put out against them, they sailed back again to Aegospotami when it grew late in the day. Thereupon Lysander ordered the swiftest of his

ships to follow the Athenians and when they had disembarked to observe what they did and report it to him and he did not disembark his men from their vessel until these scout-ships had returned. The Athenians continued to sail over and offer battle for four days and Lysander continued the same practice .... And now Lysander on the fifth day the Athenians sailed over against him told his men, who followed them back, that as soon as they saw that the enemy had disembarked and had scattered up and down the Chersonese—and the Athenians did this far more freely every day, not only because they bought their provisions at a distance, but also because they presumed to think lightly of Lysander for not putting out to meet them—they were to sail back to him and hoist a shield when midway in their course .... Straightway Lysander gave a signal to the fleet to sail with all speed .... Now when Conon saw the coming attack he signaled the Athenians to hasten with all their might to their ships. But since his men were scattered here and there some of the ships were entirely empty. (Eight Athenian Ships alone escaped.) But all the rest Lysander captured on the beach. He also gathered up on the shore most of the men of their crews. (Xenophon, *Hellenika* 11.1.20–28)

The full effect of the stratagem is best stated in Plutarch's words:

Lysander took three thousand men prisoner together with the generals and captured the whole fleet .... He had wrought a work of the greatest magnitude with the least toil and effort, and had brought to a close in a single hour a war...which had surpassed all its predecessors .... Yet it was brought to a close by the prudence and ability of one man. (*Lysander* 5)

Just as the Hebrew author says of Judith (15:10), "you are the glory of Jerusalem, the heroine of Israel ... with your own hand you have done all this"

Thus it would appear that the author of Judith drew as much on a knowledge of Greek history as of Jewish history in rendering his narrative humanly plausible, i.e., in his representation of an ancient myth or folktale as recent history in the interest of romanticized propaganda.

ADDITIONAL SOURCES*

Astell, A. W.
 1989   Holofernes's Head: Tacen and Teaching in the Old English Judith. Pp. 117–33 in *Anglo-Saxon England* 18, ed. P. Clemoes, et al. Cambridge: Cambridge University.

Bal, M.
  1994   Head Hunting: "Judith" on the Cutting Edge of Knowledge. *Journal for the Study of the Old Testament* 63: 3–34.
Craven, T.
  1983   Tradition and Convention in the Book of Judith. Semeia 28: 49–61.
Day, P. L.
  1991   Why is Anat a Warrior and Hunter? Pp. 141–46 in *The Bible and the Politics of Exegesis*, ed. D. Jobling. Cleveland: Pilgrim.
Henten. J.
  1994   Judith as a Female Moses: Judith 7–13 in the Light of Exodus 17, Numbers 20, and Deut 33:8–11. Pp 33–48 in *Reflections on Theology and Gender*, ed. F. van Dijk-Hemmes. Kampen: Kok Pharos.
  1995   Judith as Alternative Leader: A Rereading of Judith 7–13. Pp. 224–52 in *A Feminist Companion to Esther, Judith and Susanna*, ed. A Brenner. Sheffield: Sheffield Academic.
Meltzer, E. S.
  1972   Horus *dn* "cutter" "severer" (of heads?). *Journal of Near Eastern Studies* 31: 338–39.
Milne, P. J.
  1993   What Shall We Do With Judith? A Feminist Reassessment of a Biblical "Heroine." *Semeth* 62: 37–58.
Moore, C. A.
  1990   Judith: The Case of the Pious Killer. *Bible Review* 6: 26–36.
Philpot, E.
  1993   Judith and Holofernes: Changing Images in the History of Art. Pp. 80–97 in *Translating Religious Texts*, ed. D. Jasper. New York: St. Martin's.
Stocker, M.
  1990   Biblical Story of The Heroine. Pp. 81–102 in *The Bible as Rhetoric*, ed. M. Warner. New York: Routledge.
White, S. A.
  1992   In the Steps of Jack and Deborah: Judith as Heroine. Pp. 5–16 in *No One Spoke Ill of Her: Essays on Judith*, ed. J. Vanderkam. Atlanta: Scholars.

*The Judith story and head-huntress themes have been the topics of a number of recent studies noted here. *Ed.*

12 An Odyssey of Love and Hate

HUGH R. HARCOURT

It is necessary to heed legends, those traces of collective endeavor through the centuries, and surmise from them, as much as possible, the meaning of our destiny. There are several points of human activity around which through all time, slowly and in fine layers, legends appear. Long bewildered by what took place directly around me, in the latter part of my life I came to a conclusion: that it is futile and wrong to seek a meaning in the insignificant and yet apparently so important events taking place around us, rather that we should seek it in those layers which the centuries build up around a few of the main legends of humanity. Those layers constantly, if ever less faithfully, repeat the form of the grain of truth around which they cohere, and thus hand it down through the centuries. The real history of mankind is in tales, from them it is possible to guess, if not to discover totally, its meaning. (Ivo Andrič)[1]

Since 1983 an excavation of the ancient city of Marion on the west coast of Cyprus has been proceeding under the auspices of the Princeton–Cyprus Archaeological Expedition (Princeton University). As the excavation is still in progress, the final report of its findings is not yet available. Nevertheless, some partial reports of its discoveries have been published, and these are sufficient to merit serious consideration in this essay. Marion was an important and flourishing city especially in the Archaic and Classical periods (ca. 750–325 BC) It was one of the ancient kingdoms of Cyprus. Its strong links with mainland Greece, especially Athens, are clearly evident. It was also an important commercial center linking trade routes from Greece and other western trading centers, including the Levant, Syria,

Egypt and Anatolia. These trading relations were inevitably accompanied by a very rich flow of artistic, cultic and other cultural influences.[2]

Among the material evidence produced by the Marion excavations are over ten thousand terra-cotta figurines. They show a wide variety of artistic styles commensurate with the diverse cultural influences impinging on this cosmopolitan commercial center. It is their cultic referents that are of interest to us here. Clear evidence has been uncovered of two distinct religious sites existing in the same urban complex for several centuries. The two sites are material embodiments of two separate but merging religious traditions. The greater number of figurines are associated with the slightly later religious structure and identified with the emerging cult of Aphrodite. Dr. Nancy Serwint has identified a terra-cotta statuette from this site of a draped Aphrodite with a nude Eros, ca. 35 cm in height, which she is convinced is adapted from the Aphrodite and Eros group from the east frieze of the Parthenon (Serwint 1992; 1993).

The remains of the nearby second sanctuary have yielded material evidence of the existence of a cult devoted to a fertility goddess of Near Eastern lineage. A terra-cotta figurine from this sanctuary is identified as a representation of Astarte, one of the Near Eastern versions of the Mesopotamian Inanna–Ishtar. The preliminary conclusion of the excavations in progress is that this slightly older sanctuary flourished from the late eighth century to the beginning of the fifth century BC, and for most of this period contemporaneously with the second sanctuary of the emerging Aphrodite cult. This earlier cultic center apparently declined in popularity until it finally was abandoned in favor of the Aphrodite cult that assumed its now celebrated dominance on Cyprus. What is to be remarked on here is that there is no evidence of a destruction of the older Near Eastern cult center by the devotees of the younger cult nor of any pronounced conflict between the votaries or officials of the two cults. They apparently cohabited amicably for several centuries. (The city and its sanctuaries were destroyed by the violent rivalries that rent the Hellenistic world following the death of Alexander.)

The cult of Astarte was probably introduced in Cyprus at least by the middle of the ninth century BC (Serwint 1992, 13). There is disagreement among scholars about the nature of the one thousand or so figurines found at the older site. They are certainly objects brought to the sanctuary by votaries but what they represent is not certain. They show a simply executed female figure looking aloft and with outstretched arms. This very common type is usually referred to in the literature as "the goddess with uplifted arms." Desmond Morris insists that a more sensible interpretation is that the figure is that of a votary beseeching the goddess for some favor or mercy (Morris 1985, 175). What is not in dispute is the Levantine lineage of the cult, its Mesopotamian ancestry and the universally accepted relationship between the Oriental cult and the Cypriot cult of Aphrodite.

The cult and myths of Aphrodite are, of course, the heirs of several lines of ancestral descent. These have been firmly established. A well-balanced review of the evidence for these lines of descent can be found in Paul Friedrich's *The Meaning of Aprodite*, Chicago: University of Chicago, 1978. With the rare exception of a work such as D. D. Boedeker's *Aphrodite's Entrance Into Greek Epic*, Leiden: Brill, 1974, which attempts to establish on narrow philological grounds a strictly Aryan pedigree, there is a solid scholarly consensus on the indubitable Mesopotamian and Near Eastern ancestry of Aphrodite. I do not intend to question this scholarly consensus but I am concerned with what it *means* to affirm that Inanna–Ishtar–Astarte became or merged into or were transmuted into Aphrodite. I will argue finally that the distinctions between the symbolic *foci* of these two traditions, the Oriental and the Greek, have perennial and not merely antiquarian significance.

Extant texts and figurative representations of the Sumerian original Inanna, and her Akkadian manifestation, Ishtar, present us with one of the most passionately complex and compelling of all divine beings in Near Eastern and Mesopotamian mythological and cultic tradition. In a sense, the authors of *Gods, Demons and Symbols of Ancient Mesopotamia* are correct in describing three main symbolic dimensions of the figure of Inanna–Ishtar: Love, War and the "morning (evening) star" (Venus) (Black and Green, 1992, 108–109).

This over-simplification has a certain justification. Thorkild Jacobsen has argued that the function of the goddess is far more complex. He points out that in some texts she is called "Nin-me-sharra" meaning "Lady of a myriad offices" (Jacobsen 1976, 141). Jacobsen claims to identify some one hundred separate functions and duties ascribed to the goddess. The wonder then, is that it was possible from such a burden of functions to conceive of a divine character that is so vividly alive and compellingly credible as a single "person." This was achieved by distinguishing between those "offices" or duties that are merely assigned to Ishtar as responsibilities exterior to her person and those symbolical realities that are embodied in her character that distinguish her as a singular unique living being whose presence compels belief. It is this powerful character that appears to us in poetic fragments and above all in the *Epic of Gilgamesh*. Here I will follow N. K. Sandars' reconstruction of the Gilgamesh texts and her edition of some of the poetry in *Poems of Heaven and Hell from Ancient Mesopotamia* (1971; 1973).

The two essential character traits of Ishtar that I wish to underline are commonly referred to as "love" and "war." These labels may obscure as much of the vivid reality of Ishtar as they reveal. Sandars quotes a hymn from 1600 BC that describes the alluring sexuality of Ishtar: "Reverence the queen of women, the greatest of all the gods; she is clothed with delight and with love, she is full of ardor, enchantment, and voluptuous joy, in her lips she is sweet, in her mouth is Life, when she is present felicity is greatest; how glorious she looks, the veils thrown over her head, her lovely form, her brilliant eyes" (Sandars 1973, 26).

This dimension of Ishtar's character is beyond dispute, but the clear evidence of the epic should dissuade us from limiting the function of love to the allurement of sexuality and the promise of fertility.

The people of Uruk can no longer tolerate the "Alkibiadian" rampages of Gilgamesh who ravishes all the brides and leaves the city in a state of constant fearful turmoil. The people plead with the gods to send someone who is the equal of Gilgamesh to distract him and absorb his undisciplined energies. The gods send powerful Enkidu but they send him as a being who is at home only among the wild beasts of the field. Before Enkidu can be brought into the city to confront Gilgamesh he must be civilized and domesticated. He must be transformed from a beast to a *human* being. The means by which this humanization is accomplished, step by step, is through the harlot who is sent to tame Enkidu. That the harlot is one of the official prostitutes from Inanna-Ishtar's "Temple of Love" is not incidental, nor is the fact that the temple was central to the life of Uruk. The harlot seduces Enkidu with a brazenness that does justice to her divine patroness. She lies six days and seven nights with Enkidu after which he is now a stranger and even an enemy to his former companions, the wild beasts. What the sexual experience produces in Enkidu the story makes unavoidably explicit. "Wisdom" was in him and "the thoughts of a man were in his heart." He now longed for a comrade, i.e., human company (Sandars 1973, 65). But he is not yet able to enter Uruk to challenge Gilgamesh. First he must learn how to bathe and anoint himself with oil to eat bread and drink wine as a human rather than as an animal. All these things the harlot teaches him. When he finally enters Uruk and challenges Gilgamesh, the two have a spectacular wrestling match but this ends in a bond of life-long comradeship that is broken only by the death of Enkidu.

The point to be stressed here is that all this happens through the "agency" of sexual love. It is true that Ishtar herself is not a participant in the action of this part of the story, but the harlot is surely her "deputy." The meaning of the episode then is that sexual love is the fundament of human reality both in its individual and social dimensions.

"The thoughts of a man" about sexuality are utterly different from, and as the story makes clear, incompatible with the existence of animals. It is this relationship with Ishtar's "deputy" that alone makes possible the acquisition of the behavior patterns of humans. It is her efforts that finally result in the lasting bond of friendship and cooperation that makes society viable rather than perilous. It is tempting to suggest that it is due to the "agency" of Ishtar that justice itself is finally brought to Uruk, but there is no need to press the argument this far. It is sufficient to take cognizance of the fact that the strong theme of sexual love symbolized in the *persona* and *cultus* of Ishtar cannot be reduced to a matter of immoral extramarital dalliance. The moralistic incomprehension of the significance of Mesopotamian Love temple cultus may have begun with Herodotus (*Hist.* I.199) and it continues in more than one modern commentary on the subject.

Although Ishtar is on all accounts revered and feared as the Goddess of War, we do not actually meet her in this manifestation in the Gilgamesh texts. What we discover instead is something more fundamental, namely, the death-loving passion that fuels the fires of war. In Ishtar this awful passion is so intimately connected with the passion of love as to be inseparable from it, even though the two passions can be temporally distinguished in the narrative.

Gilgamesh has washed the dirt of battle from his body and his weapons (presumably after the fight with Humbaba) and donned his royal robes (Sandars 1973, 85). At the sight of him, Ishtar is seized by an urgent erotic passion for him. She beseeches him to be her bridegroom, promising untold riches for him and his household, fecundity for his flocks and vast political power over other kings and princes. Gilgamesh's answer is at first shrewd and calculating. He is no atheist. He willingly offers her the gifts appropriate to a goddess from a human, but he protests that since he is only a human, how could he ever offer the gifts appropriate to a divine consort, i.e., he refuses to serve her alone. To put his response in a modern formula, Gilgamesh assuredly believes in Ishtar but he just as firmly refuses to have faith in her. He then goes one step too far. He recounts the sad end to which each of Ishtar's lovers has come. This exposure of Ishtar's "abominable behavior, (her) foul and hideous acts" (Sandars 1973, 87) instantly exposes the opposite dimension of her essential character. She flies into a towering rage that can only be quenched by the destruction of its object. She demands that her father Anu give her "the Bull of Heaven" to destroy Gilgamesh. If this demand is not granted she promises to open the gates of the underworld and bring up the dead to mix with the living, thus bringing death and famine to the face of the earth. Her wish is granted, but much to her horror and escalating rage Gilgamesh and Enkidu slay the Bull. Rage is now contagious. Ishtar curses Gilgamesh for escaping punishment, whereupon Enkidu tears out the Bull's right thigh and flings it in Ishtar's face along with the vow that if he could only lay his hands on her, he would do with her as they had done with the Bull, adding the picturesque desire to tear out her entrails and lash them to her side. The flaming anger of Ishtar and the corresponding anger it has provoked in the heroes, has disordered the very councils of the gods who now decree as a punishment the death of Enkidu. His death shatters the whole world of Gilgamesh. It deprives his life of all meaning and purpose.

The power of love that Ishtar represents is that wide embracing means by which the bond of comradeship, social solidarity and unbreakable loyalty was created. The implacable overweening fury of this same Ishtar is the force that destroys the bond that united the heroes, leaving the survivor desolate and inconsolable.

Ishtar is indeed the Goddess of War. The *Gilgamesh* story allows us to see why. Pictorial representations of Ishtar can depict her arrayed in battle dress and brandishing the weapons of death. The Gilgamesh story allows us to peer through the battle gear and see the driving force that precipitates and sustains War. It is a complex of emotions, rage, bitterness, a thirst for revenge, a lust for destruction and contempt. The story does not try to catalog all the dark emotions; it does better. It lets Ishtar appear before us and no more needs to be said. The term Hate is merely the shorthand term to denote this complex dimension of Ishtar's character.

In view of the ever present possibility of destruction by war and famine, which terrible Ishtar embodies, it is worth noting that her votaries still found a final affirmation of life in Ishtar's dealings with humans, but only after the pain and despair, never without them. At the end of the Flood story, when even the gods, who had set out to rid themselves of noisy troublesome mankind, are cowering with fear on high ground as the waters rise, Ishtar relents of her wrath. "Alas the days of old are turned to dust, because I commanded evil; why did I command this evil in the council of all the gods? I commanded wars to destroy the people, but are they not my people, for I brought them forth? Now like the spawn of fish they float in the ocean" (Sandars 1973, 10).

The dominant character traits of Ishtar were transmitted westward to her "daughters" in the myths and cultus of Syria and Egypt. These character traits seen during the second millennium BC seem to have been dispersed among several goddesses. The most prominent of these were Anat, Atart and Astarte. Both Anat and Astarte are clearly identified as goddesses of love (fertility) and war, while Atart seems to have had an even more supreme status in the Near Eastern pantheon of the second millennium. Whether it is consistently possible to distinguish three or even more separate divine identities in this period is an issue that does not affect the burden of the line of interpretation I am here pursuing.[3] Anat seems to have been celebrated especially for her furious temper, her youthful eroticism and her love of warfare. A possible epithet points to her Mesopotamian ancestry as "Harlot of the People" (Böhm 1990, 127). Astarte bore epithets that continually associated her with horses and war chariots. Both goddesses were venerated in the New Kingdom period in Egypt as fierce war-like beings from "the East" who could protect the Egyptian rulers as foreign "mercenary" deities.

By the first millennium BC the personages and characters of the several Near Eastern goddesses have been condensed and focused into the now dominant being of Astarte. She is a fiery war goddess full of vengeance but also of erotic passion (Böhm 1990, 128; Pritchard 1943, 82). She can bestow the prosperity of fertility and sensuous enjoyment and in a sudden change of mood, the destruction and desolation of conflict. She is a worthy descendant of her Mesopotamian forebear, Innana–Ishtar. It is the cult of this Astarte that was brought to Cyprus early in the first millennium by Phoenician traders and settlers but Cyprus was not the only place to which Astarte was carried by her devotees.

The testimony of ancient chroniclers supports the general consensus concerning the oriental ancestry of the figure of Aphrodite although this testimony may be overstated or anachronistic. Herodotus (*Hist.* I.105) claims that the oldest temple of the "heavenly Aphrodite" was in Askalon and that it was the Phoenicians who introduced her cultus to Cyprus, which assumes that Herodotus believed that Aphrodite and her oriental forebears were simply one and the same with no distinctions. The Phoenician identity of the cult is also underlined by Herodotus (*Hist.* II.112) when he describes the temple of "the stranger Aphrodite whose imported cultus at Memphis is located in the "Camp of the Tyrians." Where Herodotus thought that this Phoenician "heavenly Aphrodite" was known by other names east of the Levant, he still implies that these are merely labels in different cultures for essentially the same Aphrodite. The Persians venerated her as Mitra. They learned of her from the Assyrians who called her Mylitta and the Arabians who called her Alilat (I.131 and 199) where the "foul custom" of the Babylonians is described. In this latter passage the gossip he has picked up about the immoral proceedings in the Mesopotamian temples clearly baffles him and he connects these stories with what he has heard about similar practices on Cyprus, perhaps at Amathus. Pausanias (I, Attica, 5–7) may be using Herodotus as a source in reporting that the cult of Aphrodite was established first by the Assyrians and then passed on to the Phoenicians and Paphians of Cyprus. It is curious that from none of his sources of information does Herodotus seem to have heard the name Astarte in any of its forms, nor Ishtar, Inanna–Ishtar.

The importation and implantation of an Astarte cult in Cyprus is beyond dispute, as is the scholarly consensus that Astarte became or merged with or was transmuted into Aphrodite. The process by which this occurred is obscure. It obviously transpired over an extended period of time. It is for this reason that the two adjacent sanctuaries at Marion are valuable in exemplifying a process that must have taken several centuries.[4] (Marion was not the most important center of either the Astarte or Aphrodite cults. Kition, Kouklia and Paphos were more prominent as cultic centers.)

The Cypriot origin of the Aphrodite cult is itself misleading. What probably happened is that immigrants from the Greek mainland brought with their cultus the characteristics we now attribute to Aphrodite to Cyprus late in the second millennium. These were grafted onto a much older indigenous female deity native to the island.[5]

What causal factors account for the transformation of Astarte into Aphrodite are difficult to determine.[6] The results of this transformation can confidently be identified and it is to these we shall now turn.

The personality of Astarte was not unaffected by her journey from the mainland of Asia to Cyprus. Flemberg has noted how her war-mongering passion was softened as she traveled west (Flemberg 1991). It is also clear that one early strand of the Aphrodite tradition bore the militant marks of her Near Eastern lineage. It was the representation of an "armed Aphrodite." But this tradition also gradually softens until the weapons of the goddess become almost playthings or casual adornments. In any case this atrophying tradition of an armed Aphrodite was never the dominant form of her mythological and cultic career (Flemberg 1991).[7] These considerations do not diminish seriously the drama of Astarte's transformation into Aphrodite.

The transformation of Inanna–Ishtar–Astarte to Aphrodite can be marked immediately in the visual representations of the deities. The difference between the representations of Ishtar and Astarte armed and ready for battle or flaunting their aggressive sexuality, and the "classical" statues of Aphrodite with the soft delicately flowing lines and her pristine beauty is not merely one of differing artistic styles or aesthetic sophistication. It is a serious difference between the conceptual content of the images. This can be illustrated textually by the action in Book V of the *Iliad* (ll. 290).

Diomedes "of the great war cry" has cornered the Trojan hero Aeneas in the swirl of battle. Hurling a huge stone at him, Diomedes severely wounds Aeneas who would surely have perished had not "Cyprian" Aphrodite intervened to save her son. Aphrodite saves Aeneas by wrapping her beautiful white robe around him and then spiriting him away. Never one to hold back in the face of divine intervention, Diomedes takes off after the goddess herself. Here Homer tells us explicitly that Diomedes knew very well that Aphrodite was not a goddess like those others, Athena for example, who actually take part in the fighting. Aphrodite had no fighting ability, no war-craft, at all (lines 330–333). Diomedes hurls his spear at the goddess and actually succeeds in wounding her, whereupon she drops her injured son. If Apollo had not been close by to rescue Aeneas that would have been the end of him. As the goddess flees bleeding and frightened from the battle, Diomedes hurls a contemptuous taunt at her: "Give way, daughter of Zeus, from the fighting and the terror. Is it not then enough, that you lead astray women without war-craft? Yet, if still you must haunt the fighting, I think that now you will shiver even when you hear some other talking of battles" (lines 348–351).[8]

As she is led to safety she comes upon her brother violent Ares, the God of War, on her way back to the safety of Olympos. Stirred up by Apollo, Ares returns to the battle, inflames the fighting spirit of the Trojan forces and himself challenges Diomedes, no doubt to avenge the unforgivable assault on his beloved sister. With very timely help from Athena, Diomedes adds to his previous conquest by dealing Ares himself a severe wound. Now it is Ares who must also withdraw from the battle to rest and recuperate on Olympos.

It is now possible to delineate some of the important alterations that have occurred in the tradition. There has been a rationalization and distillation of the divine persona. The Near Eastern goddess has been "divided" into two divinities, each with a very specific and limited character and function. The dimensions of Love and War (including all the attendant violent emotions) are now both symbolized in separate divinities but also still bound inseparably to each other as brother and sister. (I am not overlooking the fact that various other dimensions of the divine essences of Near Eastern goddesses have been dispersed into other Olympian deities such as Athena, Hera and Artemis. But the focus of our attention here is restricted to those forces that can be subsumed under the rubrics of Love and War-Hate. It is a mistake to conceive of the essence of a Near Eastern goddess as dispersed only into other female deities, to "feminize" the divine essence in this way is to diminish its broader human significance.[9] Another strand of mythological tradition describes a scandalous liaison between Ares and Aphrodite that produces a child named Harmonia [sic].

The epithets of Ares, "the war god" or "the god of war," may be misleading. He is certainly not the only god that takes part in the battles of the *Iliad* nor is he the most skillful or successful of the divine warriors. Athena fells and humiliates him in book XXI, 385–414. He is severely wounded by the mortal Diomedes or Athena, depending on how one interprets the text in book V. Ares is distinct from all the other gods who take part in battle in that they all have other, sometimes many other, functions or dimensions of being. Aside from his passion for Aphrodite, Ares has only one obsession, war and all its destruction, terror, suffering and death; in short, its madness. Other gods may do battle in anger but it is always a focused anger. That is, they always intend to achieve some definite purpose or end by their violent intervention: the triumph of one side or the other, revenge for an insult or the glory of a favorite hero. Athena may be the clearest example of this focused anger. Her later epithet "defender of cities" attests to this continuing character trait. By contrast Ares' passion for war exists for nothing beyond itself. He does side with Aphrodite but this is fortuitous to the issues at stake in the conflict. I suggest this attachment to Aphrodite is probably an echo of their common and unitary Oriental ancestry. In more than one passage in the *Iliad* a god or a hero observes that Ares can back either side or hero just so long as there is violence, bloodshed and death to be enjoyed. For example, V, 830. and XIII, 298–303. In XV, 128–129, his wrath is described as "mindless" and "undisciplined." When any two heroes close with each other in death-dealing rage they are both, in Nicole Loraux's felicitous phrase, "the disciples of Ares" (Loraux 1995, 96). Ares is "the god of war" in the sense that all aims, reasons, justifications and tactics of war have been stripped away and we are left with that irreducible mindless passion that drives men to war and its terrible consequences.

Important for an understanding of the diffusion of the tradition is also the scene in the household of the gods when brother and sister withdraw wounded from the battle before the gates of Troy. When Aphrodite arrives home she is immediately embraced and comforted by her mother Dione. She is then given an account of the many instances in which ungrateful cruel men have assaulted and insulted the gods on the apparent assumption that misery loves company. Finally, she is brought before Father Zeus. He smiles indulgently at her and speaks these soothing words: "Warfare is not for you, child. Lend yourself to sighs

of longing and the marriage bed. Let Ares and Athena deal with war"
(Fitzgerald 1974, 123).

Man-slaughtering, blood-stained, wall-storming Ares then arrives
with the same claim for comfort as his sister. He gets none of it. Instead
Zeus rounds on him:

> Do not come whining here, you two-faced brute, most
> hateful to me of all the Olympians. Combat and brawling
> are your element. This beastly, incorrigible truculence
> comes from your mother, Hera whom I keep but barely in
> my power, say what I will. You came to grief, I think, at her
> command. Still, I will not have you suffer longer. I fathered
> you, after all; your mother bore you as a son to me. If you
> had been conceived by any other and born so insolent, then
> long ago your place would have been far below the gods
> (Fitzgerald 1974, 137).

The bond between divine brother and sister still holds, yet the
symbolic gap between them widens. Aphrodite is indulged and loved
because she is indulgence and love. Ares is hated because hatred is his
driving force. (It is impossible to take either of these unequivocal
attitudes towards Ishtar or Astarte). Zeus declares that were it not for a
certain paternal responsibility, violent Ares would be cast out to a place
"far below the gods." All that Ares stands for is a threat to any sort of
orderly existence. His character expresses no other virtues that are
necessary for the life of gods or men (as do Hera, Athena and Apollo).
Hate, violence and all the other savage passions have been distilled into
one single divinity. They ought to be dispensed with, and yet somehow
they cannot be. They remain, and the gods (to say nothing of humans)
must somehow deal with them. (In two otherwise admirably sound and
scholarly articles, Daszewski (1982, 198, 201; 1994, 155) suggests that
the atrophying of the marginal tradition of an armed Aphrodite is
evidence of the gradual "humanization" of Aphrodite. The clear
assumption here is that love, tenderness, gentleness, beauty are
"human," but that war, violence and hatred are somehow "inhuman" or
"non-human." It is a beautiful and inspiring thought. (There is only
one thing wrong with it. It is false.)

Another strand of mythological tradition describes a proper
respectable marriage between Aphrodite with Hephaestos. It has been

suggested that this reflects the connection between the goddess of beauty and the beautiful metal products of the forge (see e.g. Flemberg 1991, 13). A more likely basis for the marriage of Aphrodite and Hephaestos is their mutual connection with the island of Cyprus. Aphrodite's Cypriot origin was a firm piece of conventional mythological wisdom, and the metallurgical importance of Cyprus as a source of copper in the ancient Mediterranean world is very clear. It has further been suggested that the power of fertility expressed in the person of Aphrodite extended to the inorganic activity of mining. In at least two excavations, evidence has been found of the cultic orientation of copper mining in Cyprus in the late bronze age. A figure of a smithy god (or a warrior-protector god) and a figure of a female fertility goddess, who may be either an Astarte or an early Aphrodite, have been claimed to be connected with this cultic aspect of the copper industry. It is possible that we have here material evidence for the origin of the Hephaestos–Aphrodite marriage legend and perhaps even a transition to the Aphrodite–Ares relationship.[10]

Whatever the mythological origins and the geographical and metallurgical contexts for the legitimate marriage of Aphrodite and Hephaestos, it ends in a spectacular scandal. Aphrodite deserts her bandy-legged husband for the charms and the bed of "ruinous Ares" (*Odyssey*, Book VIII, 305–320). The jilted husband howls his protest at father Zeus and demands the return of his bridal gifts. The meaning of the messy domestic scandal is important. As the proper wife of the smithy-god Aphrodite's significance is in a sense limited by geography and the artisanship of the forge. As the incestuous lover of the god of war, her vocation is universal.

The extant fragments of the earliest philosophers in the Greek speaking cities of the Mediterranean world, contain the evidence of an entirely new way of understanding the world of nature and society, freed from the received mythological naïveté. In the fragments of some of these pre-Socratics there is an explicit mixture of scorn, contempt and ridicule directed at Homer's account of the Olympian deities (Xenophones and Heraclitus). It is easy to overestimate the cultural importance of this anti-Olympian reaction. The pantheon of the gods as Homer described it remained the official cultus of the Greek cities for centuries and was diffused through the rise and flowering of Roman culture. Skepticism about religion was no harmless intellectual pursuit as the example of Socrates makes sufficiently clear. Just because the rejection of Olympian religion was such a peripheral phenomenon, at least in the sixth and fifth centuries BC, it is instructive to refer to one of its most intriguing exponents to discover what now is philosophically possible when the gods have atrophied for a "lover of wisdom."

One of the most fascinating of the pre-Socratic thinkers, both in his thought and in his person is Empedocles of Acragas (Latin Agrigentum) in the middle of fifth century BC. Fragments of his two serious philosophical poems are extant. In them the gods survive as poetic referents for the speculative motifs of Empedocles' philosophy rather than as vital personages in a mythological pantheon. The symbolic content of Aphrodite and Ares takes on a cosmic significance far beyond what they had in the Olympian pantheon. The other more powerful gods of Olympos may have been retired. Aphrodite and Ares are now in a sense the lords of the universe. Empedocles realized that the one major problem that was left unsolved in the thought of his philosophical predecessors was how to account for the indubitable reality of both unity and diversity in the universe. To solve the problem he postulated a double process (which a modern philosopher would describe as "dialectical"). There are two dynamic processes forever at work in every aspect and item of reality however minuscule or vast. One is a continuous movement toward unity, and the other a continuous movement toward diversity. Any single thing exists, whether a person or a planet or a blade of grass, because the elements that comprise it tend to flow together, to unite or to coalesce. Everything that exists is also discrete. It is itself and not anything else because the opposite force is at work, pulling things apart, disrupting unities. The spatial poetic metaphors Empedocles uses enable us to say that one of the forces is centripetal and the opposing one centrifugal. The uniting force is always towards the middle or the center and the disrupting divisive force is always towards the periphery or the furthest boundary. The uniting force he calls Aphrodite as a concession to popular beliefs. The centrifugal force he names directly as "Hate."[11] The dialectical balance of forces is continually at play within every entity. A human being is, for example, both a unity that coheres and a diversity of constituents that preserve their diversity. If there were in the universe only Aphrodite/Love, then everything would be one single motionless undifferentiated Being, which was precisely the philosophical position of Parmenides and the Eleatics. If there were only Hate, then nothing at all could ever come into existence.

> But I will go back to the path of song which I formerly laid down, drawing one argument from another: that (*path which shows how*) when Hate has reached the bottommost abyss of the eddy, and when Love reaches the middle of the whirl, then in it (*the whirl*) all these things come together so as to be One—not all at once, but voluntarily uniting, some from one quarter, others from another. And as they mixed, there poured forth countless races of mortals. But many things stand unmixed side by side with the things mixing— all those which Hate (*still*) aloft checked, since it had not set faultlessly withdrawn from the Whole to the outermost limits of the circle, but alas remaining in some places, and in other places departing from the limbs (*of the sphere*). But in so far as it went on quietly streaming out, to the same extent there was entering a benevolent immortal in rush of faultless Love. And swiftly those things became mortal which previously had experienced immortality, and things formerly unmixed became mixed, changing their paths. And as they mixed, there poured forth countless races of mortals, equipped with forms of every sort, a marvel to behold. As they came together, Hate returned to the outermost (bound). (Freeman 1948, 56–57, fragments 35, 36).

Hate is necessary for the diversity and thus the continuation of existence. Yet there is here the echo of that impetus toward rejection, that desire to see Hate (or Ares) pushed out to the furthest limits or cast out entirely. The attitude in Empedocles' metaphysical vision is still the moralistic one of Homer's father of the gods. A decisive rejection is impossible. Ares is still "one of the family."

Hate is necessary for the separate existence of things. (This theme is repeated with even more emphasis by Heraclitus who argues that all things would pass out of existence if it were not for war (fragments 43, 44, 45, and 47).

In all serious speculative systems, human reality is an integral element in the cosmos. Explanations of the structures and behavior of humans must be congruent with those of the cosmos as a whole. In the midst of an explication of the effects of the centripetal force throughout the cosmos, Empedocles admonishes his hearers, "observe her with your mind and do not sit with wondering eyes! She it is who is believed to be implanted in mortal limbs also; Through her they think friendly thoughts and perform harmonious actions, calling her Joy and Aphrodite. No mortal man has perceived her as she moves in and out among them, but you must listen to the undeceitful progress of my argument" (Freeman 1948, 53–54, fragment 17). The instinctual function of this force is here not restricted to sexual desire and activity. It is rather responsible for all that brings harmony, joy, cooperation and friendship within and among humans.

The "rejected" presence of Hate is attested to in another fragment (115) that has always intrigued later readers.

> There is an oracle of Necessity, an ancient decree of the gods, eternal, sealed fast with broad oaths, that when one of the divine spirits whose portion is long life sinfully stains his own limbs with bloodshed, and following Hate has sworn a false oath—these must wander for thrice ten thousand seasons far from the company of the blessed, being born throughout the period into all kinds of mortal shapes, which exchange one hard way of life for another. For the mighty Air chases them into the Sea, and the Sea spews them forth on to the dry land, and the Earth (drives them) towards the rays of the blazing sun; and the Sun hurls them into the eddies of the Aether. One (Element) receives them from the other, and all loath them. Of this number am I too now, a fugitive from heaven and a wanderer, because I trusted in raging Hate. (Freeman 1948, 65, fragment 115)[12]

All beings detest hate but try as they may, they cannot finally be rid of it, for it is ineradicably a force in the nature of things.

In his thought-provoking hypothesis on the common sociological origin of both Greek mythology and earliest Greek philosophy, Cornford (1957) argued that the original substratum of both was primitive tribal solidarity. This original datum of myth and philosophy was fractured when the tribe grew too large to maintain its unity and thus began to disperse itself into "fratres" within the now looser tribal structure. It was then that this multiform tribal structure was represented as a separation of sky and earth and the other natural phenomena. Out of this dispersion of the parts of the whole came the separate gods and the separate forces of Love and Hate (strife) of Empedocles' cosmic vision. If one concentrates only on the representational details of Olympian mythology and the two "forces" of Empedocles' poems, then Cornford's argument is persuasive. The gods can be said to be posterior to and consequent upon the break up of the original tribal solidarity. But if one reflects instead on the energies and forces that are represented by the mythological and philosophical symbols, it can be argued that these are ontologically and causally prior to the original tribal solidarity. Cornford's suggestion that the original tribal solidarity fractures rather as mercury does when it is spread too thin is not very convincing. Cornford never asks what caused the original tribal solidarity. Empedocles' poetic vision of the forces of Love and Hate provides a theoretical explanation both for the original tribal solidarity as well as for its fracturing.

At the popular cultic level, the Olympian gods flourished in Roman togas along with the inherited Republican deities and the profusion of exotic foreign cults imported from an expanding empire. At this cultic level, the survival of Aphrodite/Venus and Ares/Mars needs no demonstration. More interesting testimony is provided by ancient religion's most eloquent and passionate enemy, Titus Lucretius Carus.

In his epic philosophical poem, *De Rerum Natura*, Lucretius sought to expand and apply the basic materialist insights of the Greek thinker Epicurus to all reality, cosmic, organic, sociological and psychological with metaphysical ingenuity and poetic brilliance that still commands admiration. Lucretius explains how every conceivable reality is to be understood as a complex of the two single universal constituents of "atoms" (solid material "seeds" or "generative particles") and empty space. The utterly mindless movement of the atoms and their random and accidental combinations explain everything that is and exclude everything that cannot be. The consistent purpose of this metaphysical explication is to bring to his fellow humans the light of understanding, for it is only rational understanding of the way things really are that can banish from men's minds the fear and uncertainty that is at the root of their unhappiness. The sole purpose of human life (not a purpose imposed or decreed from some supernatural authority) or as Lucretius puts it, what Nature demands is a mind free from fear and a body free from pain for the enjoyment of pleasurable sensations. Of all the forces inimical to human tranquility and pleasure, the worst culprit is religion in any and every form. It is with a blend of disgust, contempt and moral outrage that Lucretius reminds his readers of examples of gross folly and cruelty perpetrated in the name of religion or at the supposed command of this or that god (Lucretius 29–30).[13]

Well aware of the difficulty of eradicating from men's minds all belief in divine beings of some sort, Lucretius allowed a very limited tongue-in-cheek existence to the gods as a concession to inevitable human mental weakness. Since everything that exists consists of solid material particles and empty space, the gods can be no exception. The gods are composed of the very finest lightest particles and vacuum; but they dwell very far from our earthly realm. These Epicurean gods did not create us. They never had and can never have any contact with us. They neither forgive nor punish us. They do not even think of us. Their indifference towards us is complete and eternal. They have only one relevance to the human condition. In their blissful undisturbed self-absorbed tranquility, they may serve as ideal models for the goal of the happiness for which we should seek (Lucretius 175–177).

In the light of this materialistic banishment of the gods and the polemics against the phobias of religious superstition, both of which are so important to his philosophical project, the opening lines of the epic poem have caused a certain uneasiness and interpretive scrambling among the admirers of Lucretius. "Mother of Aeneas and his race, delight of men and gods, life-giving Venus, it is your doing that under the wheeling constellations of the sky all nature teems with life" (Lucretius 27). There follows an effusion of praise and gratitude for the alluring power of love that reproduces all the species of animals and plants as well as humans. To Venus is even ascribed the soothing forces of inorganic nature that moderate the weather and calm the seas. "Since you (Venus) alone are the guiding power of the universe and without you nothing emerges into the shining sunlit world to grow in joy and loveliness, yours is the partnership I seek in striving to compose these lines *On the Nature of the Universe* (Lucretius 27–28). A few lines later the invocation to Venus becomes more urgent:

> Meanwhile, grant that this brutal business of war by sea and land may everywhere be lulled to rest. For you alone have power to bestow on mortals the blessing of quiet peace. In your bosom Mars himself, supreme commander in this brutal business, flings himself down at times, laid low by the

irremediable wound of love. Gazing upward, his neck a prostrate column, he fixes hungry eyes on you, great goddess, and gluts them with love. As he lies outstretched, his breath hangs upon your lips. Stoop, then, goddess most glorious, and enfold him at rest in your hallowed bosom and whisper with those lips sweet words of prayer, beseeching for the people of Rome untroubled peace (Lucretius 28).

This is of course poetic license, but the label is not an adequate interpretation. The translator of this excellent Penguin version, R. E. Latham, suggests that Venus is here merely a "conventional guise" for an impersonal, blind, soulless natural force that could dispense with any personal attributes (Lucretius 13). This may be true, but it is difficult to know how this dumb instinctual force could subdue Mars. What these lines express may best be understood as a grave soberfaced Roman version of what the genius of Aristophanes offered to his Athenian audience in the *Lysistrata:* a deadly serious struggle in the form of an obscenely comic piece of art. It is the struggle of all the forces of love that alone can overcome the devastation and horror of war. At the conclusion of the *Lysistrata* (lines 1288–1289) the chorus calls upon the highest rank of the gods to witness and praise the peace and harmony that Aphrodite has brought to Athens and Sparta. Both Lucretius' sober version and Aristophanes hilarious one present the overcoming of the forces of war by the forces of love in the imagery of an erotic triumph. There could also have been in Lucretius's historical consciousness the legend of the Sabine women who in spite of having been seized, ravished and forced into marriage with their Roman captors, nevertheless thrust themselves in the midst of battle between the Romans and their Sabine kinsmen to bring peace and reconciliation to the two peoples. (Plutarch's *Lives*, I, XIX, 1–5.)

Venus was for a good Roman like Lucretius always the mother of Aeneas and the focus for all those forces that tend to unite the people and oppose those destructive forces of civil strife that tore Rome apart in the first century BC. Therefore, Venus and Mars are not utterly transcendent diaphanous beings enjoying perfect tranquillity far beyond human affairs and concerns. They are the symbolical personages that show us the most basic and imminent of earthly and human realities. There are sound philosophical grounds for dispensing with the gods, but it is not so easy to dispose of Venus and Mars.

There is yet a further ambiguity in the symbolical presence of Venus. The high praise she merits as the source of sexual allurement is not unmixed. She ensures the regeneration of all species. She also is responsible for much painful loss of tranquility among humans (Lucretius 163–66). Those who suffer the torments of love might well wish that Venus would let them alone and retire out of touch in the distant company of the other gods.

Within a few centuries after Lucretius' polemic against established religious beliefs, cults and their gods, the whole edifice collapsed through its own entropy and the intolerant zeal of the latest oriental cult, Christianity. But Aphrodite/Venus and Ares/Mars did not die or retire docilely to the museum of ancient cultural phenomena. They went underground for two millennia to surface again with undiluted promise and menace in the brooding reflections of Sigmund Freud on the human condition. At the end of his life, Freud published a brief but wide ranging statement of the conclusions about human social existence to which his years of clinical and academic work had led him. The work, *Das Unbehagen in der Kultur* (1930), appears in English as *Civilization and Its Discontents* (1962).

In Freud's thought the two forces are now unequivocally declared to be instincts. They are the most basic determinants in all human beings in all times, places and conditions. The biological origin of these instincts and the extensive clinical investigation of their manifestations at the individual level no doubt render them meaningful for modern scientifically oriented minds. It is worth noting, however, how easily and naturally Freud employs archaic mythological designations in referring to these "heavenly powers" or "immortal" and "eternal" forces (1962, 92 and *passim*). Freud's standard designations for the two instincts are Eros and Thanatos (death). His theoretical formulation has the further virtue of reducing the operation of the instincts to convenient formulae that do not trivialize the extreme and often disguised effects of their presence. Eros is the instinct that ever seeks to create unities. Thanatos is the antithesis of Eros that ever seeks to destroy unities and reduce organic life to inorganic chaos. As Freud states on several occasions, he only came late and reluctantly to the conclusion that there are two powerful instincts rather than just one at work in the human psyche. It was, he says, only after he had finally accepted this dualistic conclusion that he discovered it was not original with him.

In the midst of a technical discussion of psychoanalytic problems he suddenly departs from his subject to acknowledge the prior achievement of Empedocles (Freud 1953, 348–50). Freud is extravagant in his praise of the achievement of his ancient precursor. Freud's theory of the instincts has a biological basis and is couched in the phrases of a modern scientific theory. The theory of Empedocles is a "cosmic fantasy" that postulates an explanation for the dialectic of combining and separating, for all reality. Freud's theory of the instincts cannot serve as an explanation for the existence and changes of inorganic matter because modern science has compartmentalized our understanding of existence. Nonetheless, Freud enthusiastically declares that "the two fundamental principles of Empedocles—*philia* and *neixos*—are both in name and function, the same as our two primal instincts Eros and destructiveness" (Freud 1953, 349).

Freud concludes his encomium with the thought that no one can tell in what guise the essential truth contained in the thought of Empedocles will present itself in the future to man's self-understanding (Freud 1953, 350). The point is worth further reflection. The basic "truth" was not a discovery of Empedocles. It was deeply embedded in the mythological traditions of Mesopotamia, the Near East and the cultures of Greece and Rome, which is not to belittle the genius of Empedocles. The basic "truth" appeared in a "guise" with Empedocles, no more or less so than in its ancient mythological personifications. These are all symbolic ways of representing truth in forms that will be meaningful to humans of different cultures and ages. Whether or not Freud would admit it, his reduction of the truth to two biologically based instincts is simply yet another way of representing the truth in symbols that will prove meaningful to modern scientifically inclined minds. Freud's formulation is no less symbolic than any other, although a symbol that is truly meaningful to any generation does not appear as a symbolic representation but rather as the literal truth. To paraphrase Hobbes, other people believe in symbols. We believe in the truth.

The attempt to express a truth in the logical conventions of scientific theory requires a drawing of precise distinctions that were not the same burden for mythological drama. Freud struggles with this requirement in *Civilization and Its Discontents*, and his conclusions were appropriately provisional. The single goal that all human beings seek is "happiness" defined as libidinal or sensuous pleasure. The problem is that this goal is unachievable except for brief fleeting moments. The animus of nature and the decay of our own bodies continue to frustrate human efforts to reach happiness (Freud 1962, 23 *et passim*). The instinct that drives humans toward the goal of happiness/pleasure is Eros, but the function of this instinct is itself problematic both individually and socially. Freud's conception of pleasure is a very broad one containing all sorts of libidinal excitation beyond explicitly sexual pleasure. However, he insists that the paradigmatic experience of pleasure is sexual fulfillment and thus Eros becomes a problem to itself (Freud 1962, 29, 48). In the first place, humans are nowhere more defenselessly exposed to unhappiness and disappointment than in individual emotional relationships. Secondly, society does not allow the unrestricted fulfillment of the instinctual drive for sexual pleasure. All sorts of curbs must be placed upon it. The instinct of Eros so defined as the striving for sexual pleasure must be deflected, sublimated or otherwise diverted into the constructive pursuits that build up, strengthen or enhance society (politics and science and art for example.) All the activities that create social "unities" are thus disguised sexual activities. There is a further problem with this conception of Eros. It might be thought that once Eros has drawn two individuals together in a unity, it could then expand its quest to create larger and larger unities to form a community. But this further creation of unities is inhibited by the fact that the sexual unity of two individuals is sufficient unto itself. Eros not only does not need to move beyond the immediacy of individual libidinal enjoyment, it looks upon all third parties, even a child born of the union, as superfluous. Any larger third party, such as society with its requirements, is definitely an enemy of Eros (Freud 1962, 55). Thus there exists within each individual as well as within each society a continual conflict between the divergent demands of Eros: the happiness of the individual and the unification and enhancement of the community. To describe this as the state versus the individual misconstrues the issue. It is a conflict between the polar claims of Eros, and its resolution is possible though difficult within what Freud calls "the economics of the libido" (Freud 1962, 88).

Freud's analysis of Eros is too solidly based and carefully articulated to be dismissed out of hand, but it has to be pointed out that all the problematic and conflicting aspects of the conception are traceable to his insistence that the explicitly sexual experience of the individual is the paradigm for Eros. Is it possible that the looser, less rigorous representations of the ancient myth makers and cosmic speculators were a closer approximation to the truth? No ancient or modern thinker who has sought to express the reality of the forces of love and hate in whatever symbolic form would deny or doubt for a moment the centrality of sexuality in the vocation of the powerful instinctual force of Eros. But to make human sexual fulfillment its benchmark is to create for it more problems than can be universally demonstrated to exist throughout the whole range of differing human societies. Even if the conflicts of a problematic Eros as described by Freud are perceptible in European or Western societies, are they so clearly evident elsewhere?

Freud understands that the greatest threat to Eros, its achievements in the individual and society, comes not from its own ambiguity but from its old opponent, the death instinct, with its manifestations of hate, aggression, destructiveness and a longing for chaos. Here Freud's explication of the vocation of the instincts goes far beyond the representations of his ancient precursors but is still congruent with them.

The instinct of Eros is easily discernible because its activity is largely directed towards objects in the outer world from which the self can derive pleasure and from the ever widening circle of unities that Eros creates. The death instinct is originally directed inwards towards the dissolution of the unity of the self, and we only perceive its operations clearly when it is diverted outwards toward the destruction of unities beyond the self. In this outward turning of the death instinct its presence is betrayed by hate, violence, destructiveness and all their correlates. This outward direction uses only part of the force of the otherwise inwardly directed force of dissolution (Freud 1962, 65–66).

Freud understands what his ancient precursors as far back as the Sumerians understood, namely, the intimate relationship between Eros and the death instinct. They are obviously alloyed in sadism where the death instinct is turned outward to provide a libidinous satisfaction and in masochism where that same urge toward destruction is turned inwards. Nevertheless, he claims that he was finally compelled by the evidence to postulate the *separate* existence of the death instinct. This evidence was the fact that emotions and actions characterized by hate, rage, and violence, often had no demonstrable connection with erotic, i.e. sexual, satisfaction. Freud is correct about the evidence, but more than one conclusion can be drawn from it. It may indicate that Thanatos is a separate self-subsisting instinct. It may also indicate that the model of Eros with which Freud is working is too paradigmatically determined by explicit human sexual activity. If Eros were understood as a drive to create unities that centrally *includes* human sexuality but is not determined by it, then there might be no compelling reason to view the death instinct in all its manifestations as separate.

The conflict between Eros and Thanatos is irreconcilable. The fact that civilization somehow survives in spite of this conflict of "the giants" means that ways have been found to divert Thanatos from its real aim and even to make constructive use of it in the service of civilization. Here the way in which Freud extrapolates the individual personality theory to psycho-social theory is acute. In the individual, a portion of the death instinct's outward manifestations, (hate, condemnation and punishment) is introjected back into the individual to provide the energy for the superego, the agency of conscience, guilt and shame. At the communal and civilizational level, an analogous process occurs. A portion of the corporate death instinct is communally introjected to form the enforcing energy of the group's super-ego with its laws, taboos, prohibitions, and commandments.

Civilization for Freud is a constant battle between these two terrible and "blind" forces. Human beings cannot choose to love and hate or to dispense with either or both of these "immortal giants" as Freud liked to call them. Humans can only exercise a very limited control over the direction of these forces and the objects among which they are dispersed. Freud in 1930 was not sanguine about the future of civilization caught in the battle of these two instinctual titans for world dominion, and the evidence of World War II was yet to come.

The terms Love and Hate have been used here as convenient shorthand denotations for two dense clusters of emotions, forces, patterns and sources of behavior. The difference between the forms in which Love and Hate are represented, as dramatic myth, as "cosmic fantasy," or as instincts, is not really important. It is true that these fundamental human realities are instincts. That is to say, a scientific theory based on clinical and theoretical psychological analysis will be meaningful to many a modern mind. This way of speaking will make more sense than some other way because it opens the subject to further scientific investigation (for example, Konrad Lorenz *et al.* on the subject of aggression).

It is also true that Love and Hate are gods. That is to say, they are very real ubiquitous and overpowering forces that ancient peoples have mythopoeically represented in epic and dramatic fashion. As gods they are completely natural, all too natural in fact.[14] To most sane and reflective peoples of the ancient Near East the idea of a "supernatural god" would have sounded as absurdly droll as would the idea of "supernatural instincts" to the ears of a modern scientist. It is also possible that even a sober modern mind may find a dramatic or poetic representation of Love and Hate more pregnant with meaning than a scientific theory that must dispense with evocative literary metaphors. Freud's own account is rich with literary references (ancient and modern), as poetic formulae for scientific facts.

It might be suggested that Freud's tracing of Hate and its correlate emotions and behavior patterns to the death instinct is a significant advance on ancient myth. But this would be to overlook the very strong traditions concerning Ishtar–Inanna's journey to the underworld (the realm of the dead) and her threats in the Gilgamesh story to open the underworld and mix the dead with the living, a threat that appalls even the gods.[15]

Even where a modern psychological theory proceeds on the assumption that human behavior is impelled by forces quite different from the forces that explain the dynamism of (non-human) nature, the contrast with an ancient unified understanding of human and non-human phenomena may only be provisional because the conclusions of modern science are provisional. Freud himself noted this difference between his theory and Empedocles' unified world view and did not think it should be unduly stressed.

Some of the associations and functions that adhere to the ancient divinities do not travel well because they are culturally and historically relative to the values and conditions of specific societies. Insofar as ancient deities embody the complex realities of Love and Hate, these deities do travel across geographical and cultural space and across expanses of time because they do not represent what is relative and transient but what is enduring in the human condition. They dramatically represent human self-understanding, not just facets of ancient civilizations. They will continue to travel well across space and time because, as Empedocles expressed it in speaking about Love and Hate, "as they were formerly, so also will they be, and never, I think, shall infinite Time be emptied of these two" (Freeman 1948, 53, fragment 16).

There is a difference between these various representations of Love and Hate that does deserve further reflection. It has to do not with their literary form but with their conceptual content. The Mesopotamian and eastern mythopoeic representations present us with a single figure that dramatically embodies both forces. With the appearance of the Olympian pantheon, this single figure "divides" to become two separate, contrasting or even antithetical figures that nonetheless remain inexorably related to one another. Whether this "splitting" was caused by sociological dynamic such as the development of more patriarchal social structures or economic or other causes is beyond the scope of this essay. What is clear is that from the Olympian gods to Freud and beyond we are presented with what may be called a "western" cultural conviction about the duality of these realities. The duality is consistent over two and a half millennia whether the forces appear as gods, cosmic dynamism or instincts. The serious weight of this tradition, especially with Freud's scientific refraction of it, is not to be dismissed lightly even though in the case of Freud, as was observed above, the dual formulation may be due in part to his insistence on explicitly sexual satisfaction as the determining model for Eros.

However there is still a case to be made for the more ancient unified representation, in short, for Ishtar: "Oh, star of lamentation, brothers at peace together you cause to fight one another, and yet you give constant friendship" (Sandars 1973, 26). If, to a modern mind, the concept of instinct is more meaningful than that of divine power, it may be useful to look again at the action of the *Epic of Gilgamesh* as an instinctual drama. No sooner has the bond of human solidarity and civilization been created between Enkidu and the harlot than Enkidu's first urge is to overthrow Gilgamesh and establish a "new order." After Enkidu is subdued by Gilgamesh and the strong bond of solidarity has been created between them they must go out into the forest to cut down the trees for no apparent constructive purpose and kill Humbaba because he is evil. When they finally reach Humbaba he turns out to be neither a threat to humans nor evil in any sense of the term but merely a guardian of the forest against the destructive encroachments of humans.

Humbaba is no match for the aggressive heroes. He pleads pitifully for his life when the heroes close in for the kill, but Enkidu and Gilgamesh must kill him because they have previously declared him to be "evil" and sworn to kill him. Their brutal slaying of Humbaba and their declared justification are inexplicable apart from an understanding of an overpowering urge towards destruction and death within them. The fact that the story clearly shows Humbaba not to be evil simply illustrates the maxim that if the enemy does not exist he must be invented. This intimate conjunction of Love and Hate in the lives of the heroes is a reflection of the essential being of Ishtar.

Instead of constructing a representation on the initial basis of individual psychological evidence, if sociological phenomena were the initial focus, the unitary hypothesis would appear persuasive. I cite here only two superficially different phenomena, the first in which the forces of Love and Hate (and their collaterals) have been socially blunted, domesticated and channeled into communally beneficial actions and the second in which the forces are dangerously out of control.

The gladiatorial combats of modern athletics, especially where team "contact" sports are involved, present a neat example of the forces under control for constructive ends. The bonding unifying dynamic of a competitive athletic team is so inextricably and proportionately related to the hostility, aggression and controlled violence against the opposing team that the postulation of two separate forces at work seems to violate Occam's law. The bonding and the aggression cannot possibly be sundered, and there is no reason to divide the explanation of the single force that is manifestly present. There is here a very good example of a successful "domestication" of the forces that is evidenced by the catharsis of dangerous instincts. The catharsis occurs for both athletes and spectators and is directly proportional to the extent of violence that the rules of any particular sport allow. This example will appear frivolous only to someone who has not ever been a party to athletic combat as a player or supporter or has never bothered to think seriously about the underlying significance of what goes on in the popular culture of sport.

The other example provides no grounds for cheering. Its importance cannot be ignored because the evidence is unavoidable. The formation, unification and strengthening of numbers of humans around a nationalist, religious, racial or ideological focus appears everywhere to be conjoined necessarily with hostility, aggression, and violence towards those outside the defined perimeter of the group.[16] The more intense the consciousness of unity the more violent the rejection of "the other." No one who monitors contemporary world events will need to have the examples listed. Conversely, philanthropic tendencies among individuals and communities or nations appear to be proportional to a weakening of their unifying dynamics. The homiletical rhetoric of religious communities will, of course, present us with just the opposite claims about the unity of the faithful and the love of mankind, but the weight of present and past history belies the homily. Here again the depressing mass of evidence is perhaps more satisfactorily accounted for by the postulation of a single force or instinct with the awful quicksilver duality of an Ishtar.

There seems to be no way of determining with confidence whether a single or dual representation of these realities is finally the more accurate one. Perhaps there is no need finally to choose one form of representation and reject the other. Might it not be that those Iron Age Cypriots of ancient Marion had wisdom on their side when for several hundred years they refused to reject one representation for the other. Instead they maintained two sanctuaries side by side, bringing offerings and supplication to each or both divinities as the occasion demanded. They surely understood what their wise successors for the next two and a half millennia understood; it is unwise to be too hasty or casual in assessing the reality of these two immortal powers. It is, after all, a matter of life and death.

NOTES

1. As quoted in Mukrji (1955, 30–31). The quote is from an imaginary conversation with the dead Goya and can be found also in a slightly different translation in Andriç (1992, 16).
2. See Serwint (1992, 10–13; 1993, 207–11). I am indebted to Dr. Serwint for calling my attention to the Marion excavations and for generous assistance in locating the preliminary reports that have so far been published.
3. A fuller recent discussion of the complex and often overlapping essences of the Near Eastern female deities in this period can be found in Böhm (1990, 127). See also Haussig (1965, 250–52), and Pritchard (1943,

65–82). A wonderfully explicit description of the blood thirsty war-loving passion of Anath is to be found in Gordon's translation of a hymn from Ugarit in Gordon (1966, 50–51):

> Knee-deep she plunges in the blood of soldiery
> Up to the neck in the gore of troops.
> Until she is sated she smites in the house
> Fights between the two tables
> Shedding—the blood of soldiery.

4. Although the line of interpretation pursued in this essay assumes without argument that the definitive transformation of Astarte to Aphrodite occurred on Cyprus during the first millennium BC, the geographical specificity is not essential to my argument. A case can be made for the change having been made in the Levant at Afqa or Byblos. See, for example, Haussig (1965, 252) and Pritchard (1943, 70–71). Since the evidence cited is from the Hellenistic period, it may be that any Levantine transformation occurred through the import of Aphrodite to Asia rather than through the export of Astarte westward.

5. The definitive work on the indigenous female deity is J. Karageorgis (1976). A very good English summary of the Aphrodite cult on Cyprus is to be found in J. Karageorgis (1984, 358–72).

6. J. Karageorgis (1976, 112) summarizes the theory of J. E. Dugand, which suggests that the name Aphrodite may be a corruption of Astarte. The suggestion is highly speculative, but may have more to recommend it than the widely held theory that the name "Aphrodite" means "risen from the foam" for which there seems to be no linguistic evidence. An English summary of this possibility is to be found in Karageorgis (1984, 359, 361). Martin Bernal claims that both the derivation of the name Aphrodite and the prototype of the goddess are Egyptian (see Bernal 1987, 65–66). This claim is only summarized in vol. I, and its full explication is promised as having been proved in vol. III. Unfortunately at the present time vol. III has not yet been published. Thus the reader is left to wonder how Bernal deals with the evidence that clearly shows a Near Eastern derivation for the goddess. Herodotus is otherwise so important for Bernal in re-establishing what he calls "the ancient model." Robert Graves' *The White Goddess* underlines the importance of the difference between matriarchal Near Eastern societies and patriarchal Western (Greek) societies in the alterations of the nature and function of the respective female deities. The difference in social structures is undoubtedly part of the causal explanation, but it does not account satisfactorily for all the mythological phenomena. Mesopotamian and Near Eastern myths had supreme male gods, and although Zeus is the Olympian patriarch, Hera and Athena, to name but two, are by no means docile submissive females.

7. Flemberg's study is a very thorough review of all the textual and material evidence for the traditions of an armed Aphrodite–Venus. See also his suggestion that representations of an androgynous Aphrodite also echo her Near Eastern ancestry (1991, 13–14).
8. I have adopted the simpler, though inaccurate, Latin spelling of Aeneas in order to avoid the difficulty of trying to render Greek vowels into English.
9. As Böhm apparently does (1990, 140).
10. The connection between the bronze figurines in question was argued first by H. W. Catling in what subsequently proved to be a very fruitful article (1971). The argument is carried further by Karageorgis (1976, 58–69 and 74–76).
11. That Empedocles makes use of the goddess' name here and those of the other gods as merely poetic conventions rather than objects of conventional belief can be seen from fragments 27a, 28, 132, 133, and 134, pp. 56 and 67. His rejection of popular religiosity and his theological affirmations echo the thought of both Xenophanes and Parmenides.
12. Cornford may be right in suggesting that this oracular passage may indicate a belief in the immortality of the soul, but this still does not seem certain to me (see Cornford 1957, paragraph 120).
13. Although this translation by R. E. Latham is in prose, it really preserves more of the poetic elegance and drive of the original than do most verse translations.
14. F. M. Cornford's otherwise admirable analysis is unfortunately marred by his repeated description of the ancient gods, and occasionally even the material elements, as "supernatural" (Cornford 1957, paragraphs 68, 102, 109, *et passim*). In spite of this, Cornford's interpretation of the famous passage in Plato's *Gorgias*, where the "Cosmos" is described as a harmony of gods and humans, does put the human and the divine properly in perspective within the "natural" order of things (paragraph 112).
15. For the journey to the underworld see Sandars (1971, 135–50).
16. See Eibesfeldt (1972, 69) on the "spontaneity" of aggression, which is not triggered by any specific or predetermined stimulus. Eibesfeldt marshalls a great deal of evidence on the relationship between "bonding" and aggression (1972, 74–77). Although his analysis is based on the unexamined "Western" assumption of two separate instincts.

REFERENCES

Andrič, I.
    1992   *Conversation with Goya Bridges Signs*, London: Menard.
Bernal, M.
    1987   *Black Athena* I. New Brunswick, NJ: Rutgers University.

Black, J., and Green, A., eds.
1992   *Gods, Demons and Symbols of Ancient Mesopotamia An Illustrated Dictionary.* London: The Trustees of the British Museum.

Böhm, S.
1990   *Die Nackte Göttin.* Mainz: von Zabern.

Catling, H. W.
1971   A Cypriot Bronze Statuette in the Bomford Collection. Pp. 15–32 in *Alasia*, under Mission Archeologique d'Alasia, dirigee, par Claude G. A. Schaeffer. Leiden: Brill.

Cornford, F. M.
1957   *From Religion to Philosophy.* New York: Harper & Row.

Daszewski, W. A.
1982   Aphrodite Hoplismene from Neo Paphos. Pp. 195–201 in *Report of the Department of Antiquities.* Nicosia, Cyprus: Department of Antiquities.
1994   Marble Sculptures in Neo Paphos. Pp. 153–61 in *Cypriote Stone Sculpture*, eds. F. Vandenabeele and R. Laffineur. Brussels-Liege: Rije Universiteit Brussel-Université de Liège.

Eibesfeldt, I. E.
1972   *Love and Hate.* New York: Holt, Rinehart and Winston.

Freeman, K.
1948   *Ancilla to the pre-Socratic Philosophers.* Oxford: Blackwell.

Flemberg, J.
1991   *Venus Armata, Studien zur bewaffneten Aphrodite in der griechisch-römischen Kunst.* Stockholm: Svenska Institutet i Athen.

Freud, S.
1962   *Civilization and Its Discontents.* Edited by James Strachey. New York: Norton.
1953   Analysis, Terminable and Interminable. Pp. 316–57 in *Collected Papers*, vol. V, ed. James Strachey. London: The Hogarth Press.

Gordon, C. H., trans.
1966   A Hymn from Ugarit. In *Ugarit and Minoan Crete.* New York: Norton.

Graves, R.
1992   *The White Goddess.* New York: The Noonday Press.

Haussig, H. W.
1965   *Wörterbuch der Mythologie.* Stuttgart: Ernst Klett.

Jacobsen, T.
1976   *The Treasures of Darkness: A History of Mesopotamian Religion.* New Haven: Yale University.

Karageorgis, J.
  1976   *La Grande Deesse de Chypre et Son Culte.* Lyon: Maison de l'Orient Publications.
  1984   Mythology and Cult. Pp. 358–75 in F. G. Maier and J. Karageorgis, *Paphos, History and Archeology.* Nicosia: A. G. Leventis Foundation.
Karageorgis, V.
  1976   *Kition.* London: Thames and Hudson.
Lucretius
  1951   *On the Nature of the Universe.* Translated with an introduction by R. E. Latham. Harmondsworth: Penguin.
Lattimore, R., trans.
  1951   *The Iliad of Homer.* Chicago: University of Chicago.
Loraux, N.
  1995   *The Experiences of Tiresias.* Princeton: Princeton University.
Morris, D.
  1985   *The Art of Ancient Cyprus.* Oxford: Phaidon.
Mukrji, V. S.
  1955   *Ivo Andriç: A Critical Biography*, Jefferson, NC: McFarland.
Pritchard, J.
  1943   *Palestinian Figurines In Relation to Certain Goddesses Known Through Literature.* New Haven: American Oriental Society.
Sandars, N. K., ed.
  1971   *Poems of Heaven and Hell From Ancient Mesopotamia.* Harmondsworth: Penguin.
  1973   *The Epic of Gilgamesh.* Harmondsworth: Penguin.
Serwint, N.
  1992   Terracotta Treasures from Ancient Marion. *Minerva* 3/4: 10–13.
  1993   An Aphrodite and Eros Statuette from Ancient Marion. Pp. 207–22 in *Report of the Department of Antiquities.* Nicosia: Department of Antiquities.

13 Strabo, Pliny, Ptolemy and the *Tabula Peutingeriana*: Cultural Geography and Early Maps of Phoenicia

HENRY INNES MACADAM

INTRODUCTION: A REMINISCENCE OF AL GLOCK

In the late spring of 1979 I met Al Glock for the first time at the Albright Institute in Jerusalem. I had crossed into Israel from Jordan at the Allenby Bridge the previous day and, after a lengthy interlude at the border, took a "service" taxi to Ramallah where I stayed with old friends Hugh and Shirley Harcourt, former colleagues at the American University of Beirut. They and Al were on the faculty at Birzeit University, then closed for an indeterminate amount of time by the military governor of Ramallah. Hugh and Shirley had contacted Al on my behalf and were glad I could "service" into Jerusalem the following morning to meet him. That was not my only chance to make his acquaintance, but it is special to my memory because the topic of my contribution is directly related to it. It was also significant because Al was at that time "wearing two hats": one as head of the Albright Institute and the other as Professor of Archaeology at Birzeit University in the West Bank.

Al was waiting in the Director's Office and immediately made me feel welcome. He wanted to know if there had been any problems at the border, and whether the Old City had changed much since my last visit. I answered affirmatively to both questions. Al knew I had last been in east Jerusalem in 1966, fourteen months before the Israeli annexation during the "Six-Day War." He wanted me to fill him in on the situation in Lebanon, where the civil war was entering its fifth year. He asked me what my latest project was. I said "researching the geography of Lebanon." Al had a few maps of "The Holy Land" in his office and we made small-talk about them.

We had lunch at the Albright Institute and he drove me out to the new campus of Birzeit University. Bulldozers and scaffolding were the main features then, as the architect's plan began to take shape in the warm, white sunshine of a May afternoon. Al was enthusiastic as he conjured up images of the completed buildings that would house the classrooms and laboratories and storage area of his fondest dream, a new archaeological center. Later we drove the few kilometers to the old campus, within walking distance of where I was staying. A few administrators were there, but classes were suspended. The atmosphere was tense and uncertain.

Al was happy that I had read his recently published article "*Homo Faber*: The Pot and the Potter at Taanach" (*BASOR* 219 [1975]), a thought-provoking and articulate essay that explored aspects of what he termed his "philosophy of archaeology through ceramics." I mentioned that the Latin portion of the title (meaning "Creative Man") evoked the anthropological expression *Homo Habilis* ("Handy Man") given to an early branch of hominids who fashioned tools and weapons. He was pleased that I made the connection and we spent the remaining time together discussing the role of pottery in the evolution of archaeological techniques from the earliest typology sequences almost a century ago through the development of thermoluminescence, then still a sophisticated ceramic dating process in the experimental stages.

That led to the discovery that we both shared an interest in the relentless curiosity of Thomas Jefferson, who "excavated" an American Indian burial mound on his estate at Monticello. "Today it seems to be the American expatriates who know more than just the outlines of American history," he said. I suggested that it was no longer politically correct to dig into cemeteries whether they were in Virginia or in Israel. Al laughed. "In Jefferson's day no one understood that. He was interested in the *culture* of those who had lived on his property long before he settled there. His notebooks indicate that he had a rough idea of *stratification* within that mound. Not bad for the late eighteenth century, hmm?"

Al's digression on the Enlightenment's contribution to archaeology was, I learned subsequently, just one facet of his active mind. He expressed concern that his students at Birzeit develop a "Palestinian focus" for the fieldwork they did, realizing it was limited by the political situation that then obtained in the West Bank. I was also struck by his interest in the archaeology of the early Islamic period. He knew that Prof. Dimitri Baramki at the A.U.B. was one of few Palestinians who had turned to archaeology as a vocation during the British Mandate period. Baramki's 1940s excavations at the Umayyad-built "Palace of Hisham" (Khirbit al-Mafjar) had been "groundbreaking" in more than one sense.

In the late afternoon we said our goodbyes. Al had to drive back to Jerusalem and I would be departing the next day for the return trip to Amman. He asked, "what are you going to do with all those old maps of Lebanon?" I answered, "write up an article when I make sense of them." We shook hands and he slid behind the wheel of his car. "Don't forget," he added, "maps are more than just geography, more than just lines on a paper. They have some cultural information to convey as well. About the past as well as the present." I smiled. "Jefferson would've understood," I said.

That double emphasis on culture, I learned, was typical of Albert Ernest Glock. He had a highly developed sense of how the present might inform or instruct us in the way we understand the past, and how the past could teach us about the present. It was his legacy to his profession, to his students, to his colleagues, and to his friends and family. It is a worthy legacy of a good and gracious man.

This paper is dedicated to Al's respect for "the culture of archaeology" and "the culture of old maps." He himself, since that visit, has become part of the "cultural geography" of the Palestine he loved and, in a very real sense, to which he dedicated his life. As someone who had lived and worked a large portion of his adult life in the Near East, he understood that ancient Palestine and Phoenicia were not just contiguous regions.

They formed then a closely related cultural area; language was only one aspect of their symbiosis. Iron Age Phoenician and Biblical Hebrew were dialects of the older Canaanite lingusitic matrix. Language is simply a reflection of the culture from which it has come, and the Palestinian–Phoenician cultures of antiquity were almost indistinguishable at some levels. For that reason it seems appropriate to explore, in Al's honor, the topic of this essay.

THE PHOENICIAN HOMELAND

What the Phoenicians themselves thought and wrote about their "homeland" is almost totally unknown. Commentaries written by Marinus of Tyre (ca. AD 75–140), had they survived complete, might have offered some insights.[1] There is no reference to physical geography or topography in the fragments of Philo of Byblos' *Phoenician History* (published ca. AD 125). Perhaps the echo of a native voice praising the Phoenician countryside can be heard in some passages of the Old Testament (e.g. portions of Canticles, certain Psalms). This would be appropriate in light of the close cultural ties (fostered by economic and dynastic bonds) between Iron Age Phoenicia and Palestine. That material is best examined separately since it represents a "local" tradition and its context is poetic allusion rather than prose description.

From the Late Bronze Age through the end of classical antiquity there is mention of the Phoenicians (*Kinnaḫu, Chna, Phoinikês, Poeni, Chanani*) in written sources. Homer's "Sidonians" are evident in many pages of the *Iliad* and the *Odyssey* but nowhere is there a descriptive passage referring to their homeland. Herodotus (*Hist.* 2.44, see also 1.1; 7.89) related a visit to Tyre during a "tour" of the Levant (mid-fifth century BC), but it is not until the beginning of the Hellenistic Age (330–30 BC) that the first important *descriptive* accounts begin to appear in the aftermath of Alexander the Great's extended conquest.

Gradually we gain a fairly detailed picture of the Phoenician landscape, one that combines familiar characteristics with sometimes disconcerting images. For most minor sources, physical geography is incidental to some other purpose, e.g. descriptions of flora and fauna, the narrative of a military campaign, the production of purple or glass. Those noted here are representative, not exhaustive.

Three comprehensive accounts of Phoenician geography survive complete in portions of Strabo's *Geography*, Pliny the Elder's *Natural History* and Ptolemy's *Geography*. All three works are prefaced by statements of intent, the details and clarity of which vary. It will be worthwhile to outline here what all three had to say, so that the objectives of each can be compared and contrasted. This will also permit us to check the details of their descriptions against those stated intentions. It will also allow us to compare and contrast all three accounts against the evidence of an important, and probably independent source, the *Tabula Peutingeriana*. Though this document in its present form is a medieval copy of a map produced in late antiquity, portions of it may indicate that a prototype existed some centuries earlier.

Strabo held that the utilitarian aspects of geography should be of interest to "statesmen and governments, because they can conduct their affairs with greater satisfaction if they comprehend a country's size, its position and its unique features" (*Geog.* 1.1.1 with 1.1.16). Pliny's approach was equally pragmatic. He believed that the study of the natural world (*rerum natura*) would educate men of influence in the Roman state (*HN* Praef. 13).

Ptolemy's task was somewhat different, since his handbook (*hyphêgêsis*) was not a prose descriptive geography. Thus he first defines the term geography as "a representation (*mimêsis*) in pictures (i.e. maps) of the entire world and the phenomena therein" (*Geog.* 1.11) and then goes on to say that the geographer is obligated to portray his world accurately, to establish the boundaries of regions, to note the peoples, cities and physical features peculiar to each region, and to plot by longitude and latitude the location of each (*Geog.* 1.19).

These introductory comments do not touch upon what modern anthropologists would call the "social landscape" of a region: the relationship of geography to culture, the influence of a particular physical environment on the historical development of its human inhabitants. Such concerns are not modern, but they were never fully expressed in antiquity. Some pre-Socratics (e.g. Xenophanes) hinted at potential aspects of what we term "cultural anthropology." Perhaps no one in antiquity came closer to defining them than Herodotus, but even he stopped just short of exploring the link between environment and "national identity."

Herodotus had counted the Thracians potentially among "the greatest" of peoples (*Hist.* 5.3) of his day, but never speculated that the physical limitations imposed by their Balkan homeland could have thwarted the chances for unification and the development of a powerful nation-state.[2] In like manner he devoted all of Book 2 to Egypt, offering copious observations on Egyptian topography, ethnography, botany and climate. When he summarized this wealth of detail, his conclusion was that the changeless climate and "the gift of the river" (i.e. the Nile) produced the great differences between Egyptians and Greeks (*Hist.* 2.35; cf. 2.5; 2.77). But we must infer that it was those contrasting characteristics that made Egypt such a great nation for so long.

We look in vain for that kind of detail concerning Phoenicia. Precisely where we expect to find it there is only anecdote. That occurs when Herodotus breaks off his narrative of Egypt to tell us of a visit to Tyre. That visit (*Hist.* 2.44) produced one paragraph of information on the Phoenicians consisting of what he saw and heard in Tyre. Not a single word is devoted to the Phoenician landscape or national characteristics (apart from a sense of historical *tradition*) of the people. The latter comes, also in the form of anecdote, elsewhere in the *Histories*.

Even if he had apportioned as much space to Phoenicia as to Egypt or Persia, it is doubtful that any connection would have been drawn between the physical setting and the achievements of its people. Fortune and the Gods, he constantly reminds us, determine a person's and a nation's destiny, not Nature. Polybius might have been the one source from whom we could expect an analysis of geography's effect on history. Certainly he was concerned with the cause and effects of wars (*Hist.* 3.6–8) and had we all of Book 24 instead of the fragments gleaned from later writers (particularly Strabo and Pliny) that theme of cause and effect might have included geography and imperialism.

The caveat is clear: we should not ask more of our sources than they were meant to provide. Concomitantly no single source is consistently accurate, but the margin of error, be it the distance from seacoast to inland lake, or the location of a river's source, is sometimes astonishingly small. That can only be judged by comparison with the results of modern geographic surveys of the same region. For just such a purpose it would be prudent to begin a review of Phoenician geography in ancient sources with a brief account of the region as it appears on maps today, to review the important written evidence, and then to come full circle and examine last the land of Phoenicia as it appears in ancient maps.

EXCURSUS: A SKETCH OF LEBANESE GEOGRAPHY

The mountains of modern-day Lebanon (Arabic *Lubnân*, "White") are among the major features of middle eastern geography (fig. 1). The coastal range (Jebal Lubnân, Mt. Lebanon), parallel to its inland counterpart, extends some 175 km from north to south, with many of its western foothills reaching the Mediterranean. The loftiest tip (elev. 3,083 m) in this range is Qurnat Sawdâ᾽ (Black Nook) southeast of Tripoli. The inland range (Jebal Lubnân Sharqî, Mt. Lebanon East) is nearly equal in length with its highest point (elev. 2,814 m) at Mt. Hermôn (Holy Mountain), southeast of Tyre. This is the Jebal Shaykh ("Mt. Greybeard") of early Arabic geographers, so named as much for its imposing authority on the surrounding countryside as for its perpetual snow. The northern foothills of both ranges reach almost to Homs (ancient Emesa) in the Orontes valley. The Lebanon range presents a monolithic façade to the Mediterranean coast with no natural passes (other than difficult gorges) to the interior between Mt. Carmel in the south and the Eleutheros River valley to the north. Travel inland went over, not through; a day's journey in either direction consisted of a long, laborious ascent followed by a lengthy but somewhat less arduous descent.[3]

In Graeco-Roman antiquity those parallel ranges were referred to simply as the Lebanon and Anti-Lebanon and the plain between them as the *Aulôn* (Valley) of Syria or *Koilê* Syria ("Hollow" Syria). Today that valley is called in Arabic *Biqâ᾽* (the "hollow" or "depression"; Wild 1973, 290–91; cf. Joshua 11:17 [*Biqât ha-Libânôn* "Valley of Lebanon"]). It is roughly 17 km wide and 160 km in length, at an average elevation of 800 m. Two modest but lengthy rivers, the Nahr al-ʿAsi (ancient *Orontes*) and the Lîtanî (ancient *Litas*), flow north and south respectively from springs and a major watershed in the upper (northern) end of the Biqâʿ (Abel 1933). Two riverine systems flow from the Anti-Lebanon range, the Hasbâni/Jordan to the south (from Hermôn) and the Nahr Baradâ (Bardines, Chrysorhoas) to the east (from Jebal Shaykh Mansûr).

Numerous rivers, none navigable inland, are born on the western slopes of the Lebanon range. Many reach the Mediterranean through gorges of often spectacular beauty, e.g. the valley of the Nahr Qadîsha ("Holy" River) southeast of Tripoli. The ancient name (Graeco/Roman

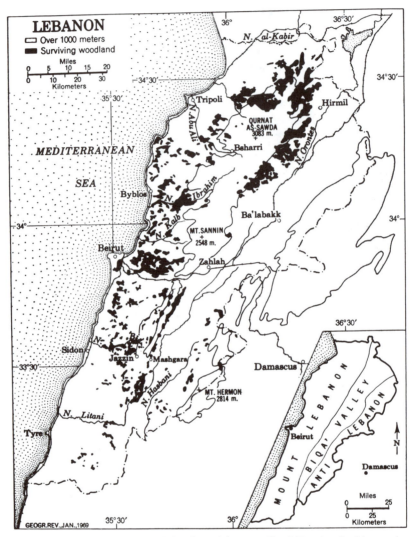

Fig. 1. Lebanon, generalized relief and surviving woodland. Reprinted with permission of *Geographical Review.*

or Semitic) of most is known. From north to south the principle rivers are the Nahr Kabîr (Eleutheros), Nahr Ibrâhîm (Adonis), Nahr Kalb (Lycus), Nahr Beirut (Magoras), Nahr Dâmûr (Damouras or Tamyras; also Leôn)[4] and Nahr Awwali (Bostrenus). The oldest stone bridges in Phoenicia are Roman, though it is possible that wooden bridges were constructed before then. Until bridges were built, a day's journey along the coast was nearly as difficult as taking the inland route. Even when men and animals did not have to ford the rivers and streams, they still had to tackle the narrow walkways or "ladders" (Greek *klimakês*; Latin *scala*) around the headlands (Arabic sing. *râs*) that protruded into the sea in half a dozen places. The *Scala Tyriorum* (Ladders of Tyre) at Râs Nâqûra was only the most famous of those. Sailing was a much faster and commercially much cheaper way to communicate along the coast. For a country bereft of any good natural harbors, it was a strong incentive to build both ships and ports. Before they developed an alphabet and were called Phoenicians, the inhabitants of the Canaanite littoral must have perfected a *lingua nautica*.

The Lebanese mountains were celebrated in antiquity as a place of beauty, a source of water and timber (fig. 2), a sanctuary for refugees, a base of operations for brigands and a home for the deities of Phoenicia. Quite understandably they became part of the folklore of the indigenous Canaanites and the neighboring peoples. For outsiders from lowlying and arid regions near or far, the first sight of such majestic mountains, especially in winter, must have been memorable. Some episodes of the Sumero-Babylonian *Epic of Gilgamesh* may be located in the Lebanese mountains[5] and the Old Testament abounds with references both historical and mythological.[6]

PHOENICIA IN THE HELLENISTIC PERIOD

Two of Aristotle's pupils had a firsthand acquaintance with Phoenicia and its fabulous geography. Alexander the Great was forced

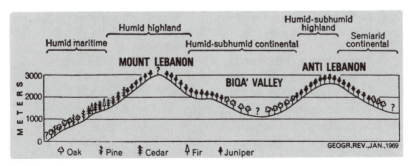

Fig. 2. Profile of primordial or potential forest cover. Reprinted with permission of *Geographical Review*.

to lead a punitive expedition into the mountains behind Tyre to counter "guerillas" who harassed his troops during the great seige of that city in the summer of 332 BC. All accounts[7] of this raid have Alexander and a "flying column" cross the Biqâ῾ Valley as far as "Arabia" (i.e. the territory in the Anti-Lebanon range [and farther east] controlled by Arab tribesmen). The military objective may have been more than a display of force; one scholar has suggested that the raid was intended to open a much-needed supply line to the agricultural interior (Engels 1978, 56). Plutarch's biography of Alexander highlights this episode by inserting an account of hand-to-hand combat with Lebanese mountaineers, an incident Plutarch borrowed from the memoires of Alexander's chamberlain or Master of Ceremonies, Chares of Mytilene:

> In the middle of the seige [late April–early May, 332 BC] he made an expedition against the Arabs who lived near Antilibanus and he ran into danger because of Lysimachus his *paidogogos* (for Lysimachus accompanied him, saying he was as good as and no older than Phoenix). When Alexander reached the hill-country and, leaving his horse behind, advanced on foot, the others went a long way ahead; but when Lysimachus began to grow weary and faint, though evening was coming on and the enemy were near at hand, Alexander refused to leave him; and encouraging him and helping him along with a few companions he unexpectedly found himself cut off from the main body and obliged to spend the night in a wild spot in darkness and extreme cold. Then he saw, at a distance, a number of scattered fires of the enemy burning; and trusting to his own nimbleness and endurance, while himself continually encouraging the despairing Macedonians, he ran up to the nearest party that was burning a fire; with his dagger he struck at two barbarians who were sitting over the fire, and snatching up a firebrand returned with it to his companions; they built a large fire and immediately frightened some of the enemy into flight and turned back a party that attacked; and so they passed the night safely. This at least is the story Chares has told. (*Alex.* 24:6–8).[8]

Plutarch's editorial remark is worth noting. He may have doubted the veracity of the incident, but it was too colorful to pass over in silence. Certainly the ambiance is evocative of Lebanese mountain weather in mid-spring, balmy and invigorating during the day but still dangerously cold at night. Substantial pockets of snow remain in shaded ravines at the higher elevations until early summer. Though some details of this episode were undoubtedly embroidered, it has the aura of versimilitude if not verifiable authenticity.

Another Aristotelian protegé, Theophrastus, left a vivid description of aromatic plants that grew in the *Aulôn* ("the Valley") of Lebanon, i.e. the Biqâ`. So vivid is his presentation that one suspects we are reading the words of an observant traveler who described what he saw ca. 300 BC:

> Sweet-flag (*calamus*) and ginger-grass (*schoinus*) grow beyond the Libanus between that range and another small range, in the depression (*aulôniskos*) thus formed; and not, as some say, between Libanus and Antilibanus. For Antilibanus is a long way from Libanus, and between them is a wide, fair plain called "the Valley" (*Aulôn*). But, where the sweet-flag and ginger-grass grow, there is a large lake, and they grow near it in the dried-up marshes, covering an extent of more than thirty *stadia* (6 km) ... as you approach the spot, immediately a sweet smell strikes you. However it is not true, as some say, that the fragrance is wafted to ships approaching the country [i.e. Phoenicia]; for indeed this district is more than 150 *stadia* (30 km) from the sea. (*Inquiry into Plants* 9.7.1–3).[9]

The location within the Biqâ` of this *aulôniskos* (literally "little valley") and its fragrant lake has occasioned some debate.[10] The figure of "more than 30 km" from the sea given in Theophrastus' account may be explained as a straight line distance. If so, it is remarkably accurate. The modern road-distance from Beirut directly east to Shtoura, on the western edge of the Biqâ`, is exactly 45 km. As the crow flies a figure of "more than 30 km" for that same distance is quite reasonable. Theophrastus' account is devoid of any village or town names and his "generic" designation for the central valley, *Aulôn*, may mean that the indigenous name for this segment of the Great Rift Valley was unknown to him or his source. Besides his botanical observations, Theophrastus also left us commentary on limestone and limeburning in Phoenicia, the forest-cover and royal "parks," the names of Phoenician winds, and Tyrian law.

Less than half a century later, a reference to the same valley under the name *Massyas* occurs in a papyrus document discovered in the discarded archives of the Finance Minister under King Ptolemy II of Greek-ruled Egypt. The document (*Papyrus Cairo Zenon* #59093 of 257 BC) records various legal and illegal transactions and customs-difficulties involving the purchase and transshipment of Phoenician and other goods (including slaves) from Phoenicia to Egypt. In passing, there is a reference to an expedition for the purpose of securing horses "in Massyas [Valley]." Whatever was purchased (or rustled) eventually found its way into the cargo of an Alexandria-bound merchant ship soon departing from Sidon or Tyre.[11]

Later still, Polybius relates a series of military campaigns during the Fourth Syrian War with Egypt (221–217 BC) in which Seleucid forces attempted to enter Ptolemaic Palestine either through the "Marsyas" (sic) Valley or along the Phoenician coast road. His description of the Lebanese Biqâ' is dramatic and accurate:

> From this town [Laodiceia-under-Lebanon] the king [Antiochus III] took the offensive with his whole army and crossing the desert entered the defile (*aulôn*) known as Marsyas, which lies between the chains of Libanus and Antilibanus, and affords a narrow passage between the two. Just where it is narrowest it is broken by marshes and lakes from which the perfumed reed (*calamus* = sweet-flag) is cut, and here it is commanded on the one side by a place called *Brochoi* ("Springs") and on the other by *Gerrha*, the passage between being quite narrow. After marching through this defile for several days and reducing the towns in its neighborhood, Antiochus reached Gerrha" (*Hist.* 5.45.7–5.46.2).[12]

The Ptolemaic commander of Gerrha secured his position with ditch and stockade; a frontal assault by Seleucid forces failed to breach the defences. That signal failure, plus trouble in the northern portion of his kingdom, persuaded Antiochus to abandon the enterprise. In the spring of 219 BC he again attacked the garrisons at Brochoi and Gerrha (*Hist.* 5.61.5–10). Leaving a sizeable force to besiege them, Antiochus out-maneuvered the enemy by a coastal attack into Palestine. It took a third campaign the following year to occupy Palestine and Transjordan. But an attempt to invade Egypt itself in 217 BC resulted in a disastrous defeat at the battle of Raphia. The Biqâ⁣ᶜ and coastal Phoenicia south of the Eleutheros River remained in Ptolemaic hands.

Polybius leavened his central discussion of politics and matters military with an occasional excursus on descriptive geography. He knew, for instance, that the source of the Orontes River lay in Phoenician territory. His detailed account of Seleuceia (the port of Antioch) includes a note to that effect. Polybius states that the city lay at the mouth of the Orontes:

> [A river] which, rising in the neighborhood of Libanus and Antilibanus and traversing what is known as the plain of Amyce [in modern Syria that plain is still called *'Amq*], passes through Antioch carrying off all the sewage of that town by the force of its current and finally falls into the Cyprian Sea near Seleuceia. (*Hist.* 5.59.10–12 [Loeb trans.]).

While the Ptolemies controlled Phoenicia, the already ancient shrine of Baᶜalbak was renamed Heliopolis. When Phoenicia eventually passed under Seleucid rule, one or more members of that Macedonian dynasty planned to develop the site as a major Hellenistic sanctuary.[13] The project was inherited, unfinished, by the Roman governors of Syria who took office after Pompey the Great (63 BC) brought much of the Near East within the imperial domains. On the foundation blocks of a shrine (presumably originally dedicated to Apollo Helios) begun by the Seleucid kings, the Emperor Augustus later caused to be raised a temple of awesome dimensions and spectacular appointments that was dedicated to Jupiter of Heliopolis.

It was there that Trajan (perhaps in the company of his architect Apollodorus of Damascus) came ca. AD 115 on the eve of his Parthian war to consult the Oracle (Macrobius, *Saturnalia* I.23.14–16). The remaining six columns of this colossal temple still dominate the skyline of the northeastern Biqâᶜ Valley. Until the outbreak of the Lebanese civil war in 1975 these and other equally imposing ruins served as the setting for the international Baᶜalbak Festival where, of a summer's evening, one could enjoy a concert by Ella Fitzgerald, a performance by the Bolshoi Ballet, or a play by Euripides.

PHOENICIA IN THE ROMAN PERIOD

In the twilight years of Seleucid rule the Ituraean Arabs[14] from east and south of the Anti-Lebanon established a capital at the site Polybius called Gerrha (modern ʿAnjar, perhaps the *Chalkis* ["Bronze"-town][15] of later writers) in the southern Biqâʿ Valley and a secondary stronghold in the ancient Bronze Age city of Arca (Tell ʿArqa) northeast of Tripoli. They proceeded to terrorize the coastal communities and the inland farms of Phoenicia until Roman forces under Pompey infiltrated the hill country, stormed the bandit headquarters and executed the ringleaders.[16]

Evidence that endemic banditry survived in the Phoenician mountains is given by a Latin inscription dating from the time of the famous "census of Quirinius" alluded to in Luke 2:1–5. A military prefect serving under Quirinius (consular governor of Syria 9–6 BC) attests that he carried out a census of Apamea in Syria and led an expedition "against the Ituraeans of Mt. Lebanon (*in Libano monte*) and captured a castle of theirs" (*Inscriptiones Latinae Selectae* #2683). Eventually the Romans suppressed these desperadoes. The Ituraean stronghold of Arca later achieved fame, under the romanized name of *Caesarea ad Libanum*, as the birthplace of the third century emperor Alexander Severus (AD 225–233; Starcky 1971/72).

The mountains of Phoenicia attracted the attention of the Roman historian Tacitus. In the early years of the second century AD he penned this brief but evocative description:

> Of the mountains, Lebanon rises to the greatest height, and is in fact a marvel, for in the midst of the excessive heat its summit is shaded by trees and covered with snow; it likewise is the source and supply of the river Jordan. (*Hist.* 5.6 [Loeb trans.]).

It would seem that Tacitus conflated descriptions of the higher peaks of the coastal mountains with Mt. Hermôn at the southern edge of the interior range. This makes sense in the context of his narrative point of view: his comments are part of a sketch of Judaea and adjacent regions. The beauty of the forest, the grandeur of its ambience, the magic of its summer snow, the gift of its waters to an arid land: all that is parenthetical background to his now-lost account of the Roman capture of

Jerusalem in AD 70. Turn the seasons around and one would expect to find somewhere in ancient sources a description of Phoenicia in winter. There is none. That was left to the Ministry of Tourism in the modern Republic of Lebanon: colorful posters advertising "sea and ski" in the same winter day, featuring lifts and lodges just a few hours' drive from sun-dappled Mediterranean beaches (and Beirut nightclubs in the evening).

But the great, green forests are now secluded groves, melancholy reminders that much has been lost. Defoliation is not a modern phenomenon; its effects in Phoenicia were noticeable not long after the time of Tacitus. The pragmatic Hadrian (AD 117–138), near the end of his reign, designated specific areas of the coastal mountains as an imperial forest, and delineated its extent with boundary-markers at intervals along the western and eastern flanks of the coastal range. The motivations were not purely ecological, but it was evident even then that some of the Mediterranean forests were in danger of extinction.

PHOENICIA IN THE BYZANTINE PERIOD

In the early Byzantine period, Eusebius of Caesarea (ca. 325) remarked in his *Chronicon* (trans. and commentary in Brown 1969, 82–84) that proof of the biblical Flood could be seen in fossilized sea-life in the Phoenician mountains. About a century later, St. Jerome affirmed that snow from Mt. Hermôn was welcomed as a summertime luxury by certain residents of Tyre.[17] A Graeco-Egyptian poet named Nonnus, a contemporary of Jerome, wrote the *Dionysiaca*, an epic describing the adventures of the god Dionysus in his travels to India and back. Part of the poem describes the seasonal pattern of life for "a farmer of Libanus."[18] A still-later Byzantine text notes that:

> Democritus records a natural signal, and advises the planting [of wheat and barley] at the setting of *Corona* [*Borealis*—the northern constellation]. Not only are abundant rains likely to fall then, but the earth has a natural receptive tendency to render fertile the seeds sown at that time. The setting of *Corona* in the regions of Phoenicia takes place roughly speaking on the 7th day before the *kalends* of December [November 25]." (trans. Brown 1969, 20 with commentary)

The tenth century AD compiler of this text cited a number of earlier sources, among them a *Collection of Farming Occupations* by Vindanius Anatolius of Beirut (fourth century AD?) from which this notation is probably taken. Perhaps it was belated recognition in the Byzantine age that the pagan, celestial deities still had some influence upon the activities of man, especially upon those who farmed the Phoenician littoral and the great inland valley. The Democritus of this text may or may not be the fifth century BC "pre-Socratic" credited with the "atomic" theory of matter and scolded by Pliny (*Natural History* 30.9) for popularizing "magical works" discovered in the tomb of "Dardanus the Phoenician." Strabo reported (*Geog.* l6.2.24) a tradition known to Poseidonius of Apamea that "the ancient doctrine concerning atoms is [that] of Mochus of Sidon, born before the time of the Trojans." There is a complex web of literary and "scientific" tradition involved in this that cannot be unraveled here and is best discussed in another context.

Even so brief a review of literary/historical references may serve to demonstrate the constant interest evoked by the physical geography of Phoenicia throughout antiquity. Two other sources must now be examined: comprehensive descriptions and pictorial representations (i.e. ancient maps). As will be shown, there are detailed but conflicting descriptions of Phoenicia in Strabo's *Geography* and Pliny the Elder's *Natural History* and a schematic account in the text of Ptolemy's *Geography* (see Appendices). The extant maps of Phoenicia are also a mixed blessing. We can study medieval copies of two Graeco-Roman maps that illustrate vividly how Phoenicia appeared to anyone in antiquity with access to such documents.[19] Here again the evidence is contradictory. Let us begin with the descriptive accounts.

STRABO AND PLINY ON PHOENICIA

Strabo probably set down what he knew about Phoenicia during a sojourn in Alexandria between 24 and 20 BC It was evident to him that the mountains were the most distinctive features of the country and, accordingly, they dominate his account (*Geog.* l6.2.15–34). His descriptive point of view is from the seacoast looking inland. Mt. Libanus, he says, *runs inland from the headland of Theouprosôpon* ("God's Face," modern *Râs Shakka*) just south of Tripoli. The Anti-

Libanus range *runs parallel to it from the coast near Sidon*. Both ranges terminate "above" (i.e. beyond) Damascus in the Syrian interior.

Between them lies a plain (part of "Hollow [*Coele*] Syria"), 200 *stadia* (40 km) wide and 400 *stadia* (80 km) long. This plain is well-watered by rivers, among them the Jordan, the Chrysorhoas ("Gold-Flowing", modern Wadi Baradâ) "rising (*arxámenos*) in the city and *territorium* of Damascus," and a third called the *Lycus* ("Wolf," modern Nahr Kalb), which empties into the Mediterranean. Strabo states that both the Lycus and the Jordan are navigable inland and are used for transport by ship, particularly merchant-vessels from the island-city of Aradus (now Ruʿad island within modern Syria).

His description becomes even more detailed when the single great plain between the mountains is shown to be composite. There are in reality two plains, the *Macra* or *Macras*-Plain near the seacoast and the *Massyas* inland. The latter in places is mountainous, with Chalkis as "the acropolis, so to speak, of the Massyas." Beyond Massyas is a "Royal Valley" about which we are told nothing, and farther yet is the city and territory of Damascus. But then he summarizes his discussion by saying,

> the entire country south of Seleuceia [the coastal district of Syria], as far as Egypt and Arabia, is called *Coele Syria*, but the part delimited by the Libanus and Anti-Libanus is given that name in a special sense. The remainder [of Coele Syria] from Orthosia [near Aradus] to Pelusium [in the eastern delta of Egypt] is called Phoenicia, a narrow corridor of land, some of which projects into the sea.

Pliny, writing no later than AD 77, is also aware of the Phoenician mountains. The Libanus range, he says, begins behind Sidon and extends to Zimyra (near Aradus), some 1,500 *stadia* (300 km) away. "Opposing [Libanus], with a valley between, is Antilibanus, once connected [to Libanus] by a wall" (*NH* 5.77). East of the Antilibanus range is the region of the Decapolis; south of Antilibanus is Palestine. The Orontes River, he notes, "rises (*natus*) between Libanus and Antilibanus next to Heliopolis" (*NH* 5.80). His list of coastal cities belonging to Phoenicia begins, as does Strabo's, with Aradus in the north but ends with Caesarea (Straton's Tower) in the south.

Pliny implies that he considers the great interior plain and the Antilebanon range as parts of Greater Syria, since he uses the term

Coele Syria to describe the Orontes Valley north of the Biqâ'. It is evident that he read Theophrastus' account of the aromatic plants from the Aulôn since his own discussion of *calamus* notes that it is found in "a medium size valley ... about 150 stades from *Mare Nostrum* (the Mediterranean) between Libanus and another low mountain—not, as some think, Antilibanus" (*NH* 12.104). Pliny locates the river Jordan in Palestine, and knows that it flows south to the Dead Sea.

There is little hope of reconciling these two conflicting descriptions of Phoenicia. The garbled account of Strabo testifies to his own ignorance. Somehow he managed to travel to and from Egypt bypassing Phoenicia, since even in his detailed sketches of Aradus (16.2.13–14) and Tyre (16.2.23–24) his information is attributed not to a named historian or geographer but to an anonymous "(as) it is said." Throughout the *Geography* he credits Poseidonius and Polybius for specific geographical information, but his sources for Phoenicia remain unknown to us.

In the face of that, one is at a loss to explain such basic errors in Strabo as the east–west alignment of the mountain system, his estimate of the size of the intervening valley, and his comments on certain rivers. Strabo's Massyas plain is approximately twice the width and half the length of the Biqâ'. Worse yet, the width of the valley should correspond to the distance between Theouprosôpon and Sidon (120 km), western terminal points (as Strabo tells us) of the Lebanon and Antilebanon ranges. Yet he gives the breadth of the valley as only one-third that figure.

Were it not for those fundamental mistakes, the details of his description would appear less bizarre than they do. There is today a large plain northeast of Tripoli, the 'Akkâr ("Dark," perhaps from deposits of alluvial silt), which corresponds in name and location to Strabo's Macras.[20] The Royal Valley beyond the Massyas is recognizable as *Abilenê*, a tetrarchy (princedom) tucked in a fold of the eastern Antilebanon and known to Josephus (*Antiquities of the Jews* 19.5.1; *Jewish War* 2.11.5) and the author of the Gospel of Luke (3:1).[21]

Chalkis is identified as the key strategic site in the Biqâ'. In an earlier passage (*Geog.* 16.2.10), Strabo correctly associates Chalkis and Heliopolis. Strabo's account of the Jordan River reaching the Mediterranean coast is difficult to understand unless one makes the desperate effort of emending the Greek text to read *Orontes* instead of

Iordanes.[22]   But there is no semantic fig leaf that will hide the embarrassment of his observation that Damascus is the source, rather than the gift, of the Chrysorhoas River.

The source of Pliny's more accurate description is not noted in his text but it is obvious he did not consult Strabo or Strabo's source(s). Neither does it seem that he ever traveled to Phoenicia, in spite of attempts to restore his name in an honorary inscription from Aradus.[23] There are well-documented instances where Pliny utilized military records available to him (e.g. *NH* 6.l4) or had access to maps prepared to accompany campaign accounts—especially the eastern campaigns of Cn. Domitius Corbulo and C. Licinius Mucianus (*NH* 6.40). It is very probable that he made use of such reports, some as recent as the Jewish War of AD 66–74 which Pliny knew of as a conflict in progress.

Pliny's note on the source of the Orontes at Heliopolis/Baʿalbek is accurate (and unique), but his estimation of the length of the mountain ranges is almost double what it should be. Remains of the "connecting wall" between the Lebanon and Antilebanon ranges have been traced on the ground (Ghadban 1981, 143–68, esp. 158–59).[24] There is no mention in Pliny of the fortress town of Gerrha.

Neither Strabo nor Pliny attempts to define the political situation obtaining at the time he wrote. Phoenicia was part of geographical Syria; for Pliny this includes the Massyas Valley (unnamed in his account). Strabo's belief that Phoenicia included coastal Palestine (*Philistia*) as far as Pelusium agrees with the statement in Josephus (*AJ* 15.5.1) that Antony gave Cleopatra the Phoenician cities (except Sidon and Tyre) "between the Eleutherus River and Egypt." That exaggerated view may mean that "Phoenicia" and "Coele Syria" (the latter in its broadest geographical context) were for them (or their sources) synonymous.

PTOLEMY OF ALEXANDRIA AND PHOENICIA

It would be useful now to compare the evidence of ancient maps with the testimony of Strabo and Pliny. Some caution must be expressed at once since our sources are very meagre and in every case the original map is no longer available for consultation. Indeed, a healthy dose of skepticism concerning the practical value of Graeco-Roman maps and itineraries has very recently been voiced (Bekker-Nielsen 1988). But even so, the evidence of maps cannot be ignored. Maps drawn to illustrate Ptolemy's *Geography* were probably produced in his lifetime. Many facsimile editions have appeared since the medieval period (with Latin or Greek notations),[25] but since all are based on the figures compiled in Ptolemy's handbook, the variations are minimal (fig. 3). Their value lies entirely in the visual image, the ability to render in a meaningful pattern the dry list of place-names and coordinates of the *Geography*.

Ptolemy's "Phoenicia" appears twice (as a district of Syria) under the heading *Phoinikê*. First is a list of twelve coastal cities (*Geog.* 5.14.3–4), from Simyra to Dora, and features of physical geography. The latter include four rivers (the Eleutheros, Adonis (modern Nahr Ibrahîm), Leôn and Chorseos), the promontory of Theouprosôpon near Tripoli, and Mt. Carmel. A supplementary list (*Geog.* 5.14.17) gives four "inland" towns. The source of the river Jordan is correctly located at Caesarea Panias (modern Banias in Upper Galilee), one of those "interior" towns. Aradus and Tyre are listed as "islands adjacent to Syria" in a separate entry (*Geog.* 5.14.21).

So far we appear to be on firm ground. But a close comparison of handbook and map reveals some disturbing discrepancies. Under the heading Laodicenê (*Geog.* 5.14.16) are the names of two towns, Laodiceia (further identified as *Scabiosa* [= "Rough"] by Ptolemy) and Paradisus (in the upper Orontes Valley) associated with Phoenicia. Another town, Iabruda, he places in the tetrarchy of Abilenê. The Chrysorhoas River inexplicably flows *northwest* (!) to Damascus from the distant interior of Syria. The town of Palaeobyblos is located inland between Botrys and Byblos instead of on the coast between Byblos and Beirut.

But these oddities, however disconcerting, are minor compared to the disposition of the Lebanon and Antilebanon mountains. These are not associated with "Phoenicia" but are named (and their coordinates given) in a separate entry (*Geog.* 5.14.6–7) listing "the notable mountains of Syria." When their coordinates are actually plotted, Ptolemy's map shows the "Libanos and Antilibanos" mountains parallel to each other *but at nearly right angles to the Mediterranean*. Their latitudes correspond to those of Theouprosôpon and Sidon respectively, but the twin ranges begin at a considerable distance inland and terminate east of Damascus. This rearrangement actually places the

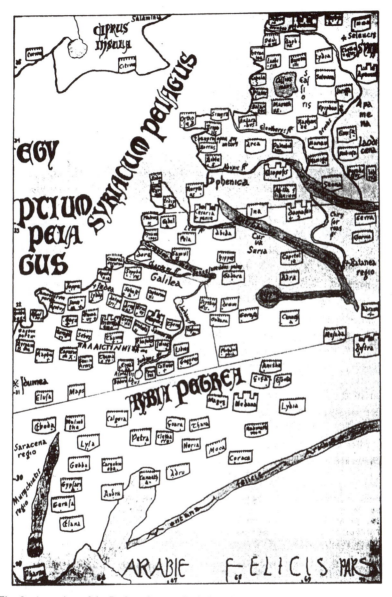

Fig. 3. A portion of the Ptolemaic map depicting the Near East based on the medieval copy of the Ptolemaic map in the *Vatican Urbinas Greek Codex* 82, ed. J. Fischer (Leiden: Brill, 1932). The physical features are copied from Fischer's pl. 19, but the Latin forms of most Greek names are taken from his pl. 46. Map enlarged from that given in R. North, *A History of Biblical Map-Making* (1979, 65 fig. 12). Reprinted with permission of L. Reichert Verlag.

mountains and their valley within *another* district of Syria called by Ptolemy "Coele Syria and the Decapolis." The latter entity (*Geog.* 5.14.18–19) includes eighteen cities, though it is not stated which belong to Coele Syria and which to the district or region called the Decapolis. Among the eighteen Ptolemy lists are Heliopolis, Abila (capital of Abilenê) and Damascus in west to east order between "Libanos and Antilibanos." Still farther east is another district named *Batanaea* (*Geog.* 5.14.20–21) in which a "Gerrha" is located. Such extraordinary disposition of topography, towns and territory associated with Phoenicia demands some explanation. Ptolemy has introduced an aspect of what might be called social or cultural geography.[26]

PHOENICIA IN THE *TABULA PEUTINGERIANA*

The eleven sheets comprising the *Tabula Peutingeriana* or Peutinger Maps are also of medieval vintage (fig. 4).[27] The map is a linear representation of the known world with the major emphasis on exact distances between towns and cities. The sheet on which northern Britain, the Iberian peninsula and the western half of North Africa were depicted is missing. The remaining portions of the map measure about 7 m in length by about one-third of a meter in width, an elongated rectangle (with inevitable distortions) showing the roads and major stopping-places between southern Britain and the Far East. Christian notations related to biblical place names clearly show that the Peutinger Map, or at least its Near Eastern segments, was in use from the fourth century AD Internal evidence demonstrates that the prototype of some segments (if not the entire map) dates from the first century AD. It is possible that the ultimate prototype was the famous *Orbis Terrarum* attributed to Marcus Agrippa (10 BC), which Pliny the Elder observed on the walls of the Agrippan Portico in Rome (NH 3.2.17).[28]

Fig. 4. (Opposite.) The *Peutinger Table*, enlarged segment showing Palestine, Lebanon, and Syria (K. Miller, *Die Peutingersche Tafel*, 2nd edition, 1929). Dark areas are the sea and light areas are land. Road distances and major stations are shown. The central portion of the lower third of the map shows two mountain ranges; the legend *PALESTINA* runs between them. Roman roads from Damascus (bottom, just right of center) run to Heliopolis (Baʿalbek) and thence to Berytus, or from Damascus via Caesarea Paneas through the costal range to Tyre. There is no indication of a Roman road *through* the Biqâʿ (i.e., from Heliopolis to Caesarea Paneas). Reprinted with permission.

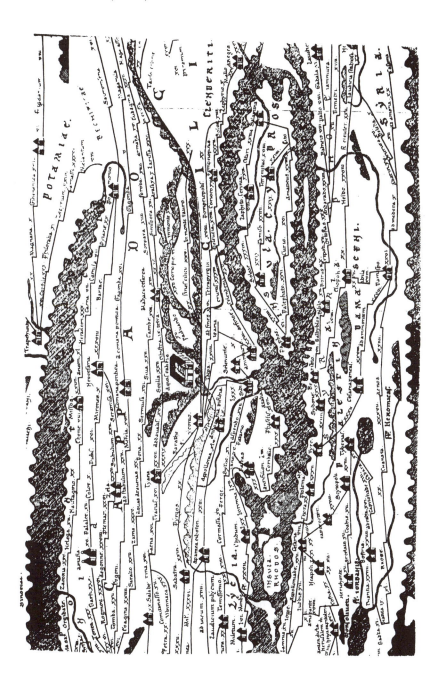

However that may be, the map as we have it dates from some centuries after Ptolemy. *Syria-Phoenici* is clearly labeled along the Mediterranean coast on Segment 10 of the map, extending as far north as the upper Orontes valley. The towns and cities of the Phoenician coast are shown as vignettes featuring the façade of a building. Parallel mountain ranges (unlabeled and not directly opposing each other) are shown inland, the outer (easternmost) running considerably farther north. The annotation *Palestina* obtrudes from the south into the valley between those mountains. Beyond the eastern range is *Damasceni*.

Two rivers are associated with Phoenicia: the Eleutheros with its mouth between Antarado(s) and Balneis (Balnea) on the northern coast and another, unnamed river, perhaps the Belus (*Nahr Naʿmân*),[29] debouching between Ptolemaide (Ptolemais) and Cesaria (Caesarea) on the southern coast. The coastal road is marked with appropriate stops and the mileage between each.

Two roads run inland from the coast, one from Tyre directly through the Lebanon range to Caesarea Paneas (the *Caesarea Philippi* of the New Testament), a distance of thirty-two Roman miles (47 km). The other runs from Berytus around the northern edge(?) of the Lebanon range to Eliopoli (Heliopolis). The distance shown is 108 Roman miles (158 km) with no stops indicated. That road bifurcates at Heliopolis, one branch going north to Laudicia (sic) Scabiosa and the other east to Abila and Damascus. The Jordan River, marked as such, flows directly from Lake Tiberias to the Dead Sea.

CONCLUSION

The descriptive geographies of Strabo and Pliny, and the Ptolemy and Peutinger Maps, represent four independent accounts of Phoenician geography. There are some superficial resemblances between texts and maps. This is most apparent when Strabo and Ptolemy err in the orientation of the Lebanon and Antilebanon or when Pliny and the Peutinger Map concur on the correct alignment of those mountains. But the discrepancies far outnumber the agreements. Strabo's Jordan reaches the coast, Ptolemy's flows to the Dead Sea. Pliny's Orontes and Jordan Rivers have their headwaters near Heliopolis and Caesarea Panias respectively. On the Peutinger Map the source of the Orontes is shown near Emesa and the Jordan is created by, instead of creating,

Lake Tiberias. In short there seems to be no reason, other than occasional coincidence of detail, to connect Strabo with Ptolemy, or Pliny with the Peutinger Map.

Where we might expect the descriptive accounts to draw some important parallels between the physical geography of Phoenicia, and the historical and cultural development of the Phoenicians, there is silence. That silence is all the more noticeable in light of the lofty intentions of both Strabo and Pliny set out in the prefaces to their respective works.[30] Pliny does at least manage in passing to note the contribution of the Phoenicians to Mediterranean culture when he states (*NH* 5.67) that "the Phoenician race has glorified itself by innovations in the alphabet, astronomy, navigation and the art of warfare."

Not a word there of how or why that came to pass. A few pages later (*NH* 5.76) we find this bittersweet remark for the city that founded Lepcis Magna, Utica, Gades and Carthage: "Now all of its glories reside in a mollusc and its purple." Such is his epitaph for Tyre. Strabo is also aware of Phoenician glories won and lost and notes (*Geog.* 16.2.23) that seamanship and dyemaking were the two skills in which "the Phoenicians excelled beyond all peoples." He is also careful to add (*Geog.* 16.2.24) that Greeks attribute to Phoenicians knowledge of astronomy and arithmetic "and many other philosophies from their cities."

PLINY, *NATURAL HISTORY* V, 15–17

A tergo eius Libanus mons orsus MD stadiis Zimyram usque porrigitur Coeles Syriae quae² cognominatur. huic par interveniente valle mons adversus Antilibanus obtenditur quondam muro coniunctus. post eum introrsus Decapolitana regio praedictaeque cum ea Tetrarchiae et Palaestines tota laxitas; in ora autem subiecta Libano fluvius Magoras, Berytus colonia quae Felix Iulia appellatur, Leontos Oppidum, flumen Lycos, Palaebyblos, flumen Adonis, oppida Byblos, Botrys, Gigarta, Trieris, Calamos, Tripolis quam Tyrii et Sidonii et Aradii optinent, Orthosia. Eleutheros flumen, oppida Zimyra, Marathos, contraque Arados septem stadiorum oppidum et insula ducentis passibus a continente distans; regio in qua supradicti desinunt montes: et interiacentibus campis Bargylus mons.

XVIII. Incipit hinc rursus Syria, desinente Phoenice. oppida Carne, Balanea, Paltos, Gabala, promunturium in quo Laodicea libera, Dipolis, Heraclea, Charadrus, Posidium. dein promunturium Syriae Antiochiae; intus ipsa Antiochia libera, Epi Daphnes cognominata, Oronte amne dividitur; in promunturio autem Seleucia libera Pieria appellata. super eam mons eodem quo alius nomine, Casius, cuius excelsa altitudo quarta vigilia orientem per tenebras solem aspicit, brevi circumactu corporis diem noctemque pariter ostendens. ambitus ad. cacumen xix p. est, altitudo per directum iv. at

in ora amnis Orontes natus inter Libanum et Antilibanum iuxta Heliopolim. oppida Rhosos—et a tergo Portae quae Syriae appellantur, intervallo Rhesiorum montium et Tauri,—in ora oppidum Myriandros, mons Amanus in quo oppidum Bomitae. ipse ab Syris Ciliciam separat.

Behind Sidon begins Mount Lebanon, a chain extending as far as Zimyra in the district called Hollow Syria, a distance of nearly 190 miles. Facing Lebanon, with a valley between, stretches the equally long range of Counter-Lebanon, which was formerly connected with Lebanon by a wall. Behind Counter-Lebanon inland is the region of the Ten Cities, and with it the tetrarchies already mentioned, and the whole of the wide expanse of Palestine; while on the coast, below Mount Lebanon, are the river Magoras, the colony of Beyrout called Julia Felix, Lion's Town, the river Lyeus, Palaebyblos, the river Adonis, the towns of Jebeil, Batrun, Gazis, Trieris, Calamos; Tarablis, inhabited by people from Tyre, Sidon and Ruad: Ortosa, the river Eleutheros, the towns of Zimyra and Marathos: and facing them the seven-furlong town and island of Ruad, 330 yards from the mainland; the region in which the mountain ranges above mentioned terminate; and beyond some intervening plains Mount Bargylus.

XVIII. At this point Phoenicia ends and Syria begins again. There are the towns of Tartus, Banias, Bolde and Djebeleh; the cape on which the free town of Latakia is situated; and Dipolis, Heraclea, Charadrus and Posidium. Then the cape of Antiochian Syria, and inland the city of Antioch itself, which is a free town and is called 'Antioch Near Daphne,'ᵃ and which is separated from Daphne by the river Orontes; while on the cape is the free town of Seleukeh, called Pieria. Above Seleukeh is a mountain having the same name as the other one, Casius, is so extremely lofty that in the fourth quarter of the night it commands a view of the sun rising through the darkness, so presenting to the observer if he merely turns round a view of day and night simultaneously. The winding route to the summit measures 19 miles, the perpendicular height of the mountain being 4 miles. On the coast is the river Orontes, which rises between Lebanon and Counter-Lebanon, near Baalbec. The towns are Rhosos.—and behind it the pass called the Gates of Syria, in between the Rhosos Mountains and Mount Taurus,—and on the coast the town of Myriandros, and Mount Alma-Dagh, on which is the town of Bomitae. This mountain separates Cilicia from Syria.

STRABO, *GEOGRAPHY* XVI, 15–18

15. Μετὰ δὲ Ὀρθωσίαν ἐστὶ καὶ τὸν Ἐλεύθερον Τρίπολις, ἀπὸ τοῦ συμβεβηκότος τὴν ἐπίκλησιν εἰληφυῖα· τριῶν γάρ ἐστι πόλεων κτίσμα, Τύρου, Σιδῶνος, Ἀραδου· τῇ δὲ Τριπόλει συνεχές ἐστι τὸ τοῦ Θεοῦ πρόσωπον, εἰς ὃ τελευτᾷ ὁ Λίβανος τὸ ὅρος· μεταξὺ δὲ Τριήρης, χωρίον τι.

16. Δύο δὲ ταῦτ᾿ ἐστὶν ὅρη τὰ ποιοῦντα τὴν Κοίλην καλουμένην Συρίαν,¹ ὡς ἂν παράλληλα, ὅ τε Λίβανος καὶ ὁ Ἀντιλίβανος, μικρὸν ὑπερθεν τῆς θαλάττης ἀρχόμενα ἄμφω· ὁ μὲν Λίβανος τῆς κατὰ Τρίπολιν, κατὰ τὸ τοῦ Θεοῦ μάλιστα πρόσωπον, ὁ δ᾿ Ἀντιλίβανος τῆς κατὰ Σιδῶνα· τελευτῶσι δ᾿ ἐγγύς πως τῶν Ἀραβίων ὁρῶν τῶν ὑπὲρ τῆς Δαμασκηνῆς καὶ τῶν Τραχώνων² ἐκεῖ λεγομένων εἰς ἄλλα ὅρη γεώλοφα καὶ καλλίκαρπα. ἀπολείπουσι δὲ μεταξὺ πεδίον κοῖλον· πλάτος μὲν τὸ ἐπὶ τῇ θαλάττῃ διακοσίων σταδίων, μῆκος δὲ τὸ ἀπὸ τῆς θαλάττης εἰς τὴν μεσόγαιαν ὁμοῦ³ τι διπλάσιον. διαρρεῖται δὲ ποταμοῖς ἄρδουσι χώραν εὐδαίμονα καὶ πάμφορον, μεγίστῳ δὲ τῷ Ἰορδάνῃ. ἔχει δὲ καὶ λίμνην, ἣ φέρει τὴν ἀρωματῖτιν σχοῖνον⁴ καὶ κάλαμον, ὡς δ᾿ αὔτως καὶ ἕλη· καλεῖται δ᾿ ἡ λίμνη Γεννησαρῖτις. φέρει δὲ καὶ βάλσαμον. τῶν δὲ ποταμῶν ὁ μὲν Χρυσορρόας, ἀρξάμενος ἀπὸ τῆς Δαμασκηνῶν πόλεως καὶ χώρας, εἰς τὰς ὀχετείας ἀναλίσκεται σχεδόν τι· πολλὴν γὰρ ἐπάρδει καὶ βαθεῖαν σφόδρα·⁵ τὸν δὲ Λύκον καὶ τὸν Ἰορδάνην ἀναπλέουσι φορτίοις, Ἀράδιοι δὲ μάλιστα.

17. Τῶν δὲ πεδίων τὸ μὲν πρῶτον, τὸ ἀπὸ τῆς θαλάττης, Μάκρας καλεῖται καὶ Μάκρα πεδίον· ἐν τούτῳ δὲ Ποσειδώνιος ἱστορεῖ τὸν δράκοντα πεπτωκότα ὁραθῆναι νεκρόν, μῆκος σχεδόν τι καὶ πλεθριαῖον, πάχος δ᾿, ὥσθ᾿ ἱππέας ἑκατέρωθεν παραστάντας ἀλλήλους μὴ καθορᾶν, χάσμα δέ, ὥστ᾿ ἔφιππον δέξασθαι, τῆς δὲ φολίδος λεπίδα ἑκάστην ὑπεραίρουσαν θυρεοῦ.

18. Μετὰ δὲ τὸν Μάκραν ἐστὶν ὁ Μασσύας, ἔχων τινὰ καὶ ὀρεινά, ἐν οἷς ἡ Χαλκίς, ὥσπερ ἀκρόπολις τοῦ Μασσύου· ἀρχὴ δ᾿ αὐτοῦ Λαοδίκεια ἡ πρὸς Λιβάνῳ. τὰ μὲν οὖν ὀρεινὰ ἔχουσι πάντα Ἰτουραῖοί τε καὶ Ἄραβες, κακοῦργοι πάντες, οἱ δ᾿ ἐν τοῖς πεδίοις γεωργοί· κακούμενοι δ᾿ ὑπ᾿ ἐκείνων ἄλλοτε ἄλλης βοηθείας δέονται. ὁρμητηρίοις δ᾿ ἐρυμνοῖς χρῶνται, καθάπερ οἱ τὸν Λίβανον ἔχοντες ἄνω μὲν ἐν τῷ ὅρει Σίνναν καὶ Βόρραμα καὶ ἄλλα τοιαῦτα ἔχουσι τείχη, κάτω δὲ Βότρυν καὶ Γίγαρτον καὶ τὰ ἐπὶ τῆς θαλάττης σπήλαια καὶ τὸ ἐπὶ τῷ Θεοῦ προσώπῳ φρούριον ἐπιτεθέν, ἃ κατέσπασε Πομπήιος, ἀφ᾿ ὧν τήν τε Βύβλον κατέτρεχον¹ καὶ τὴν ἐφεξῆς ταύτῃ Βηρυτόν, αἳ μεταξὺ κεῖνται Σιδῶνος καὶ τοῦ Θεοῦ προσώπου.

---

15. After Orthosia and the Eleutherus River one comes to Tripolis,¹ which has taken its name from what is the fact in the case, for it is a foundation consisting of three cities, Tyre and Sidon and Aradus. Contiguous to Tripolis is Theuprosopon,² where Mt. Libanus terminates; and between the two lies Trieres, a kind of stronghold.

16. Here are two mountains, Libanus and Antilibanus, which form Coelê-Syria, as it is called, and are approximately parallel to each other. They both begin slightly above the sea—Libanus above the sea near Tripolis and nearest to Theuprosopon, and Antilibanus above the sea near Sidon; and somewhere in the neighbourhood of the Arabian mountains above Damascenê and the Trachones,¹ as they are called, the two mountains terminate in other mountains that are hilly and fruitful. They leave a hollow plain between them, the breadth of which, near the sea, is two hundred stadia, and the length, from the sea into the interior, is about twice that number. It is intersected by rivers, the Jordan being the largest, which water a country that is fertile and all-productive. It also contains a lake, which produces the aromatic rush² and reed; and likewise marshes. The lake is called Gennesaritis. The plain also produces balsam. Among the rivers is the Chrysorrhoas, which begins at the city and country of the Damasceni and is almost wholly used up in the conduits, for it irrigates a large territory that has a very deep soil; but the Lycus and the Jordan are navigated inland with vessels of burden, mostly by the Aradians.

17. As for the plains, the first, beginning at the sea, is called Macras, or Macra-Plain. Here, as reported by Poseidonius, was seen the fallen dragon, the corpse of which was about a plethrum¹ in length, and so bulky that horsemen standing by it on either side could not see one another; and its jaws were large enough to admit a man on horseback, and each flake of its horny scales exceeded an oblong shield in length.

18. After Macras one comes to the Massyas Plain, which contains also some mountainous parts, among which is Chalcis, the acropolis, as it were, of the Massyas. The beginning of this plain is the Laodiceia near Libanus. Now all the mountainous parts are held by Ituraeans and Arabians, all of whom are robbers, but the people in the plains are farmers; and when the latter are harassed by the robbers at different times they require different kinds of help. These robbers use strongholds as bases of operation; those, for example, who hold Libanus possess, high up on the mountain, Sinna and Borrama and other fortresses like them, and, down below, Botrys and Gigartus and the caves by the sea and the castle that was erected on Theuprosopon. Pompey destroyed these places; and from them the robbers overran both Byblus and the city that comes next after Byblus, I mean the city Berytus,² which lie between Sidon and Theuprosopon.

NOTES

1. For Marinus' contribution see MacAdam (in press).
2. The tragic modern parallel is the present situation in what used to be known as Yugoslavia. There, the combination of cultural diversity and divisive physical geography is manifest. The closer we come to the beginning of the twenty-first century, the more the map of Europe begins to resemble the map of Europe precisely a century ago. In 1900 there was no Yugoslavia, no Soviet Union, and no Czechoslovakia; Germany was then (and is again) united.
3. A concise and colorful introduction to Lebanese geography can be found in Hitti (1967, 11–24). The best maps available are the series prepared during the French mandate and tabulated by Brown (1969, xxv). A useful bibliography of maps is given by Ghadban (1981, 143–45, n. 2). For the etymology of Lebanese (and some Syrian) place-names the standard work is now Wild (1973). It has not completely eclipsed its predecessor, Freyha (1972).
4. Wild (1973, 273), who overlooked Ptolemy's (*Geog.* 5.14.3) reference to the river of that name. Some modern writers (e.g. Hitti 1967; Jones 1971, map V opposite p. 226) have incorrectly identified the River Leôn ("Leontes") with the Litâni. Strabo (*Geog.* 16.2.22) and Pliny (*NH* 5.74) note a "Leontopolis" near the river Tamyras.
5. The relevant texts are in Pritchard (1969, 78–81). See also Brown (1969, 167) for commentary.
6. References are collected in Brown (1969, 164, 167, 172 [mythological]; 180–81, 201–203 [historical]).
7. Arrian, *Anabasis of Alexander* 2.20.4; Quintus Curtius, *History of Alexander* 4.3.1; Polyaenus, *Strategems* 4.3.4; Plutarch, *Alexander* 24.6.
8. Pearson (1960, 56). Chares (or Plutarch) seems to distinguish between the *Arabes* of the Antilebanon and the *barbaroi* ("non-Greeks") of the Lebanon. Curtius (4.3.1) refers to Alexander's antagonists more specifically as *Arabum agrestes* ("Arab peasants"). Both terms must refer to the Ituraeans of a later time (see n. 14 below and Brown [1969, 32 n. 15]).
9. Loeb translation. On the basis of this and other references to Phoenicia in Theophrastus, Brown (1969, 15) believes the botanist actually saw what he described, or at the very least drew upon an eyewitness account (verbal or written).
10. Rey-Coquais (1964, 296–301), plausibly situates it in the southern Biqâ'.
11. For translation and commentary see Harper (1928, 28–29).
12. Loeb translation. For commentary see Walbank (1957, 577). Gerrha has long been identified with modern 'Anjar; the identity of Brochoi is less

certain. On the latter especially see Rey-Coquais (1964, 289–96). Though *Brochoi* has a Greek meaning relevant to its location, it probably is a fortuitous transliteration of an indigenous place name (e.g. the nearby modern sites of Barûq and Baraka). ʿAnjar is probably elision for ʿAyn Gerrha (sing.) or ʿAyûn Gerrha (pl.), i.e. the Spring (or Springs) of Gerrha. It is just possible that "Brochoi Gerrha" may mean the same thing and that Brochoi is modern Majdal ʿAnjar and Gerrha is ʿAnjar proper.

13. See Ragette (1980, 28) with sketch. See also Rey-Coquais (1976), s.v. "Heliupolis."

14. On the Ituraeans see Schürer (1973, Appendix I); Schottroff (1982, 125–52).

15. The identification Gerrha/ʿAnjar is virtually certain: Wild 1973, 254 s.v. "ʿAnzar." Restoration of the place-name *Ain(garr)ia* in a Greek inscription (*Supplementum Epigraphicum Graecum* 1.545) found near ʿAnjar has more recently (*Inscriptions Grecques et Latines de la Syrie* 6.2986) been disproved. Gerrha must be the ancient place name *Garis* on the upper reaches of the River Litas (modern Nahr Litâni) where a battle was fought between Muslim forces in AD 743 (Theophanes, *Chronographia*, translation and commentary in Brown 1969, 70–71). The identification *Gerrha/Chalkis* is doubted by Rey-Coquais (1981, 171–72).

16. For Pompey's submission of the coastal cities see Strabo, *Geog.* 16.2.8. A parallel account in Flavius Josephus (*Antiquities of the Jews* 14.38–40) describes an inland campaign through the Biqâʿ.

17. Jerome's commentary on Eusebius, *Onomasticon* s.v. "Aermôn" (translation and commentary in Brown (1969, 55).

18. *Dionysiaca* 42.282–312 at line 282; translation and commentary in Brown (1969, 4–6).

19. Talbert (1989) has argued that a "uniform absence of map-consciousness" was characteristic of the Graeco-Roman world. That parallels the general belief that only a small percentage of the population in classical antiquity enjoyed literacy. The modern world may not be as "map conscious" as we suppose. Our advantage lies only in having accurate maps to consult, not in any enhanced awareness of their value.

20. *Macra* is Greek for "Big"; the modern name for the nearby Eleutheros River is Nahr Kabîr, "Big River." But Strabo's Macras (*Pedion* = "Plain") probably transliterates the original Semitic name of that coastal plain, of which ʿAkkâr is an echo (cf. Arabic ʿakâra = "sediment", *mu ʿakkar* = "muddy" and associated meanings in Freyha (1972, 117).

21. *Abilenê* (the valley of the upper *Wadi Baradâ*) seems the logical location (following R. Benzinger, *Realencyclopädie* 2.2 [1896] col. 2414) based on Strabo's "seacoast to interior" progression of valleys. Abilenê was

rejected by Dussaud (1927, 399), which proposes the southern Biqâ', and by Rey-Coquais (1964, 301–306 and Appendix 2) which argues for the upper Jordan valley (Nahr Hasbani).

22. As was done by Rey-Coquais (1965).

23. IGLS 7.4011—see especially Rey-Coquais' judicious commentary on this much-published inscription.

24. Ghadban proposes that the wall (at the northern entrance of the Biqâ'; photos *planche* VIII), represented the political and physical border between Ptolemaic and Seleucid territory. This barrier is also mentioned by Strabo (*Geog.* 16.2.19), where it is called "the Egyptian Wall", i.e. the former frontier between Seleucid (northern) Syria and Ptolemaic (southern) Syria, the latter belonging administratively to Egypt.

25. A representative sample of maps produced from Ptolemy's text (or copied from other maps) can be seen in Fischer (1932) with other facsimiles in a supplementary volume. For purposes of easy consultation, and comparison with a modern physical map on the same page, see Müller (1901, 35–36 [Near East—one section of this is reproduced here]).

26. On two specific instances of how Ptolemy shows an awareness of cultural geography, see MacAdam (1989, 306–307, discussing Judaea [Palestine] and Nabataea [Arabia]).

27. See the facsimile edition in two volumes (Weber 1976). On the rationale of this and other ancient maps see Levi (1981).

28. Moynihan (1985, 153–56 and 162), has argued unconvincingly against this view. On the Agrippan map and Pliny's description of it see Bowersock (1983, 164–67).

29. The Belus is also called the *Pacida* (Pliny *NH* 5.75; 36.190; Josephus, *JW* 2.10.2). See also the comments by Rey-Coquais in *IGLS* 7 #5050 n. 3 (p. 79).

30. The intentions of each are discussed in MacAdam (1989, 295–97 [Strabo] and 290–91 [Pliny]).

REFERENCES

Abel, F.-M.
    1933   Oronte et Litani. *Journal of the Palestine Oriental Society* 13:
                147–58.
Bekker-Nielsen, T.
    1988   *Terra Incognita: The Subjective Geography of the Roman
                Empire.* Pp. 148–61 in *Studies in Ancient History and
                Numismatics presented to Rudi Thomsen*, eds. A. Damsgaard-
                Madsen et al. Aarhus: Munksgaard.

Bowersock, G.
1983   *Roman Arabia.* Cambridge, MA: Harvard University.

Brown, J. P.
1969   *The Lebanon and Phoenicia, Vol. I: The Physical Setting and the Forest.* Beirut: American University of Beirut.

Dussaud, R.
1927   *Topographie historique de la Syrie antique et médievale.* Paris: Geuthner.

Engels, D.
1978   *Alexander the Great and the Logistics of the Macedonian Army.* Berkeley: University of California.

Fischer, J.
1932   *Claudii Ptolemaei Geographia Codex Urbinas 82: Pars altera, tabula geographicae LXXXIII, Graecae-Arabicae Latinae e Codicibus LIII selectae.* Leiden: Brill.

Freyha, A.
1972   *A Dictionary of the Names of Towns and Villages in Lebanon* (Arabic). Beirut: Librairie du Liban.

Ghadban, C.
1981   Les frontières du territoire d'Héliopolis-Baalbeck à la lumière de nouveaux documents. Pp. 143–68 in *La Géographie Administrative et Politique d'Alexandre à Mahomet,* ed. T. Fahd. Paris: Geuthner.

Harper, G., Jr.
1928   A Study in the Commercial Relations between Egypt and Syria in the Third Century Before Christ. *American Journal of Philology* 49: 1–35.

Hitti, P.
1967   *Lebanon in History* (3rd ed.). New York: Macmillan.

Jones, A. H. M.
1971   *Cities of the Eastern Roman Provinces,* 2nd ed. Oxford: Clarendon.

Levi, A., and Levi, M.
1981   Map Projection and the Peutinger Table. Pp. 139–48 in *Coins, Culture and History: Numismatic Studies in Honor of Bluma L. Trell,* eds. L. Casson and M. Price. Detroit: Wayne State University.

MacAdam, H.
1989   Strabo, Pliny the Elder and Ptolemy of Alexandria: Three Views of Ancient Arabia and its Peoples. Pp. 289–320 in *L'Arabie Préislamique et son Environnement Historique et Culturel,* ed. T. Fahd. Leiden: Brill.

in press   Marinus of Tyre and Scientific Cartography: The Mediterranean,
            The Orient and Africa in Early Maps. *Graeco-Arabica* 7/8.
Moynihan, R.
1985   Geographical Mythology and Roman Imperial Ideology.
            Archeologia Transatlantica 5: 153–62.
Müller, C.
1901   *Claudii Ptolemaei Geographia (Vol. 3: Tabulae)*. Paris: Didot.
Pearson, L.
1960   *The Lost Histories of Alexander the Great.* New York:
            American Philological Association.
Pritchard, J. B., ed.
1969   *Ancient Near Eastern Texts Relating to the Old Testament* (3rd
            ed.). Princeton: Princeton University.
Ragette, F.
1980   *Baalbek.* London: Chatto & Windus.
Rey-Coquais, J.-P.
1964   Notes de Géographie syrienne (2): Le lac aux roseaux
            aromatiques de Théophraste et la Vallée Royale de Strabon.
            Mélanges de la Université St. Joseph 40: 296–306.
1965   La navigation fluviale des aradiens. *Mélanges de l'université
            Saint-Joseph* 41: 226–35.
1976   Heliupolis.   Pp. 380–82 in *The Princeton Encyclopedia of
            Classical Sites*, ed. R. Stillwell. Princeton: Princeton University.
1981   Les Frontières d'Hélioupolis: Quelques Remarques. Pp. 171–72
            in *La Géographie Administrative et Politique d'Alexandre à
            Mahomet*, ed. T. Fahd. Paris: Geuthner.
Schottroff, W.
1982   Die Ituräer. *Zeitschrift des Deutchen Palästina Vereins* 98:
            125–52.
Schürer, E.
1973   *A History of the Jewish People in the Time of Jesus Christ Vol. I*,
            rev. and ed. F. Millar and G. Vermes. Edinburgh: T. & T. Clark.
Starcky, J.
1971/72   Arca du Liban. *Les Cahiers de l'Oronte* 10: 103–13
Talbert, R.
1989   Review of *A History of Cartography* Vol. I.   *American
            Historical Review* 94: 407–408.
Walbank, F.
1957   *A Historical Commentary on Polybius* Vol. 1. Oxford: Oxford
            University.
Weber, E.
1976   *Tabula Peutingeriana, Codex Vindobonensis 324: Vollständige*

Faksimile-Ausgabe im Original format.   Graz: Akademische Druck und Verlagsanstalt.

Wild, S.
  1973   *Libanesische Ortsnamen: Typologie und Deuting.* Weisbaden: Steiner.

APPENDICES

Albert E. Glock in his office at the Palestinian Institute
of Archaeology, Birzeit University, 1987.

Appendix 1

Archaeology as Cultural Survival: The Future of the Palestinian Past[1]

ALBERT E. GLOCK

P alestine's rich cultural past has been a focus of considerable archaeological activity. Much of this work has been done by western scholars in search of evidence to support and illustrate the Bible, perceived as a major source of western cultural values. In Palestine the result has been an alienation of the Muslim and Christian Arab population from its own cultural past. I will describe efforts to help recover a usable past, including helping develop a corps of Palestinian archaeologists.

There are at least four forces that have contributed to the divergent versions of the Palestine story today. First, the canonical Palestine story for the Anglo-American and European world is based largely on biblical tradition as interpreted by western Christian nations to inculcate in their youth what are presumed to be Judaeo-Christian values. Second, European rivalry for control of the Levant generally and Palestine in particular generated a considerable knowledge of the land to serve western military, economic and cultural needs. As a cover, the data were used to illustrate and amplify the canonical story. Third, the calculated decimation of the native Palestinian population in order to provide a home for Jewish refugees from European persecution prevented the Arabs of Palestine from becoming an independent political community, as had neighboring Arab states following World War I. As displaced refugees with a culture bound to a specific parcel of land, cultural survival depended on continued social cohesion that was obviously much threatened. Whether physical or emotional refugees, or both, Palestinians were engaged now in a life-and-death struggle. This resulted in the forceful rejection by Palestinian intellectuals of the canonical story of Palestine as a calculated justification of their refugee status. Fourth, the deliberate confiscation of Arab cultural resources by Israelis, such as the large library of Dr. Tawfiq Canaan in 1948 and the Palestine Archaeological Museum in Jerusalem and its library in 1967, as well as the destruction of cultural property in the form of more than four hundred villages between 1948 and 1949, combined to disinherit Palestinians from their own land. As a consequence, it has been difficult for the Palestinians to encourage archaeologists and historians to generate an unabridged version of their own story, revising the current abridged story by including a sympathetic account of the Arab contribution to the cultural history of Palestine.

The immigrant rulers of today's Palestine fear the native Arab population, a fear of revenge for having taken in this century the lives of many, the homes, land and livelihood of most, and the honor of all. Zionist leaders taught the world to believe that Palestine was a land without people for a people without a land. There might also be fear that someday the world would learn that in 1914 Palestine was the most densely populated region in the eastern Mediterranean, 22.29 persons per square mile compared to 8.53 in Syria and Lebanon and 10.67 in Asiatic Turkey (Weinstock 1979, 52). It is therefore no mystery why the Israelis prefer to have the Arab past in most of Palestine empty of the frightening details of actual life. Arab past in Palestine, Arab cultural traditions, Arab history in the land, when acknowledged to exist, is regarded as peripheral. The connection of the past with the present that counts for Israel and her supporters is the biblical land, post-biblical Jewish life and conflict with the non-Jewish sectors of the region, never mind the thirteen centuries of Arab cultural presence. This undisguised ethnocentrism distorts pubic awareness of the rich history of Palestine.

Nevertheless, the past is vividly and deeply remembered by the Arab Palestinians in song (Mustafa Kurd, Thatir Bargouthi), in poetry (Mahmud Darwish), in novels (Emil Habiby, Anton Shamas) and short stories (Ghassan Kanafani), in drama and dance (the Marj ibn ʿAmr Group), in film (Michael Khalifeh), in painting (Suleiman Mansour) and ceramics (Vera Tamari), but also in documented histories (Walid and Rashid Khalidi), social (Rosemary Sayej) and economic studies (Sami Hadawi). Most of this memory, however, accounts for only the last fifty years, some a bit more in time but very little reaches even as far back as the nineteenth century. The link to the one hundred centuries of Palestinian history is the last thirteen when Palestine was mostly villages, a few towns, and fewer cities. There is in Palestinian cultural tradition a strong tilt toward the arts on the one side and hard sciences on the other. Between the two a deep gap seems to exist and that is where history, both an art and a science, best fits.

In this study I will show how one of the primary resources exploited to construct, support and embellish that "history," namely, the "archaeological record," has been selectively used to document and sometimes to defend the version of the past required by Christian and Jewish Zionists to justify the present occupation of Arab Palestine. Since archaeology deals with the present and future as well as the past, I will outline what can be done to correct the present bias in the story of Palestine.

INTRODUCTION

Palestine has very limited natural resources. Efforts to find gas or oil in commercial quantities have not been successful. What few mineral deposits once existed are virtually exhausted. For modern industrial production most raw materials must be imported. By contrast, Palestine has almost unlimited cultural resources. Much, but not all, is preserved underground. The method by which this resource is uncovered and made available is summed up in the term "archaeology," an academic discipline that begins with systematic excavation of the primary data. Because the material remains are often the products of the thought and action of ancestors, the resulting information documents the past lifeways of the descendant population. All over the world this resource is controlled by the government as public property. The purpose of government control is to protect this non-renewable public resource from destruction or sale for private gain, and misuse or mismanagement by artifact predators.

The first excavations in Palestine were conducted by foreign archaeologists. Before and after World War I the British dominated the archaeology of Palestine. In the fifty years between 1865 and 1914 the

British were responsible for ten excavations and two important surveys; the Germans, six excavations and the Americans only one (Macalister 1925). Of these, the most important were probably the work of Flinders Petrie (British) at Tell el-Hesi in 1890 and George Reisner (American) at Sebastiyeh between 1908 and 1910, important in that these excavations developed the fundamental procedures of field work that were later refined and have endured (Wright 1969).

During this period, Palestine was a province of the Ottoman Empire. Permission to excavate required a firman from the Sultan in Istanbul. In the judgment of one of Palestine's early excavators Turkish permits were issued "based on the sound principle ... that national monuments must not be removed from the country ... their possession must remain with the people of the country whose they are" (Macalister 1925, 54). In view of the Ottoman's demonstrated lack of interest in the Arab population of Palestine this statement requires many qualifiers. Nevertheless, when compared to what happened to Arab Palestine and its past in the hands of the British Mandate, some small virtue may yet be reserved for Ottoman rule.

In order to determine the position of Arabs in the development of archaeology in Palestine, I will look at two centers of archaeological activity and scholarship, first, the Department of Antiquities and second, the Palestine Oriental Society. In each case I will examine the personnel roster and the publications of these two organizations that theoretically at least were open to Arab participation. There were five foreign schools of archaeology in Jerusalem: French, American, German, British and Italian. We will not consider these centers since Arabs were not normally related to these institutions as archaeologists.

THE HISTORICAL BACKGROUND 1919–1967

After World War I the story of archaeology in Palestine was similar to that in other parts of the colonized Middle East with one significant difference. In Iraq, Syria and Jordan the Arabs sought and gained independence from the British and French. In these countries there had been established during the Mandates government agencies to preserve, excavate, publish and exhibit the material culture remains of national pasts. These agencies as well as the government itself were staffed by Arabs whose land and past were now under their control. It was anomalous at best that a similar pattern did not occur in Palestine. To be sure, there was a Department of Antiquities staffed by British, Arabs and Jews. But, and this is the "significant difference," there was no serious effort by Mandate authorities to train and encourage Arab archaeologists to become professionals. The burden of the Mandate was the commitment to encourage such circumstances as would facilitate the creation of a Jewish National Home. Development within the Jewish community was left to the Jews themselves. In education and most other aspects of community life the Jews maintained separate institutions. The Jewish Palestine Exploration Society had been founded already in 1914. Its first excavation, however, was not until 1921–1922, at Hammath-Tiberias. Hebrew University opened its doors in 1925. By 1928 E. L. Sukenik was head of the Archaeology Department. For the Arab population, still a three quarters majority in Palestine, there was no association or university supporting archaeology. The only possibilities lay in the British Mandate's Department of Antiquities and the British School of Archaeology in Jerusalem. Early in 1920 already the latter institution was "making active preparation for the training of archaeologists .... No modern religious or political question will be allowed to affect the policy of the School ... which is conceived on the broadest lines in an organized effort to cope with the existing national need" (*Palestine Exploration Quarterly* 1920, 54). It seems the "national need" was British. No Arab students benefited from this educational opportunity.

The Department of Antiquities of Palestine was first established during the period of British civil administration in 1919, prior to the Mandate. Article 21 of the Mandate stipulates that an Antiquities Law should be prepared within a year (Allen 1974, 628–29). It seems, however, that the first law was not published until 1929 (Luke *and Keith-Roach* 1930, 86). This law stated that any artifact or architecture dated to AD 1700 or earlier was a protected "antiquity." Human and animal remains earlier than AD 600 were protected by the law. One significant difference from the Ottoman law was that the Mandate allowed the expedition director half of the portable finds to be distributed among sponsoring institutions in order to encourage foreign investment in the archaeology of Palestine. The Ottomans, on the other hand, had required that all recovered artifacts be deposited in the Imperial Museum in Constantinople. The Director of the Department of Antiquities as well as the Advisory Board was appointed by the High Commissioner from the British, French, American and Italian Schools of Archaeology in Jerusalem. In addition two Arabs and two Jews were to be appointed to represent the interests of Muslim and Jewish cultural heritage. The Department was organized in five subunits: inspectors, a records office and library, a conservation laboratory, a photographic studio and the Palestine Museum.

That the British were deeply interested in the Archaeology of Palestine is evident from the immediate organization of a British School of Archaeology in Jerusalem and a Department of Antiquities for Palestine. These two organizations occupied the same building until 1930 though already in 1926 the directorships had been separated. From 1930 until after World War II the British School was housed with the American School of Oriental Research. The salvation of the Department of Antiquities was a gift in 1928 of two million dollars to establish the Palestine Museum. Half of the sum was for construction of a building and half was to remain as an endowment. The building was dedicated in 1938.

If we examine the numbers, positions, and contributions of Arabs and Jews in each of these organizations devoted to the Archaeology of Palestine we come to the following conclusions:

1. An inspection of the records of the Department of Antiquities for 31 March 1947 shows ninety-four persons on the payroll. Of these six are British Christians, twenty-two Arab Christians, six Armenians, fifty-one Arab Muslims and nine Jews.

2. The preponderance of Arabs can best be explained on the grounds that most of the land was owned by Arabs and archaeological sites were on land. In addition, though the percentage of Arabs in the population diminished during the Mandate, by 1948 it was still double the Jewish population.

3. Arabs have commonly served as guards at sites around the country. They have also been museum guards and attendants, messengers, cleaners, and also inspectors. In fact, of the six inspectors commonly mentioned three are Arab: D. Baramki (1927–1948), S. A. S. Husseini (1930–1948) and N. Makhouly (1922–1948). In addition, Stephan H. Stephan was a self-taught scholar who worked in the library (1920–1948).

4. Only two of these four, a fraction of the seventy-three Arabs
    (seventy-nine if the Armenians are included) had a university
    education: Baramki had a B.A. from London and Husseini a B.A.
    from Beirut. This contrasts with the nine Jewish employees of
    whom six had a university degree: three had doctorates, one from
    Rome, one from Florence and another from Basel. One had a
    Hebrew University M.A. (Ruth Kallner) and two had B.A.s from
    London.
5. Jews were employed in jobs for which their European education
    made them more acceptable to the British. S. J. Schweig was the
    chief photographer (1934–1947).   Michael Avi-Yonah was
    employed as site recorder attached to the library (1931–1947).
    Immanuel Ben-Dor was librarian and excavator (1936–1947).

An inventory of the authors of articles published in the fourteen
volumes of the *Quarterly of the Department of Antiquities of Palestine*
(*QDAP*)—the scholarly voice of the Department of Antiquities,
published between 1932–1950—shows that fifteen were British, six
Jewish and six Arab, one American and one Swede. The last two as
well as three British scholars were nonresident. The Arabs include the
brothers Dimitri and Jalil Baramki, S. Husseini, N. Makhouly, N. G.
Nassar and S. H. Stephan who contributed thirty-three titles out of a
total of 163 while the six Jewish scholars contributed thirty-nine.
Among the Arab scholars Dimitri Baramki was the most prolific. He
joined the Mandate Department of Antiquities at age 18 in 1927 where
his major contribution was the thirteen-year excavation of Qasr Hisham
(1935–1947). After the collapse of the Mandate in 1948, Baramki
worked on excavations emanating from the American School in
Jerusalem before moving to a teaching post at the American University
in Beirut in 1951. He received a doctorate from London in 1953. His
dissertation was based essentially on the results of his excavation of
Khirbat al-Mafjar, erroneously labeled Qasr Hisham. The most active
Jewish archaeologist was Michael Avi-Yonah who immigrated to
Palestine from today's Austria in 1919. He worked as assistant
librarian and Records Officer in the Palestine Museum from 1931 to
1948 and began teaching at Hebrew University after 1949, receiving his
doctorate from London in 1958. All of the remaining Jewish
archaeologists who had published in *QDAP* before 1948 became
professors at Hebrew University at one time or another.

Parallel to and contemporary with the founding of a Department of Antiquities was the formation of the Palestine Oriental Society in 1920, largely due to the energy of Prof. A. T. Clay of Yale University who was Annual Professor at the American School of Oriental Research in Jerusalem that year. In its twenty-eight years of existence, the Palestine Oriental Society published twenty-one volumes of its *Journal of the Palestine Oriental Society* (*JPOS*). The first eighteen volumes appeared annually from 1921 to 1939. The beginning of World War II and the post-war struggle for Palestine caused delays so that volume 19 appeared in 1941, volume 20 in 1946 and volume 21 in 1948, by which time six of the nine articles were by resident Jews. Arabs who had consistently published in the journal were not represented. The membership of the Society had always been dominated by foreigners, mostly non-resident. In 1932, for example, out of 191 members, ten were resident Arabs, thirty-three resident Jews, forty-two resident foreigners and 117 nonresidents. Arab membership fluctuated from a high of nineteen in 1926 to five in 1934. Of 335 articles published, fifty were by seven Arab scholars, or 16.8 percent of the total. The two most prolific were Dr. Tawfig Canaan who published twenty-five articles and Stephan Hanna Stephan who published nineteen. Ninety-two articles were published in the Journal by twenty-six resident Jewish scholars, or 30.8 percent leaving 52.4 percent of the material produced by foreigners most of whom were connected with German, French, British or American institutions based in Jerusalem or abroad. A preliminary comparison of resident Arab and Jewish scholars indicates that almost all of the latter had received doctorates in Europe or America before or after immigrating to Palestine. To my knowledge, the Arabs were all born in Greater Syria before World War I and only Tawfig Canaan had a doctorate, a medical degree from the American University in Beirut in 1905.

The difference between the purposes and organizations supporting these two journals is important. The *QDAP* was a Mandate government publication dedicated to reporting excavations sponsored by the Department of Antiquities and research dealing with the collection in the Palestine Archaeological Museum. It was necessarily dominated by the British. By contrast the Palestine Oriental Society was open to anyone with a scholarly interest in what may broadly be called "palestinology." Thus, for example, Stephan dealt largely with Arabic and Turkish inscriptions or texts in *QDAP* while in *JPOS* he had numerous articles on the folklore of Palestine. On the other hand, D. Baramki published only in *QDAP* while T. Canaan only in *JPOS*, the former excavation reports and the latter Palestinian folklore, as well as a series on the architecture and social context of the village house and another series on Muslim shrines. In general, the Arabs focused on living cultural traditions in Arab Palestine while Jewish scholars in the Palestine Oriental Society researched the topography of biblical sites and the interpretation of difficult biblical texts. There were exceptions, particularly in the 1920s, when Stekelis in prehistory and L. A. Mayer on Muslim texts and artifacts appeared on the scene.

Not reflected in *QDAP* but clear in *JPOS* is that Jewish immigration had a significant impact on the growing weight in numbers of Jewish scholars in archaeology while the number of Arab scholars remained relatively stable and then declined. In the first two volumes of *JPOS* (1921, 1922) Arabs contributed eight articles, in the last two volumes (1946, 1948), none, reflecting the increasing judaisation of scholarship on and from Palestine.

From material published by Arab Palestinians in both *JPOS* and *QDAP* it seems clear that there were Arabs both learned and capable of dealing with both the archaeology and ethnography of Palestine. Of the many reasons they did not flourish after the 1948 disaster two seem to be paramount: (a) the turmoil resulting from the influx of refugees inside a sealed border, now one-third of the former Palestine, and (b) the lack of local academic institutions supporting scholarship in the Arab community.

Following the 1948 debacle, Jordan annexed the West Bank and reorganized the Department of Antiquities with its headquarters in the Roman Theater in Amman. The Director then was G. L. Harding who had earlier served a decade in that capacity when Transjordan was detached from Palestine as a separate Mandate under the British. In 1956 he and all other British holdovers from the Mandate period were dismissed. The Annual of the Department of Antiquities (of Jordan) did not begin publication until 1951. Between that date and 1968, thirteen volumes were published in nine issues, four being double volumes. The emphasis on the East Bank is very clear. Except for one report on Qumran, one on el-Jib, two on Sebastijeh, three tombs near Nablus and one in Beit Sahur, all other excavations and studies reflect the focus on the East Bank.

The one center of archaeological activity that might have provided a base for Palestinian archaeologists was the Palestine Archaeological Museum in Jerusalem. The British remained in control of what was now East Bank–West Bank Jordan archaeology until 1956. The more sophisticated West Bank Palestinians' demand for representation in the new government was suppressed by Jordanian politicians. It is nevertheless not clear why persons like Dimitri Baramki were not able to continue their work as archaeologists employed by the Palestine Museum. It was under the control of trustees made up of the directors of the several foreign schools of archaeology in the city and not Jordan. The Museum was nationalized by Jordan only months before the June War of 1967 for which reason it was regarded by the invading Israelis as theirs by right of conquest.

In the first part of this discussion I will search for explanations that will help understand the quality and quantity of Arab participation in the development of the Archaeology of Palestine emerging from the data cited above. In the second part I will discuss what I think should be done to increase Arab participation in particular as well as to improve the quality of the Archaeology of Palestine in general.

THE INTELLECTUAL CONQUEST OF PALESTINE: THE ARCHAEOLOGY OF PALESTINE AS A CONSTRUCT OF WESTERN CHRISTIANS

Several different intellectual traditions have converged to form the study of the past that we today call "archaeology." One powerful stimulus was the Renaissance revival and enthusiasm for Greek classical tradition in plastic arts and architecture. It was the scholarship of Johann Winckelmann (1717–1768) that gave archaeology an art historical tradition (Leppmann 1970). A second source was the eighteenth and nineteenth century development of the science of geology out of which three concepts emerged which were important for archaeology: stratigraphy, prehistory, and uniformitarianism (Daniel 1975). The association of stone tools and "human" remains in sealed deposits led to the discovery of the antiquity of hominids and thus prehistory. This led inevitably to the view that the natural forces that created the sediments that formed the landscape we know today were still at work so that an understanding of today provides the key for interpreting the natural events of the past. Applying this rule to cultural change is much more difficult than it is for natural change. Nevertheless, early attempts to understand the parallel existence of preliterate and literate societies, farmers and hunter-gatherers grew out of uniformitarian assumptions (Orme 1981). All of these developments occurred in Europe at a time when the people of Palestine were suffering the consequences of Ottoman weakness. The "Arab awakening" did not occur until the late nineteenth century.

With the basic intellectual components in place by the beginning of the nineteenth century, archaeology moved to the Middle East as European nations, particularly England and France, while vying for position in the collapsing Ottoman empire, explored their own cultural origins, encouraged by the search for biblical connections. The process began in 1798 with Napoleon Bonaparte's failed expedition to Egypt, which included a host of savants who published the monumental *Description de L'Egypte* in nineteen massive folio volumes (1809–1828) and continued in Mesopotamia with collecting art treasures from mounds in the area of Mosul by Paul Emile Botta (1802–1870) and Austin Henry Layard (1817–1894) (Fagan 1979, 85–137). These sculptures turned out to be Assyrian, a people known from the Bible to exist but little more could be said with certainty. In the process Europe discovered evidence for the several high cultures in the Middle East, many predating biblical history. By the end of the nineteenth century the ancient Near East was divided into numerous specialized fields of study dealing with the language, literature and archaeology of each of these areas. The physical remains were often expropriated by Europeans for the edification and education of westerners assuming that the living populations of Mesopotamia, Anatolia and Egypt were not sufficiently educated to appreciate their unique and ancient heritage. Indeed, westerners laid claim to ancient Near Eastern cultural treasures as their own heritage, not that of the peasants and town dwellers of nineteenth century Middle East. By the end of the nineteenth century it seemed clear that while Europe was a cultural cross of Athens and Jerusalem, the high cultures of the ancient Near East laid the foundations of Athens and Jerusalem.

Once established, archaeologists began to collect masses of new data, but in Palestine the picture began to be confused. By a rigorous application of typological methods W. F. Albright (1891–1971), in his publication of the Tell Beit Mirsim excavation (1932–1943), put order into the sequence of pottery types (Van Beek 1989). But it was not until 1952 when Kathleen Kenyon (1906–1978) introduced into Palestine stratigraphic methods for excavating natural deposits that it was possible to order with confidence the layers of tells in Palestine. Since that time there have been constant refinements in field methods and recording. These developments had little bearing on the motivations for excavation in Palestine which remained for the most part tied to biblical connections and western languages. Elsewhere in Europe and America there was considerable ferment in the ranks of archaeologists about problems of archaeological interpretation. American archaeologists were trained in an ahistorical anthropological approach while Europeans regarded archaeology in one way or another as a contributor to historical science. It was therefore for different reasons that both began to consider seriously the theoretical constructs that lay at the foundations of the archaeological enterprise as currently practiced. Very little of these developments have had an impact on work in Palestine, Israel, or Jordan except for persons in prehistory.

Since archaeology was a discipline that grew up in Europe and many of the Jewish immigrants to Palestine had received part or all of their education in Europe, they found archaeology intellectually congenial and, from a nationalistic point of view, essential to establishing their identity with the land. Nahum Slouschz (1871–1966), founder of the Jewish Palestine Exploration Society had been trained at the Sorbonne in Paris; also Moshe Stekelis (1898–1967), the prehistorian, who had immigrated from the Ukraine in 1928. Eliezer Lipa Sukenik (1889-1953) had arrived in 1912 from Poland as did Michael Avi-Yonah (1895–1974), who joined the Hebrew University in 1953. Leo Ary Mayer (1895–1959) specialized in Islamic culture. He had immigrated from Poland in 1921, served as inspector, librarian and record keeper at the Department of Antiquities until his appointment at Hebrew University in 1925. Clearly the foundations of archaeology as a discipline in the Israeli community were laid in Europe. Among the Arab Palestinians who could be classified as archaeologists in the pre-1948 period only Dimitri Baramki (1909–1984) studied in London. After 1967 there were a number of Palestinians now living in Jordan who did archaeology degrees in Europe and the U.S. but none in the West Bank or Gaza where there was no Department of Archaeology at a university. In recent times the Israeli Department of Antiquities has been willing to hire at best a not too ambitious Arab B.A. In short, those Arabs who did enter archaeology drank from the well of Euro-American scholarship on the assumption that they were dealing with objective reality. For the Arabs what was missed was the intellectual connection with Islamic tradition, in part because the most active Arab archaeologists in Palestine came from Christian backgrounds and in part because, even for the Muslims, there had been no eighteenth or nineteenth century precursor to suggest that in the search for the past one could well begin with views of history generated by Arab scholars such as Ibn Khaldun.

What have been the consequences for the Palestinian Arabs? There are at least three: (a) Arabs educated in the West have adopted the western agenda for archaeological research where the emphasis is on proto- and prehistory, Bronze and Iron ages, sometimes Hellenistic and Roman periods. (b) In the matter of Islamic Archaeology Arab scholars, following their western instructors, have emphasized the art historical aspects. (c) Since archaeological sites can be expropriated by the government and the Palestinians have not been permitted a government, land owners fear archaeologists. We will examine each of these consequences in more detail.

(a) There is little doubt that the archaeology of Palestine has been dominated by what has been called "Biblical Archaeology." It has not been easy to define the boundaries of this rather amorphous study since W. F. Albright. He regarded the biblical world as virtually the entire Middle East, and succeeded in mastering an incredible number of disciplines focusing on the ancient Near East which he used to "illuminate" the general historical background as well as specific problems of interpretation. British, American, German and French involvement in the archaeology of Palestine was generated by the Bible. Except for the British most archaeologists were biblical scholars. Since for the British the Bible was the "national epic," the geography of the Bible was more familiar than that of Europe, so special training was not required. When one examines the journals devoted to the archaeology of Palestine, most of them beginning in the late nineteenth century, the clear emphasis is on biblical background and interpretation. After 1948 The Jewish Palestine Exploration society became the Israel Exploration Society which sponsored major excavations at such biblical sites as Dan, Hazor and Beersheba. Even in the West Bank where Jordan was in control, the momentum of biblical archaeology brought foreign excavations to Tell Balata (Shechem), Tell el-Tell (ʿAi), Tell Taʿannek (Taanach) and Tell el-Sultan (Jericho). Arab participation in these predominantly American expeditions was limited to representatives of the Department of Antiquities of Jordan assigned to each of the foreign excavations. They were to monitor the excavation and to gain field experience. Two of these persons became leading archaeologists—Muawiya Ibrahim who participated in the Tell Taʿannek excavation, and Fawzi Zayadine who worked at Sebastiyeh. The former was later trained in Berlin and the latter in Paris. Both are today accomplished students of traditional archaeology, now focusing their attention on Jordan where they live and work. Though neither concentrates on the Bible they have also not been able, or not thought it necessary, to change the direction of archaeological research. This may in part be due to their not working in and for Palestine as a geographical and national entity. Since 1967 Jerusalem has become the center of biblical archaeology. The first International Congress on Biblical Archaeology was held there in 1984 celebrating the 70th anniversary of the Israel Exploration Society. The proceedings were published as *Biblical Archaeology Today* (Amitai 1985). The next congress occurred in the summer 1990.

(b) The emphasis on fine arts in Islamic Archaeology appeals to Arabs because it reveals the remarkably advanced technical skills of craftsmen and architects during the flowering of Islam. It is a heritage that elicits pride. But for Palestine this is a disaster because it focuses on Jerusalem to the exclusion of 95 percent of the land occupied by towns and villages, many of them of considerable importance. The villages of Palestine are ignored and thus the real character of Palestine is not yet studied.

(c) The need of a benevolent Arab government is imperative if there is to be freedom to explore the Arab past of Palestine. Since there has never been a Palestinian government, the resources required to tell the Arab story have not been properly collected or preserved. Nor has the material culture evidence been adequately protected or where possible, restored. In the last forty-two years, however, these resources have suffered calculated decimation, whole villages destroyed, libraries and documents confiscated, unique agricultural installations dislodged by force to be incorporated in Israeli museums. Increasingly there is public awareness among Arabs in Israel and all of the occupied territories that symbols of the past must be somehow preserved in order, if nothing else, to keep alive the memory of a rich past for the next generation. Private museums have been organized in some towns. Collections of regional costumes have been published. Domestic architecture has been described. This is not enough, however, if an adequate public account of Arab cultural traditions is to become an integral part of the very long story of Palestine. What is required is a documentation center as well as access to the deep and rich archaeological record, the still buried resource required to document and illustrate the Arab past in Palestine.

In Palestine a serious problem arises because (i) of the density of evidence of the past on the landscape, and because (ii) the antiquities law allows the state to expropriate land registered as a historical site. The Jordanian Provisional Antiquities Law No. 12 of 1976, Article 5, Paragraph D reads as follows: "The Government may expropriate or buy any land or antiquity if it is in the interest of the Department to expropriate or buy it." The Israeli Antiquities Law of 1978 (Law 885), Chapter 8, deals with expropriation: "An antiquity site whose expropriation is necessary, in his [the minister's] opinion, for the purposes of preservation or research," or "any land whose expropriation is necessary, in his opinion, in order to facilitate excavation therein." These laws are based on the assumption that antiquities, movable or immovable, are the property of the state. Since for Palestinians the state is an imposed "legality," and since the state has used as much "law" as is available to expropriate land in the past, one cannot be surprised at the unwillingness of Palestinian Arabs to encourage the identification of archaeological sites. It is evident, however, that even the existence of a Palestinian state will not automatically solve the problem. What will be required is a policy that will not block the growth and development of established communities and at the same time not destroy the subterranean cultural resources.

STEPS TOWARD INDEPENDENCE:
PALESTINIAN ARCHAEOLOGY

There are formal elements in the inherited archaeology that are 'versally valid and can be adopted without loss by Palestinian archaeologists. There are also some substantive issues of common interest. It is, however, with substantive questions that most differences occur. These differences are a reflection of sensitivities deriving from both education and the explicit questions of cultural identity raised by the Palestinian community. I will outline some of these similarities and differences.

1. The similarities between the inherited and the locally derived archaeological agenda are technical and methodological. Basic to all archaeological recovery is attention to the bedding lines of sediments. The development of stratigraphic excavation methods that have occurred in the work of foreigners in the Middle East can, with suitable adaptation, be said to be universally applicable. A by-product of sedimentary analysis is now site formation, a study particularly important in interpreting the deposits that form a tell. On the other hand, the technical analysis of artifact formation processes are especially useful, whether dealing with pottery, glass or metal artifacts. It is not common that such analysis be done but indigenous archaeologists are probably more interested than others because such information often has direct relevance for the interpretation of local cultural traditions and by implication for present self-understanding and local development. These analyses are usually labor-intensive and expensive and, thus, foreigners might be restrained from participating. When, however, there is a clear present value to such information the cost factor may not appear as important. Finally, one may find in literary sources descriptions of conditions in Palestine, particularly after the eleventh century BC. The correlation of material evidence and literary texts requires critical examination of both data types, a system of analysis that also is universally applicable.

2. The differences between the archaeological agenda inherited from the western Christian and Jewish scholars and that generated with a view to the needs, values and interests of the native Arab population of Palestine are of course critical to the character of Palestinian archaeology. Adaptations of this list of research interests can be found in many other nations of the world.

If we begin with the definition of archaeology as the study of the material expression of human thought and action, we are not confined to the past as an etymological definition of the term would suggest. We can therefore begin with the present, which can be supported by both national and methodological arguments. Where continuity of the present with the past is a reasonable assumption, elements of the deeper past are still alive in traditional village settlement patterns, architecture of domestic and public building, subsistence systems and social organization. In order to understand the changes that have occurred, it is necessary and possible to move backwards through time. For the living population who are heirs to that tradition it is therefore logical to begin the process of exploring the past with the immediately preceding period, in Palestine, the period of Ottoman rule. It is not astonishing that no archaeologist has done this if in fact the native population of Palestine has not been in control of their own archaeological record. This, then, is the most significant difference between the foreign focus on "biblical archaeology" and the Arab version, Palestinian Archaeology.

In countries where archaeology is a serious government program, the first task is to make an intensive survey of existing physical remains of the past. It has become a required feature of archaeological surface surveys to collect not only evidence of the remains of past human activities but also to gather from local oral tradition place names and the known function of buildings and installations, at least in secondary use (Miller 1980, 712). The Israel government has an ambitious survey program. Maps are being produced at a scale of 1:20,000. The area inside the Green Line will be covered in 267 volumes (Yeivin 1967). The first volume published covered 56 sq. km along the coast south of Haifa in the area of ʿAtlit (Ronen and Olami 1978). Two villages destroyed in 1948 were included, ʿAin Haud and al-Mazur (Ronen and Olami 1978, 56, 63–65). The pottery on both sites is read as Byzantine and Arab. Fifty-five of 145 sites are said to have "no antiquities." These sites include many lime kilns, caves, ruins of a building, wells and other evidence of human working. Amazingly 110 of the 145 sites have no names. I say "amazing" because Arabs have a name for every plot of land, hill, spring, and any unusual feature on the landscape. These toponymics are often part of the local oral tradition not found on published maps. In Palestine where the Arab population has been expelled the oral tradition has gone with them. The expulsion of the Arab population of hundreds of villages in 1948 has created a gap in the understanding of Palestine that will forever remain a lacuna in the knowledge of the land.

There is a second significant difference between the inherited perspective and that of the native of Palestine. It has been a common assumption that Palestinian culture is borrowed, largely from the great centers of urban culture in Egypt and Mesopotamia. This is based on the assumption that the population of Palestine was non-urban and unsophisticated. R. A. S. Macalister, an important early excavator, concluded a description of work at Tell Zakariya saying: "The experience at Tell el-Hesy was repeated; the excavator was working in the remains of a people of low culture, entirely dependent on Egypt and the Aegean, to a lesser degree on the empires of Mesopotamia, for its arts and civilization" (Macalister 1925, 56). And again reflecting on Sellin's excavation at Tell Taᶜannek, "there was the same complete absence of any evidence of a native-born civilization" (Macalister 1925, 64). Thus, for example, it has been assumed that the *terre pise* mounds that surrounded the city defenses the second quarter of the second millennium BC were brought to the land by the Hyksos (Kenyon 1979, 166), and that the casemate defence system and ashlar construction was an innovation introduced in the tenth century BC from Anatolia via Phoenicia (Aharoni 1978, 198-9). Based on recent excavations in Palestine itself we now know that none of these construction techniques were imported from abroad, that in fact all these systems were native to Palestine. Against such hyper-diffusionist perspectives, the Palestinian archaeologist will search for the evidence for the adaptive systems engineered by the native inhabitants in the different ecological zones of the land. Archaeology is then a tool that can be used to identify the specific forms of cultural expression linking the present with the past.

3. What are some of the obstacles to village study? 1) More than half of all the Arab villages in Palestine were destroyed by the Israelis between 1948 and 1950. 2) During the British Mandate, house-by-house plans of all of the villages were drawn. These plans are not now accessible since many of these plans are of destroyed villages. 3) The population of the West Bank today is suspicious of the motives of anyone collecting information about their villages. They find it difficult to believe that such study can be of value to them. More likely, in their view, the researcher will provide the occupation with information that could be used to their disadvantage. 4) Village study requires a team composed of an anthropologist, architect, archaeologist, photographer and historian. Such a team would require a permit from the occupation that would be difficult to receive. 5) In

addition such a project would be long-term and expensive though its benefits would extend far into the future. 6) Highly desirable would be the excavation of a destroyed village. Receiving a permit would be virtually impossible because of adverse nationalistic publicity such an endeavor would generate among the Palestinians.

One other human settlement type on the recent landscape of Palestine deserves the archaeologist's attention, namely, refugee camps, some of which in the Jericho region are virtually abandoned. Refugees are not new to Palestine. Ordinarily traces of their presence are ephemeral and today can be bulldozed easily from the surface of the land and erased from memory. Refugee Archaeology is a research subject that would make a significant contribution to understanding the real world of Palestine today.

4. A critical step toward intellectual independence of the Palestinian archaeologist is his or her education. The ultimate aim of such a process is not only an effective handling of the tools of the profession but also sensitivity to community needs and the willingness to lead. I will limit myself here to the strictly archaeological aspect of education, assuming that what is said above provides some indication of the kinds of projects that will help create a more accurate picture of the cultural history of Palestine.

Now I want to outline some of the experiences and skills required to successfully work on these projects. The profile of an archaeologist requires one to be physically and mentally robust, able to endure the long hours of outdoor activity, which includes observation and recording of minute details that ultimately are sewn together into a seamless whole, the story of a site. Included in this profile is a space-time sensitivity, that is, on the one hand intuitive three-dimensional imaging that helps recreate the whole from the part remaining and on the other hand ability to see these fragmented forms changing through time. All of these qualities are best tested during several seasons of field excavation and survey. It is in the context of an excavation where the ability to work under pressure and still function as a member of a team is demonstrated. It is essential to be able to organize one's own work and that of a team, to think clearly and record details accurately, in short, to teach by example because a team will inevitably include students among whom some will see a future in archaeology.

Once the field work is completed, another level of work begins. The data collected must be analyzed, interpreted and then synthesized, that is, the story told. Since no one person can analyze all of the data, a team of specialists is required who, in the best of all worlds are also familiar with the need for and meaning of stratigraphic separation. The essential special skills are in sediment analysis, ceramics, lithics, botanical and faunal identification, and historical sources where applicable. If these six persons can be assisted by appropriate technicians, all working together with mutual respect for each others' efforts, we will find a formidable archaeological team.   Finally, the future archaeologist should have the opportunity to follow the process from field recovery through analysis to writing and publication.

5. A Palestinian archaeology must be created. Since up until recently the archaeology of Palestine can be said to have focused largely, if not exclusively, on biblical archaeology, a segment of the past reconstructed to support Jewish claims to Palestine, it can be argued that Palestinian archaeology is but the other side of the coin, also political in intent.   This claim would have merit if in Palestinian Archaeology there were a conscious effort to efface the record that relates to the Jews, Jerusalem in the tenth or second century BC, or synagogues in the fifth and sixth centuries AD, for example. But this is not the case. Palestinian Archaeology, assuming the general veracity of written records, acknowledges the polyethnic nature of Palestinian cultural history. Indeed, research into the distinctive features of ethnic diversity is an important feature on the research agenda of Palestinian Archaeology. As in all good science, we do not favor one answer or the other. We will test for multicultural indicators as a hypothesis, and it is no more than that, to determine the probability of its truth.

How does the rationale for Palestinian Archaeology differ from that which has been promoted by western archaeologists? First, if archaeology is the study of the materialization of human thought and action then it is not chronologically bound. In other words, archaeology is not merely the study of what is old, though it certainly includes antiquity, but attempts to correlate the adaptation of materials and space to human needs. Second, since the past is dead, it can be interpreted only by analogy with human experience. The valid experience is obviously that which is closest in both time and space to what I want to interpret and that brings us again to the traditional villages of Palestine. I am not forgetting the towns but for the sake of abbreviating the argument we will stay with the village on the assumption that what we are currently excavating was once a village. Just as I excavate backwards through space and time, so I interpret backwards going from the known to the unknown. To be sure, there are many problems along the way. Even today with much improved means of communication there are significant regional and class differences in Palestine and within each district and segment of society. Language continues to preserve long nurtured regionalisms. For example a *hawsh* in the Bir Zeit district is a house, including the courtyard. To the west near Ramleh it is only the courtyard but still very much a part of the beit. On the desert edge in Taqu'a the *hawsh* is the courtyard separated from the house. Animals are penned in the *hawsh*. In any case, these examples are twentieth century, close to our experience. To study the forces compelling change that are close in time and where the documentation is controllable makes it possible to generate explanatory hypotheses about the deeper past than can be tested by a close inspection of the archaeological record. This means that Palestinian Archaeology is not only more relevant to living Palestinians but also is qualitatively better archaeology.

NOTES

1. This paper is dated April 1990. A shortened version appeared as Glock 1994.

REFERENCES

Aharoni, Y.
    1978   *The Archaeology of the Land of Israel.* London: SCM.
Allen, R.
    1974   *Imperialism and Nationalism in the Fertile Crescent: Sources and Prospects of the Arab-Israeli Conflict.* New York: Oxford University.
Daniel, G.
    1975   *One Hundred Fifty Years of Archaeology.* 2nd ed. London: Duckworth.
Fagan, B.
    1979   *Return to Babylon. Travelers, Archaeologists and Monuments in Mesopotamia.* Boston: Little Brown.
Kenyon, K.
    1979   *Archaeology in the Holy Land.* 4th ed. London: Methuen.

Leppmann, W.
1970   *Winckelmann.* New York: Knopf.
Luke, H. C., and Keith-Roach, E., eds.
1930   *The Handbook of Palestine and Trans-Jordan.* London: Macmillan.
Macalister, R. A. S.
1925   *A Century of Excavation in Palestine.* London: The Religious Tract Society.
Miller, D.
1980   Archaeology and Development. *Current Anthropology* 21: 709–36.
Orme, B.
1981   *Anthropology for Archaeologists.* London: Duckworth.
Ronen, A. and Olami, Y.
1978   *ʿAtlit Map.* Vol. 1. Jerusalem: The Archaeological Survey of Israel.
Van Beek, G.
1989   W. F. Albright's Contribution to Archaeology. Pp. 61–73 in *The Scholarship of William Foxwell Albright: An Appraisal.* Atlanta: Scholars.
Weinstock, N.
1979   *Zionism—False Messiah.* London: Ink Links.
Wright, G. E.
1969   Archaeological Method in Palestine—An American Interpretation. Pp. 120–33 in *Eretz-Israel.* Jerusalem: Israel Exploration Society.
Yeivin, S.
1967   Israel's Archaeological Survey. *Ariel* 18: 80–85.

Appendix 2
Cultural Bias
in Archaeology[1]

ALBERT E. GLOCK

... there is no great harm in a little honest prejudice. It may
at least stimulate the wiser judgment of those critics who are
devoid of bias (Wheeler 1956, 228).

I should preface this discussion of the problem of bias with an
autobiographical statement that will help to understand my
interest in this problem. I live among people whose past as history
and whose present as the remains of an ancient tradition has been of
more interest to Christians and Jews in Europe and America than it has
been to themselves. Two forces have isolated Palestinians from
anything other than a legendary past, and have prevented their
development of a serious attempt to reconstruct their own past. The
power centers that have attempted to control Palestine have for four
thousand years either been elsewhere or in the hands of an immigrant
population. Palestinians have been forced therefore either to flee into
exile for fulfillment, or to bargain for survival with the foreign rulers.
The development of an independent self-understanding based on the
historical and archaeological record would be perceived as either a
threat or irrelevant. As a consequence there are seven foreign
archaeological schools in Jerusalem, many with long histories and
impressive publication records while the Palestinians themselves have
nothing. Since 1977 I have attempted to develop a Department of
Archaeology at Birzeit University, the only such department among the
seven universities in the West Bank. Our purpose has been to train
archaeologists and to encourage research in the complete archaeological

history of Palestine. What kind of problems do we face and what kind of solutions do we propose to deal with them?

Let me first describe the kind of bias I will *not* be talking about. I will call it operational bias because it refers to the anatomy of the archaeological record and techniques of recovery. The archaeological record is biased by a particular climate and sediment cover as well as the presence or absence of scavenging living communities. Both natural and cultural forces distort the archaeological record. Inadequate techniques of recovery as well as observational blindness limit the recovery capability of the excavator and thus fractionalize an already fragmented archaeological record (Schiffer 1983, 1987). All this produces a biased or distorted image of material culture, its sedimentary context and its ability to reflect human thought and action. I want rather to discuss the cultural bias of the archaeologist that distorts our understanding of the past.

INTRODUCTION

One of the very positive developments in archaeology in recent years is the increasing awareness of "bias" in the processes of selecting, collecting, and especially interpreting the archaeological record (Gero *et al.* 1983). The cultural and academic soul-searching that has been experienced in the Anglo-American west in recent years has focused on the numerous distortions that can be traced straight back to the political and economic interests of those who paid the research bills (Trigger 1980; Patterson 1986). Deceptively clothed in the finery of scholarly "objectivity," archaeologists and historians alike, assuming they had more to teach than learn from the past, equally convinced and comfortable with their inherited values, disconnected Blacks, Aborigines and Native Americans from the achievements of their respective pasts, in order to continue their domination of the present (Ucko 1983; Hall 1984; Trigger 1985). The impact of the colonial period on the archaeology of regions alien to its rulers has, however, only been slightly measured. Even more important, in regions where archaeology has been taken over by the people whose past is under investigation, little has been done to examine the difference between the old and new styles of archaeology or the problems resulting from adopting an academic skill developed elsewhere. I shall attempt to explore what real difference it makes to the archaeology of a region when its own people do the archaeology.

"Bias" may be defined in many ways. In very general terms, the uneven sampling of the total data possibilities produces "bias." Translated into the practical terms of the archaeology this means that we excavate and save only what we today think is important. What we save we analyze, classify, and describe, often only in terms that we inherit, or on a more sophisticated level, narrowly limit to answer explicit questions. Our interpretation usually relates the new data to old questions, often with little more than a quantitative expansion of knowledge. In this way the investigator enlarges bias as an inherited or acquired scholarly tradition. A devastating loss of consciousness is sometimes induced—most effective when it comes from the charismatic scholar—by the assertion that archaeology is above politics. For this person bias may be an operational problem but certainly not cultural and least of all political. Such persons are unaware that the ethnocentrism and political interests of the investigator produce bias in archaeology. Does this mean that the archaeologist should have no ethnic identity or political agenda when he or she works in the field and wishes to be "scientific"? My thesis is that it is impossible not to be biased, that bias can and should be chosen to serve the needs of the people whose past is being investigated and whose cultural self-understanding is at stake, but that such bias can be both explicit and controlled. First we must, however, examine more closely the evidence for bias in the work of the archaeologist. We may then be able to judge the value of suggestions for controlling this inevitable academic reality.

I shall attempt to illustrate bias in the selection of what to excavate, the collection of what to analyze and the interpretation of what is meaningful. Most of my illustrations will come from Palestine where, according to Mortimer Wheeler (1956, 30, 53), "more sins have probably been committed in the name of archaeology than on any commensurate portion of the earth's surface ... (an) unfailing source of cautionary examples."

A. SELECTION

It has been asserted that bias in the selection of what site to excavate and what problem to research is a function of an intellectual agenda created by the ruling elite whose cultural, political, religious and social-economic interests are thereby supported (Fowler 1987). I submit that there will be a measurable distance between such an agenda, if archaeologists possessing a social consciousness are working on their own past cultural traditions, and the agenda developed by foreign scholars for execution in a foreign country serving an alien social or academic need (Glock 1987). This can be illustrated by reference to the history of excavation in Palestine.

Palestine is a small land, about 10,000 square miles under the British Mandate. The 1922 census revealed a population of 757,182 persons, of which 79 percent were Muslim, 11 percent Jewish and 10 percent Christian (Luke 1930, 5). As of 1944, 2,048 abandoned sites and tells (Amiran 1953, 68) were registered as protected monuments. At the same time we should include 1,051 living villages, many of which were located on ancient sites. By the end of the Mandate, 3780 antiquity sites had been recorded (Anonymous 1976). In addition, since 1944, intensive surveys have mapped thousands of additional sites. In the sparsely populated desertic Naqab alone, an area of ca. 4600 square miles, between 1980–1985 almost 10,000 new sites had been identified. Obviously, the definition of what constitutes an archaeological site now includes small encampments. These known abandoned sites represent only some of the possibilities for archaeological investigation. However, apart from salvage excavations, most of the major expeditions have not only focused on biblical sites (one or more of the six hundred plus settlements mentioned in the Bible) but were also directed by archaeologists from England, Europe or the U.S. Even though mostly Christian they can hardly be said to have represented the 10 percent Arab Christian population, although perhaps a very small fraction of the 11 percent Jewish population. The almost 80 percent of the population that was Muslim Arab, most of whom had lived in Palestine for hundreds of years, and whose cultural traditions were visible everywhere, were represented only by uneducated laborers who assumed that the foreigners were unsuccessful in their search for gold.

Since mid-century the cultural connection of Palestinian Arabs to ther past has deteriorated significantly. More than half of their villages have been razed, their inhabitants turned into refugees. Towns for immigrant colonists have replaced the destroyed villages. In one instance where the abandoned buildings were left standing—Lifta, near

Jerusalem, presumed to be on the site of the biblical Mei Neftoah—a government agency is restoring the buildings in order to create a natural history and study center emphasizing the Jewish connection. The message of the extant architecture constructed by the refugeed Arab population, may, it is reported, receive passing attention, if any (*The Jerusalem Post* 13.2, 1987). It is clear that the story communicated by the winners is heavily biased, filtering out the unwelcome "noise" of the vanquished. If indeed it is true that cultural heritage of a land is the possession of all its inhabitants, then it seems certain that agencies, needing less to bias the record than governments eager to defend their claims to legitimacy, ought to be assigned the task of excavating, interpreting and presenting the archaeological evidence of the past. This should be the responsibility of university scholars representing the diversity of living cultural traditions in any one land, while governments should continue the task of protection and preservation.

   Guidelines for the first serious attack on the archaeology of Palestine were announced in June 1865 in London when the PEF (Palestine Exploration Fund) was established. The principles of the organization required it to be scientific, non-religious and non-controversial. It was, however, no accident that the centenary exhibition of PEF at the Victoria and Albert Museum was entitled, "World of the Bible," rather than "Palestine through the Ages" or the like. Until 1925 when the first evidence of Pleistocene hominids appeared, all excavation focused on biblical sites of interest to Jews and Christians, the people whose religious attachment to Palestine generated the required financial support for PEF projects. The chief interest of the supporters of the PEF was the illumination and illustration of biblical texts. Even the late nineteenth century survey of Jerusalem by Warren and Conder (1884; Besant 1886, 48–62), then largely a Muslim built city, appears interested in the third most sacred space in Islam, the Haram, only to the extent that it was presumed to be the original site of the tenth century BC temple of Solomon rebuilt by Herod in the late first century BC. The British anxiety about the authenticity of the Bible supported such early excavators as Petrie (Tell el-Hesi in 1890 and Tell el Ajjul, 1931–1938) and Macalister (Gezer in 1902–1905, 1907–1909), the research aims of the German Old Testament scholar Sellin at Tell Taʿannek (1902–1904), Tell el-Sultan (1907–1909), and Tell Balata (1913–1914, 1926–1927). Indeed, the interests of supporters of the

American excavators Reisner and Fisher at Sebastiyeh (1908–1910) included little that might have stimulated the cultural and historical awareness of the majority Muslim population that had existed in Palestine for the past thirteen hundred years.

Since 1925 the interest of excavators has broadened only slightly to include post-biblical sites. Some few Islamic sites or strata have been excavated and published but none with the care required to be certain even of the date of the ceramics. No site of the four hundred year Ottoman period immediately preceding the British Mandate has been excavated with the possible exception of our own work at Tiʿinnik (1985–1987) which was designed to attack this gap in the cultural history of Palestine. There can be no doubt that this hiatus is a function of a strong cultural bias against the values of Muslim tradition on the part of the foreign excavators. The negative view of the native population of Palestine, largely Muslim, reflected in the accounts of pilgrims since the fourth century AD, climaxed in the nineteenth century by both travelers and students who emphasized the squalor of living conditions and the duplicity of the native inhabitants (Drake *et al.* 1881). The Arab people of Palestine were not prepared for the cultural conquest of the archaeologist. We cannot, however, allow them to be the losers if we are to protect and preserve an adequate understanding of the role of Palestine in the cultural history of the Middle East. To this day we do not have a history of Palestine that allows for a documented understanding of the native Arab contribution. There is little or no appreciation of the powerful Palestinian cultural traditions that succeeded in preserving the integrity of the community in all its rich diversity through at least the last millennium. Archaeology has been allowed to contribute virtually nothing to the refinement, testing or elaboration of this understanding of Arab Palestine. Until this picture is rectified the popular image of Palestine is biased by the chronological provincialism of the archaeological establishment that depends for its support on patrons interested in elaborating the biblical connections.

B. COLLECTION

Bias in the collection of physical evidence in the process of excavation or survey is subtle, and may appear to be a function of technical competence but is actually as culturally deliberate as is the section of what site to excavate. What observations and records, samples or even photographs the excavator collects or does not collect reflects his or her tutored point of view regarding the nature and form of the archaeological record as well as the possibilities of cultural variability under investigation.   In an excavation the source of the collected data is the archaeological record. For the field archaeologist the "archaeological record" is both the preserved and retrieved fraction, and the part of the latter that is observed and measured becomes the database. For today's archaeologists the collected evidence is artifacts, ecofacts, plans of architecture and installations, section drawings, photos and written observations systematically transferred from a stratigraphically excavated sedimentary matrix to a laboratory for further analysis and synthesis (Patrik 1985; Sabloff *et al.* 1987). The key word is "selected." What is selected and why? The answer to the first question is relatively straightforward while the answer to the second may reflect one of many constraints or contingencies. But it may also indicate a limited understanding of what is possible or necessary to accomplish the stated aims of the excavation, which ultimately means that the reasons for selection and deselection are hidden in the implicit philosophies of archaeology at work in the individual investigator.

The research agenda, topics considered a contribution to current discussion, is the generative force for data collection. It could be argued that the archaeology of Palestine today has several research agendas. Even a cursory review of articles in the leading journals, however, reveals that the central tendency in the research agenda continues to be strongly influenced by the desire to settle questions that influence biblical interpretation. By and large, the research agenda has been established by biblical rather than archaeological scholars, though in Palestine today this distinction must be used with caution. The recent work of young anthropologically trained archaeologists has emphasized the value of data relation to social and economic systems of cultures that remain the focus of a biblically oriented scholarship public, but it has not yet had a significant impact on that focus.

To illustrate, it may be useful to cite those topics that continue to enjoy prime research time and support. It may also be illuminating to observe issues that are not regarded as important and are therefore rarely discussed.

The topics commonly researched, regularly published, and widely discussed, are the following:

1. The development of urban and pastoral Bronze Age culture focusing on evidence that provides a foil against which Israelite traditions are viewed.
2. The transition between Late Bronze and the Iron Age, the period of the formation of the 12-tribe league called Israel, the destruction of cities and formation of villages in the mountains of central Palestine presumed to be Israelite.
3. Distinctive artifacts and architecture of the Iron Age through the Byzantine period that are presumed to represent the Israelite and later Jewish occupation of Palestine.
4. Formal, macroscopic, two-dimensional studies of artifacts, especially pottery, viewed as static symbols of culture change.

The topics that receive scant attention, are not discussed, and for which data is usually not collected, are these.

1. Studies in the background of the material culture traditions of the living Arab villages in Palestine today.
2. The transition between the Byzantine and Umayyad and between the two succeeding Islamic periods; tribal boundaries and groupings as well as the nature of village life in these periods.
3. The distinctive material culture traditions of the polyethnic communities that formed the population base of Palestine in most periods to the present.
4. Ethnographic and technological studies of artifact groups that emphasize social and economic implications.

In summary, two further examples may be helpful. The degree to which the sediments that hide the artifacts and architecture are observed and recorded with increasing detail is certainly a measure of a developing interest in accuracy both of description and interpretation. In the case of a reexcavation the result is often much the same as earlier except that now it is possible to demonstrate the results more clearly (compare the Marquet-Krause and Callaway excavations of the "sanctuary" at Tell el-Tell) though in many cases considerable redating has resulted (e.g., Jericho, Taʿannek, Gezer). In other cases the data are catalogued but rarely exploited to the full and even less synthesized. Note the refined locus description catalogs in the Gezer reports that have relatively little impact on the interpretation of the stratigraphy. In both cases we are dealing with the reexcavation of prime biblical sites. The aim was to reevaluate the earlier work, making the archaeology more reliable and more usable in a more scientific age. The understanding of the purpose of archaeology in Palestine implied in this aim, however, rarely goes beyond its value for the interpretation of history in Palestine during the biblical periods, primarily the last three millennia BC.

The increase of detail is making a cultural history of Palestine more possible though the few who are using the data for that purpose are often motivated by the desire to connect the Israeli present to the Jewish past in the land to the exclusion of the resident Palestinian Arabs. There may be evidence of maturation in excavation technique while the purpose of Archaeology in Palestine continues to be inspired by the Bible. The result is an even more potent biblical bias, which manifests itself in an intense interest in correlating cultural details on the basis of an agenda established by the need to interpret biblical statements. This is not to say that some archaeologists are not interested in inter-site and intra-site settlement patterns, in the history and technology of various features of the archaeological record, both artifact and architecture. The perspective, however, from which all of this work proceeds continues to be the affirmation of a Judaeo-Christian heritage that satisfies the needs of history-minded Christians and Jews, predominantly western in origin and orientation. In such an archaeological tradition, Muslim Arabs, also a part of the population of Palestine, are culturally ignored and displaced. By implication, the later periods are not important and therefore little data is collected. In this way the biblical archaeologist has disinherited the Palestinian Arab by a process of carefully selected data collection. One indication that this is so is that no general survey of the archaeology of Palestine discusses the Byzantine and Islamic periods with as much detail as the preceding biblical periods and rarely reports their existence at all. The people who affirm that archaeology in Palestine today is a process of objective and scientific data collection and therefore not political in the broad sense will be the same who will deny that today it remains essentially biblical though less explicitly so than in the past.

C. INTERPRETATION

The ultimate impact of bias is on the interpretation of the data collected from the archaeological record. In Palestine where the chief interest is often to relate the new data to the Bible and where the Bible is today the chief source of political ideas and language in the dominant culture, the main interest is in success stories mainly from the first millennium BC. In such an atmosphere, there is a limited tolerance of diverse interpretive scenarios. This has produced a data glut. The vast amount of new data types cannot be accommodated without more flexible social constructs. The result is a final field report containing many autonomous essays by specialists with little attempt to produce an integrated picture of a living society. Even where an attempt is made to include results of the analyses of diverse material evidence in summing up the dominance of history as essentially "conquest" and "settlement" of alien land by a distinctive ethnic population emphasizes the broadly political to the virtual exclusion of serious interest in alternatives (Finkelstein 1986). There may be disagreement in details but the need for broad consensus and support for national aims permits little tolerance for reassessment.

To illustrate the problem I would like to review briefly current interpretations of the archaeology of the thirteenth to eleventh centuries BC in Palestine. In biblical terms this is the period of the Israelite "conquest" and "settlement," in archaeological terms, the end of Late Bronze II and the beginning of Iron Age I. The 75th anniversary symposium of The American Schools of Oriental Research held in Jerusalem in 1975 focused on this period (Cross 1979). Ten years later, in 1984, the 70th anniversary of the Israel Exploration Society was celebrated with an International Congress on Biblical Archaeology in which the first session after general considerations of the state of Biblical Archaeology today dealt with "The Israelite Settlement in Canaan" (Amitai 1985). The image of the Conquest of Palestine described in the Bible functioned for long in the Christian west as a powerful myth. It was used, for example, to support the self-understanding of the New World colonists who thought "of their own people as constituting a New Israel and of the native Anericans as Canaanites whose possessions God was delivering into their hands" (Trigger 1985, 13).

The Bible describes a systematic conquest of Palestine west of the Jordan River by the united tribes of Israel led by Joshua. This event presumably occurred in the late thirteenth century BC at a time when, according to literary sources, there is a general collapse of preexisting social, economic and political structures in the eastern Mediterranean accompanied by demographic displacement. Three explanatory models are currently used to interpret the literary (mainly biblical) and archaeological evidence: conquest, immigration and revolt (Weippert 1971). Conquest is the traditional view of scholars who regard the biblical story as essentially correct and find that the collapse of Canaanite cities in the late thirteenth century is confirmation (Malamat 1979). This view was also supported by the false assumption that nomadic life on the desert edge was precarious and there was a natural desire to settle on arable land, the so-called conflict between the desert and the sown. Others interpret the biblical account of the "conquest" as an ahistorical ritual explanation from a later time when the land was politically unified (Weippert 1979, 31–34). Still others, drawing on sociological studies of periods of turmoil and change, found the key in the "outright rejection of the agrarian tributary system by which city-state apparatuses exacted taxes of compulsory labor, military service and in kind from their peasant subjects" (Gottwald 1985, 36).

The archaeological record in this period reflects change, sometimes drastic. The evidence is always uneven and the sample is inevitably small. What is evident, however, is the eagerness of many to identify all recently identified unfortified villages in the mountain country as Israelite (Mazar 1985; Finkelstein 1986, 201–204). A few years ago it was common to hear that the four-room house, the collar-rim storejar, plastered cisterns and field terraces were markers of Israelite villages of the twelvth to eleventh centuries. Today we know that most of these markers were found also earlier or in areas that were presumably not occupied by Israelites. Gradually the force of new evidence and less need to rely on the biblical symbol compels revision of entrenched interpretations. What is important here is to see how much a religious document, itself composed in Palestine, now interpreted to satisfy western interests, has made demands on the interpretation of the archaeological record. This has led some scholars to insist that unless archaeology is independent of the biblical myth it will not be able to contribute an authentic picture of the cultural history of Palestine (for example, see Glock 1986).

Of importance is the stout resistance of many archaeologists to any but a literal interpretation of the biblical record and the vehemence with which the issue is dicussed. One reason for this appears to lie in the bias of western scholars who regard the Bible as an essential source of their cultural traditions (Parkes 1959). Modern archaeology was developed within western culture and made some of its early spectacular discoveries in the Middle East a means of strengthening the *status quo* by demonstrating the antiquity of the cultural roots of the West. Palestine, especially Jerusalem, was an early though disappointing focus of archaeological attention because it was the scene of most biblical events. Never mind that 80 percent of the population is Muslim and 90 percent Arab and thus only peripherally connected with western culture. After the founding of the State of Israel in 1948 and the ensuing military conquest, perceived by many as a fulfillment of biblical prophecy, the Bible became even more crucial than before as the source of symbolic language and deeds (Dayan 1978). Not least among these deeds was the "conquest" of Palestine under Joshua. The scholarly defence of the biblical story became an essential means for preserving the vision and the meaning of the current conquest of the land; any view that diminished the heroic stature of Joshua and his deeds was perceived as hostile (see, for example, Yadin 1979).

D. CONTROLLING BIAS

If it is true that cultural bias distorts one's picture of the real world and distortion is undesirable, and if it is also true that cultural bias is inevitable in the selection, collection and interpretation of the archaeological record, then how is it possible to deal responsibly with this "crack in the mirror?" (Ruby 1982). I have seven suggestions for controlling bias, kinds of knowledge that involve commitment to action. Some are cognitive, others interactive. Knowing the problem of bias is relatively easy; solving the problem requires a change of mind and behavior, and is quite another matter (Lindblom and Cohen 1979, 18). We must because we are in search of a usable archaeology.

The first step in controlling cultural bias is to acknowledge that it exists and know how it affects our work as archaeologists. It is much easier to reject an influence, an idea or a position you know exists in yourself. Thus, for example, I was once a professor of Old Testament History and Literature. It is easier for me to identify the influence of the Bible in my work as an archaeologist because I know precisely the nature of biblical categories so common in the thinking and work of archaeologists in Palestine. On the other hand, the fact that I am a skeptical white American tending to minority views presents a set of cultural conditions that is more difficult to analyze the way it affects my interpretation of the archaeological record. Unfortunately, even the most penetrating minds are often unable or unwilling to be explicit about their biases. The violent debates among scholars, for example, revolving around the historicity of the so-called "conquest," is due less to clear understanding of the different philosophies of history that inform the debates than to non-academic considerations. I suspect, for example, that Yadin rejects the views of Weippert and Alt regarding the so-called "conquest" largely because he believes that no one has the right to impugn the integrity of the biblical record, least of all a German, and because he believes the Bible is crucial to the identity of the Jewish citizens of Israel (Yadin 1979).

The second step is to be explicit and specific in stating our assumptions and aims as we prepare a research design for any field work we attempt. Proper homework, however, means that we should go one step further and identify the particular philosophical perspective that requires such assumptions and promotes and supports the kind of aims that we announce. It is important that we make a conscious choice. More often than not we accept uncritically an intellectual tradition that supports the ruling elite without knowing or even asking if this is really going to produce useful new knowledge. If, in fact, after examining the options, we prefer to be eclectic, it will be necessary to construct some sort of system so that the potpourri of views are consistent and fit together. Only in this way will a coherent research program emerge with most of its biases clearly visible.

A third step is the insistence that we begin the archaeological task by first dealing with an examination of the living cultural traditions closest to the elements of earlier extinct or nearly extinct societies to be investigated. Ethnoarchaeology has become a field of study by itself. It is my contention here that the perils and pleasures of this program contain significant insights and stimuli for all forms of archaeology precisely because it deals with a living and present reality which is inevitably the starting point for all study of the material expression of human thought and action. Archaeology divorced from the living present produces a fiction, dangerous because it is unaware of the source and limits of interpretive ideas. Most of our ideas about the past are generated in the present and are of value only to the living.

The fourth step should be an effort to see that no period or part of the cultural landscape of a country receives less attention because it is of no value to [a cultural or political *Ed.*] *status quo.* Archaeology should have the capability of stimulating the reevaluation of the justice of the establishment view of the past. A usable archaeology in a land with a deep past will place emphasis on continuity and change through all time. Australia, South Africa, the U.S. and Israel will acknowledge that their cultural traditions were born in Europe and not attempt to diminish by neglect or undervaluation indigenous traditions. In a land of rich diversity the archaeology of each ethnic, religious or cultural tradition should be treated sympathetically. It is not possible to do everything but the choices to be made must be subjected to the demands of a valid representative sample.

The fifth step requires accepting the responsibility to test the hypothesis that there exists in each region or land distinctive culture traits. This does not deny the possibility of diffusion but seeks to search out the generative centers of cultural creativity that exist everywhere. In Palestine, for example, there is considerable evidence that during the last five hundred years of Ottoman rule each region possessed a political identity strong enough to resist the posting of Turkish civil servants and require the appointment of local notables to collect taxes. The impact of these internal power centers on the material culture traditions of sixteenth to nineteenth century Palestine has never-been investigated by archaeologists and yet therein may be one key to the distinctive nature of Arab Palestinian cultural history. It has been the prevailing opinion that because Palestine was a hinterland in the Islamic world it was a cultural borrower rather than a generator. The nature of foreign influence should be evaluated. In U.S. archaeology the period when foreign settlements intruded on the tranquility of the long-term original inhabitants is investigated as the Contact Period. The way in which the invasion is resisted may highlight the distinctive nature of the indigenous culture, and what changes least is more important than what changes most.

A sixth step is to provide for an estimation of error and find ways to validate results. Randomized error is less dangerous than systematic or regular error (Watson et al. 1984, 169). Cultural bias is certainly a source of systematic error. Though this process implies the quantification of data, common enough in archaeology today it will often allow cultural bias to surface. Our cultural pasts train us to differential observation, often severely biased. This problem may be observed among researchers doing their own ethnoarchaeology who have had little experience with an alien culture. This world is so familiar to the observer that much is taken for granted. Contrariwise, a foreign observer may collect much irrelevant data. Not adequately familiar with the language he or she has little ability to test observations.

Finally, a seventh step is to advocate the purposeful involvement of selected foreign persons in planning and executing an archaeological project. The research program is under the supervision of the native scholar. The purpose of foreign involvement is consciously to engage in debate regarding the value of the proposed project for the living people whose past is being investigated. The reasoning is that only in the confrontation of opposing aims will the real nature of the working local and foreign biases emerge to full view. There exist numerous examples of joint local and foreign archaeological research programs. I know of none, however, that have consciously pursued these suggested aims. It is difficult enough to create a working team even when the members have a common cultural background (Butzer 1975), the more so when the national backgrounds are diverse. Nevertheless, we must attempt by a variety of means to force to the surface for clear reflection the biases that inhabit our work programs. For some regions of the world this is the only way to recover from a long and devastating period of colonialism.

CONCLUSION

The recent symposium of the Australian Academy of the Humanities on the subject of "Who owns the past?" produced several essays documenting the impact of western European bias on the protection, recording and interpretation of Aboriginal cultural traditions (McBryde 1985). It is no surprise that "the organizations (that) aimed at preserving the European heritage have a long history, are widespread, have strong popular support, and pay little attention to the Aboriginal heritage .... Aboriginal sites have never effectively been regarded as part of the Australian heritage" (Sullivan 1985, 144–45). Nothing demonstrates so clearly the bias of the ruling elite as the suppression of that part of the cultural past that does not support the *status quo*. Responsible archaeologists will not merely protest but find ways to help confront the real world we struggle to live with.

The past, like memory, is selected to support the present. The brutal fact is that the past is always distorted by our analysis to fit the needs of the present. The archaeologist must ask, whose "present"? A land of multiple traditions has many pasts. National interest requires that none be ignored if the condition of the present struggle is to be an honest reflection of our dialectic debate with the past. To call the past an anachronism is to pronounce it dead and dismiss its meaning in the present. To produce a past that is comfortable to the present is to ignore the change that is today's agony. The tangible artifacts of the past are identified, displayed, protected, reconstituted, and duplicated, all changes that reshape the past to make it attractive to the present (Lowenthal 1985, 263–362). Archaeologists who control a significant body of data from the past must decide what kind of use should be made of the evidence to provide for us a future.

NOTES

1. This paper is dated November 1987. *Ed.* A shortened version appeared as Glock (1995).

REFERENCES

Amiran, D.
   1953   The Pattern of Settlement in Palestine. *Israel Exploration Journal*: 3: 65–78, 192–209, 250–60.

Amitai, J., ed.
   1985   *Biblical Archaeology Today. Proceedings of the International Congress on Biblical Archaeology.* Jerusalem: Israel Exploration Society.

Anonymous
   1976   *Geographical List of the Record Files, 1918–1948.* Jerusalem: Israel Department of Antiquities.

Binford, L.
   1962   Archaeological Perspectives. In *New Perspectives in Archaeology*, ed. S. R. Binford and L. R. Binford. Chicago: Aldine.
   1972   *An Archaeological Perspective.* New York: Seminar Press.

Butzer, K.
1975   The Ecological Approach to Archaeology: Are we Really Trying? *American Antiquity* 40: 106–11.

Clarke, D.
1978   *Analytical Archaeology.* 2nd ed. revised by Bob Chapman. London: Methuen.

Cross, F. M.
1979   *Symposia.* Cambridge, MA: American Schools of Oriental Research.

Dancey, W. S.
1981   *Archaeological Field Methods. An Introduction.* Minneapolis, MN: Burgess.

Dayan, M.
1978   *Living with the Bible.* New York: William Morrow.

Deetz, J.
1977   *In Small Things Forgotten.* Garden City, NY: Anchor Books.

Drake, C. F. T.; Claremont-Ganneau, C.; and Finn, E.
1881   The Peasantry of Western Palestine. Pp. 309–51 in *Survey of Western Palestine: Special Papers.* London: Palestine Exploration Fund.

Finkelstein, I.
1986   *'Izbet Sartah.* Oxford: BAR International Series 299.

Fowler, D. D.
1987   Uses of the Past: Archaeology in the Service of the State. *American Antiquity* 52: 229–48.

Gero, J. M.; Lacy, D. M.; and Blakey, M. L., eds.
1983   *The Socio-Politics of Archaeology.* Research Report Number 23. Department of Anthropology, University of Massachusetts: Amherst.

Glock, A. E.
1986   Biblical Archaeology: An Emerging Discipline? Pp. 85–101 in *The Archaeology of Jordan and Other Studies*, ed. L. T. Geraty and L. G. Herr. Berrien Springs: Andrews University.

1987   Prolegomena to Archaeological Theory. *Birzeit Research Review* 4: 4–39.

Gottwald, N. K.
1985   The Israelite Settlement as a Social Revolutionary Movement. Pp. 34–46 in *Biblical Archaeology Today*, ed. J. Amitai. Jerusalem: Israel Exploration Society.

Hall, M.
1984   The Burden of Tribalism: The Social Context of Southern African Iron Age Studies. *American Antiquity* 49: 455–67.

Hodder, I.
1982   *Symbols in Action: Ethnoarchaeological Studies of Material Culture.* Cambridge: Cambridge University.

Lindblom, C. E. and Cohen, D. K.
1979   *Usable Knowledge: Social Science and Social Problem Solving.* New Haven: Yale University.

Lowenthal, D.
1985   *The Past is a Foreign Country.* Cambridge: Cambridge University.

Malamat, A.
1979   Israelite Conduct of War in the Conquest of Canaan. Pp. 35–56 in *Symposia*, ed. F. M. Cross. Cambridge: American Schools of Oriental Research.

Mazar, A.
1985   The Israelite Settlement in Canaan in the Light of Archaeological Excavations. Pp. 61–71 in *Biblical Archaeology Today*, ed. J. Amitai. Jerusalem: Israel Exploration Society.

McBryde, I.
1985   *Who Owns the Past?* Melbourne: Oxford University.

Parkes, H. B.
1959   *Gods and Men: The Origins of Western Culture.* New York: Knopf.

Patrik, L. E.
1985   Is There an Archaeological Record? Pp. 27–62 in *Advances in Archaeological Method and Theory*, Vol. 8. New York: Academic Press.

Patterson, T. C.
1986   The Last Sixty Years: Toward a Social History of Americanist Archaeology in the United States. *American Anthropologist* 88: 7–26.

Ruby, J., ed.
1982   *A Crack in the Mirror: Reflexive Perspectives in Anthropology.* Philadelphia: University of Pennsylvania.

Sabloff, J. R.; Binford, L. R.; and McAnany, P. A.
1987   The Archaeological Record. *Antiquity* 61: 203–9.

Schiffer, M. B.
1983   Toward the Identification of Formation Processes. *American Antiquity* 48: 675–706.

Sullivan, S.
1985   The Custodianship of Aboriginal Sites in Southeastern Australia. Pp. 139–74 in *Who Owns the Past?*, ed. I. McBryde. Melbourne: Oxford University.

Trigger, B.
  1980   Archaeology and the Image of the American Indian. *American
            Antiquity* 45: 662–76.
  1985   The Past as Power: Anthropology and the North American
            Indian. Pp. 11–40 in *Who Owns the Past?*, ed. I. McBryde.
            Melbourne: Oxford University.

Ucko, P. J.
  1983   Australian Academic Archaeology. Aboriginal Transformation
            of its Aims and Practices. *Australian Archaeology* 16: 11–16.

Weippert, M.
  1971   *The Settlement of the Israelite Tribes in Palestine.* London:
            SCM.
  1979   The Israelite "Conquest" and the Evidence from Transjordan.
            Pp. 15–34 in *Symposia*, ed F. M. Cross. Cambridge: American
            Schools of Oriental Research.

Wheeler, M.
  1956   *Archaeology from the Earth.* Harmondsworth: Penguin.

Wylie, A.
  1985   Putting Shakertown Back Together: Critical Theory in
            Archaeology. *Journal of Anthropological Archaeology* 4:
            133–47.

Yadin, Y.
  1979   The Transition from a Semi-Nomadic to a Sedentary Society in
            the Twelfth Century B.C.E. Pp. 57–68 in *Symposia*, ed. F. M.
            Cross. Cambridge: American Schools of Oriental Research.

Appendix 3
Divided We Stand:
The Problem of Palestine[1]

ALBERT E. GLOCK

To explore the roots of the problem of Palestine, I will discuss the kinds of biases westerners have regarding Palestine and how these predispositions effect what we read and hear about Palestine. I will also examine the grounds for the assertion that Christians may ultimately be responsible for many of the injustices that the Arab people of Palestine are experiencing today.

My aim is to show the difference between Palestine as perceived in the west and what actually exists in the real world on the ground in the east. I want to leave no doubt that the religious views that informed the western perspective were and are in large measure responsible for the virtual extinction of Arab Palestinian culture and population. What remains of this heritage deeply rooted in the land of Palestine continues to live in the memory and imagination of Palestinians in Diaspora, now transformed by the bitterness of an increasing alienation.

The east–west polarity is adopted for convenience (Lewis 1964; 1982). While it is true that the nineteenth century saw the importation of nationalistic spirit to the east, the impact was superficial. World economy and politics were dominated by Europe and America. The crumbling Ottoman Empire was sundered by the burden of a rigid rule of a richly diverse ethnic population bound by an isolationist tradition that was unable to accept rapid change. Weakened by nationalistic fragmentation, the archaic lifeways in the Middle East contributed to the easy manipulation of parts of the former Ottoman Empire by Britain, France, and Russia, the dominant European powers. In this context Palestine, of special significance to the west, was singled out for special treatment. Combined with its strategic location, it was of course the Palestine of the past that had meaning for the West. The contemporary people of Palestine had no meaning. It was in this east–west encounter that the Palestine Problem of today emerged.

A. PALESTINE IN THE WESTERN MIND

The trauma of 1948 remains the single most powerful event in the modern history of Palestine. The political force that produced the 1948 war was the political Zionists' interpretation of the Balfour Declaration of 1917 that was incorporated in the charter of the British Mandate over Palestine. While the timing of the Balfour Declaration may or may not have been connected with British attempts to keep Russia as an ally in World War I (Rodinson 1973, 46–48), it certainly was an outgrowth of the attempt to create a reliable buffer state to protect the Suez Canal, lifeline to India, the crown of the British Empire. The fact that the Declaration was made at all ultimately is rooted in Christian tradition.

What was the Balfour Declaration? It was actually a private letter addressed to Baron Lionel Walter Rothschild by British Foreign Secretary Arthur Balfour with a message to be relayed to the Zionist Federation. The final version reads in part: "His Majesty's Government view with favour the establishment in Palestine of a national home for the Jewish people, and will use their best endeavours to facilitate the achievement of this object, it being clearly understood that nothing shall be done which may prejudice the civil and religious rights of existing non-Jewish communities in Palestine, or the rights and political status enjoyed by Jews in any other country." Of the three elements in this statement only the first two are of interest here.

1.   The phrase, "a national home for the Jewish people ... in Palestine" was interpreted by Zionists to mean a state following Herzl's ideas in the pamphlet entitled, *Das Judenstaat*, first published in 1896. Dr. Chaim Weizmann, a leading advocate of Zionism, argued that "Palestine should be just as Jewish as America is American and England is English" (Sidebotham 1937, 65). In the face of considerable Arab protest the British Government issued a White Paper in 1922 that attempted to clarify for both Arabs and Jews the meaning of the phrase, "a national home for the Jewish people." On the one side the White Paper addresses the fears of the Arabs:

Unauthorized statements have been made to the effect that
the purpose in view is to create a wholly Jewish Palestine.
Phrases have been used such as that Palestine is to become
"as Jewish as England is English." His Majesty's
Government regard any such expectations as impracticable
and have no such aim in view. Nor have they at any time
contemplated ... the disappearance or the subordination of
the Arab population, language, or culture in Palestine.
(Ingrams 1972, 164).

On the other hand, to allay Jewish fears that the British are
withdrawing their support, the White paper continues:

When it is asked what is meant by the development of the
Jewish National Home in Palestine it may be answered that
it is not the imposition of a Jewish nationality upon the
inhabitants of Palestine as a whole, but the further
development of the existing Jewish community ... in order
that it may become a centre in which the Jewish people as a
whole may take, on grounds of religion and race, an interest
and a pride. But in order that this community should have
the best prospect of free development of right and not on
sufferance ... recognised to rest upon ancient historic
connection (Ingrams 1972, 165).

At the Paris Peace Conference in 1919 both Arab and Zionist
delegates argued their respective cases. It was not until the following
year at the San Remo Conference that the League of Nations agreed to
assign the Mandate of Syria to France and of Palestine together with
Iraq to the British. When the terms of the Mandate for Palestine were
completed in 1922 they incorporated not only the Balfour Declaration
in the second paragraph of the preamble but added the following:
"whereas recognition has thereby been given to the historical
connection of the Jewish people with Palestine and to the grounds for
reconstituting their national home in that country." During the process
of draft revision the then Foreign Secretary, Lord Curzon, objected to
the inclusion of any statement supporting Jewish claim to Palestine: "I
do not myself recognise that the connection of the Jews with Palestine,
which terminated 1200 years ago, gives them any claim whatsoever.
On this principle we have a stronger claim to parts of France" (Ingrams

1972, 98). Nevertheless, it was Curzon himself who revised the wording as given above. The notion promoted by others in the Foreign Office was that Dr. Weizmann said he needed such a statement in order to stir interest and raise funds to support the Zionist cause.

2. The second element in the Balfour Declaration reads, "it being clearly understood that nothing shall be done which may prejudice the civil and religious rights of the existing nonJewish communities in Palestine." It was seen by some but too late by those in power that it was impossible to create conditions favorable to establishing a national home for Jews in Palestine and at the same time protect the rights of the native Arab population. In the first census of the Mandate dated October 1922 there were 83,794 Jews in a total population of 757,182 that was overwhelmingly Muslim and Arab (Luke 1930, 37). Little wonder then that on the first anniversary of the Balfour Declaration there were Arab protests against Zionist demonstrations in Jerusalem celebrating the event (Ingrams 1972, 33–34). Between 1917 and 1920 Palestine was controlled by a British Military Government that attempted to maintain the *status quo ante bellum*. Dr. Weizmann wished, however, to create facts in Palestine which would strengthen Zionist hands at the upcoming Peace Conference (Ingrams 1972, 33). Forty Zionist schools were opened to support the demand that Hebrew be at least parallel to Arabic as the language of Palestine (Smith 1984, 43). Most outrageous of all for Muslims of Jerusalem was Weizmann's attempt to purchase the space in front of the Western Wall, which was inalienable *waqf* property (Storrs 1943, 346–47). The British, however, were being supportive. Already in 1920, two years before they had been granted the Mandate of Palestine, they established a civilian government and appointed Sir Herbert Samuel, a "practising Jew by religion and a genuine Zionist" (Sidenbotham 1937, 147; Sachar 1969, 196–97), as governor. Two years later when the conditions of the mandate for Palestine were approved by the League of Nations and granted to Great Britain the Balfour Declaration was incorporated into the charter.

It is not necessary to look far for the ancestry of the Balfour Declaration. From the seventeenth through the nineteenth century in Britain alone there were frequent books and pamphlets advocating the resettlement of Jews in Palestine. Most of these publications were generated by a mixture of religious zeal and political strategy, the fulfillment of biblical prophecy and the need to protect the route to the eastern reaches of the Empire. Already in the seventeenth century there were at least twelve English publications that advocated the return of the Jews to Palestine (Hyamson 1950, 2). In the prelude to Napoleon's abortive invasion of Syria he issued a proclamation in May 1799 in which he promised the restoration of the Jewish state in return for support from the Jewish community of Africa and Asia (Guedalla 1925, 31). During the nineteenth century many such proposals emanating from England were motivated by fear that France might succeed in establishing herself in the Middle East at the cost of Great Britain. Other proposals were motivated by efforts to encourage the second coming of Christ. In 1839 Lord Shaftesbury presented a formal communication to the Palmerston government outlining reason for and methods by which to support the restoration of a Jewish state in Palestine. As a consequence a British consulate was established in Jerusalem with the specific mission of protecting the 9,690 Jews then living in Palestine (Parkes 1949, 229–32; Tuchman 1956, 175–207). Some years later Bishop Russell argued that the greatly increased knowledge of that land "has also added, in many minds, to the conviction of anticipated change, and induced students of prophecy to examine anew the predicted signs of Israel's restoration to the land of their fathers" (1860, 471). Throughout the century articles in "The Times" suggested that more Christians than Jews were interested in reestablishing a Jewish state in Palestine.

Consider now the western view of the indigenous Muslim population of Palestine. In an effort to grasp the background and implications of the Balfour Declaration it is necessary to include a commentary by Balfour himself who wrote the following in an August 1919 memorandum: "in Palestine we do not propose even to go through the form of consulting the wishes of the present inhabitants of the country.... The Four Great Powers are committed to Zionism. And Zionism, be it right or wrong, good or bad, is rooted in age-long traditions, in present needs, in future hopes, of far profounder import than the desires and prejudices of the 700,000 Arabs who now inhabit that ancient land" (Ingrams 1972, 73). It is evident that the principle of consent of the governed or self-determination in the formation of any new government in the Middle East, as stipulated by the League of Nations, did not, as far as the British government was concerned, apply to Palestine. Why not? I will propose three reasons, all of which combined to produce inevitable injustice.

1. European fear of Islam degenerated into hate which by the seventeenth century, when Europe advanced rapidly to a dominant position, automatically led to its manipulation of Middle Eastern peoples to serve imperial purposes. In the ninth century at least fifty Christians living in Cordova (Spain) under Muslim rule were martyred (Daniel 1975, 23–48). Muslims tolerated Jews and Christians when they refrained from slandering Islam. The records of Spanish martyrs, however, suggest that they deliberately flaunted Muslim tolerance. Christians were simply not able to live peaceably with another religion. When Christians were dominant, as they were in thirteenth century Spain, they not only searched out and tortured heretics but also issued a decree on 31 March 1492 expelling all Jews from the country (Wiesenthal 1973, 188–90). What Europeans learned of Islam from returning crusaders and other sources rarely reflected Muslim realities. Each side was extremely ignorant of the other, each regarded the other as polytheists and idolaters (Hill 1977). The prophet was maligned, the ritual ridiculed. In short, Muslims were viewed as enemies of God (Daniel 1975, 230-48). Christian Europe would be at war with the Muslim Arab world. The eloquent preaching of St. Bernard provided support. "we altogether forbid," he wrote, "that for any reason they should enter into alliance with (the Muslims), neither for money nor for tribute, until with the help of God either their religion or their nation has been destroyed" (cited in Daniel 1975, 252).

2. Memoirs of pilgrims, scholars and mere travelers to Palestine show the biblical past to be a greater force in the consciousness of western Christians than the Muslim population of the land. Descriptions of the contemporary landscape are sometimes detailed, living villages are almost always "miserable" and never described in detail. This may be in part because villagers were often hostile to foreigners. On return from his 1697 visit to Jerusalem Henry Maundrell passed through Jenin where he had to pay his "caphars," a tax due from travelers. We learn that Jenin "is a large old town ... (that) has in it an old castle, and two mosques, and is the chief residence of the emir Chibly." Maundrell was kept waiting sleepless for twenty-four hours and finally departed for Nazareth at midnight "to get clear of these Arabs" (Maundrell 1963, 150). An incident in John Lloyd Stephen's

1836 visit to ʿAin Yabrud illustrates both the wariness of villagers and their natural hospitality. Neither the sheikh nor the villagers were prepared to welcome the foreigner. After making friends of the brother of the sheikh he learned that "the reason of their unwillingness to receive us, namely, that they thought we were officers of Mohammed Ali, sent to spy out their condition and ascertain the number of their men able to bear arms" (Stephens 1970, 417). For the most part only those towns which called to mind biblical events were visited and described. When, however, biblical towns were out of the way they were rarely visited. Such was the case with Taanach which lies on the edge of the plain 10 km northwest of Jenin. The only visit recorded seems to be that of a certain Rev. Wolcott, who on 5 April 1842 "arrived at 8.50 at the village of Taʿannuk, the ancient Taanach. This lies five minutes west of the road, on the south side of a small hill, with a summit of tableland. It is now a mean hamlet. There is a Wely here, evidently ancient, with sculptured door-stones, and the capital of a column lying on its floor" (Wolcott 1843, 76).

3. In the nineteenth and twentieth centuries the politically ascendant powers of Europe needed Palestine for its geopolitical location and its cultural-historical resources. This view is supported by the cynical promises of independence to the Arabs, including the Arabs of Palestine, in order to gain their support for the war and then imposing three and finally four mandates on the region. More specifically, the isolation of Palestine as a National Home for the Jews and the simultaneous promise to the Arab Palestinians that their interests would not be threatened was a manifestly unworkable manipulation of a little understood population. During the nineteenth century Britain and France vied for power in the Levant, well aware that each was attempting to prevent the other from capitalizing on the weakness of the Ottomans. When the British forced Muhammad Ali out of Palestine the French supported the Egyptian Pasha. It was the Crimean War of 1853–1856, however, that showed that France and England feared Russia more than each other (Rich 1985). The wedge used to legitimise economic and political interference in the affairs of Syria was religion, the Russians as protectors of the Orthodox Church, the French as defenders of the Latin Church and, the British as supporters of the Jews.

SEVENTY YEARS OF PALESTINE
ON THE GROUND IN THE EAST

We have attempted to understand the underlying causes for the unilateral expropriation of Palestine and protecting the process by which it was converted into a Jewish state without even considering to consult the indigenous Arab population. The emphasis has been on the mind of the West. I will now attempt to describe briefly what in fact occurred on the ground in Palestine. This might be considered a commentary on the views of George Kidston in the foreign office when he read Balfour's views cited above: "Palestine is to go to the Zionists irrespective of the wishes of the great bulk of the population, because it is historically right and politically expedient to do so. The idea that the carrying out of ... (this programme) will entail bloodshed and military repression never seems to have occurred to him" (Ingrams 1972, 74).

(a)   Whatever views and forces were at work to modify the movement toward the formation of a Jewish state in order to accommodate Arab Palestinian political aspirations, cultural traditions and physical presence, were inevitably suppressed in favor of creating a state as Jewish as England is English. The historical context of this included first, the Jewish community and the struggle between political and non-political Zionists, second, the struggle between the two major families within the Arab community, the Nashishibi's and the Husseini's, and third, the British attempts to accommodate these conflicts and at the same time achieve its own imperial purposes.

(b)   The nineteenth century fruits of the late eighteenth century French Revolution were romanticism, a growing intellectual freedom from religious constraints (the Enlightenment), and nationalism tainted with Aryan racism. As Jews gained freedom (Emancipation) they began to assimilate into secular European culture. It was, however, the 1881 pogroms in Russia following the assassination of Nicholas II that taught Jews that for them at least, this new freedom, both civil and intellectual, was an illusion. In this context Jewish Zionism was born, twice born, in Europe and exported to Palestine. From the beginning the tension between political and religious Zionism divided the Jewish community. It was the political Zionism espoused by Herzl that ultimately gained the day as a secular messianism. The two streams created the paradox that, though denying God, Zionists insisted "that they could rebuild the Jewish nation only on the land He had promised to Abraham" (Hertzberg 1970, 75). Though not defined with any precision, the Balfour Declarations's support of a National Home for the Jews in Palestine was to accept Zionism. Herzl had assumed that western liberal democracies would solve the "Jewish problem" by supporting Zionism. The British proved him correct.

Between 1919 and 1948 there are thirty fateful years. Picture Palestine when its population was 90 percent Arab and 10 percent Jewish, and when it was technologically underdeveloped in comparison to Europe. Now, almost suddenly, Jewish immigration introduced an average of 10,000 new persons annually, a high of 33,800 in 1925, mostly from Europe. Due to economic depression in 1926, drought and a devastating earthquake in 1927, the next two years saw increasing emigration so that in 1927 there was a net loss in the Jewish population of 2300. Jewish immigrants from Europe were young and visionary. They perceived themselves as "pioneers" (*hehalutzim*), reclaiming the land by the labor of their hands, as taught by Aaron David Gordon of Degania (1856–1922) (Baratz 1957, 85–95). The immigrants were supported by an international fundraising committee known as the Jewish Agency. They had their own education system, own language, health care and labor union. They had engineers who construct roads and build factories. The Jewish Agency was allowed to function as a quasi-government of the Jewish population, supporting an independent educational system, press and an unofficial military force.

(a) The implementation of the Mandate required that Britain regulate but also support Jewish immigration as well as land sales to the Jewish National Fund. As a consequence between 1922 and 1939 the Zionists were able to purchase and lease almost a million dunams of land and increase their population ratio from less than 10 percent to 30 percent (Khouri 1968, 18). Land purchase inevitably resulted in the displacement of Arab peasant families, though every effort was made by the Jewish National Fund to lay the blame elsewhere and thus to evade responsibility. In a report by John Hope-Simpson for the Mandate administration more than 29 percent of the almost 87,000 rural Arab families were landless. A recent study has attempted to show that the statistics simply do not exist to allow even an estimate of how many Arabs were displaced by Jewish land purchases (Stein 1984, 108–11). It was therefore possible to keep saying that Jewish immigration "would continue in accordance with the possibilities of economic absorption, and without dispossessing the non-Jewish inhabitants of their present habitations" (Ben-Gurion 1973, 124).

(b) In this period the Zionists invested approximately $400 million in industry. A deep sea harbor was constructed at Haifa. A pipe line brought oil from Mosul in Iraq to Haifa. Power stations were built following the creation of the Palestine Electric Corporation in 1923. The Palestine Potash Ltd. at the north end of the Dead Sea was established in 1930, production beginning in 1932. A major survey of past and future possibilities for economic development in Palestine describes the impact of Zionist policies in reactive, not cooperative terms (Horowitz 1946). Arabs, referred to as non-Jews, were never involved in the development planning that was presumably having such a positive effect on their welfare.

(c) On the other hand, the long-time Arab peasant farmer (*fellah*) was sometimes displaced from his land, unfamiliar with the new technologies being introduced. He was no longer his own master. Because he was not prepared to accept the imposed modernity he had no recourse except to violent rejection or passive acceptance. One of the more disastrous riots occurred between 23–29 August 1929 when 133 Jews and 114 Arabs were killed all over the country (Elbogen 1944, 620). With the rise of Hitler in Germany Jewish immigration into Palestine increased dramatically. Between 1933–1935 130,000 Jews entered Palestine, many of them highly skilled scientists and medical doctors. On 26 April 1936 the Arabs of Palestine began a rebellion against the British Mandate that was to last the better part of three years. They refused to work or pay taxes. Guerrilla bands roamed the hill country cutting telephone lines, ambushing police and military personnel, attacking railroads and highways.

Each revolt brought a royal commission from London to investigate the causes, the Shaw Commission in 1930 and the Peel Commission in 1937. The Shaw Commission had determined that the causes of riot were ethnic. As a result Jewish immigration was halted but only briefly. The Peel Commission's findings were more sobering. It concluded that the Mandate as defined was unworkable and should be abandoned by partitioning the country into a Jewish and an Arab state, with the British holding a permanent Mandate over the holy sites of Jerusalem, Bethlehem and Nazareth as well as a passage to the coast from Jerusalem to Jaffa. Both Arabs and Zionists, the British Parliament and the Permanent Mandate Commission, rejected the findings of the Peel Commission report. With the beginning of World War II on 1 September 1939 the problem of Palestine was temporarily put on the back burner.

Between 1948 and 1967 things turn from trauma to tragedy. On 29 Nov 1947 the United Nations General Assembly passed by a vote of thirty-three to thirteen, with ten abstentions, the recommendation of the United Nations Special Committee on Palestine to partition the country into two states, leaving Jerusalem-Bethlehem a *corpus separatus* under international supervision. This decision was accepted by the Yishuv and rejected by the Arabs. The British Mandate was to end on 15 May 1948. In preparation for that day, the underground Jewish terror groups known as the Irgun and Stern Gang drove home the message to the Arab inhabitants that they were not wanted in the new Jewish state. On 4 January a powerful car bomb in Jaffa destroyed the municipality and generated the first wave of Arab evacuees. On 9 April both the Stern Gang and Irgun attacked Deir Yassin on the western edge of Jerusalem, murdering 250 men, women and children. Menahem Begin, leader of the Irgun, later declared that this operation did more to spread the fear that cleared Israel of Arabs than any other single military action (Begin 1951). On 21 April the Haganah launched an offensive on the Arab population of Haifa that resulted in early May in the flight of 66,000 of the 70,000 Arabs of the city. On 25 April the Irgun began a major assault on Jaffa, further demoralising the Arab population. By the time the British interceded there was no stopping the flight of refugees who were painfully aware of the plight of the Haifa Arabs as well as the departure of the British in a few weeks.

(a) It is clear that all Arabs were regarded as potential enemies. For long it was the Israeli explanation for the flight of the Arabs that the refugees were responding to the call of the Arab Higher Committee to evacuate so that Arab civilians would not be harmed when their troops entered the land after 15 May to push the Yishuv into the sea. A recent major study based on released Israel Defence Force archives has shown that for the most part both the Arab Higher Committee as well as Arab states had in fact urged the Palestinian Arabs to stay put and that it was the often explicit, always implicit, policy of the Jewish military to clear the land of Arabs (Hitchens 1988; Morris 1987). There is little doubt that leaders of the Yishuv such as Ben-Gurion, Chairman of the Jewish Agency, and Yosef Weitz of the Jewish National Fund Lands Department were delighted with the Arab exodus.

Nothing shatters the myth of voluntary Arab flight as much as the story of how the Nazareth population stayed put. The town was taken on 16 July by the 7th Brigade commanded by Canadian Ben Dunkelman. The town's notables signed a surrender document. In return "Dunkelman solemnly pledged that no harm would befall the civilian population" (Kidron 1988, 86). Two days later an order arrived requesting that the civilians of Nazareth be evacuated. Dunkelman refused to obey the order. He was relieved of command but before departing insisted that the pledge of safety for the citizens of Nazareth be kept. It seems that Ben-Gurion had canceled the expulsion order of the commander of the Northern Front, Moshe Carmel. The cabinet was later told, " the army must be given strict instructions to behave well and fairly towards the inhabitants of the city because of the great political importance of the city in the eyes of the world" (Morris 1987, 202).

(b) While in Nazareth people and buildings were spared, such was not the case elsewhere, not even in the Nazareth subdistrict. Six of the nineteen Arab villages in the region were demolished. Where before 1948 there were no Jewish settlements in that subdistrict, by 1977 there were twenty-one. A few more examples will serve to indicate the nature of the demographic changes following 15 May 1948 through 1977. All of the twenty-six Arab villages in the Jaffa subdistrict were demolished. Up until 1977, twenty-six new Jewish settlements had been built on these sites (Nijim 1984, 66-8). In the Gaza subdistrict all forty-six villages were destroyed. Prior to 1948 there were thirteen Jewish settlements on Gaza lands. Between that date and 1977, eighty-three new Jewish settlements had been established in this area (Nijim 1984, 70–72). In the Ramleh sub-district fifty-six Arab villages existed before 1948 all of which were demolished. Added to the twenty-five pre-1948 Jewish settlements in the region were an additional seventy-five by 1977 (Nijim 1984, 54–56). Of the seventy-two Arab villages in the Haifa subdistrict in 1948, forty-five were destroyed. By 1977, thirty-nine Jewish settlements were added to the previously existing sixty-four (Nijim 1984, 457). Seventy-eight of the eighty-three Arab villages in the Safad subdistrict were destroyed and thirty Jewish settlements were added to the previous twenty-six (Nijim 1984, 25–29); The Tiberias subdistrict fared no better. Of twenty-nine Arab villages, twenty-four were destroyed and eleven Jewish settlements were added to pre-existing twenty-seven (Nijim 1984, 30–33).

Ultimately it was Ben-Gurion who authorized the destruction of villages, the settlement of Jews in the evacuated space, and the prevention of the return of the refugees. He was wise enough to never write explicit memoranda on the subject. Nevertheless the records of close associates, particularly Yosef Weitz, testify to the existence of a Transfer Committee to oversee making the new Israel "Araberrein" (Morris 1987, 135–70). A token population of between 120,000 or 130,000 remained.

Though statistics are only estimates, the 1948 war resulted in between 600,000 and 760,000 Palestinian refugees, largely a consequence of forced expulsion and between 437 and 472 of their villages deliberately obliterated. The code name for Plan D, the military plan of the Haganah that went into effect following the withdrawal of British forces, was "MATATEH" (the broom) (Saleh 1987, 16).

Between 1967 and 1989: from Occupation to Intifada. As a consequence of the 1967 war, Israel occupied the West Bank, formerly governed by Jordan, and the Egyptian-ruled Gaza Strip, as well as the Egyptian Sinai and Syrian Golan Heights. The Sinai was returned to Egypt in 1982 following the signing of a peace treaty in 1979. The Golan Heights was annexed by Israel in 1981 over the protests of its remaining Druze inhabitants. Israel has decreed that the West Bank is now officially Judea and Samaria, presumably a part of Greater Israel (Metzger et al. 1983, 32). Maps of Palestine provided tourists as well as elementary school children are now maps of Israel showing the eastern border as the Jordan River.

It was the Balfour Declaration that assured the world the Jewish National Home would not be at the expense of the indigenous Arab population. In the seventy years between the first Zionist Congress and the war of 1967 there was ambivalence in the Jewish community. Some of the leadership worked with the assumption that there was room for two peoples in Palestine. Those who had argued for a bi-national state, as Martin Buber and Judah Magnes, were long gone by 1967 with almost no progeny, certainly few in the Knesset (Mendes-Flor 1983;

Goren 1982). Today there are two parties in the Knesset that advocate the "transfer" of the Arabs out of the occupied territories, Tehiya and Moledet. Gershon, the political secretary of Gush Emunim, declared on 2 November 1979, "it is impossible for two people to have a right to the same piece of land. We have an absolute right to this land and the Arabs have none whatsoever" (cited in Metzger et al. 1983, 34). After 1967 Israel had added another million plus Arabs to its responsibility.

What was Israel going to do with the additional Arab population? Would the pattern of 1948 be repeated? The political mythology of Israel is bound up with the view that with the founding of the state in 1948 the Jews entered the Third Temple Period. The earlier temples had been destroyed but this one remains to be built. As with all myth, if given divine authorization, it becomes a self-fulfilling prophecy. It is only a minor obstacle that today the Qubat el-Sahra stands on the site of the earlier temples. Pointing to the Dome of the Rock the guide tells fundamentalist Christian tourists:

> There we will build our third temple. We have all the plans drawn .... Even the building materials are ready. They are hidden in a secret place. There are several shops ... making the artifacts we will use in the new temple .... In a religious school called Yeshiva Ateret Cohanim ... rabbis are teaching young men how to make animal sacrifice (Halsell 1986, 90).

Nothing divides Israel more than the political implications of the move to judaise the Temple Mount (Lustick 1988, 173–76). Yet such a move is supported by 40 million fundamentalist Christians who see the rebuilding of the temple as the prelude to the second coming of Christ (Halsell 1986, 91).

(a) Most of the 150,000 Palestinians who fled eastward across the Jordan in the 1967 war had been refugeed once before in 1948. In contrast to 1948 most of the villagers and town dwellers stayed put, leaving only 8 percent of the land abandoned. This did not pose an obstacle to the Israeli "occupation" which devised "legal" ruses to justify expropriation so that by 1985, 52 percent of the West Bank was controlled by Israelis (Benvenisti 1986a, 25–36). Much of this land is so-called "state land" for exclusive Israeli use. No Arab is permitted to exploit the potential of this land for private or communal needs as can the Israeli. Further, on land that remains in Palestinian hands there are strict limitations of use. Thus, for example, according to Military Order 1015 issued in 1982 "no fruit tree may be planted in an orchard without written permission by the authorities." The same applies to vegetables and grapevines (Benvenisti 1986b, 120). Private Palestinian land adjacent to Israeli settlements cannot be used. By contrast, there are no such limits for use on land controlled by the Israelis. Finally, planning of the use of all "occupied" land is in the hands of a government "High Planning Committee" representing only Israeli interests. Master Plan 200, for example, covers ca. one million dunams of the Mateh Binyamin Regional Council land in which are 95 Arab villages with a population of more than 150,000 and 22 Jewish settlements occupied in 1985 by 6,180 settlers. Thus the future of this region is controlled by the 4.1 percent of the population who are immigrant settlers while the 95.9 percent who are Palestinians have no voice in planning "roads, watergrids, sewerage, garbage disposal, electricity, communication, industrial and agricultural development" (Benvenisti 1986a, 34; 1988, 59–60, 95).

(b) As of 1987 the Israelis had established 109 settlements in all parts of the West Bank, excluding Jerusalem, with a population of about 67,000 (Benvenisti 1988, 32–3, 138–40).[2] The purpose of settlements is to create facts that will make it impossible to return the West Bank to Arab rule. If this was not the intention of the Allon Plan submitted as early as July 1967, it is certainly true today with the uncompromising settlement philosophy promoted by the ultranationalist Gush Emunim (Bloc of the Faithful), ideological descendants of the Jewish Zealots of Roman times. Gush Emunim rejects the conventional Zionist view that the Jews will become a nation like other nations when they have their own land and develop their own culture. With this anti-semitism will disappear. Rather, Gush Emunim ideology asserts that the Jews are and will always be abnormal because they are the *am segula*, the chosen people of God (Genesis 17:7, 8). Therefore the moral laws of nature do not apply to the Jews. Thus, "from the point of view of mankind's humanistic morality we were in the wrong in (taking the land) from the Canaanites. There is only one catch. The command of God ordered us to be the people of the Land of Israel" (Shlomo Aviner, cited in Lustick 1988, 76). Arab objections are understood as the hostility of the world, like all anti-semitism, in opposition to Israel's mission to save the world. The Palestinians have the same three choices as Joshua offered the biblical "Canaanites:" flee, fight or accept Jewish rule. To oppose the Jews is suicide. The goyim (gentiles) are inevitably enemies of the Jews because "in the final analysis our moral values contradict the basis upon which the people of the world build their lives." So Shlomo Aviner, a leading Gush Emunim ideologist (cited in Lustick 1988, 80). Therefore, a negotiated peace will inevitably fail.

(c) The story of the West Bank and Gaza Strip in these seventy years is that it has never been allowed to develop itself thanks in large part to the commitment of the U.S. and Great Britain to create a National Home for the Jews in Palestine. Britain was not willing to invest in the economy of the Palestinian Arabs. Jordan encouraged development of industry and agriculture only on the East Bank and at the same time ruthlessly suppressed nationalist leaders in the West Bank (Smith 1984, 122–43, 176–202). They preferred local leaders with a regional base at best, as Sheikh Ja'bari of el-Khalil (Migdal 1986, 37). The Israelis follow a similar policy of political fragmentation to allow control of the economic development of the West Bank. Israel is a high-income, capital-intensive economy while the West Bank is a low-income, labor-intensive economy. In order for the victor not to be threatened by the loser, the victor is bent on maintaining the Palestinians as perpetual losers. Little wonder, twenty-three years after the "occupation" began, the Arab family consumes less than half the electricity and water of an Israeli family. In 1983 there were 1.8 hospital beds per 1000 Arabs, 6.4 beds per 1000 Israelis. Wages in Israel for Jews in industry are four times higher than for Arabs in the same job (Benvenisti 1986b, 10, 36).

The economy of the West Bank is largely agricultural. In the first thirteen years of Israeli occupation agricultural production had not reached the level of 1966, the last full year of Jordanian rule (Metzger et al. 1984, 102). Highly productive irrigated land was reduced from 322,000 dunams in 1965 to 85,000 in 1985 or 73 percent, of which 87 percent was now in the hands of Jewish settlers (Samara 1988, 83, 91). It is not possible to receive a permit to export surplus from the West Bank to Israel unless the products are either in short supply there or not grown at all. On the other hand no permit is required for Israeli producers to dump as much surplus as they wish, often inferior grade products, on the West Bank. Government subsidies for Israeli farmers make it impossible for the West Banker to compete who, of course, has no government subsidy. The price of water for the Palestinian farmer is four times higher than for the Israeli (Samara 1988, 81). Palestinians can dig wells 100 m deep while Israelis can dig wells 600 m deep. Until 1980 only two permits had been granted to Arabs to drill for water (Shehadeh and Kuttab 1980, 113–14). In this way the economy of the West Bank is integrated into that of Israel on Israeli terms. Before 1967 the West Bank exported one-third more than it imported. But a decade after occupation it was importing 11 percent more than it exported merely to sustain life (Metzger et al. 1985, 105). In short, under the Israelis as under the Jordanians, the West Bank was economically peripheral to the center of development (Samara 1988, 116–32). Today the planners' strategy is to answer one question: Is it good for Israel? Answers are anchored in ethnics.

(d) The core of the problem faced by the Palestinians is that the Israelis do not regard their presence in the West Bank and Gaza Strip as a "temporary military occupation" which would be constrained by the Fourth Geneva Convention of 1949 for the Protection of Civilians in Time of War. They argue that this Convention assumes that the preexisting government was legitimate. Israel asserts that Jordan's annexation of the West Bank in 1950 was recognized only by Great Britain and Pakistan and therefore was not legal (Shehadeh and Kuttab 1980, 10–11). This means that Israel is not occupying but administering territories that she has liberated since the Jews have a historic "right" to Palestine or, now, Eretz Israel. As a consequence the Fourth Geneva Convention does not apply. What law, then, does apply? To apply Israeli law, the logical consequence of the above argument would entail great problems. If the Palestinians of the West Bank and Gaza were allowed to vote they would soon control the country. There would also be an international protest since most countries assume that the Fourth Geneva Convention does in fact apply and therefore guarantees the maintenance of the *status quo ante bellum*. What seems to be happening is that Jordanian Law serves as the legal base amended now beyond recognition by hundreds of Military Orders.

The Israelis have also adopted the Defence (Emergency) Regulations issued by the British Mandate in 1945 to suppress anti-British activity. These Regulations allow for deportation (over 2000 since 1967), administrative detention up to six-months (the Israel

Defence Force admits 9000 during the first two years of the Intifada; others put the number much higher), blowing up houses of suspected terrorists (over 1500 excluding the villages of Yalu, Beit Nuba and Immwas), and censorship of all copy, including cartoons, published by newspapers, thus justifying by law Israel's repressive rule of the West Bank and Gaza Strip (Benvenisti 1986b, 86–87). The Palestinian experience is not the rule of law but the rule by law (Shehadeh and Kuttab 1980). The attack on Palestinians as individuals and as community is ordinarily within the framework of some original "law," as often as not amended by a Military Order. The Intifada which began on 9 December 1987 brought to the surface not only the Palestinian frustration with years of arbitrary military occupation but also the basic human rights violations which have characterized the occupation from the beginning (Punishing 1989). Statistics, inevitably incomplete, tell but a fraction of the story. For one kind of statistic there is a fatal finality. In the first two years of the Intifada more than 750 Palestinians were martyred, almost 38,000 wounded either by the army or settlers. Of the number slain more than 156 were under 14 years of age.

CONCLUSION

I would like to end by making five points. First, in a recent issue of the "New Yorker," Amos Elon reports on the so-called Israeli peace movements, chiefly Peace Now. At the end of the article he describes a meeting between the philosopher Avishai Margalit, a Peace Now activist, and Yitzhak Rabin, then the hardline Minister of Defence. Elon writes, "Rabin, irritated, at one point turned to Margalit and snapped, 'Who are you to tell us what to do? How many votes does Peace Now have?' Margalit, according to a witness, replied, 'Maybe we don't have the votes. We do have the historians. They will have the last word in the future, when today's disorders will be tidied up into books." Rabin, according to this source, seemed taken aback (Elon 1990, 101). If the study by Benny Morris, which destroys the government-sponsored deception that the population of Palestine was refugeed at the behest of their leaders, is any indication of what historians can do with the past, then it is clear that the true story will eventually be known. But will it be too late?

Second, from the perspective of the victims the events of the last seventy years have resulted in nothing less than a calculated genocide.

The destruction of hundreds of Arab villages, the blotting out of Arabic place names in favor of biblical toponymns, often erroneous, not planning or allowing for the development of the Arab sector in the society forces ambitious and talented persons to emigrate in order to find satisfying employment. Palestinians are heavily taxed with no representation in government. The effect has been to unify the Palestinian population. Whereas military service socialises Israeli youth, prison life has been the socialising force in the Arab community.

Third, the beliefs and political-economic contribution of nineteenth century British and twentieth century American Evangelicals played a significant role in providing the Zionists with the support required to realise Jewish statehood in Palestine. At the same time popular Christian antagonism to Islam supplied western political interests with the approval required to dehumanise Arab peoples generally and Palestinians particularly. How is it that the negative stereotype of the Arab continues to appear with impunity while that of the Jew and Oriental is taboo (Terrey 1985)? The language, policies and actions of today's Christian Zionists are almost precisely parallel to that of the Jewish messianic activist settlers known as the Gush Emunim (Halsell 1986).

Fourth, it has wisely been said that, "biblical promises are not recognized as being internationally binding" (Metzger *et al*. 1983, 62). To attempt to translate a biblical promise, whatever its original context and intended meaning, into modern politics, is, as Gush Emunim ideologists make clear, putting divine right over human right, to brutally impose a religiously derived "military order" to dominate or expel a population that has lived in Palestine for centuries. Such a movement makes the Hague or Geneva Convention truly "academic." Yet what else is it that causes people to argue for Israel as *sui generis*? Does she alone among the nations of the world today have the right to enlarge her living space by conquest?

Fifth, the struggle against the illusion and myth generated by biblical tradition, and the fight for the sanity of facing political reality in the dangerous late twentieth century, are illustrated in part by the current peace efforts of the Palestinian leadership; and also in part among the Israelis, by the recent study of The Jaffee Center for Strategic Studies. The latter study explored six options in the search for peace: the *status quo*, autonomy, annexation, a Palestinian state, Gaza withdrawal and

Jordanian-Palestinian federation. These options are examined through the filter question: What's good for Israel? The qualified answer is that no option is acceptable without great risk (Jaffee Center 1989a). In a parallel document the same group proposes a hopelessly vague and drawn-out solution by mini-confidence-building steps evolving from direct negotiations, leading perhaps to a Palestinian state. It is also suggested that Israel may ultimately have no choice but to talk to the PLO. As if in despair the document wonders if the only hope is a Palestinian or Arab "Sadat"! (Jaffee Center 1989b, 19) It seems not to have occurred to Israeli politicians that Arafat may be that person. Perhaps the Palestinian "Sadat" has appeared, as once the messiah, and not recognized for who he is. If that is too much, is an Israeli "Sadat" a possibility? If the Jaffee Center study had invited contributions from Palestinian analysts the process of negotiation might already have begun.

NOTES

1.   This paper is dated March 1990. It has not been previously published. *Ed.*
2.   As of 1998, there are over 140 Israeli settlements in the West Bank housing approximately 150,000 Israeli settlers. *Ed.*

REFERENCES

Al Haq
  1988   Punishing a Nation: Human Rights Violations During the Palestinian Uprising, December 1987–December 1988. Ramallah: Al-Haq (*Law in the Service of Man*).
Aronson, G.
  1990   *Israel, Palestinians and the Intifada: Creating Facts on the West Bank*. London: Kegan Paul.
Baratz, J.
  1957   *A Village by the Jordan: The Story of Degania*. New York: Sharon Books.
Begin, M.
  1951   *The Revolt: The Story of Irgun*. London: Allen.
Ben-Gurion, D.
  1973   *My Talks With Arab Leaders*. New York: The Third Press.
Benvenisti, M.
  1986a   1986 Report. *Demographic, Economic, Legal, Social and Political Developments in the West Bank*. Jerusalem: The West Bank Data Base Project.

1986b   *The West Bank Handbook. A Political Lexicon.* Jerusalem: The Jerusalem Post.

1988   *The West Bank and Gaza Atlas.* Jerusalem: The West Bank Data Base Project.

Daniel, N.

1975   *The Arabs and Mediaeval Europe.* London: Longman.

Elon, A.

1990   Letter From Jerusalem. *The New Yorker* 23 April: 92–101.

Goren, A. A., ed.

1982   *Dissenter in Zion. From the writings of Judah l. Magnes.* Cambridge: Harvard University.

Guedalla, P.

1925   *Napoleon and Palestine.* London, Jewish Historical Society.

Halsell, G.

1986   *Prophecy and Politics. The Secret Alliance Between Israel and the U.S. Christian Right.* Chicago: Lawrence Hill Books.

Hertzberg, A.

1970   *The Zionist Idea. A Historical Analysis and Reader.* New York: Atheneum.

Hill, R.

1977   The Christian View of the Muslims at the Time of the First Crusade. Pp. 1–8 in *The Eastern Mediterranean Lands in the Period of the Crusades*, ed. P. M. Holt. Warminster: Aris and Phillips.

Hitchens, C.

1988   Broadcasts. Pp. 73–83 in *Blaming the Victims: Spurious Scholarship and the Palestinian Question*, ed. C. Hitchens and E. Said. London: Verso.

Horowitz, D.

1946   Arab Economy in Palestine. Pp. 55–65 in *Palestine's Economic Future: A Review of Progress and Prospects*, ed. J. B. Hobman. London: Percy Lund Humphries.

Hyamson, A.M.

1950   *Palestine Under the Mandate 1920–1948.* London: Methuen.

Ingrams, D.

1972   *Palestine Papers 1917–1922. Seeds of Conflict.* New York: George Braziller.

Jaffee Center for Strategic Studies

1989a   *The West Bank and Gaza: Israel's Options for Peace.* Report of a Study Group at the Jaffee Center for Strategic Studies Tel Aviv University.

1989b   *Israel, the West Bank and Gaza: Toward a Solution.* Report of a Study Group at the Jaffee Center for Strategic Studies Tel Aviv University.

Khouri, F. J.
1968   *The Arab-Israeli Dilemma.* Syracuse: Syracuse University.

Kidron, P.
1988   Truth Whereby Nations Live. Pp. 85–96 in *Blaming the Victims: Spurious Scholarship and the Palestinian Question*, ed. C. Hitchens and E. Said. London: Verso.

Lewis, B.
1964   *The Middle East and the West.* London: Weidenfeld and Nicolson.
1982   *The Muslim Discovery of Europe.* London: Weidenfeld and Nicolson.

Lustick, I. S.
1988   *For the Land and the Lord. Jewish Fundamentalism in Israel.* New York: Council on Foreign Relations.

Maundrell, H.
1963   *A Journey From Aleppo to Jerusalem in 1697.* Beirut: Khayats.

Mendes-Flor, P. R., ed.
1983   *A Land of Two Peoples. Martin Buber on Jews and Arabs.* New York: Oxford University.

Metzger, J.; Orth, M.; and Sterzing, C.
1983   *This is Our Land: The West Bank Under Israeli Occupation.* London: Zed.

Migdal, J. S.
1980   *Palestinian Society and Politics.* Princeton: Princeton University.

Morris, B.
1987   *The Birth of the Palestinian Refugee Problem, 1947–1949.* Cambridge: Cambridge University.

Nijim, B., ed.
1984   *Toward the De-Arabization of Palestine/Israel 1945–1977.* Dubuque: Rendall/Hunt.

Parkes, J.
1949   *Whose Land? A History of the Peoples of Palestine.* Penguin: Harmondsworth.

Rich, N.
1985   *Why the Crimean War? A Cautionary Tale.* Hanover: University Press of New England.

Rodinson, M.
1973   *Israel, A Colonial-Settler State?* New York: Monad.

Russell, M.
  1860   *Palestine; Or the Holy Land.* New ed. London: T. Nelson and Sons (1st ed., 1837).

Sachar, H. M.
  1969   *The Emergence of the Middle East: 1914–1924.* New York: Alfred A. Knopf.

Saleh, A. J., and Mustafa, W.
  1987   *Palestine. The Collective Destruction of Palestinian Villages and Zionist Colonisation 1882–1982.* London: Jerusalem Center for Development Studies.

Samara, A.
  1988   *The Political Economy of the West Bank 1967–1987: From Peripheralization to Development.* London: Khamsin.

Shehadeh, R., and Kuttab, J.
  1980   *The West Bank and the Rule of Law.* Geneva: International Commission of Jurists.

Sidebotham, H.
  1937   *Great Britain and Palestine.* London, Macmillan and Co. Ltd.

Smith, P. A.
  1984   *Palestine and the Palestinians 1876–1983.* London: Croom Helm.

Stein, K.W.
  1984   *The Land Question in Palestine, 1917–1939.* Chapel Hill: The University of North Carolina.

Stephens, J. L.
  1970   *Incidents of Travel in Egypt, Arabia Petraea, and the Holy Land.* Norman, OK: University of Oklahoma.

Storrs, R.
  1943   *Orientations.* Definitive ed. London; Nicholson and Watson.

Terry, J. J.
  1985   *Mistaken Identity: Arab Stereotypes in Popular Writing.* Washington, D.C.: American-Arab Affairs Council.

Tuchman, B.
  1956   *Bible and Sword. England and Palestine from the Bronze Age to Balfour.* New York: New York University.

Wiesenthal, S.
  1973   *Sails of Hope: The Secret Mission of Christopher Columbus.* New York: Macmillan.

Wolcott, S.
  1843   Researches in Palestine. Pp. 2–88 in *Bibliotheca Sacra*, ed. Edward Robinson. New York: Wiley and Putnam.

Appendix 4
Bibliography of Albert E. Glock

PUBLICATIONS

1961   Review of James B. Pritchard, *Archaeology and the Old Testament*. Princeton, NJ: Princeton University, 1958. *Lutheran Education* April, 1961: 414–15.

1964   Tell Taʿannek. *Aid Association for Lutherans*. Appleton, WI: Winter. 5 pp.

1966   Reviews of Claus Westermann, *The Praise of God in the Psalms*, 1965; Waller G. Williams, *Archaeology in Biblical Research*, 1965; Gaalyahu Cornfeld, *Pictorial Biblical Encyclopedia*, 1964. *Lutheran Education*. February, 1966: 272–74.

1967   Study and Interpretation of the Old Testament. *Concordia Theological Monthly* XXXVIII.2: 90–108.

1970a   Covenant and Law in Early Israel. *Concordia Theological Monthly* XLI; 593–97.

1970b   Review of Heinz Skrobucha, *Sinai*, 1966; Helmer Ringgren, *Israelite Religion. Lutheran Education* February, 1970: 305.

1970c   Early Israel as the Kingdom of Yahweh. *Concordia Theological Monthly* XLI.9: 558–605.

1971   A New Taanach Tablet. *Bulletin of the American Schools of Oriental Research* 204: 17–30.

1972   Review of Hans Kosmala et al., eds. *Annual of the Swedish Theological Institute*, Vol. VIII, 1972. Leiden: Brill.

1973a   *Problems in Biblical Archaeology*. River Forest, Illinois, Offset. Copyright 1975 Albright Institute of Archaeological Research, Jerusalem. 70 pp.

1973b   Review of R. De Vaux, *Histoire ancienne d'Israel; des origines a l'installation en Canaan. Journal of Biblical Literautre* 92.2: 285–87.

1974   Review of Joseph A. Callaway, *The Early Bronze Age Sanctuary at Ai (et Tell). No. 1.* 1972. *American Journal of Archaeology,* 78.2: 187–88.

1975   Homo Faber: The Pot and the Potter at Taanach. *Bulletin of the American Schools of Oriental Research* 219: 9–28.

1976   Taanach. Pp. 854–55 in *Interpreters Dictionary of the Bible,* Supplementary Volume. Nashville, TN: Abingdon.

1977   Field Notes—Israel. *Archaeological News* VI.2: 51–52.

1978   Taanach. Pp. 1138–47 in *Encyclopedia of Archaeological Excavations in the Holy Land Vol. IV,* ed. M. Avi-Yonah and E. Stern. Jerusalem: The Israel Exploration Society and Massada Press.

1982a   Ceramic Ethno-Techniculture. Pp. 145–51 in *Studies in the History and Archaeology of Jordan,* ed. I. A. Hadidi. Amman: Department of Antiquities.

1982b   Jericho. *Encyclopedia Americana.* Danbury, CT: Grolier.

1983a   Texts and Archaeology at Tell Taᶜannek. *Berytus* XXXI: 57–66.

1983b   Use of Ethnography in an Archaeological Research Design. Pp. 171–79 in *Quest for the Kingdom of God: Studies in Honor of George E. Mendenhall,* ed. H. B. Huffmon *et al.* Winona Lake, IN: Eisenbrauns.

1985   Tradition and Change in Two Archaeologies. *American Antiquity* 50:2, 464–77.

1986   Biblical Archaeology: An Emerging Discipline. Pp. 85–101 in *Archaeology of Jordan and Other Studies: Essays in Honor of Siegfried Horn,* ed. L.T. Garaty. Andrews University.

1987a   Archaeology of Palestine. *Birzeit Research Review* 4. Guest Editor. Birzeit: Birzeit University.

1987b   Excavating Palestine Today: Part I. *Birzeit Research Review* 4: 124–49.

1987c   Prolegomena to Archaeological Theory. *Birzeit Research Review* 4: 4–39.

1987d   Where to Draw the Line: Illustrating Ceramic Technology. *Newsletter of Department of Pottery Technology,* University of Leiden, the Netherlands 5: 93–110.

1990a   Excavating Palestine Today: Part II. *Afaq Filistiniyya: Birzeit Research Review* 5: 3–44.

1990b   Linking Past and Present. Review of Neil Silberman, *Between Past and Present: Archaeology, Ideology and Nationalism in the Modern Middle East. Journal of Palestine Studies* 77: 134–35.

1991   A Short History of Palestine. Pp. 147–50 in *Passia,* Diary & Directory, Jerusalem, 1992.

1992a   *All That Remains.* Associate Editor with Walid Khalidi *et al.*

Washington, D.C.: The Institute for Palestine Studies.

1992b   Taanach. Pp. 678–80 in *The Anchor Bible Dictionary Vol. III*, ed. D. N. Freedman *et al.* New York: Doubleday.

1992c   Jenin. Pp. 287–90 in *The Anchor Bible Dictionary Vol. VI*, ed. D. N. Freedman *et al.* New York: Doubleday.

1994   Archaeology as Cultural Survival: The Future of the Palestinian Past. *Journal of Palestine Studies* XXIII.3: 70–84.

1995   Cultural Bias in the Archaeology of Palestine. *Journal of Palestine Studies* XXIV.2: 48–59.

1997   Ta'anach. P. 149 in *Oxford Encyclopedia of Archaeology in the Near East Vol. 5*, ed. E. Meyers. Oxford: Oxford University.

UNPUBLISHED REPORTS AND PAPERS RELATED TO EXCAVATIONS AT TELL TA'ANNEK AND TELL JENIN

1964*   Report of the Excavation of the South Slope of Tell Ta'annek, 1963. Unpublished MS. 30 pp.

1967*   Report of the Excavation of the South Slope of Ta'annek, 1966. Unpublished MS. 40 pp.

1967*   Copy for Preliminary Report on Excavations on the South Slope in 1966. Unpublished MS. 11 pp.

1969*   Report for 1968 Season at Ta'annek. Unpublished MS. 50 pp.

1970   Reports I–VI to the Concordia Committee for Archaeological Studies in the Near East and the Ta'annek Core Staff. Unpublished MS. Private Circulation only. 49 pp.

1971   A System for Drawing and Describing Pottery and Objects from Taanach. Unpublished MS. Private Circulation. 9 pp.

1972   Taanach 1972: Interim Technical Report. Unpublished MS. 20 pp.

1986   Ta'annek in the Ottoman Period—The 1985 Excavation. With Ghada Ziadeh. Birzeit. 34 pp.

1989   Archaeology of the Village of Ti'Innik, Palestine. Part 2: Digging up the Story. With Ghada Ziadeh. Birzeit. 75 pp.

*   Submitted to and used by Paul Lapp for Area A sections of Preliminary Reports on Excavations at Tell Ta'annek in Bulletin of the American Schools of Oriental Research, 173 (1964), 185 (1967), 195 (1969) respectively.

MISCELLANEOUS UNPUBLISHED MANUSCRIPTS

1963   Haggai. For the Popular Commentary. Unpublished MS. River Forest, IL. 34 pp.

1968   Warfare in Mari and Early Israel. Dissertation, Ph.D. University of Michigan, Ann Arbor, Michigan. Unpublished ms. 337 pp.

1974   Archaeological Systematics. Jerusalem. 24 pp.

1977   The Purpose of the Past. Jerusalem. 6 pp.

1981   Intercontinental Culture: Archaeological History and Tradition in the Southern Levant. Jerusalem. 23 pp.

1986   The Archaeology of Palestine and the Palestinians. Jerusalem. 10 pp.

Contributors

William G. Dever is Professor of Near Eastern Archaeology and Anthropology at the University of Arizona. He was Director of the Hebrew Union College in Jerusalem (1968–1971) and the W. F. Albright Institute of Archaeological Research (1971–1975), and he served as editor of the *Bulletin of the ASOR* (1978–1984). He has research interests in the history of Biblical and Syro-Palestinian archaeology, the Bronze and Iron Ages of the Southern Levant, and religion and cult in ancient Israel. He has authored more than twenty books and three hundred articles.

Albert E. Glock (1925–1992) was professor of Archaeology and Director of the Institute of Archaeology at Birzeit University (1976–1992). From 1970–1980 he was affiliated with the Albright Institute of Archaeological Research in Jerusalem and served as its Acting Director from 1978–1980.

Henk Franken is emeritus professor at the University of Leyden. He specializes in the Old Testament, cultural anthropology, and the archaeology of Palestine, and has published twelve books and numerous articles in both Dutch and English on these topics.

Hugh R. Harcourt has taught Humanities and Philosophy at Beirut College for Women, American University of Beirut, Portland State University, and Birzeit University. He is now retired and lives with his wife in Cyprus.

Tomis Kapitan is Professor of Philosophy at Northern Illinois University. He taught philosophy and cultural studies at Birzeit University from 1981–1986. He is the editor of *Philosophical Perspectives on the Israeli-Palestinian Conflict* (1997) and the author of several essays in metaphysics, logic, international ethics, and the philosophy of language.

Ann E. Killebrew is a lecturer in the Department of Archaeology, the Zinman Institute of Archaeology at the University of Haifa, Israel. Her areas of interest and research include the Bronze and Iron ages in the Levant and ancient ceramics. She has excavated extensively at numerous sites in Israel, including Tel Akko, Tel Beth Shean, Tel Miqne-Ekron, Deir el-Balah and most recently at Tel Megiddo.

Nancy Lapp has recently retired from teaching Archaeology and Biblical Hebrew at the Pittsburgh Theological Seminary. She serves as Curator of the Bible Lands Museum, and continues field work, research, and publication of excavations and field work in Palestine.

Henry Innes MacAdam taught Classical history and Archaeology at the American University of Beirut between 1968–1985. He has participated in archaeological projects in Greece, Cyprus, Lebanon, Jordan, and Syria. His publications include three books, three dozen articles, and a dozen reviews. He currently resides in central New Jersey.

Walter Rast is Senior Research Professor at Valparaiso University and a Research Associate at the Oriental Institute of the University of Chicago. He is now retired from teaching in the Department of Theology at Valparaiso University. He is the author of several books and articles on archaeology and Biblical studies, among which are studies of the Iron Age pottery from Tell Taʿannek and the cemetery material excavated at Bab edh-Dhraʾ. Currently he is working on the final volumes of the Expedition to the Dead Sea Plain.

Thomas Ricks is an associate professor of Modern Middle East history in the Center for Arab and Islamic Studies and the Director of International Studies at Villanova University. Currently, he is completing the Third Edition of his co-authored textbook, *Middle East: Past and Present* (Prentice-Hall), and an oral history project on the social history of Palestinians and the mission schools in Palestine (1905–1995). Dr. Ricks has lived, worked, and carried out research in Iran and Palestine, having taught for two years in Mashhad and Mahabad, one year at the Tehran International School, and two years at Birzeit University (1983–1985).

Hamed J. Salem has been a lecturer in the Institute of Archaeology at Birzeit University since 1987. He studied with Al Glock at Birzeit University and received a Masters of Arts from the University of Arizona. He has published articles dealing with ceramic analysis and Palestinian archaeology and a book entitled *Archaeological Excavations and Surveys* (in Arabic).

Neil Asher Silberman is an author and historian with a special interest in the history, archaeology, and politics of the Near East. He was trained in Near Eastern Archaeology at the Hebrew University of Jerusalem. He is a contributing editor for *Archaeology* magazine, a frequent contributor to archaeological and general-interest periodicals, and the author of seven books.

Patty Jo Watson is the Eward Mallinckrodt Distinguished University Professor of Anthropology at Washington University. She has authored or edited ten books, and authored or coauthored over seventy articles and twenty book reviews in the areas of early agricultural economies, cave archaeology, and archaeological theory and method. She has served as editor of *American Antiquity*, and as the editor for archaeology of *American Anthropologist*.

G. R. H. Wright is the author of several books and essays dealing with the archaeology and culture of Palestine, Jordan, Cyprus, Iran, and India. He currently resides in Avignon, France.

Ghada Ziadeh-Seely has taught archaeology at Birzeit University, and was a research assistant to Albert Glock. A specialist in the archaeology of Ottoman Palestine, she has co-directed excavations at the village of Ti'nnek, supervised excavations at Tell Jenin, and published several papers in the area. She is currently living in the United States.

Index

OLD TESTAMENT